W9-BLW-290

SPEECH AND SOCIETY IN TURBULENT TIMES

This volume explores how societies are addressing challenging questions about the relationship between expression, traditional and societal values, and the transformations introduced by new information communications technologies. It seeks to identify alternative approaches to the role of speech and expression in the organization of societies, as well as efforts to shape the broader global information society. How have different societies or communities drawn on the ideas of philosophers, religious leaders, or politicians, both historical and contemporary, that addressed questions of speech, government, order, or freedoms and applied them, with particular attention to applications in the digital age? The essays include a wide variety of cultural and geographic contexts to identify different modes of thinking. The goal is to both unpack the "normative" Internet and free-expression debate and to deepen understanding about why certain Internet policies and models are being pursued in very different local or national contexts as well as on a global level.

Monroe Price is founder of the Programme in Comparative Media Law and Policy at Oxford University. He directed the Center for Global Communication Studies at the University of Pennsylvania's Annenberg School for Communication and helped develop centers for media policy studies in Moscow, Budapest, New Delhi, and elsewhere. An international media Moot Court established at Oxford bears his name. His most recent book is *Free Expression, Globalization and the New Strategic Communication*.

Nicole Stremlau is Head of the Programme in Comparative Media Law and Policy at the University of Oxford and Research Professor in the Humanities at the University of Johannesburg. She previously worked for a newspaper in Ethiopia, and has researched new technologies and innovation in Somalia and Somaliland and media and election violence in Kenya. She is the recipient of a European Research Council Starting Grant and her research and work has also been funded by the Open Society Foundations, Google, the UK Foreign and Commonwealth Office, and the United Nations, among others.

Speech and Society in Turbulent Times

FREEDOM OF EXPRESSION IN COMPARATIVE PERSPECTIVE

Edited by

MONROE PRICE
University of Pennsylvania

NICOLE STREMLAU
University of Oxford and University of Johannesburg

CAMBRIDGE
UNIVERSITY PRESS

CAMBRIDGE
UNIVERSITY PRESS

University Printing House, Cambridge CB2 8BS, United Kingdom

One Liberty Plaza, 20th Floor, New York, NY 10006, USA

477 Williamstown Road, Port Melbourne, VIC 3207, Australia

314–321, 3rd Floor, Plot 3, Splendor Forum, Jasola District Centre, New Delhi – 110025, India

79 Anson Road, #06-04/06, Singapore 079906

Cambridge University Press is part of the University of Cambridge.

It furthers the University's mission by disseminating knowledge in the pursuit of education, learning, and research at the highest international levels of excellence.

www.cambridge.org
Information on this title: www.cambridge.org/9781316640319
DOI: 10.1017/9781316996850

First published 2018

Printed in the United States of America by Sheridan Books, Inc.

A catalogue record for this publication is available from the British Library.

ISBN 978-1-107-19012-2 Hardback
ISBN 978-1-316-64031-9 Paperback

Contents

PART V CONCLUSION

Contributors

Altug Akin is an associate professor in the Faculty of Communication at Izmir University of Economics, Turkey. His work has been published in leading journals, including the *International Journal of Communication* and *Journalism: Theory, Practice & Criticism.*

Ali Allawi was a research professor at the National University of Singapore. He has been at various times a fellow at Harvard, Princeton, and Nanyang Technological University, and a senior member at St. Antony's College, Oxford University, as well as serving in a number of senior cabinet posts in the post-2003 government of Iraq.

Rohit Chopra is an associate professor of Communication at Santa Clara University, California. His research interests include the relationship of global media and cultural identity, memory work, and South Asian politics.

Yoel Cohen is an associate professor in the School of Communication, Ariel University, Israel. His areas of research interest include news media and religion, and foreign news. His publications include *God, Jews & the Media: Religion & Israel's media* (2012).

Rogier Creemers is a researcher at the Leiden University Law Faculty and Institute for Area Studies in the Netherlands. He holds degrees in Chinese Studies, International Relations, and Law. His main research interests are Chinese technology regulation and legal theory.

Richard Danbury is a former practicing lawyer and investigative journalist. He has a doctorate in media law from the University of Oxford and currently runs the Channel 4 MA in investigative journalism at De Montfort University, Leicester.

Stephen M. Feldman is the Jerry W. Housel/Carl F. Arnold Distinguished Professor of Law and Adjunct Professor of Political Science at the University of Wyoming. His publications include *Free Expression and Democracy in America: A History* (2008), and *American Legal Thought from Premodernism to Postmodernism: An Intellectual Voyage* (2000). He was a visiting scholar at Harvard Law School during the Fall 2016 semester.

Iginio Gagliardone is a senior lecturer at the University of Witwatersrand in Johannesburg, South Africa, and an associate of the Programme in Comparative Media Law and Policy, University of Oxford, where he was a Research Fellow for several years. His most recent book, *The Politics of Technology in Africa*, was published by Cambridge University Press in 2016.

Cherian George is an associate professor in the journalism department of Hong Kong Baptist University, where he also serves as director of the Centre for Media and Communication Research. He is the author of four books, including most recently *Hate Spin: The Manufacture of Religious Offense and Its Threat to Democracy* (2016).

William Gould is Professor of Indian History at the University of Leeds. He has published three monographs: *Hindu Nationalism and the Language of Politics* (Cambridge University Press, 2004), *Bureaucracy, Community and Influence* (2011), and *Religion and Conflict in South Asia* (Cambridge University Press, 2012).

Baogang He is Alfred Deakin Professor and Chair in International Relations at Deakin University in Australia. He graduated with a PhD in Political Science from Australian National University in 1994 and has become widely known for his academic work on Chinese democratization and politics, in particular the deliberative politics in China and issues pertaining to Asian regionalism, federalism, and multiculturalism.

Julien Mailland is Assistant Professor of Communication Science at Indiana University's Media School. He received his PhD at the University of Southern California and law degrees from New York University School of Law and the University of Paris (Assas).

Monroe Price is an adjunct full professor at the Annenberg School for Communication and the Joseph and Sadie Danciger Professor of Law and Director of the Howard M. Squadron Program in Law, Media, and Society at the Cardozo School of Law.

András Sajó is a judge at the European Court of Human Rights in Strasbourg. He is also a University Professor at Central European University in Budapest, Hungary, where he was the founding dean of Legal Studies.

Elena Sherstoboeva has a PhD in Journalism and is an associate professor in the Media Department of the Higher School of Economics in Moscow, Russia. Her research focuses on media and entertainment law in Russia and other post-Soviet countries.

Nicole Stremlau is head of the Programme in Comparative Media Law and Policy, Centre for Socio-Legal Studies, at the University of Oxford and Research Professor in the Humanities at the University of Johannesburg.

Foreword

In the newsrooms and courtrooms of many countries, journalists, lawyers, and judges, in particular, tend to take fundamental rights like freedom of speech for granted. Once a principle like the individual right to free speech is recognized as an axiom, little thought goes into the reasons behind its acceptance. But this is changing. Long-dominant frameworks for internationally accepted norms are now more frequently questioned. And even where there is some rough acceptance of the established tenets of free speech, proponents of national sovereignty often undercut what has long been prevailing thought by drawing on idiosyncratic cultural concerns. This book responds to the present moment by putting this contemporary questioning in comparative context. The contributors to this volume each strive to find the roots of varying approaches to international norms within long-contrived differences among states and regions.

The language of universal and fundamental rights often exists in its own ideological echo room, at times impervious to the complex social system of communication in which it functions. This leads to limited and odd effects. The very proposition that a right is fundamental means that its foundational principles are surrounded by a kind of taboo, a taboo that limits more careful considerations of context and contingency, but helps preserve the overall framework. This kind of taboo is convenient. Calling a claim or interest a "fundamental right" helps avoid recurring and repetitive soul-searching and mind-boggling analysis. Of course, there is still a place for recalibration in the balancing act needed in measuring competing rights. But in societies where freedom of expression is elevated to a human right or a fundamental constitutional right, there is frequently very limited debate about the legitimacy and priority of the rights claim. The foundational justifications, even if originally shaky or contradictory, have been rarely challenged and nor are such challenges taken particularly seriously in judicial and regulatory decisions. Such cracks as may exist in the doctrine of free speech remain hidden under the face powder of triviality and respect for the status quo.

Today, however, wrinkles appear in this Enlightenment makeup, wrinkles that indicate cracks in the body politic as public debates threaten old axioms and create new assumptions. Such debates throw grave doubt upon prior faiths such as the belief that in a free marketplace of ideas, truth will ultimately prevail, hardened and secured. Even where there has been long established acceptance of the underlying principles, new coalitions or ideologies, often linked to national sovereignty, begin to undercut what has long been prevailing thought. The grand tradition of free speech may be dominant but not universal, despite claims to the contrary.

This book is about the gulf between the dominant and the universal and it comes at a time when "universal" assumptions are more questioned than ever. The consequence of this questioning is that most of the discourse concerning free speech issues concerned the permissibility of certain restrictions within the existing parameters of the scope of the right. The debate did not concern itself with the status of freedom of expression among the venerable social values in a democracy, nor was it linked to broad and deep cultural differences among societies. Freedom of speech comes "naturally"; at least until one is offended or afraid of it. After all, speech is a human default, and silence is abnormal. Humans pertain to a gabby species. Silence is the result of drilled-in conditioning, even if coated in politeness and civility. It is a product of oppression, even if censorship is the act of alleged responsibility, as was argued during the Inquisition. Communication is the default for humans, but not all default situations amount to a right.

Of course, freedom of expression can be very limited. There are "no entry" zones for free speech principles in the organization of our social institutions. "Elites" and "power holders" build a reality where freedom of expression is squeezed out and the boundaries of the zones of free speech are in constant shift. Privacy is one of those areas of shifting boundaries. There are domains or fiefdoms where those who control communication are able to block imagination: at any given time, there are spheres of communication that are simply not imagined as areas where free speech is appropriate. Silencing and imposed views are the rule here. It is perhaps ironic that in democratic societies, speech in national parliaments occurs in one of the most restricted spaces. Freedom of expression is often legally limited where freedom of religion prevails; that is, within the religious community. Expression is commonly restricted in schools, the army, state bureaucracy, and in the workplace. Where established, these zones of "no entry" are the subject of constant challenge, a challenge that was made unseen in the normalizations provided by regulatory process. For example, this is the case with state secrets and confidential information. But it is also true that new "free speech zones" are carved out by new social sensitivities turned into social conventions. And while much has been made of the so-called democratizing or empowering abilities of social media to give voice and greater power to ordinary citizens, such spaces are proving easily manipulated, echo-chambers where it is not only the gatekeepers of communication who can limit freedom of expression but determined individuals or small groups as well.

Moreover, as this volume indicates, the self-confident axiomatic assumption made by over-confident democracies that freedom of expression is a right, although universalistic in its aspiration, runs into its own limits. Freedom of speech assumed relatively rational adults, open to arguments. Freedom of expression works "for the calmer and more disinterested bystander," as J. S. Mill argued. In many respects, though, these assumptions about the individual for an effective free speech regime fail, not because of illiteracy or imposed nonage, but increasingly for socio-psychological reasons as people prefer to live in bubbles of self-selecting information where the bubble looks more and more a bunker with cave-mentality inhabitants. This is how despotism disguised as paternalism operates: government and other dominant powers determine what is "proper" information: citizens are taken only to be in need of *proper* information. Information gatekeepers cater such select information relying on the limited deliberative capacity of the citizen.

For whatever reasons, the assumption about the importance of freedom of expression (in particular beyond trade and science) is not accepted in many cultures. In a globalized world with new, selective technologies of communication that do not allow time and distance for reflection, where mediation is replaced with the fake money of the slogan of "equal value of all utterances," the foundations of freedom of expression (and with it constitutional democracy) lay bare. The cultural foundations of free speech are not shared anymore where information is a threat to security and the likelihood that the information is false grows ever higher. Cultures (including political cultures) that did not cherish free speech are now taking their revenge. One form of despotism, the one that stars populists, makes a particular use of this cultural force. With the legitimation of an absolutist popular sovereignty, it justifies a new censorship as defender of national cultural habits. Nationalism, relying on the primacy of sovereignty, claims that in its disregard of universal norms, it is only protecting local culture. This *is* despotism *disguised* as nationalism presented as reclaiming sovereignty. All this has rather well-known censorial effects. Of course, all information regulation (including regulation by architecture) is censorial but not all censorships are equal.

This backlash (a term that will likely have become overused by the time this volume is published) seems to resonate most among those who build their identity as being victims of globalization. It grows in the sentiments of those unwilling to tolerate uncertainty who rally behind populists in the evisceration of the "mainstream media."

While this volume clearly demonstrates the local cultural differences in creating and limiting free speech, it begs the question how these reservations to the international human rights law narrative of freedom of expression became suddenly much more forceful and respectable. Because the multi-layered constitutional regime was transnationally open, it was malleable. For a while, constitutionalism and human rights reached vulnerable countries that had to adapt to these developments, but once the governments in these countries (riding, very often, local nationalist and populist winds) became more self-conscious and powerful (for economic and military reasons), they could to some extent reverse the circulation of expectations and standards. Freedom of expression that was accepted at least as "best practices" within a rule of law package is gradually replaced with "anything that stands for national security practices goes." And this was encouraged by shifts in those countries which formally stood (and claim to continue to stick) to the position that open communication and freedom of expression is part of their culture. Sovereignty is again the talk in town, and sovereignty facilitates the culture of censorship. Open communication across borders has become a threat, the international law protecting it looks suddenly obsolete, and the nation-state of impermeable borders promises protection of the shelter.

Phenomena related to the Internet and social media give an opportunity, be it a pretext or a moral urge, to challenge the very legitimacy of free speech as we know it. The rise of these new modes of communication have caused challenges to the justification of free speech, exposing, among others, the anthropological foundations of free speech justifications (that people are truth seeking, fully rational beings) as well as the very foundations of democratic social institutions. The critiques refer to online experiences, and dubious findings of neuroscience, claiming that the assumptions relied upon in freedom of expression are not sustainable. Humans, at least online, are irrational, instinctively aggressive, and their sociability is perverted, so the criticism goes. Weak humans find each other's company discomforting and human weaknesses reinforce that tendency. Extremists will break through their isolation and will mutually encourage and radicalize each other. This observation leaves out of the equation that all sorts of vulnerable and powerless people too will likewise benefit from online empowerment. Empowering the powerless, however, does not necessarily lead to liberation; certainly not without mediation.

Among the challenges to traditional free expression justifications, I would single out one as of critical and (to my mind) dangerous importance. Breathtakingly short, the argument is that the free flow of ideas has the potential *itself* to restrict democracy, and now more so than ever. Therefore, as the criticism goes, "proper" regulation of speech is needed; such regulation, it is argued, will enhance democracy and increase social justice. As a related matter, lying or dissemination of false information becomes a ground for "screening" the free flow of information and it may be that it will develop into a legitimate ground for a tactic of national security to spread false information for the sake of militant democracy. This, in itself, raises a traditional problem, namely that of the dangers of governmental regulation of speech. There are too many people of influence who are cocksure what "proper" means when it comes to regulation. While some view the government as exercising judicious and enlightened regulation, governmental regulation of speech is inherently limited to the viewpoint of the regulators.

It is now also increasingly argued that there is nothing special about speech that would grant it priority, the kind of priority that would require the government to provide compelling reasons to justify an interference. In this dubious approach, there is nothing to justify the privileged treatment of speech among other liberties and interests, for example security and good morals. After all, until the 1960s, even in the United States, speech was just one among the many constitutional concerns that was handled in balancing with other interests, a position toward which Europe is moving dangerously close, in view of recent ECtHR judgments.

Why is freedom of speech to be provided special protection that is not accorded to other forms of conduct? Why are resulting harms, and in particular risks of harm, which would otherwise be unacceptable, at least tolerated, just because freedom of expression is elevated to a human right?

The standard political argument in the justification of free speech was one of democracy. Democracy as choice cannot exist without the alternatives provided by free speech. The Internet seemed to open up democracy, promising more robust, interactive participation. In other words, democracy becomes more accessible, and the government becomes more transparent or at least easier to control. It creates a kind of citizen press, which makes information more easily and rapidly available than it was with broadcast news. News becomes more democratic. Online communication is more democratic in the sense of participation than the broadcast model, where a select few talk to an invisible and manipulated mass audience. Online democracy is much more individualistic and individual liberty enhancing. That has been the hope.

Internet and social media–based democracy is, or can be, trans-political. As the American legal scholar Jack Balkin has demonstrated, Internet speech is of a populist nature. (He may have hoped for a different kind of populism: but this is the nature of people that is brought to light in social media.) It was hoped that this populist speech will be innovative and will create new communities. And it did: we have virtual communities but hardly to the benefit of a democracy of fairness. Participation in decision making in these communities and societies composed of such partly virtual communities results in a democracy that is polarized and merciless, if it can be considered democracy at all.

In the justification of dethroning the primacy of freedom of expression, it is argued that it is one-sided; free *speech* disregards the audience and privileges the speaker. After being silenced for a long time in many countries, the censor dares to ask it once again: what about the communicative rights of the audience to receive information? The empirical experience with online speech seems to add weight to these speech skeptics. On the other hand, equality for all speakers (to destroy the communication monopoly of conspiratorial elites) – this is the self-destructive argument of populist democracy.

One has to admit that when more information is available, faster and from so many sources, the likelihood of misinformation (including deliberate political and governmental manipulation and systematic lies) increases. There might be a need to take steps to reduce the prevalence of this misinformation. But this is, by the traditional democratic free speech definitions, dangerous as it denies a previously cherished principle that more information and better information will drive out lies. Until there is compelling evidence of a Gresham Law dynamic in speech where "bad money drives out good money," or in our case that false news prevails against critical facts, the presumption generated by the free-speech principle should still apply.

This volume suggests that Gresham's Law maintains some (increasingly threatening) power in contemporary communication. Not the first time in the history of manipulation.

Consequentialist arguments supporting freedom of expression collapse once the assumed consequences do not materialize. Of course, this is not a theoretically relevant objection once freedom of expression has an inherent value but politicians and the public do not believe in values that they consider to be relative. One cannot argue successfully that free speech is part of human autonomy (self-development or self-fulfillment) when people are afraid of autonomy, or even detest it for that reason.

Non-consequentialist justifications should not be immune to a reality check. A belief in human rationality and goodness underlies both consequentialism and non-consequentialism. These justifications, at least in the world of prac-tical considerations, depend on anthropological facts. What if humans are simply unable to act autonomously? What if anonymous speech that helped Jonathan Swift (though not his printer, who died in prison) results in a mass online disinhibition effect? Speech is liberating – but how do people behave once they are liberated in their bias-reinforcing chatrooms?

This volume, with its essays written with impassionate critical scholarship, does what freedom of expression promises: it enables us to use our rational judgment. The value choice in matters of censorship is ours.

András Sajó
Judge at the European Court of Human Rights, Strasbourg
University Professor, Central European University, Budapest

Introduction: Speech and Society in Comparative Perspective

Monroe Price and Nicole Stremlau

This book identifies how different states, with different traditions and different political, economic, and social realities, conceptualize and practice the role of speech and information in society. How, the authors ask, have countries drawn upon the ideas of philosophers, religious leaders, and politicians who have ruminated on questions of speech, government, order, and freedom, and how have states applied the lessons learnt to governance? This question provides the book's primary objective: to identify the processes or combination of ideas concerning speech and information that are articulated as governments seek to maintain or extend power, with particular attention paid to applications in the digital age. These essays underscore how difficult and delicate a process it is to establish universal values and distinguish among normative approaches. This focus on the specificities and peculiarities of each state aids a secondary objective: by focusing on political ideologies, the philosophical or religious underpinnings of communal approaches to the regulation of speech, we seek to add context to global debates that are often characterized by polarizing dichotomies.

The essays included in this volume are, by design, eclectic, with authors bringing different ways of thinking, which draw on their varying disciplinary, epistemological, and professional backgrounds. Intended to be a truly polyphonic book, this approach has been taken to enrich the vocabulary of global discussion and to both unpack the prevailing "normative" Internet and free-expression debate and to deepen analyses in very different local or national contexts as well as on a global level. This requires a conversation across disciplines and between scholars of law, philosophy, anthropology, communications, politics, and international relations.

In part, this is also an exercise in archaeology: to understand the present one must also look backwards and ask how various societies evolved in their approaches to the role of speech and of the press. Those who have set foundational principles for speech and those who have succeeded in realizing them have variously described the importance of creating cohesion, commanding loyalty, and maintaining peace for nation building while, in some cases, acknowledging the role and values of free expression in underwriting creativity or improving governance. This collection of essays roots itself in these historically fraught debates seeing the legacies and continued influence of prominent thinkers, philosophical or religious approaches, and moments in disparate societies from Confucius and Gandhi to the role of Islamic law.

It is often assumed that new technologies bring with them new modalities of interaction and that new technologies alter the outer bounds of justifications for the role of speech in society. New technologies may underwrite heightened dependence on tried and true rhetoric or create opportunities for new ways of framing speech and information. Radical political changes or political crises over information management may lead to revolutions in thinking about the role and management of speech in society; or they can also turn into restorations, with new regimes repackaging old theoretical and practical approaches. This can be seen from a structural perspective (how modes of speech, expression, or control persist with the advent of new technologies) as well as from a contingent perspective (who is in control or designs particular projects and whether they are taking a "legacy" approach from a pre-digital generation). In many cases, older logics and historical experiences of controlling, harnessing, or encouraging certain modes of speech dominate.

In the litigation and advocacy mode – and because of law's role as a repository of values – there is often the tendency, or need, to depend on legal analyses or international legal norms when discussing free expression. Often these norms are enlisted in an opportunity to highlight the deviations and shortcomings of particular governments or leaders in power. This book respects that tradition but supplements the tendency to rank by focusing on the ideas, philosophies, and values that underlie and inform the speech rules that a government or community institutes. In many cases justifications for restricting speech may simply be excuses for governments to maintain their hold on power, or to weaken adversaries, but too often the debate is polarized and political projects and ideals that underlie policies are misunderstood or ignored.

A common theme running throughout the chapters of this book is the role of ideology in framing speech practices in a society. First published in 1956, the long-time bible of comparative approaches to speech and society, *Four Theories of the Press*, analyzed systems not so much as they functioned, but in terms of their relationship to a set of categories: authoritarian, libertarian, communist, and what the authors referred to as "social responsibility," which lies between the libertarian and authoritarian theories whereby the media has freedom but is also subjected to external controls such as a code of conduct (Siebert et al. 1973). Endeavoring to improve on the mostly theoretically based structural analysis of *Four Theories*, Daniel Hallin and Paolo Mancini (2004) wrote their acclaimed *Comparing Media Systems: Three Models of Media and Politics*, in which they sought a far more empirical approach to differentiating one national approach from another, but largely focusing on Western countries.

Following a more empirical approach, we argue that ideologies matter but they are not always determinative. Authoritarian systems can have and strive toward restrictive characteristics, but they can also be authoritarian and have significant, though hardly perfect, characteristics of openness, as Cherian George's chapter on Singapore shows. A system can be influenced by Confucian principles of deliberative culture, but maintaining power can be overarching as a factor, as Baogang He discusses. In Elena Sherstoboeva's chapter on Soviet and Russian history, we see that Lenin's theories of the function of the press in realizing a new society casts an interesting shadow on current media developments in Russia. And, while ideology may have had a central role in shaping a media system under new governments, there can also be the decline of ideology, as Nicole Stremlau's chapter on Uganda demonstrates. The conclusion from these studies is that ideology is useful when studying speech and information in society, but ideologies alone are often misleading and certainly not totalizing. Simply stated, a libertarian approach defends Isaiah Berlin's negative liberty and the core idea of a significantly limited state, but consolidation, corporate power, and the lure of control, even in democratic societies, has often acted as a brake on the libertarian dream in practice. Understanding the conceptual limits of ideology for our purposes thus provokes a further question: are there alternate modes of considering the role of speech in society?

In this volume, this question has been answered in various ways. In Julien Mailland's chapter on France and Iginio Gagliardone's chapter on Ethiopia, we see how two very different state structures, underpinned by two very different intellectual and ideological heritages, both struggle with the implications of statist tendencies. William Gould's chapter on India finds grounding in the history of representation and the construction of monuments as a guide to thinking of emerging patterns of speech and society. Of course, the chapters in this book are only a sample of insights into the question of alternate theories and their implications for political structures. We might as easily have found space to interrogate Nasser's ideas of the role of the press in an Egypt-led United Arab Republic, and analyzed theories on the role of communication in Japan, both in a wartime 1930s "home" and in its Pacific expansion. To explore these questions in an even greater whole, one might ask how Canada saw the building of a media system that would undergird a nation and differentiate it from the United States. Or one could think of the role of information management in theocratic societies, including in Puritan Massachusetts, where concepts of speech became more closely tied to the demands of governance than bound to the demands of scripture. Plural societies, like modern-day Belgium or much of the twentieth-century Netherlands, forged media systems that reflected and reinforced pillarization as the basis for government organization.

CHALLENGING ASSUMPTIONS OF FREEDOM OF EXPRESSION

Theories of speech and society are invariably constructed on a framework of assumptions about the function of the society's institutions. Inevitably, this framework is subject to historical change, challenging the commonsense assumptions of the day. In the Netherlands, for example, a comprehensive, carefully developed and ingenious approach manifested, whereby each major or minor group in society that could claim proportionate media time began to collapse as technology and the development of a European market and media standards undermined the state's ability to maintain its system. When the Soviet Union dissolved, the media systems left in its wake dangled as new political institutions formed and attempted (or not) to alter the roles for press and speech in society. Frequently, the institutions and the language used to describe them adapt to changing circumstances, often giving a veneer of intellectual continuity. Richard Danbury, in his chapter, discusses this process of adaptation in relation to the Miltonian assumption of divine assistance in finding a "Revealed Truth." The marketplace-of-ideas metaphor is often used to justify the role of more speech in countering divisive or dangerous speech, but some aspect of the core meaning of John Milton's observation has been altered by changes in the context in which similar words are used.

Advocates of freedom of expression must therefore be careful in their arguments, avoiding attaching their strategies to edifices that are crumbling remnants of a previous world or superficial portents of a seeming new age. Epistolary practices once served as an undergirding of discourses, and coffeehouse cultures have famously played a role in forging a public sphere, as Jürgen Habermas (1991) has detailed; and now the Internet and other technologies challenge normative assumptions about freedom of expression. Important shifts could be taking place contrasting the self-generated contributions from a newly virulent civil society with the directed, overt, and disciplined imposition of information flows from highly organized strategic communicators.

Each shift will have consequences; each may lead to the reassertion of state power, in some cases, or the weakening of such power in others. In some circumstances, the state may properly be called on to act as a meaningful referee, regulator, or even partial sponsor of the public debate. In a crowded, global, highly competitive context, the state may seek a more public role in which it seeks to assert its own voice. Terror and national security concerns have become increasingly salient and defining.

The point is that the extraordinary phenomenon we call "free expression" is not only a set of principles and practices but is also inextricably bound to a set of institutions. And a similar conclusion could be drawn for other architectures of speech in society. These institutions include the mechanisms that exist in a society for the production and diffusion of information through which people process information as they function as citizens or as members of a community. They incorporate the rules and norms of governments and other actors who affect the interplay between principles and actions. Most importantly, they encompass the enduring and slowly eroding rivulets through which changing bits of information flow quickly over long periods of time. Of course, principles may endure while the phenomena in which those principles live may change. That, after all, is what makes for overarching principles. But even if principles are constant, how they can be achieved – indeed, whether they can even be optimally applied – differs when the mechanisms of daily life are materially altered. Change any one element of an existing equation and all other elements are affected as well.

These institutions or architectures of speech and society have always and are always altering with often complicated and far-reaching repercussions (Lyn and Atkin 2007; Marvin 1988). The institutions changed with the development of institutionalized mail services and again with the telegraph; they changed with the industrialization of society and with the coming of the railroad. Satellites altered patterns of communication profoundly. Can one argue that the current rounds of change – including the Internet and the growth of social media – is of a more dramatic impact on our institutions, bringing unprecedented change that affects assumptions of freedom of expression in ways that are qualitatively different from anything that has occurred before? That seems to be the music of the moment. A more modest claim is that whenever such transformational changes take place, it is important to re-examine the fit between speech principles and their structural and practical underpinnings.

The main point, however, for this book is that the set of assumptions and the way they change are different in different societies. What, then, are some examples of fundamental assumptions or practices that undergird a system seeking to support a particular role of speech in a society? These assumptions are basic; they are what might be called the "plumbing of information flows" or the "infrastructure of communication." Some democratic societies, for example, may have an expectation about the reasonable availability of information to create a citizen sufficiently educated to exercise a franchise, and a system to provide opportunities to express views to a receptive government. These societies gain legitimacy (often in their own self-assessment) because of the self-respect and respect of others for the practice of free expression. Ideally such societies engage in critical analysis to determine whether the values they proclaim are being realized. Free expression and its exercise presuppose some value in the aggregated output of information and debate. And that presupposition may turn on a consensus (validly earned or not) that what is produced has the capacity to provide informed contributions to a public sphere.

An example of the "plumbing" of discourse involves the way speech principles are connected with political processes. A description of free speech that includes, at its heart, an electoral process, for example, may be twisted out of shape if the process becomes corrupt or the major contributors to political speech in the public space are entities from outside the polity. Confidence in free speech may depend on some perception, widespread in society, that it is a broad privilege to speak that is being protected (and perhaps exercised) and that the space for speech is not monopolized or controlled by special or exclusionary interests. In this view, the rise of social media should heighten the idea of breadth of privilege and greater equity and equality in shaping the public communicative space, while the growth of focused, powerful groups as speakers moves in the other direction. But even this assumption about the impact of trends must be examined over time.

Debates around the role of speech in particularly fragile or democratically transitioning societies where state power can be very weak are most frequently grounded in conceptions of the rule of law. In the rhetoric of this volume, the authors are fairly united in viewing the existence of a legal system that can fairly recognize and enforce limits as one of the key aspects of an institutional foundation for expression. Free expression, in the "evolved tradition" of international norms and standards, depends on the idea that judges can hold the government accountable if it oversteps its bounds and likewise – perhaps equally important – that judges can sanction individuals or groups who violate constitutional rules that set sanctioned boundaries. To the extent that the rule of law weakens, and to the extent that appropriately bargained-for or legislatively agreed-upon limitations cannot be enforced, the right itself may be at risk.

It is common in the wider literature of rights and rights enforcement to mention the function of the rule of law. Related to this is legality, understood here as the need for the government in a society to act in accordance with law – to have clearly stated and transparent law and to create a culture in which proper legal norms are actually followed. The rule of law, in this sense, is significant for free expression as an encouragement of states not to violate constitutional and international norms, not to have vagueness as a mode of obscuring the boundaries of free speech, and not to have secret ways in which speech is confined and confounded, notwithstanding appropriate public legal norms.

In this connection, what has been often underexplored is the *necessity* of law. Without a legal system that functions, rights, both positive and negative, are themselves in danger. In "Why the State?" and other writings, Owen Fiss (1987) argued against an overemphasis on individual autonomy as the basis for freedom of expression on the ground that such an emphasis leads to the domination of debate by those who control the economic and political power structures of society. For Fiss and his advocacy of a robust model, law and public intervention should be used to further public discourse. This could include positive steps like enactment of a "fairness doctrine" and the sustaining nature of public service broadcasting. Many governments have a different view of what an interventionist state should do to guard free expression against free-market logic, but the point here is not to evaluate these different proposals, but to question whether the principle underlying these proposals can be implemented and sustained. Looking historically, there is reason to suggest that this can be the case. For much of Europe during the twentieth century, a strong public service broadcasting system was a hallmark of a comprehensive approach to the structure of speech in society.

It is often argued that free expression in the United States as protected by the First Amendment is an "absolute," and the more free expression has achieved this rarefied, absolutist status, the more it has been applauded and canonized. But the ability to "freely express" is bounded by a set of practices, a collection of capabilities and limits, and law is wheeled into place as a way of defining and enforcing these limits. Few as these may be, whether they are limitations of time, place and manner, or content, or whether they are consistent with what international norms consider to be an appropriate balance, they are always present. Recognition of this fact should temper too sanctified a respect of "legal absolutism" and too immediate and conclusive packaging of it as part of international development. Without such nuance, positive and vital specific historical and political contexts tend to be obscured. Advocacy of a disputatious and theoretical "best" may conquer a necessary "good." Ready-made and sometimes absolutist approaches, inadequately considered and staged, may force states emerging from complex conflicts or messy transitions to adopt a constitutional system that is neither suitable and functional nor furthering of strong long-term advances to a more equitable and democratic society and here, often, the critique of international civil society becomes a significant factor (Lunn 2005).

Again, this goes to the question of institutional foundations needed for any concept or practice of freedom of expression. If a foundation of a scheme of freedom of expression is that its legitimate boundaries can be observed and enforced, then weakening that foundation may require some form of corresponding adjustment in the conception of the right. When Article 19 of the Universal Declaration of Human Rights was adopted internationally in the 1950s, there appeared to be bargaining on what would be listed as limitations and in what way. The *travaux preparatoires* of Article 19, paragraph 3, indicates the existence of debates particularly over controversial language such as "duties and responsibilities" and "public order." One of the notable ideas that guided the legislation-making process, as evidenced in the International Covenants on Human Rights, was "strik[ing] a balance between the rights of the individual and the requirements of society and the State" (UN General Assembly 1961). The ultimate profile of the right contains both the entitlements and the limitations. One can see limitations as an intrinsic part of the general acceptance of the formulation of the right.

Of course, the essays in this volume demonstrate a wide range of variations on the concept of the "rule of law" and where the entitlements and limitations should rest, or the role that the rule of law plays in media policy, broadly construed. There are vast differences in how to conceptualize law itself, in the enumeration of those who can invoke the law, and in the nature and independence of courts. Further widening the parameters of analysis, the effectiveness of a law often deals with the technology of its enforcement. A duly enacted law might be so clumsy in its administration or enforcement, so oppressive in its bearing on society, and distant from its authors' intent that, it ought to be nullified. Or it could be assumed that government has the responsibility for engineering its relevant world to make enforcement fairer and more feasible. Mandatory withholding and bank reporting regulations, for example, help ensure that there is greater compliance with income tax law requirements. Modern camera systems are designed to "catch" violators of traffic regulations, although there are, increasingly, constitutional limits in the United States to their use. Companies build "click" software into their programs to gain records of consent by consumers because of various legal requirements (for example, with respect to privacy). Thus, the general acceptance of principles of free expression in many, if not most, societies is based on a set of assumptions, one of which is that government has the authority *and* the power to police, subject to limits, its boundaries (including obscenity and child pornography – categories that are so solidly in this framework that some courts do not call them "speech"). This hardly means that the state always does police this border but debates on the failings and hypocrisies of government action in this area are different from arguing that it does not have the capacity to do so. Shaking this foundational assumption of free-expression theology would shake support for the principle itself.

This argument applies to language in Article 19 that sweeps in the right to receive and impart information "regardless of frontiers." That language could mean that a government cannot restrict language and images from outside its boundaries on grounds broader than those it uses to restrict language within. But such a reading is inconsistent with many government practices that seek to prefer domestic producers (often on economic or cultural grounds, such as promoting local artists or languages). And there is another consideration quite relevant to this book: what if, as a condition of modern technology, sources of information from outside a state's boundaries cannot be subjected to the restrictions applied to those within? The result could be (and perhaps already is) a kind of Gresham's Law of Information,[1] in which uncensored or unmonitored programming drives monitored, intermediated, and law-complying programming out of circulation. These oft-unexpected consequences alter the way in which a state reconceives the management of its information sphere.

CHANGING SPEECH NORMS IN THE DIGITAL AGE

One would be forgiven for happily thinking that the new social media and their transforming ilk present no or little negative challenge to the institutions of free expression, but rather provide yet another opportunity for realization of individual autonomy and other cherished goals. The rapid-diffusion capacity of social media clearly transforms information ecologies. The rise of social networks leads to a rethinking of the power of the individual in receiving information, deliberating, and mobilizing. Social networks change the balance between open and closed terrains of speech. They threaten existing intermediaries and create new ones. They are a challenge for governments, democratic or not. They alter the status quo. And social networks themselves may yet yield another newly empowered, all-seeing, all-knowing oligopoly of

[1] Gresham's Law states that bad money drives good money out of circulation.

private entities, with new names and the potentially deceptive appeal of positive change. Should this dystopian projection be realized, it would not be the first time that pioneers of progress in communications technology become the new wielders of old authority, with a transfer of power – not a radical reduction in power – as the consequence. Social networks are indeed seeking to define their relationship to the existing status quo of institutions of free expression. Facebook and YouTube threaten to become the operative gateways for new tribes transcending the borders of nation states, left to determine what controls to impose. Do they enact and replicate, enforcing old standards, or do they produce a new world? Should they act wholly independently of government or increasingly at governmental behest? The Arab Spring, seen as owing much of its early success to social media, offered a significant (though still confusing) tutorial in these questions.

In 2011, Alec Ross, then the guru of social media in the US State Department, reflected on ways in which the Internet and other "connection technologies" affected processes of change and the effectiveness of free expression in Egypt and Tunisia (Ross 2011). He counted four distinct impacts. First, these technologies "accelerated" mobilization, allowing "movements that normally would have taken years to build" to come together "in the course of weeks and months." Second, these new media processes "enriched the information environment," bringing more people into it and conveniently giving them a treasure trove of information. Third, these processes "made weak ties strong," unifying momentarily "the 57-year-old member of the Muslim Brotherhood with the 27-year-old digital hipster who is educated at the Sorbonne." Fourth, the new technology processes led to different forms of political organization. In prior "revolutions," a single hero emerged: "Lech Walesa in Poland[,] Vaclav Havel in the Czech Republic[,] or Nelson Mandela in South Africa." It was Ross's judgment that social media would lead to more distributed leadership.

Deployment of social media and related changes have already disrupted pre-existing institutional assumptions of freedom of expression through the more sophisticated surveillance that has accompanied it. Notions of privacy are profoundly affected by the information-gathering and user-identification aspects of social media. The relationship between privacy and free expression is both complex and significant. Notions of anonymity – often essential to fundamental aspects of free expression – are marginalized in the operation of the social media-era Internet. It becomes invaluable to investigators to recreate lives and relationships, sifting through thousands of posts and tweets, tracing how individual attitudes, representations, and capacities change over time. Manipulators of "big data" rely on social media-generated data to recreate a network of communication and influence. We are only beginning to fathom the impact on privacy – and consequently on freedom of expression. Disclosures in mid-2013 about the deep and wide program of the US National Security Agency and its counterparts have placed a new frame and context on the tensions (always present) over the use of the new media. Organizations such as the Global Network Initiative, with significant company representation, seek to identify principles that should guide an understanding of what privacy sacrifices are taking place and what policy modifications should occur as privacy concerns interact with freedom-of-expression principles.

A related significant impact on ideas of free expression exists because of the apparent change in the role of intermediaries. In the pre-social media world, much of media was filtered through intermediaries – newspapers, television networks, even state-related entities. Freedom of expression existed in this highly intermediated world, where the often unstated assumption was that these intermediaries would function (or would be obliged to function) as guardians of the public interest. These institutions acted as gatekeepers. There were many valid objections to intermediaries taking this role, from accusations of false guardians to over-filtering, and critiques of the democratically deficit. But it is possible to think of intermediaries as an important institutional aspect of the structure of free expression. One of the major sources of liberation, but also of current unease, lies in the rapid disappearance of familiar intermediaries – particularly those entities that can be subjected to government control and influence. Much of the debate over the responsibility and role, if any, of Facebook and Google to "counter online violent extremism," to filter or take down material (about hate speech, violence against women, and material deemed by governments insulting and destabilizing) relates to the question of the penchant for intermediaries. Governments and other strategic communicators have responded by seeking to shift the discourse from providing safe harbors for the new intermediaries to making ISPs or platforms more responsible, enlarging their roles as mediating gatekeepers or, through processes of surveillance, aiding the government. Intermediaries can also be the enforcers of territorial distinctions.

There are other major differences among states that affect theories of speech and society. Societal tolerance for free-speech principles may depend on what may be called a balance between open and closed terrains of speech. A society requires a theater of public representation of ideas, public speeches, posters, sermons, dance, art, and music. It also requires space for individuals and groups to communicate privately, beyond the surveillance of the state and other powerful forces in the society. Pluralism, for example, might depend on both the open and closed variety of speech: the open terrain allows for a society in which each citizen is exposed to many ideas; the more restricted domain allows for enriched channels of differentiated identity or political parallelism. Increasingly, with the revelation of widespread government surveillance, the assumption of the existence of an adequate closed or private terrain of speech is undermined. One can imagine a society in which the balance is not quite right, in which the open terrain of speech is barren and devoid of meaning and private discourse is hushed and paranoiac, or one in which private discourse abounds but is not allowed to blossom into the public realm. How to gauge health on such a scale has hardly been defined, but one of the unarticulated assumptions of this book is that various societies approach the question in different ways. Free speech may be that the balance is a "proper" one. As an example somewhat outside the usual scope of free expression, take the issue of the burka and facial disclosure. A general societal norm of exposed faces in Western societies comes into conflict with changing cultural practices as more and more women follow religious mandates, France being an important case study. The norm – an institutional foundation for a mode of personal expression – becomes subject to re-examination (Gey 2005).

Several decades ago, at least in some quarters, it was fashionable to talk of "cultural imperialism." For some, the world was seen as one in which the United States wielded its hegemonic control over the interpretation of information and in which an American culture industry dominated music and film and therefore shaped attitudes globally (Schiller 1976). The weakness in the "fashionable" chat on cultural imperialism was that it rendered other voices silent, voices that have always spoken back but are now more readily heard by Western commentators. Flows now seem more multipolar, and more regional nodes of power exist to regulate these flows and provide counter-flows. One could see in all of this a modification of who controls the levers of strategic communication – the rise of powerful satellite channels with Middle East parentage, the formation of a European Union that seeks to manage imagery to some extent, and the shift in ownership of the largest entertainment companies to provide more plural geographic sources of control. But this would not be the whole story. For some, it is a fundamental assumption of systems of free expression that powerful, sometimes corrupt, often state-sponsored strategic communicators are or should be offset by conditions of diversity, by independent media, or by public service media. But these are aspirations that are often unrealized. It is in this context that institutional aspects of free expression norms totter. Consider a society in a transitional phase, confronted with a series of forces of strategic communication seeking to reshape or "rehabilitate" it – convert its citizens to a different religion, alter their consuming habits, or place them under the sphere of influence of one neighboring or foreign state rather than another. The search might be for a formulation of principle or law that allows that state, assuming it has the capacity, to construct a response consistent with free-expression norms.

The existence of the state system is itself a major aspect of the structure of free expression or other conceptions of the structure of speech in society. Historically, the state has been the instrument for organizing a national definition of rights and responsibilities for speech practices. That idea, that working assumption, is in perpetual tension with ideas of globalization and technologies that make borders porous. Saskia Sassen has been original and perceptive in dissecting the changing framework of the nation state in the dynamic of globalization and its impact on rights (2008), and it is useful to apply parts of her analysis to the specific rights we denominate as the right to receive and impart information. How is our set of rights embedded in the structure of the nation state and therefore altered by changed global circumstances?

THE RISING SECURITIZATION OF THE STATE

Another institutional foundation for a system of freedom of expression is a certain level of confidence in the security of the national polity. It may well be that the level of fear or paranoia in a society is a better predictor of the extent of living, breathing freedom of expression than is the language of constitution or law. During wartime, societies steeped in a tradition of free expression engage in deep compromises, although they may also strive to maintain as much capacity for unencumbered discourse as is possible. National experiences in the World Wars and the conflicts of the twenty-first century demonstrate how a society can, at the same time, both clamp down and consciously search for ways to make expression freer and more constitutive of a democratic society. In such an environment, persuasion, peer pressure, and the government's penchant to manage information all contribute to mediating between spaces of freer speech and spaces of greater control (Stone 2004).

Some boundary of preoccupation with national security is a condition of freedom-of-expression jurisprudence, at least in common experience. "National emergencies" have been one of the most frequent reasons for suspending privileges of free expression or modifying them beyond recognition. India, Ethiopia, Egypt, Georgia, and other states have all had short or long "emergencies" in which speech regulation has been an integral and often a seriously unpleasant ingredient. Declaration of a global war on terror has been the occasion for systematic review and revision of the underpinnings of free expression – surveillance, data storage, data retention, and reexamination, declaring certain kinds of speech efforts as, themselves, acts of terrorism and therefore unprotected. Beyond direct government acts, heightened national security fears intensify self-censorship but create a feedback mechanism; legislation that would normally be implausible gains currency during periods of fear. The systemic question for our historical moment is whether there is a shift from the norm of a democratic state to a norm of a security state or some novel melding of the two. Again, the point is to determine whether the ordinary rhetoric of free expression – the models that are put forth, the limitations deemed suitable – is changing because of these geopolitical transformations. The ubiquitous deployment of terms such as "cybersecurity" and "cyberattack" (Zetter 2010) by governments are indicators of changed assumptions that could foretell further changed government practices.

Tied to these questions of security is how technology causes a shift in the plurality of citizenship. Not only the Internet and social media, but satellites as well, facilitate the retention of old loyalties and have an effect on the making of new ones. Social media occupy some of the enforcement space; Facebook, for example, establishes rules about what can be seen and what is filtered. States beseech Google to block or allow information. Altered conditions change the real-world constitution of rights, including the right to freedom of expression. Here, especially, the machinery surrounding human rights is increasingly impressive with the capacity to appeal outside territorial bounds for a declaration that international norms and laws apply. These are all elements for Sassen (2008, p. 280) of the reconstitution of the nation state: "Insofar as citizenship is at least partly and variably shaped by the conditions within which it is embedded, conditions that have changed in specific and general ways, we may well be seeing a corresponding set of changes in the institution itself."

CONCLUSION

A new age of pervasive social media use, with global community standards, often clashing with local national or cultural norms, presents circumstances the world over that call for the pressing review of the impact on a variety of theories of speech and society. In a way, such a reconceptualization is ongoing, as states, corporations, and other large-scale speakers, together with civil society, seek to understand whether and how processes of change take place and with what consequences. Speech flows may be more a function of infrastructure design than of the machinery of rights. Were this the case, practice would be more affected by architectures of the Internet, pricing mechanisms for data, the health and capacity of the printed press, or the regulation of satellite transponders and cable systems than it would be by conceptions of speech in society. The locus of control of information moves steadily to monopolies or oligopolies on the traditional media side or, in a newer world of social media, to self-generated and unmediated producers of information. Both modes fit with difficulty into the old paradigm of speech and society in which mediators or gateways were recognizable and largely accountable. The porousness of borders means that regulation, in its historic sense, is less and less effective.

The point is that when we are looking at the institutional bases for various conceptions of the role of speech in society, there are large-scale, meaningful, often neglected factors rooted within the societies themselves that should be considered. The essays in this volume are efforts to enrich such examination.

REFERENCES

Fiss, O. M. 1987. "Why the state," *Harvard Law Review* 100(4): 781–94.

Gey, S. 2005. "Free will, religious liberty, and a partial defense of the French approach to religious expression in public schools," *Hous. L. Rev.* 42(2005–2006).

Habermas, J. 1991. *The Structural Transformation of the Public Sphere: An Inquiry into a Category of Bourgeois Society.* Cambridge, MA: The MIT Press.

Hallin, D. C. and Mancini, P. 2004. *Comparing Media Systems: Three Models of Media and Politics.* Cambridge, New York: Cambridge University Press.

Lunn, J. 2005. "The power of justice, justice as power: Observations on the trajectory of the international human rights movement," *Crisis States Development Research Centre, LSE.* Discussion Paper No. 12, September. Available at: http://eprints.lse .ac.uk/28335/1/dp12R.pdf.

Lyn, C. A. and Atkin, D. J. 2007. *Communication Technology and Social Change: Theory and Implications.* Mahwah, NJ: Lawrence Erlbaum Associates.

Marvin, C. 1988. *When Old Technologies Were New: Thinking About Electric Communications in the Late Nineteenth Century.* New York: Oxford University Press.

Ross, A., interview by Esfandiari, G. 2011. "U.S. innovation adviser: 'Internet freedom is not a regime-change agenda'," *Radio Free Europe/Radio Liberty.* Last modified July 18, 2011. Available at: www.rferl.org/a/us_innovation_adviser_says_internet_ freedom_is_ not_a_regime_change_agenda/24269090.html.

Sassen, S. 2008. *Territory, Authority, Rights: From Medieval to Global Assemblages.* Princeton, NJ: Princeton University Press.

Schiller, H. 1976. *Communication and Cultural Domination.* White Plains, NY: International Arts and Sciences Press.

Siebert, F. S., Peterson, T., and Schramm, W. 1973. *Four Theories of the Press; the Authoritarian, Libertarian, Social Responsibility, and Soviet Communist Concepts of What the Press Should Be and Do.* Freeport, NY: Books for Libraries Press.

Stone, G. R. 2004. *Perilous Times: Free Speech in Wartime from the Sedition Act of 1798 to the War on Terrorism.* New York: W.W. Norton.

United Nations General Assembly 1961. "Draft international covenants on human rights, report of the third committee," Sixteenth Session, Agenda Item 35, December 5, 1961.

Zetter, K. 2010. "U.S. declassified part of secret cybersecurity plan," *Wired*. March 2, 2010. Available at: www.wired.com/2010/03/us-declassifies-part-of-secret-cybersecurity-plan/.

Part I

Revisiting International Norms

2

Islam, Human Rights, and the New Information Technologies

Ali Allawi

Freedom is to act as one's real and true nature demands and so only the exercise of that choice which is of what is good can properly be called 'free choice'. A choice for the better is therefore an act of freedom ... Whereas a choice for the worse is not a choice as it is grounded in ignorance ... it is then also not an exercise in freedom because freedom means precisely being free of domination by the powers of the soul that incites to evil. (al-Attas 1995, p. 33)[1]

Tensions and crises have punctuated the relationships between Islam and the West in the modern era. In the past three decades, Islam has been in the dock of world opinion. It has been obliged to respond to questioning and even indictment of its values and principles. Islam has been challenged over its contribution to or encouragement of the instability, violence, and mayhem caused by some of its adherents. Muslims have been put on the defensive and feel besieged by accusations and obloquy from all quarters. Age-old charges that would not have been out of place in the Middle Ages are trotted out and hurled at Muslims and Islam, to which are added new accusations that are specific to modern times. The onslaught is unremitting and no sooner is one issue resolved than another quickly emerges to replace it. There are wars everywhere: from the "War for Muslim minds" to the "War for the Soul of Islam;" from the "War on Terror" to the wars in Iraq, Syria, and Afghanistan. European parliamentarians discuss the finer aspects of Islamic jurisprudence and US presidents pontificate on the merits of the Islamic religion. Islam is the fodder for scare-mongering headlines in the gutter press, but also preoccupies the more sedate and thoughtful of the world's media. Islam has become the foil for whatever set of precepts defines the modern mind. Whenever gender issues are discussed, Islam's treatment of women becomes the other,

[1] Syed Muhammad Naquib al-Attas was a Malaysian philosopher and educator.

unacceptable alternative. Whenever freedom of speech is seen to be threatened, it is often Islam that is doing the threatening. Whenever freedom of worship is restricted, it is Islam that is condemned for its supposed intolerance of other religions and its degrading treatment of its minorities. The ancient Islamic term of protected minorities, the *Dhimmis*, is now turned against Islam as proof of its in-built discrimination. A few weeks after September 11, 2001, the Italian journalist Oriana Fallaci wrote:

> You [the Western public] don't understand or don't want to understand that if we don't oppose this, don't defend ourselves against this, don't fight, Jihad will win. And it will destroy the world that, good or bad, we've succeeded in building, changing, improving and making a little more intelligent, i.e., less bigoted or even without bigotry. And with that it will destroy our culture, our art, our science, our morality, our values and our pleasures. (Fallaci 2001)[2]

The animus against Islam could partly be explained by the hysteria that gripped the Western public after the attacks by al-Qaeda on New York and Washington. This was further exacerbated by the 2004 bombings in Madrid and those in 2005 in London. All of this fed into the vastly disproportionate military and security response of the United States and its allies to what were, after all, terrorist acts, and not a declaration of war by a state let alone a religion and civilization. However, the grounds for demonizing Islam had already been set in the past decade, or even earlier.

UNIVERSAL HUMAN RIGHTS AND ISLAM

The idea of Islam as the "Other" is of course not new. However, it lay dormant for most of the twentieth century. Its reappearance with such virulence in recent times is quite shocking. What is notably different now is the extent to which it has seeped into popular culture and the politics of the West. The "Orientalism" of earlier times was a preoccupation of narrow elites: of administrator-scholars, founders of new academic disciplines, and writers and artists of peculiar aesthetic sensibilities. It penetrated the popular mind through colonial wars and jingoism, but its duration as a factor in the public imagination was short. There were other, more pressing dangers: from internal economic collapse during the Great Depression; the threat from the totalitarian dictatorships of Europe; and finally the Cold War. For most of

---

[2]   This quote is from Fallaci's now-famous diatribe against Islam. Fallaci was not the only writer who vented her spleen against Islam after the September 11, 2001 attacks. Others were the British journalist Melanie Phillips and writer Polly Toynbee.

the twentieth century, the defeated and prostrate Islamic world was hardly fit to challenge the West in any meaningful way. No one cared much, but still, Islam was vaguely felt to be a threat or problem, even in the days immediately after World War II. As the world was convening to establish the institutions of the UN and to formulate the 1948 Universal Declaration of Human Rights (UDHR), the potential of an Islamic "exception" to the evolving doctrines on human rights was already an issue. The entire effort paid only lip service to the concerns and world views of other civilizations. No one, of course, was in a position to challenge the victorious allied powers or to engage in any serious debate about what were in essence philosophical and religious issues. The Cold War had not quite started so, although the Soviets were prevaricating, they nonetheless went along with the final draft.

The commission that was set up to oversee the process of drafting the UDHR was chaired by Eleanor Roosevelt, but the special rapporteur (or coordinator) was Charles Malik of Lebanon. He in fact wrote the preamble and was responsible for several articles that strove to ensure the document had universal import. Other members of the commission included a French legal expert, René Cassin, a Canadian UN administrator and legal scholar, John Humphrey, and P. C. Chang of China. Cassin, a noted scholar of Jewish origin, had lost members of his family in the Holocaust. He later went on to win the Nobel Peace Prize in 1968. P.C. Chang represented the Republic of China, before the victory of the communists under Mao in 1949 sent the remnants of its government into exile on the island of Taiwan. He received his doctorate in philosophy from Columbia University and his own views were heavily influenced by Confucian thought.

However, it was Malik who was the pivotal figure in the commission's work. Malik, a philosopher and diplomat, had studied under Alfred North Whitehead at Harvard. His Lebanese origins made him, as it were, a surrogate for the absent Muslim voice in the commission, but that was an erroneous assumption. Malik was not only a committed Christian, what would be termed a fundamentalist today, but held views that were deeply antithetical to Islam. In later life, he became an ideological mentor to the Lebanese Forces, a right-wing Christian militia during the Lebanese Civil War of 1975–90. He was responsible for statements such as "I believe that the Graeco-Roman-Judaeo-Christian tradition, with all its rich inner manifold and even contradictions, is the greatest and deepest and truest living historical fact in existence." (Malik 1971)[3]

---

[3]   It is noteworthy that this article is still included on the website of Lebanese Forces, a militant Christian right-wing party.

At the UN of that period, some of the states that represented "Islam," all of them impoverished, dependent, and weak in the pre-oil era, abstained from voting on the declaration. They neither appreciated its import nor were prepared, or capable, of arguing for a different, more inclusive document. The Soviet Bloc reacted to it mainly in terms of its emphasis on individual rather than social rights. In the end, Charles Malik, an indefatigable lobbyist and networker,[4] managed to neutralize the suspicions of the Soviets, partly by incorporating some of their concerns into the final draft. However, they also abstained from the final vote. The declaration was passed and became "universal," the official global statement on human rights.

The point, however, is not to disparage the UDHR, but rather to situate it in the context of the age. The document was drafted to all intents and purposes by a body dominated by Western powers with a spoiler's role for the Soviets. It became the foundation stone of the world's understanding of human rights. It has since achieved almost sacrosanct status and is a leitmotif of all discussions on human rights. At the time, very few critics of the declaration saw it as a document that was a product of a specific civilizational or cultural worldview. Superficially, it appeared to be a natural outgrowth of the "four freedoms" proclaimed by Roosevelt as the basis of the postwar order: freedom of expression; freedom of worship; freedom from want; and freedom from fear. Nevertheless, none of the authors of the declaration would have explicitly associated it with a particularly "Western" concept of human rights. The epithet "universal" that was attached to the declaration gave it finality and an elevated perch from which it could preside as the world's conscience. Human rights were indeed universal and emancipatory. Its fashioners, nearly sixty years ago, could not anticipate that the worthy principles embodied in the declaration would become a tool to challenge Islam on its commitment to or acceptance of universal human rights. Islam was simply not on their radar screens.

Are human rights universal, or are they rooted in specific Western experience? If they are indeed an outcome of Malik's "Graeco-Roman-Judaeo-Christian" basis of Western civilization, then their adoption by other civilizations, specifically Islam, affirms the "victory" of Western civilization in the modern world. These rights include the ideals of liberalism, democracy, and secularism. If Islam were to adopt them in their entirety, then the separate civilizational space that Islam could claim for itself would end. If other civilizations reject them as purely Western formulations (again, Islam is the one civilization that is seen as the recalcitrant holdout) then the West

---

4   Charles Malik's work at the UN on the UDHR is considered in the collection of essays in his honor, edited by his son (Malik 2000).

has a new civilizing mission, namely to act out its historic role as the end state of the human political order. Its values, including its definition of human rights, become the globe's values. Alternatively, if the values of the UDHR are indeed universal, then their roots must be present in all civilizations. A new consensus on human rights has to evolve from an inter-civilizational exchange that would include all the world's religions and civilizations to generate a new universal declaration of human rights. This is hardly on the cards. In fact, the proliferation of official agencies and nongovernmental organizations in the Western world devoted to human rights propagation and monitoring makes it clear that no one in the West is prepared to budge from the position that the declaration is globally applicable, if not quite yet enforceable.

Are human rights an essentially Western construct? There is little doubt that the idea of human rights can be traced to both Biblical sources and the notion of a natural law that is separate from divine revelation. The Bible talks about Man being created in the image of God, and St. Paul's letters emphasize the equality of mankind in Christ. The natural law tradition goes back to the ancient Greeks: the idea that human beings are endowed with inalienable rights that derive from an unwritten law, a higher principle. Then there is the Protestant Reformation, which asserted individual conscience as the foundation for an authentic faith. English common law and its concern with inheritable rights as such is another noted source for the ideal of human rights. The privileging of the individual over the collective is a common theme in these traditions of human rights, and underpins the UDHR. Its preamble is replete with words such as "inalienable" and "inherent." The French Revolution's Declaration of the Rights of Men and the Citizen, the Magna Carta, writs of habeas corpus, Christian theology, and the US Constitution and Bill of Rights are all sources of modern human rights. So, in this sense, human rights are indeed a product of the Western tradition.

However, it was never inevitable that this particular aspect of the Western tradition would prevail. What we have now is the end of one of the many routes that Western thought and practice on human rights could have taken before it settled on the present formulations. The appalling horrors of World War II, at least in the European theater of war, were committed in the Western sphere. Stopping their recurrence was an essential purpose of the UDHR. "Disregard and contempt for human rights have resulted in barbarous acts which have outraged the conscience of mankind," declaims the declaration.[5] Medieval Christian theology celebrated the hierarchical in nature and thus inequality within the order of things. The Protestant Reformation had deeply

---

[5] UDHR, preamble.

authoritarian features to it. Luther's spiritual equality among Christian believers did not extend to non-Christians or to a challenge to the political and social order. There exists an entire tradition in Western political and moral thought that decries individual human rights and fears them as undermining collective rights and the sense of community, and as a source of alienation. The most powerful critique of the modern notion of human rights came from the most significant religious institution in the West: the Catholic Church. It was not until the Second Vatican Council of 1965 that the Church finally made its guarded peace with the modern human rights movement. Until that time, religious freedom was a mortal sin in Catholic theology, and freedom of expression was a license for disorder and chaos. The issue of "reproductive rights" as an element of the panoply of human rights continues to be hotly disputed by the Catholic Church.

Modern human rights are situated in a post-traditional society, a society divorced from its roots in the ethics of religion or philosophy. Such rights are a feature not so much of Western civilization but rather a natural concomitant to the development and progress of modern, technologically based and market-driven societies. They are an aspect of the political debate and can be subject to variation and change. They are given a concrete reality by laws and institutions, none of which has any overarching ethical framework. Whatever stands in the way of the adoption of human rights as a hallmark of such a postmodern society is an irrelevance or, at worst, an obstacle to be ignored or removed. Human rights become "de-traditionalized." The conditional recognition of human rights by the Catholic Church is, for example, an irrelevance in practice. The Church's ethical arguments against abortion carry no weight in the political debate on reproductive rights. There are many majority-Catholic countries, especially in Europe, that pay no heed to the Church's rulings in these matters. Islam of course is doubly damned. Not only are its ethical arguments ignored entirely, but it is seen as a positively retrograde force inasmuch as it declines to participate in the postmodern order. This argument has been frequently employed by "progressive" figures in Europe who denigrate Islam as a premodern worldview that has no place in Europe. It has gained currency as Europe wrestles with the implications of "multi-culturalism" and its perceived failure to integrate Muslims into wider European society.

The UDHR, despite misgivings about its provenance, was a laudable project in many aspects. It set standards that would later confront the world of Islam with a definition of universal rights that could conflict with Islam's own possible interpretations of human rights. Some of its articles were loaded and appeared primed to elicit a negative response from Islam. Article 18 is a case in point.[6] It affirmed freedom not only to choose one's faith but to change it. It was introduced specifically by Charles Malik, knowing full well that renunciation of Islam by a born or converted Muslim has problematic consequences.

The declaration's effectiveness during the Cold War was limited, despite the frequent appeal to its principles by organizations such as Helsinki Watch that monitored the Soviet Bloc's human rights record. It mainly stayed dormant throughout the Cold War years but sprang to life again in the 1980s as the Soviet Union began to lose its grip over its east-European satellites.

In the intervening period, Muslim states had paid scant attention to or respect for the idea of human rights, lulled into a false sense of security by the certainties of the Cold War. From the Arab world's ubiquitous *Mukhabarat* to the Shah's SAVAK (*Sōzemōn-e Ettelō'ōt va Amniyat-e Keshvar* [Organization of Intelligence and National Security]), the secret police apparatuses that kept most Muslim leaders in power were deeply complicit in illegal killings, deportations, kidnappings, and torture. Their human rights abuses went unnoticed in the confrontation between the Soviet Bloc and the West.

It was only after the demise of the Soviet Bloc that Muslim countries began to notice that they had unwittingly signed up to a document, the underlying principles of which they may not have fully shared. The UDHR and the phenomenal growth of the human rights movement in the 1990s began to focus the spotlight on Muslim countries and their appalling human rights records. In 1990 they convened in Cairo and produced an alternative Islamic version of human rights. This became known as the Cairo Declaration of Human Rights. It was officially adopted in 2000 by all the countries of the Organisation of the Islamic Conference. The spirit of the Cairo Declaration is fundamentally different from that of the UDHR. It firmly sets the Islamic understanding of human rights in terms of the Quran and Sharia: human rights being derived from the dignity conferred to man by God's ascription of vice-regency to Man; and Sharia as the fundamental basis for understanding and interpreting these rights.

HUMAN RIGHTS IN ISLAM

Human rights, and their universal application, are rightly seen as a defining challenge to the principles of Islamic life and civilization. The issue is now

---

[6] The full text of Article 18 reads: "Everyone has the right to freedom of thought, conscience and religion; this right includes freedom to change his religion or belief, and freedom, either alone or in community, with others and in public or private, to manifest his religion or belief in teaching, practice, worship and observance."

highly politicized, especially with the rise of Islamophobia in Europe, outcries over the imposition of Sharia, and the war on terror that wittingly or otherwise has conflated Islam with violence in the minds of millions of people. It has become an either/or issue: either Islam accepts the universality of the rights embodied in the UDHR and subordinates its own ethical foundations to it, or it opts out of the entire matter and charts its own way to formalizing the rights of man in Islam. The collapse of the Soviet Bloc and its half-hearted attempts to present economic and social rights as an alternative axis for a human rights doctrine gave a huge fillip to the universality of the concepts underpinning the 1948 UDHR. Nearly all the European states of the former Soviet empire signed up to the dominant Western-inspired human rights movement.

Many in the Islamic world see the human rights movement as the thin edge of the wedge: under the guise of human rights the building blocks of the Islamic worldview would gradually be disassembled. This suspicion is behind the attempt to articulate an independent Islamic doctrine of human rights.[7] Although the authors of the Cairo Declaration may not then have realized it, the language used in the document was very much derived from modern pre-conceptions, garbed in the language of Sharia. Rights in Islam had previously been formulated in terms of people's duties and obligations to each other, to those in authority over them, to those subordinate to them, and above all to God. Whatever rights human beings have are thus an outcome of individuals and societies fulfilling their duties and responsibilities to each other. There are a few rights that are explicitly recognized as such in the Quran, parental rights over children for example, but most rights take the form of obligations. The rights of God over man are met through acts of worship and devotion; the right to work is because human beings have a duty to work and strive to improve their lot; the right to free expression is because man has a duty to seek the truth and its fulfillment. Even in matters that are not, on the surface, contentious, such as the right to justice, the right arises because others (the state, the judiciary, or those in power) have not fulfilled their duty to provide or dispense justice.

So, rights are attached to a nexus of obligations, responsibilities, and duties. This is the heart of Islam's perspective on rights. Unfortunately, it is barely

---

7   The Cairo document of 1990 was predated by nearly a decade, to little effect, by another attempt at formulating an Islamic perspective on human rights: the Universal Islamic Declaration of Human Rights, issued by the Islamic Council of Europe in 1981. That document was promoted by prominent individuals, including Algeria's former leader Ahmed Ben Bella, but was ignored after a polite reception at UNESCO where it was first presented. Neither the Western world, still preoccupied with the Soviet threat, nor the Muslim world were yet at loggerheads on the issue of human rights.

discernible in the Cairo Declaration. Clearly, fulfilling duties and obligations as the core to human rights is deeply antithetical to the modern individualist sensibility. It smacks too much of authoritarian states and institutions, of inflexible and burdensome religious duties, of the shackling of the Promethean spirit of man by a chain of dos and don'ts. But if these have created a culture that has seemingly been rejected by the modern Western imagination, there is no compelling reason why Islam should follow the same trajectory. Where will the human rights movement ultimately stop in its endeavor to remove all restrictions and curbs on the individual? The right to life may be diluted with time by utilitarian or even "ethical" calls for euthanasia. Many point to the destruction of the family as the fundamental building block of all societies or the redefinition of the institution of marriage.

One cannot and should not expect that such outcomes, which might be deemed "desirable" in the context of the enlargement of individual human rights, are automatically adopted by cultures that do not subscribe to such assumptions. It is in these spiritual and metaphysical constructs that the Cairo Declaration is severely deficient. As with so many other attempts to provide an Islamic gloss to global issues, it is simply a counter-argument, not particularly rooted in the Islamic experience or in any deep understanding of the issues raised. It is an inadequate response to a dominant paradigm and suffers the same fate as other "Islamic" responses to whatever challenges the modern world hurls at Muslims.

Nevertheless, however one takes the issue of human and social rights and duties, the Islamic world has been woefully poor in meeting its own standards of human rights. What is more galling is that, while there are numerous governmental and nongovernmental agencies in the Western world that monitor human rights abuses, the Muslim world has no organization or group of any consequence that does the same. The human rights movement that played a large part in galvanizing and supporting the Eastern European revolutions of the 1980s based its moral and legal authority on the human rights conventions of the UN.[8] There are few groups whose function is to ensure that Muslim countries that have signed up to the Cairo Declaration actually meet its stipulations. There are any number of human rights activists in the Muslim world who are connected with the global human rights movement and who monitor human rights abuses in the context of the UN declarations and conventions. The abuses in the Muslim world are monitored and exposed by these groups rather than by groups committed to the ideals of an Islamic human

---

[8] An example of these Eastern European movements is the Charter 77 group, founded by Václav Havel in Czechoslovakia.

rights movement, not that any actually exist.[9] Uncovered abuses are then either ignored or politicized as an example of nefarious plotting by groups determined to undermine Islam. Case upon case is uncovered, ranging from the persecution of minorities, such as the Ahmadis of Pakistan or the Baha'is of Iran, to the stoning of purported adulteresses in Nigeria and the amputation of criminals' hands in the Sudan. The unrelenting pressures on Muslim countries and individual Muslims from the torrent of allegations of human rights abuses goes a long way to explain Muslim sensitivities to the claims of the universal validity of human rights norms. However, this in no way justifies the general indifference shown by Muslims to the actual abuses going on right under their noses.

These are legion and are a real challenge to the significance of the Cairo Declaration; their sheer number makes them difficult to tackle. The Cairo Declaration decries genocide, but one of the Organisation of Islamic Cooperation (OIC) member countries, Saddam's Iraq, had only recently massacred its Kurdish population. Article 3 of the Cairo Declaration, which sets the principles of warfare, has been flagrantly ignored in most of the wars involving OIC member countries, such as the Somali and Afghan civil wars and the war in the south of the Sudan. Articles dealing with torture and the inviolability of the individual are routinely ignored when Muslim states feel under threat. The indiscriminate slaughter of civilians by the state security apparatus of Algeria in the 1990s civil conflict is a case in point, as are the measures deployed by the Egyptian government to combat militant Islamism in the same period. Article 20 bans torture and arrest without due cause and process. Torture and abuse of prisoners is a common practice in the authoritarian states of the OIC, including nearly all the Arab countries. Article 6 guarantees the dignity of womankind, only to see its stipulations flouted by innumerable cases where women have been treated in a degrading and cruel manner because of local tribal or social customs. Article 7 guarantees the rights of children. Abused, abandoned, and mistreated children, including victims of widespread child labor, are a common feature of Muslim countries such as Bangladesh, Egypt, and Pakistan. Article 8 guarantees the right to justice. Muslim countries have probably some of the worse judicial systems where corrupt judges, overloaded courts, and cumbersome and unfathomable legal systems all conspire to undermine one of Islamic civilization's key props: the delivery of fair and speedy justice by incorruptible judges with real authority. The list can go on. Nearly every aspect of the Cairo Declaration is flouted in

---

[9]   To give credibility to their reports, Muslim human rights advocates cite Amnesty International or Human Rights Watch, rather than any Islamic human rights group.

practice, with no effective mechanism, either governmental or through civil society networks, to monitor and ensure compliance with its terms.

Critics of a specifically Islamic doctrine of human rights focus on the "opt-out" clause, namely Sharia. Articles 24 and 25 of the Cairo Declaration specifically give Sharia the overriding legal and moral authority to determine the definitions of the categories of human rights. The implication is that Sharia does not see eye-to-eye on human rights issues with the universal codes adopted by the UN and other international conventions. So, it becomes impossible to achieve a universally acknowledged set of standards and rules for human rights to which all nations must adhere, and Islamic countries are afforded an opt-out from these agreements. However, this is a circular argument and leads either to the idea of cultural relativism, that is, each civilization is entitled to its standards of human rights, or the imposition of a supposedly universal standard of human rights on all cultures. The main issue so far as Muslims should be concerned is the real status of human beings in the Islamic world and whether their rights, no matter how derived, are abused or ignored.

Whether Sharia will always veer towards the same definition of human rights as in the liberal democracies is an interesting issue. In the majority of cases it does, and Muslim countries should be held accountable for their human rights records under these specifically Islamic codes. Where they might not, there are still ample opportunities to discuss and probe the limits of Sharia as it relates to the rights and duties of mankind. However, the debate over cultural relativism and the universality of human rights breeds a hostile defensiveness on the part of Muslims. They are asked to jettison a foundation of their worldview in order to conform to a universal code, to which they feel they have little to contribute. This drives many Muslim states to propose a review of the UDHR.[10]

The defense of an Islamic norm for human rights is often hypocritical. The rhetoric of an Islamic basis for human rights frequently camouflages a cavalier disregard for the very Islamic values that these countries purport to promote. The confidence that Muslims would have in their own legacy's capability of addressing human rights would be boosted immeasurably if the human rights record of the Islamic world had lived up to Islam's own codes of practice. It is hopeless to rail against a Western conspiracy to undermine Islam by imposing Western standards of human rights, if the human rights record in these

---

[10] Iran in particular has been vociferous in its demands for a review of the UDHR. See, for example, "Islamic contribution to enriching the Universal Declaration of Human Rights" (paper presented by Iran's deputy foreign minister, M. Javad Zarif, at a seminar on Islam and human rights, October 1988, Geneva). In 2014, Zarif was appointed Iran's foreign minister under President Hassan Rouhani.

countries is dreadful. Muslims must denounce abuses, demand the abandonment of unacceptable conduct, and confront governments with their human
rights record, framed, where possible, within the ethical norms of Islam.
Governments will then find it more difficult to disguise their abusive behavior using as a justification cultural norms or traditional customs; they will be
unable to reject criticism with a blanket condemnation of human rights codes
as a Western invention.

FREEDOM OF EXPRESSION

A valid and effective Islamic version of human rights would not only serve the
interests of Muslims, but might introduce a needed balance to the entire global human rights movement. The balance between freedom of expression and
incitement, for example, is tilting increasingly towards an unfettered understanding of freedom of expression. If this is the end goal of unlimited rights to
freedom of speech, then an Islamic view that gives serious weight to responsibility and accountability for what people say may be a cure for individualism
running riot. This is, of course, one of the more contentious issues that has
driven a wedge between liberals in the West and Islam. At its heart, the dispute
is whether freedom of expression is absolute: a right that emanates from the
dignity of being a human being and that should be tempered only in extreme
conditions, such as war. This is certainly the position of the UDHR and its
subsequent unfolding in modern, liberal societies of the West. When Muslims
and Muslim states are held up to these standards they are seen to be wanting.
Their response is usually expressed in the language of authoritarianism, such
as the state or religion must not be undermined by irresponsible statements
and declarations, but hardly ever in terms of their adherence to Islam's own
understanding of freedom of expression. "Reverse engineering" would help
here so that the roots of freedom of expression in Islam must be discovered
and elaborated upon in a systematic and consistent manner. Such a process
would be connected to the contemporary definition of the term "freedom of
expression" and not to one that is derived from the limited and possibly different meaning given to it in earlier times.

   This *ijtihad* (independent reasoning) must therefore both be rigorous in
scholarly terms as well as fully aware of the moral, political, and even metaphysical meanings attached to the particular freedom in modern times. Too
often, the "universal" definition is taken for granted and then reformers seek to
find the justification for it, *ex posteriori*, in Islamic jurisprudence. The results
are then hotly disputed by more traditional scholars, who reject them on the
grounds of unacceptable innovations or pandering to Western definitions.

The alternative route is also fraught with problems. Traditional scholars draw on history, precedent, and analogy to interpolate the meaning of freedom of expression, and produce rigid and narrow definitions that do not fit with the modern, broader significance of the concept.

Man's right to freedom of expression does not derive, in Islam, solely from the inherent dignity of man that entitles him or her to this right. It is also a matter of purpose. What is the purpose of a right to free expression if it does not seek to find or advance the cause of truth, Islam would ask? The Quran is replete with references to *Haqq* (the Truth) and in fact it is one of the attributes of God. It is this aspect, the purposeful aspect of the fully empowered being, that stands at the heart of freedom of expression. Of course, democratic notions of freedom of expression were also imbued with this aspect, but these have been whittled away over the past few decades.

It is not that freedom of expression in the liberal democracies is absolute. It is not. There are specific legal limits, such as the criminalization of Holocaust denial or where malicious slander is intended, but most have been removed as the definition of freedom of expression has expanded. The scope of obscenity charges, for example, has been drastically restricted in past decades. However, nonlegal constraints on freedom of expression continue to hold, prompted mainly by what public opinion determines to be the limits of free expression. While in the past these limits may have owed much to religious or moral scruples, today they are more influenced by the media and "opinion-leaders" in society. Attacks on people on the grounds of race and ethnicity are deemed unacceptable, and even criminalized in certain countries, but not so pervasively on the grounds of religion. An individual is deemed to have chosen his religion, but not his ethnicity or race.

Attacks on Islam have come from a variety of sources, but many are in one way or another related to the issues of freedom of expression in Islam. The Rushdie affair, for example, came down in the end to a clash between the advocates of unrestricted freedom of expression and Islamic notions of blasphemy. (Politically, of course, the Rushdie affair had far more to do with the disorientation and marginalization of recent migrants to the UK, and the intense, almost blind, hatred that certain members of the West's intellectual elites have for Islam.) The Rushdie affair was only the progenitor to a rash of similar confrontations that took place, mainly in Western Europe, between Muslims and advocates of absolute free expression. The Danish cartoons controversy and the murder of the Dutch filmmaker Theo van Gogh simply confirmed to the West the censorious and repressive features of Islam. Muslims of course saw it differently: a calculated, gratuitous attack on the faith of a deeply disadvantaged and politically weak minority, purposefully designed to

humiliate and incite. The massacres of cartoonists at the *Charlie Hebdo* magazine in January 2015 brought these issues once again to the fore in a gruesome
and terrifying fashion. For a moment, all of France and Europe were united
in rejecting the claims of the jihadi perpetrators, but it did not put to rest the
matter of the limits to freedom of expression. None other than the founder
and former editor of the magazine questioned the assumptions of limitless
freedoms.

There is probably little common ground between notions of absolute
freedom of expression and the desirable limits of free expression in Islam.
"Political correctness" in the Western world plays a decisive role in limiting
freedom of expression among the intelligentsia. This is partly borne from
guilt at the horrors of the Holocaust, mainly ignored or acquiesced to by a
substantial number of people, including intellectuals, during the 1930s and
in wartime Europe, and from the undercurrent of racism that was part and
parcel of colonial projects. The extent of the awareness and complicity of
Europeans, both in Western and Eastern Europe, in the decimation of their
Jewish and gypsy fellow citizens during World War II has only recently come
to light. In most of the Western world, Holocaust denial and overt racism have
become criminalized, and anti-Semitism in any form is no longer publicly
tolerated. However, this sentiment does not quite apply to Islam. For example,
a proposed bill by the British government in 2004 to criminalize incitement
to religious hatred, aimed mainly at preventing Islamophobic behavior, was
watered down. It faced a chorus of opposition from across the political spectrum, mostly couched in convoluted arguments about why freedom of speech
should not be constrained by religious sensibilities. It was clear though that
the attempt to give Muslims in Britain some legal cover against violent acts
or speech that targeted them as Muslims had little appeal, especially with
opinion-leaders, politicians, and intellectual figures.[11] So, freedom of speech
is in fact constrained in many instances in the West, but what Muslims see
is the insistence on an absolute right to speech for those who target them or
their faith.

The argument has been made that Islam not only respects but demands freedom of expression. The Quranic injunction of "enjoining the good and shun-
ning evil" is impossible to act on if human beings are not allowed to speak and
act freely. However, the concept of *hisbah*, which embodies this injunction,
has been perverted with time. It is now associated with the notorious moral
police of some Muslim countries who take it upon themselves that Muslims
conform to the outer duties of Sharia. In an erudite and comprehensive work,

---

[11]   Thus black, Asian, or Jewish Britons had legal redress under antiracism and anti-Semitism laws.

Freedom of expression in Islam, the Afghan scholar Muhammad Hashim Kamali, sets out specific principles from which an entire doctrine of free speech can be derived (Kamali 1998). These are mainly praiseworthy actions or specific license that cannot be undertaken without the freedom to express oneself. They include the proffering of sincere advice (*nasihah*), the need to consult (*shura*), personal reasoning, the freedom to criticize, the freedom to express an opinion, freedom of association, and freedom of religion.

These rights are not absolute. They are constrained both morally and legally. The moral constraints on freedom of expression are found in all the great religions. They are built-in safeguards that prevent injustice, abuse, and strife. Backbiting, slander, ridicule, and exposing the weaknesses of others are all exhortations that carry no legal, only moral, compunction. The arts of comedy or satire might suffer if these compunctions are carried to extremes, but Islam would not specifically restrict them. Islamic literature is full of irreverent and satirical poets, who caricatured rulers and the high and mighty. Some, in fact, carried their license into dangerous territory. The blind medieval poet Abu 'Aala al-Maari, for example, went so far as to denounce religion and all that was sacred in Islam. The Hajj was a pagan institution; religion, including Islam, is for knaves or fools. "Do not suppose the statements of the prophets to be true; they are all fabrications. Men lived comfortably till they came and spoiled life. The sacred books are only such a set of idle tales as any age could have and indeed did actually produce," he wrote (as quoted in Hastings 2003, p. 190). Elsewhere, al-Maari declared:

> Falsehood has corrupted all the world
> That wrangling sects each other's gospel chide
> But where not hate Man's natural element
> Churches and mosques had risen side by side.
> (Nicholson 1993, p. 321)

He even challenged the literary merit of the Quran by claiming he could equal it with his poetry. (Although he did produce a parody of the Quran, he admitted to its literary inferiority.) Al-Maari was not a hermit or recluse, which would have meant that his rank impieties and heresies would have gone unnoticed. He lived to be eighty-four and, according to the traveler and fellow poet Nasir-I Khosraw, who visited him in his home town, he was very rich, revered by the townsfolk, and had over 200 students who came to attend his lectures on literature and poetry (Nicholson 1993, p. 323).

What al-Maari and scores of other libertines and free-thinkers in Islam had done was to exercise their freedom of opinion, unrestrained by any moral compunction or special allegiance to Islam. They were not punished, as their contemporaries in medieval Christianity would certainly have been, nor were they socially censored or ostracized. Personal unbelief, even ridicule of the faith, may have been reprehensible, but it was an insufficient basis on which to condemn and punish the violators. However, there are specific instances where Sharia calls for legal restraint and in this sense can be said to limit freedom of expression. Some of these restraints, such as malicious slander or libel, would be recognizable in modern Western societies. Others, such as blasphemy, are held over from laws on the statute books in some Western countries and are not currently enforced. Speech or action that encourages *fit-nah*, or sedition and conspiracy against legally constituted authority, is a punishable offense. This would be no different from sanctions against those who conspire to overturn or undermine the legal order in any democratic state.

The modern Muslim state has ignored the wide latitude given in Islam to the exercise of freedom of expression. But this has more to do with the structures of authoritarian states and governments than Islam as such. Most of these governments attained power in ways that would be denounced by Sharia, such as through a military coup d'état or assassinations and killings. What most of the world sees are Muslims and Muslim rulers who flagrantly violate universal standards of human rights and freedoms, without pausing to consider whether these violations are in any way allowed or tolerated by Islam. It is automatically assumed that because they are perpetrated by Muslims then they must have the sanction of the religion in whose names these violations are often committed or justified. However, it is in the very special and limited issue of the Islamic position on apostasy and blasphemy that those who denigrate Islam's commitment to freedom of expression appear to have a strong case. This is typical of the clash between the values of a secular modernity and a religiously inspired world, one which has been relegated to the past in most liberal democracies. That blasphemy and apostasy can even be considered as crimes is astonishing to most secular-minded people. The idea itself smacks of heretics being burnt at the stake and massacres of innocents in religious wars, a past that is best transcended rather than relived.

However, the easy generalizations about Islam, blasphemy, and apostasy are not borne out either by history or law. Although all the major classical Islamic schools of jurisprudence agree that the death sentence is proscribed for both blasphemy and apostasy, there is a significant and growing body of dissenting opinion on this matter (Kamali 1998, pp. 212–50). The dissenters base their argument, inter alia, on the explicit Quranic verse that there is no compunction in matters of religion. In the early community of Muslims, the acts of blasphemy and apostasy clearly had political as well as religious implications. The nearest approximation to this condition in modern times would be high treason. As the nascent community of Muslims became established, so did its confidence in its survival and growth. Islamic history has only a few instances where people were tried and put to death specifically for these crimes. The scale of these incidents pales in comparison to the European wars of religion, where tens of thousands were put to death for their beliefs.[12] The rarity of these crimes in Islam may be put down to either the fear of retributive justice or the fact that the legal authorities preferred to overlook these crimes because of a general unwillingness to acknowledge that they merited the death sentence, or that they threatened the integrity of Islamic society.

In modern times, the issue of blasphemy or apostasy only sporadically materializes in the Islamic world, and when it does it is often sensationalized by the Western media and treated as a significant issue in Muslim society. It does not occur to Islam's critics that the vast majority of Muslims may not be particularly interested in changing their religion or deriding its tenets and its prophet. A basically theoretical concern about the "barbarism" of Islam's apostasy and blasphemy laws has been transposed as a defining feature of the civilization. The resources and power of parts of the media in the West, and their deliberate targeting of Islam and Muslims, frequently overpowers any attempt to provide a balanced perspective on the matter. Blasphemy and apostasy are lumped with child brides, women in burqas, stoning of adulterers, flogging of wine-imbibers, and the execution of homosexuals to generate a ghastly and frightening image of Islam. It may sell newspapers and bring audiences to television channels but it hardly serves the purpose of truth.

ON BALANCE, EQUALITY, AND JUSTICE

The issues of rights and values that are facing Islamic civilization are real enough, but they cannot be treated one-dimensionally. It is not enough to "capitulate" to the incessant calls for the implementation of universal rights; neither is it possible to hide behind an all-too-human rendering of Sharia and claim eternal validity for such rights. The middle ground, if there is one, between an aggressive universalism and a defensive parochialism is also an inadequate end result for what, after all, are existential questions. These go to the heart of what Islam means and what are its relationships to ideas of justice and equality. Whenever such issues are raised, then the proper course

---

[12] The population of the German Empire probably numbered 21 million in 1618; by 1648, at the end of the great war of religion, the population had dwindled to 13 million (Wedgwood 1961, p. 496). In one incident alone, the St. Bartholomew's Day Massacre of 1572, nearly 5,000 Huguenots were killed in an orgy of sectarian violence in Paris (MacCulloch 2004, pp. 337–40).

is to return to first principles. For example, the landmark decisions of the US Supreme Court in the 1950s and 1960s on civil rights drew on basic principles, such as equal protection, to overturn two centuries of racist and discriminatory legislation.[13] Many of these laws had been approved by the Supreme Court itself in earlier times. The continuation on the statute books of such racist and discriminatory legislation threatened to poison the politics of the United States and even destroy its foundations of democracy and the equality of its citizens under the law. The crisis in Islamic civilization is broader. It is not restricted to one or two glaring aspects of abuse that need to be overturned or addressed. There is no single authority that can do the overturning; in fact, there are numerous authorities, some self-appointed, that claim the right to interpret Islam. This process is incremental and may continue for decades before a new paradigm is established to which most Muslims would subscribe most of the time.

There are numerous passages in the Quran that discuss the matter of the median way, the balance and scale of things. Balance is one of the defining features of Islam: balance between the individual and the collective; between the physical and spiritual; between the private and the public domain; between men and women; between rights and duties. Whether Muslims like it or not, the balance inside Islam has been ruptured and the civilization has lost its poise. Retreat into a self-enclosed space is not an option. An ever-changing world is too demanding and intrusive to allow this. The values of modern societies are a constant challenge and refrain to Islam, and their main demands have seeped into the public consciousness of Muslims. They have to determine whether these values are instrumental or not to the enhancement of justice and the possibility of living the good life. Muslims also have to determine whether these rights are derivable from the Islamic legacy itself and with what modifications and changes.

Women's rights, for example, are an issue that will not be explained away by reference to how Islam honored women in the Arabia of the seventh century, how women's rights are enshrined in the Quran, or how women dominate the private space in Islamic life. All are true but they bear little relationship to the real condition of women in Muslim societies, and the raw deal that is meted out to them under the camouflage of Sharia. Seeking a balance in the male-female relationships in Islam requires not only a re-examination of the roots of inequalities but also a redefinition of the role of men according to the Quran and Sharia. Balance is not simply the halfway point between inequality

---

[13] The famous Supreme Court decision in *Brown v. Board of Education of Topeka* 347 U.S. 483 (1954), which banned segregated public schools, drew on this principle.

and equality, but a separate state which strives for a harmonious, just, and stable outcome. In the case of women's rights, it is not only women that are to observe modesty and courtesy in their outer behavior and inner disposition; men are also obliged to do the same. Men have not been, historically, subjected to the same standards of behavior and responsibility demanded of them by the Quran and Sharia. Women's rights in Islam cannot be enhanced without a parallel insistence that men must also adhere to Quranic injunctions on their behavior and conduct.

THE IMPACT OF NEW TECHNOLOGIES

The debates that had framed the decades-old exchanges between Islam and the global human rights movement were conducted mainly at the level of the elites and political and social activists. However, the advent of new technologies, especially the spread of mobile communication technologies and social media, has greatly altered the tone and balance in interactions, both between Islam and the universal human rights paradigms, as well as within Islam itself. This has produced entirely unexpected outcomes. The revolts of the so-called Arab Spring that started in 2011 appeared to herald a new world of engaged citizens mobilized by social media and wholly committed to the propositions of the human rights movement. Superficially, the calls for freedom and dignity that defined the early stages of the revolts coincided with the key tenets and claims of modern human rights. The presence of huge numbers of consciously Islamic parties and groups in these manifestations raised another intriguing possibility: the acknowledgement of the validity of human rights principles within the framework of traditionalist Islam. A reconciliation of sorts between modern human rights and Islam's classical doctrines of human duties appeared to be in the offing. However, this was short-lived.

Political chaos and social turmoil gripped the countries of the Arab Spring and decimated the political promise of the uprisings. In its wake, a new landscape emerged, facilitated in no small measure by the rapid spread of social media. The alarming and unprecedented sweep of militant Salafism, politically in the form of the military conquests of the self-styled Islamic State (ISIS) and other jihadi groups, but also culturally by its seizure of huge swathes of cyberspace, brought a completely unreconstructed literalism into focus in the human rights and duties discourse in modern Islam. Issues that had lain dormant for centuries were resurrected with a vengeance as an integral part of the worldview of militant Salafism. As ISIS extended its rule into Iraq and Syria, its treatment of non-Muslim groups, heterodox Muslims and women, was all justified by an obscurantist reading of Islamic doctrines that fundamentally contradicted and rejected the proposition of an essential concordance between Islam and modern human rights. The aggressive assertion of Sharia rulings of centuries past raised a fundamental challenge to the very principle of human rights and posed a serious dilemma to conservatively minded Muslims who nevertheless held out the possibility of an Islamically inflected view on human rights.

If slavery is not only permissible but is in fact an ordinary feature of society, then what does that imply to the essential impermissibility of losing one's freedom? If forcing Christians to convert, pay the *jizya* tax, or be put to death is mandatory inside an Islamic state, what does that mean to freedom of religion? How does anathematizing entire populations whose religions are not considered within the ambit of the protected faiths impact the notion of genocide? These questions had been allowed to slip into obscurity and irrelevance, even by literally minded Salafists, because they lay well outside one's experiences in the contemporary world. The postwar consensus on the outlawing of slavery and genocide and on freedom of religious practice was overwhelming, even though it was not always uniformly honored in reality. What made the matter of even greater significance was that the justifications for these practices by the militant Salafis of ISIS and their ilk were invariably accompanied by copious legal and jurisprudential arguments as to their permissibility, mainly carried through social media and the Internet. This is, of course, fundamentally different from the limited range and impact of previous reactionary Islamic states, such as those of the Taliban or premodern Arabia. They were greatly constrained by their isolation and inability or indifference to spreading their own version of Islam to a global audience. Cyberspace is now not only the front line for the spread of jihadi ideologies but also the preferred platform for the dissemination of Salafi literalism as it relates to human rights.

This is posing a dilemma of the first order to reform-minded Muslims who have built their case on an accommodating reading of the notion of human rights within the Islamic tradition. It raises the conundrum of the inviolability of Sharia and its timelessness around issues that were best forgotten, because they ought not to arise in a modern context. There are few ways that Sharia-minded Muslims can counter Salafi literalism when confronted with clearly sanctioned practices of eons ago, if these practices are resurrected anew. Nevertheless, one is hard put to believe that such an aberrant form of Islam can withstand the pressures of the age. It is likely that Salafi literalism will be decoupled from militant armed Salafism, but the unity of doctrine that they both share will cast a pall on the notion that an empowered Salafi literalism will behave any differently from the version embodied in jihadi Salafism. After all, the roots of ISIS's social doctrines are the same as those of the literalist Salafists.

In the end, Muslims must themselves decide what human rights mean in Islam and whether these rights must be affirmed consciously, rather than adopted under pressure or international scrutiny. However, the starting point must be whether Muslims actually want these rights for themselves, not only because they are sanctioned by jurisprudence but, perhaps more importantly, because they advance justice. The concept of 'Adl (justice) is specifically mentioned in many instances in the Quran. Justice in Islam is a universal moral truth and the creation of a just order, political as well as religious, ought to be a primary focus of any Islamic rule or government. The fact is that Muslim states pay scant attention to Quranic justice, and have not evolved a body of human rights principles that are justice-based. However, the establishment of a more just society may in fact be the way forward for an evolving Islamic doctrine of human rights. The inequality of women in society, for example, violates the concept of 'Adl in many fundamental ways. 'Adl can be used to reinterpret or challenge important rulings that have formed the Islamic position on these matters, creating a new Islamic "architecture" of human rights. Regardless of whether these rights accord with the rules of international conventions, it is crucial that they occupy a prominent place in the political and moral lives of Muslim societies.

Information technology will also play a fundamental part in the evolution of the human rights discourse in Islam. The dissemination of Salafi doctrines, whether politically or doctrinally militant in inspiration, is greatly facilitated by the undermining of traditional authorities and their channels for diffusing orthodox Islam. These have played no small part in creating the groundswell of support for and legitimization of outlying and even outlandish interpretations of Islam. However, the alienation of a large proportion of ordinary pious Muslims from the behavior and thought of militant Salafism could lead to both an erosion of religious faith and the beginning of serious push-back, if the Salafi ascendancy prevails. In this case, new information technologies will play a vital part in the process. The new forms in which Islam has to mold itself to overcome this destructive turn cannot be diffused widely and effectively except through new media; neither for that matter can the secular understanding of modern human rights.

REFERENCES

Abu 'Aala al-Maari quoted in Nicholson, R. A. 1993. *Literary History of the Arabs*. Richmond, Surrey: Curzon Press.

al-Attas, S. M. N. 1995. *Prolegomena to the Metaphysics of Islam.* Kuala Lumpur: ISTAC.

Fallaci, O. 2001. "Rage and pride," *Il Corriere della Sera,* September 29, 2001 (Italy).

Hastings, J. 2003. *Encyclopaedia of Religion and Ethics, Part 2.* Whitefish, MT: Kessinger Publishing.

Kamali, M. H. 1998. *Freedom of Expression in Islam.* Kuala Lumpur: Ilmiah Publishers.

MacCulloch, D. 2004. *Reformation: Europe's House Divided 1490–1700.* London: Penguin.

Malik, C. 1971. *God and Man in Contemporary Islamic Thought.* American University of Beirut Centennial Publications, September 13, 1971.

Malik, H. 2000. *The Challenge of Human Rights: Charles Malik and the Universal Declaration.* Oxford: Centre for Lebanese Studies.

Nicholson, R. A. 1993. *A Literary History of the Arabs.* Richmond, Surrey: Curzon Press.

Wedgwood, C. V. 1961. *The Thirty Years War.* New York: Anchor Books.

3

Closure, Strategic Communications, and International Norms

Monroe Price

This is a book about alternate visions of speech in society where the visions occur in different national settings. Often these visions are rooted in foundational norms; these are set domestically, as with the First Amendment to the United States Constitution; regionally, as in Article 10 of the European Convention on Human Rights; or internationally, as in Article 19 of the International Covenant on Civil and Political Rights (ICCPR). Resort to norms gives comfort to those who hold to a vision that conforms to them. Norms provide a justification and framework for comparing one vision against another.

One consequence is that state and non-state actors compete to define norms and to adjust those norms to fit particular visions (as well as adjust visions to conform to norms). Countless rivulets of reflection and reaction lead to gradual, glacial shifts in interpretation. Norms exude qualities of immutability, and definitely aspirations of permanence. Yet within the portrait of such norms as caught frozen in ice, there are sites and moments in which processes of adjustment take place. In the area of speech and society, the contest or competition to shape international norms is vibrant on a range of issues. Examples include debates on the definition of hate speech and the role of the state in regulating it; renewed debate about Article 20 of the ICCPR dealing with state prohibitions on propaganda for war; or the coherent international attack by many on the availability of criminal sanctions for defamation.

In this chapter, I look at one prominent site where this reinterpretation and adjustment of norms is taking place, Internet governance, where governance implies state regulation and the shaping of new or revised international institutions that affect Internet practice. The debates on this issue of governance are often esoteric, answers to fine-tuned practical questions (such as how to deal with domain names, what the immunity of intermediaries should be from liability for the use of their platform, and to what extent can states require the localization of data storage), but each of these issues is encased in a larger-scale debate embedded in normative frameworks. Decisions that appear to be local and overly technical cumulatively affect the norms themselves. Dialectically, engaged entities thus house debates both in the particular and the general. They simultaneously invoke international norms and try to refigure them to help persuade stakeholders to defend one position or another.

The Internet, as we have come to know it, is a series of institutional, mechanical, and human interactions. It has elements of revolution and disruption with widespread political and social consequences and, like the introduction of every new technology, it is surrounded by issues of definition. During moments of significant technological change, companies, countries, and civil society all vie to characterize the novel technological phenomenon, often to suit existing political realities. Norms are invoked to modulate, for example, the level of government involvement in the struggle for settlement, for assurance that a particular way of perceiving the technology becomes the surviving, possibly dominant one (McCarthy 2011, p. 90). Those for whom this process of definition is meaningful, including entities I have elsewhere placed under the umbrella of "strategic communicators" (Price 2015) seek to obtain deep and long-term support for their particular mode of thinking about the technology.

The framing of international norms becomes a vital part of this process. If, in one popular formulation, a "free and open" Internet is taken as the dominant understanding of how the Internet should function in international society, then the outliers or violators of the norm can be more easily identified and labeled in terms of censorship and privacy. But we know this process of reaching definitional closure is highly contested, and the Internet governance debate involves competing architectures of information policy contained in sets of words and concepts. Most notably, China, Russia, and Iran have substantially different models of what the Internet is and should be. Indeed, societies throughout the world, including those in the West, are all trying both to understand and to persuade the international community what iteration, what idea, and what complex relationship to government and business should characterize the Internet and other new media technologies.

The invocation of norms in the search for closure is epitomized by the way the US State Department and the White House, together with like-minded states, have sought to make "Internet Freedom" the definitive narrative of a global Internet. Hardly alone, and building on the extraordinary success of the technology's advances, US government officials have emphasized how an allegedly single, interconnected Internet, as unencumbered by state interference as possible, can fulfill hopes for realizing free expression, human rights, and democracy around the world. Creating and connecting this "Internet

Freedom" narrative to these lofty goals has provided a source of legitimacy, a legitimacy purportedly embedded in the norms of the international community. This has been a long-term effort, requiring the work of not only government but of transnational companies like Google, as well as academics and other actors. In this multi-stakeholder world, engaging diverse parties is essential.

The struggle over norms is epitomized by the international campaigns and clashing conceptions for Internet design articulated by the United States and by China in the period around 2010. Both countries had, and have, a great deal at stake domestically in terms of the evolution of Internet system design, and both sought to project their views on an international stage. Two statements from the campaigns – one from the United States, one from China – are useful touchstones: a January 2010 speech by then US Secretary of State Hillary Clinton and a China-originated Internet White Paper issued not long afterwards. These releases were presented as visions of what the future of the Internet should look like, but they were also presented as visions and reflections on the domestic society that the Internet would create or reinforce. This competition is illustrative of an oft-seen phenomenon: those advocating change in communications policy, both nationally and globally, have enmeshed their conceptions in various technological, social, and political categories to improve the chances that these policies will be adopted. They have sought to "hard-wire" their ideas of speech and society into evolving digital infrastructures. Both documents were also formulated to be read in an international context, to gain support from influential institutional audiences.

THE US "INTERNET FREEDOM" STRATEGY

In January 2010, Secretary Clinton delivered a landmark speech called "Remarks on Internet Freedom" at a temple of free speech, the Newseum in Washington, DC (Clinton 2010). As an exercise in narrative framing, the talk was a dramatic effort to define proper structuring of the Internet in a global setting. The speech threw down a gauntlet: "Both the American people and nations that censor the Internet should understand that our government is committed to helping promote Internet freedom," and this requires that the US government fight for a global policy consistent with these views (Clinton 2010; cf. Thierer and Crews 2003). In 2006, the Bush Administration had already established a Global Internet Freedom Task Force (GIFT) but the Clinton State Department pushed further still. Renaming GIFT as the NetFreedom Task Force, Clinton provided an upgraded framework to make the Internet – and US policy concerning it – a priority in bilateral and multilateral discussions and to develop grant programs, policy initiatives, and other steps to further that goal.

The Secretary's Newseum presentation provided the earmarks of a "new information" enthusiasm, celebrating the glories of the technology:

> The spread of information networks is forming a new nervous system for our planet ... Now, in many respects, information has never been so free. There are more ways to spread more ideas to more people than at any moment in history ... And even in authoritarian countries, information networks are helping people discover new facts and making governments more accountable. (Clinton 2010)

In this metaphor of a nervous system for the planet, grounds for exporting a specific form of architecture were articulated. It required some massive complex interrelatedness, a free-flowingness inconsistent with multiple sovereign interferences, and a kind of relatively invisible oversight.

Secretary Clinton's argument depended on a tree of logic in which US interests are served by an increase in democratic values in states throughout the world. Drawing on democratic peace theory, this argument rests upon a longstanding plank of US foreign policy, namely that a world that is more dependably democratic is more stable, possibly more prosperous, and less likely to lead to conflict because, it is said, democracies do not fight battles against other democracies (Doyle 1983; Smith 2007). Attendant to this is the similarly oft-held belief that democratic states open to information and observing press freedom provide a system of diffusion that empowers individuals, leads to greater accountability, and improves or enhances the demand side for democratic governance. In this context, "Internet freedom" is, at least in part, shorthand for a series of policies concerning the Internet that would advance these democratic values and expedite more democratic political outcomes. It entails a commitment to providing and fostering an "enabling environment," one where many principles and practices come together (aspects of copyright law, the spread of literacy hewing to the rule of law, and other factors) (Price and Krug 2000).

Secretary Clinton's speech clearly played on the anxiety that a great opportunity for furthering free expression globally would be lost if the United States, in concert with others, was not proactive. The Internet provided a long-hoped for "liberating technology," one that had the potential to work in a myriad of beneficial ways, increasing education, serving as the basis for stronger citizenship advancing democratic values, and promoting "freedom" itself, perhaps the core US foreign policy narrative or brand. "Internet freedom" in this sense implies some vindication for American approaches and American aspirations. Understood within this tradition, "Internet freedom" as an idea exports both a legal structure and a culture of expression that sings in harmony with more long-standing American narratives. It implies the structuring of a competitive environment for entry and reception in which US interests have historically done well. And the alternative – more closed systems – can be seen as encouraging an environment where counter-narratives have privileged if not exclusive access (MacKinnon 2012).

How does one pursue such a vision, incomplete and aspirational as it is? Clinton's speech created the prospect of a new design element, "the freedom to connect," a potential international "right to connect" (Clinton 2010). This high-minded right sought to twin rhetorical grandeur and entitlement discourse to ground a policy approach. Creating a "right" is an example of deploying international norms as a persuasive underpinning for a strategic outcome. By endeavoring to create a movement toward a "right to connect" (or an obligation to ensure a "freedom to connect")[1] – the US government sought to establish a public and external framework in which steps toward the desired Internet freedom structure would be seen as almost mandatory.

Focused on the individual's rights, this approach pointed to the heart of the US position, succinctly stated by Clinton when she said, "We stand for a single Internet where all of humanity has equal access to knowledge and ideas" (Clinton 2010). Combining the "single Internet" idea with the "right to connect" provided the basis for a legal model whereby the Internet should not be splintered into many national Internets, each with its own rules of entry and separate regulatory frameworks reflecting differences among national publics. What was desired was "One Internet" supported by the universal right to access, regardless of territoriality. Setting out this vision and encapsulating it in a pithy term is an element of rhetorical strategy. Narratives of technological closure often require the exclusion of complex details – details that might detract from the appeal of the more clearly stated idea.

In terms of more immediately serving the ultimate objective of "One Internet," the Clinton speech was the public launch of a global campaign aimed at building an international consensus for this norm. Just five months after Clinton's remarks, in June 2010, Kenneth Corbin, reporting on a speech by the then-State Department communications guru, Alec Ross, could write that the "Department had made Internet censorship a key pillar of its foreign policy and now factors the issue into its diplomatic relations with every

---

[1] The "right to communicate" was first articulated in the 1960s by Jean d'Arcy. See d'Arcy (1969). See also Fisher (1982). More recently, William McIver, Jr., William F. Birdsall, and Merrilee Rasmussen have discussed the right in the context of the Internet. See McIver, Jr., Birdsall, and Rasmussen (2003).

other nation" (Corbin 2010). Ross argued in his speech that "Internet freedom has gone from being something that's a piece of what could at best be called a piece of foreign policy arcanum – a little thing that a handful of people work on – to something becoming increasingly central in our foreign policy." But even with new resources fueled with renewed enthusiasm, the field of engagement was vast and often hostile. As Ross continued to say:

> 2009 was the worst year in history in terms of Internet freedom ... There are now literally dozens of countries with less-than-stellar Internet freedom records. And it's increasingly the case that governments view the Internet as less something built on a single end-user-to-end-user principle than something that can be sort of built to spec, that looks and feels and works more like an intranet than an Internet. (Corbin 2010)

A public conversation in February 2011 between then Assistant Secretary of State, Michael Posner, and Leslie Harris of the Center for Democracy and Technology dealt candidly with the challenges in fostering a coherent strategy (Posner and Harris 2011). Recognizing that the United States needed to think about issues of jurisdiction and power, they asked: how could there be universal standards of Internet governance, and, if achievable, how would they be enforced? Who would referee this world? This amounted to the eternal political questions of: who decides? Where should authority to make these decisions lie? In the conversation, Harris said, "We have to figure out some kind of global governance bodies that don't force us into a race to the bottom." Finding real-world solutions to these questions placed American visions on a collision course with other nations' visions and, importantly, existing forums, Harris said, threatened to make those collisions more keenly felt:

> There are some calls around the world for governance bodies, like the UN, where we would be negotiating what works on the Internet or what ought to work with countries who have very, very different values ... I'm hoping that, in the first instance, that we can reach agreement with other democratic governments on what we believe the right policy principles are, so that we can start demonstrating the way that the Internet should be governed cross borders. But the questions of who should manage the Internet in a global environment is the thorniest and the biggest challenge. (Posner and Harris 2011)

Posner, too, recited "a range of anxieties about throwing this issue and many others into the United Nations." He went on to outline the US position on these issues:

> We believe in the United Nations; it has a lot of important roles to play. But we have great trepidation that if this [Internet governance] became a

UN-sponsored initiative, all of the most – all of the governments that have the greatest interest in regulating and controlling content and protecting against dissident speech in their own countries would be very loud voices. (Posner and Harris 2011)

The confidence of this American position in suggesting new governing structures to oversee the next-generation Internet has to be seen in the context of the formative US role – the early history of the Internet and the role of national security institutions in shaping its foundations (Abbate 1999; Townes 2012; Zittrain 2008). The Internet is a creature born of various US international communication strategies in the past, and the "Internet freedom" narrative was a way to try to sustain influence on Internet governance and architecture through a re-articulation of goals. A new historical moment, and the need to develop a new constituency for Internet regulations, requires a repackaging and, to some extent, a conceptual redesign.

Elements of the new bureaucratic embodiment of the US strategy are useful to note. In addition to making the condemnation of online censorship a plank of its diplomatic work, the State Department established monitoring and reporting mechanisms to produce a more reliable picture – as in its annual Human Rights Reports (McCarthy 2015, pp. 110, 117–20; US Department of State 2015) or the largely US government-funded Freedom House Reports on Internet Freedom (Freedom House 2016). The Department accentuated its support of grassroots efforts advocating for Internet freedom or expressing dissident views in blogs and other online forums. It offered funding for research and study in how groups in repressive societies use the Internet and how Internet opportunities can be extended, and, most directly, provided funding for the production and distribution of circumvention software to avoid filtering in societies deemed unfree.[2] It encouraged the Global Network Initiative (GNI), an entity for companies to come together with NGOs to further social responsibility objectives.[3]

---

[2] This US approach to fostering "Internet Freedom" has contributed to a competitive market for resources amongst activists and resistance movements.

[3] Established in 2008, GNI "is modeled on previous voluntary efforts aimed at eradicating sweatshops in the apparel industry and stopping corruption in the oil, natural gas, and mining industry. As with those efforts at self-regulation, this one came at a time when Internet companies were seeking to polish their image and potentially ward off legislation." See Kopytoff (2011). Google, Yahoo!, and Microsoft were charter corporate participants. On the international political economy of the Internet more broadly, see Powers and Jablonski (2015).

THE CHINA INTERNET WHITE PAPER

Similarly seeking to seal their vision into favorable technological and govern-ance infrastructures, China's architectural approach to the Internet can be contrasted with that of the United States. When viewed together, what seemed to be emerging was a global competition over international norm definition. The China Internet White Paper (People's Republic of China 2010), released in June 2010, is more impersonal and cold compared with the US position as declared by Secretary Clinton (with its receptions, banners, and idealistic bell-ringing), a product more of a bureaucracy than of a tradition of advocacy and the claim to a long-standing free-speech doctrine. The White Paper was clearly the result of careful deliberation: polished and clearly manicured and, given the timing, it seemed to be a response to the American initiative. Like the American position, it was ultimately addressed to an international audi-ence but in a language only fully understandable to those who could read Chinese history, and, while oriented towards building an international con-sensus around norms and their implementation, it carefully reflected Chinese ideas of sovereignty.

China's argument in the White Paper, its distinct selling point, was based on a position attractive to many governments. China stressed the important – indeed, necessary – role of the state and the deep significance of national sov-ereignty as a means of asserting rules and imposing obligations. With controls guaranteed, the White Paper mentions both enlarging the field of expression (the way in which the Internet expands) and emphasizing industrial pol-icy (the Internet as an engine of economic growth), but more significantly emphasizes the latter. For China, the appropriate architecture of the Internet is not valued for its "openness" but rather by the extent of its harmonious inte-gration into existing society, its reach, and its widespread use.

According to the document, the Chinese Internet, far from being an example of repression, stands as a vehicle for expanded opportunities for citizenship and economic growth. The White Paper thus heralds China's Internet accomplishments on these terms, denoting the volume of citizen use and celebrating industrial policy. It highlights the achievement of goals in the country's successive Five-Year Plans. Here, then, is the essence of China's advocacy of its model: "To build, utilize and administer the Internet well is an issue that concerns national economic prosperity and development, state security and social harmony, state sovereignty and dignity, and the basic inter-ests of the people" (People's Republic of China 2010). To this end, perspica-cious administration and management, not autonomous free-market growth, is the key to making the Internet successful in society. Administration and management are the antidotes to anxiety, allowing China to simultaneously create growth while maintaining some control over the national narrative.

From the perspective of China, this set of goals and achievements demonstrates why national legal regulation is warranted, indeed central:

> The Chinese government has from the outset abided by law-based administration of the Internet, and endeavored to create a healthy and harmonious Internet environment, and build an Internet that is more reliable, useful and conducive to economic and social development … China advocates the rational use of technology to curb dissemination of illegal information online. Based on the characteristics of the Internet and considering the actual requirements of effective administering of the Internet, it advocates the exertion of technical means, in line with relevant laws and regulations and with reference to common international practices, to prevent and curb the harmful effects of illegal information on state security, public interests and minors. (People's Republic of China 2010)

This formulation was written, obviously, to appeal to other states and establishes a bias with which many other states, and their leaders, might concur:

> Within Chinese territory the Internet is under the jurisdiction of Chinese sovereignty. Internet sovereignty of China should be respected and protected. Citizens of the People's Republic of China and foreign citizens, legal persons and other organizations within Chinese territory have the right and freedom to use the Internet; at the same time, they must obey the laws and regulations of China and conscientiously protect Internet security. (People's Republic of China 2010)

It is not only in this idea of the exercise of sovereignty that the Chinese White Paper design for the Internet differs from the "One Internet" aspiration articulated by the US Department of State, although that is a significant distinction. The differences instead go deeper: each sees the evolution of Internet policy as linked to basic theories of the role of the state and issues of leadership in global matters. The US position embraces the elements of Article 19 of the Universal Declaration of Human Rights that promise the right to receive and impart information regardless of frontiers. The assertion of sovereignty in the White Paper, however, leans toward recognition of other interests and values; employing a conventional (if often caricatured) understanding of Westphalian sovereignty to advocate that governance decisions should be made in state-led forums and international organizations.[4] The tendency of the United States

---

[4]   On September 29, 2011, Wang Chen, head of China's State Council Information Office (SCIO), spoke in the United Kingdom at the Fourth UK–China Internet Roundtable. During

to disfavor the United Nations as a decision-maker in setting these standards has already been cited. In contrast, the Chinese White Paper calls for "the establishment of an authoritative and just international Internet administration organization under the UN framework through democratic procedures on a worldwide scale." As the White Paper says:

> China holds that the role of the UN should be given full scope in international Internet administration. China supports the establishment of an authoritative and just international Internet administration organization under the UN system through democratic procedures on a worldwide scale. The fundamental resources of the Internet are vitally connected to the development and security of the Internet industry. China maintains that all countries have equal rights in participating in the administration of the fundamental international resources of the Internet, and a multilateral and transparent allocation system should be established on the basis of the current management mode, so as to allocate those resources in a rational way and to promote the balanced development of the global Internet industry. (People's Republic of China 2010)

The United States and China continued their jousting on these issues as they courted allies and found opportunities for continued engagement, skirmishes Laura DeNardis well details in her work, *The Global War for Internet Governance* (2014). In 2012, the site for contestation was the World Conference on International Telecommunication (WCIT) in Dubai, held to review existing international telecommunications regulations. The United States saw the debates leading up to the WCIT as threatening a shift in Internet governance away from institutions such as the Internet Corporation for Assigned Names and Numbers (ICANN) – the entity that governs Internet names and numbers[5] – that are technical, engineer-dominated, and were designed to exist under nominal US management. The apprehension was that governance would tilt away from a multi-stakeholder approach and toward increasing intervention from the International Telecommunications Union (ITU) or other state-centric international organizations. The final document published by the WCIT included an aspiration that "All governments should have an equal role and responsibility for international internet governance," (World

---

his opening remarks, Wang noted the importance of "sovereign jurisdictions" over the Internet in various countries, and urged his counterparts to refrain from using "freedom" to seek "network hegemony." See *China Daily* (2011).

[5] This refers to the process whereby Internet addresses match specific IP numbers on the network, a register of which is kept by Domain Name Registry. Thus, www.example.com will resolve to 123.456.789 as an IP address.

Conference on International Telecommunications 2012). This seemingly ano-dyne language was, however, interpreted as masking a potential attack on existing arrangements favorable to the United States. In that context, even proposals for change that could have been interpreted as constructive were warily received. A provision, for example, on regulating spam was seen by US representatives as a Trojan Horse for a broader system of content controls for the Internet. Seemingly simple and uncontroversial "technical" solutions to the outside observer thereby took on a deeply political character.

At the Organization for Economic Co-operation and Development in 2011, the future of the Internet was largely framed in terms of innovation and the capacity to drive economic growth (Organisation for Economic Co-operation and Development 2011). The White House issued an International Strategy for Cyberspace, designed to "build an international environment that ensures global networks are open to new innovations, interoperable the world over, secure enough to support people's work, and reliable enough to earn their trust" (Schmidt 2011). It notes that US federal policy would "encourage an environment in which norms of responsible behavior guide states' actions, sustain partnerships, and support the rule of law." Google has invested in supporting the US position, including in the publication of its Transparency Report, which tracks government requests for removal of data or for user data.

CONCLUSION

It is hardly adequate to describe the clash over the future of the Internet as a duel between the United States and China. The world is neither composed of a single superpower nor is it bipolar. Other models and approaches to system architecture exist. Iran seeks to implement a "halal Internet," structured to con-form to a particular view of national and religious morals and Shari'a jurispru-dence. This would constitute a comprehensive architecture of management, a strong and severe version of what, in earlier Internet days, was called a "walled garden" approach. Elsewhere in the world, Alexey Sidorenko has written of a sophisticated means of structuring the Internet in Russia (Sidorenko 2010; 2011) while others emphasize the "Russianness" of the "Runet"[6] (Alexanyan et al. 2012). These authors point out that, unlike much of the Internet, which remains dominated by English and dependent on popular applications and services that are provided by US-based companies such as Google, Yahoo!, and Facebook, Runet is a self-contained linguistic and cultural environment

---

[6] This term is widely used within and outside Russia to denote the Russian-language Internet (both inside and outside the country), as well as the Internet in Russia.

with well-developed and highly popular search engines, web portals, social network sites, and free email services. As Sidorenko highlights, the increasing activity of the Russian government in these affairs makes the Internet environment not only "more Russian," but also more state-affiliated. The new initiatives, such as the Cyrillic domain, not only contribute to further the "Russianness" of Runet, but also to implement a higher level of state influence. Platforms and software that are supported by the government are used in the educational system. Consequently, these become part of the socialization process for the new generations of "digital natives." An emerging multipolar international system is shaping the technology of the Internet and its users, and vice versa.

In this multipolar system, all states have sought to gain entry into the debates on Internet governance, aiming to adjust interpretations of international norms so as to harmonize them with the visions and requirements of domestic societies. As a consequence, local discourses have expanded, and discussions on the "foreign policies of Internet policy," have become truly polyphonic. Forums for interaction have emerged such as the Internet Governance Forum, and there has been a growth of institutions, alliances, research institutes, and other structures where states engaged in debates and resolution. Efforts by the major competitors to influence the Internet policy of "swing states" have become noticeable.

In this chapter I have discussed a few of the myriad legal, social, and political ways in which states compete or cooperate to adjust Internet norms, often in the interest of protecting a national vision of the role of speech in society. Let me close with one final example: the activities of the Freedom Online Coalition (FOC), a group now comprised of thirty member states. Formed in 2011 under the stewardship of the Dutch government, the Coalition was envisioned as a loose agglomeration of like-minded states who, working together, would buttress the argument and strengthen the environment for desired international norms and their proper implementation in policy. At its foundation was the oft-stated principle that "offline human rights ought to apply online," a shorthand rhetorical effort to build on what was conceived as a preexisting consensus on the individual's right to "free expression, association, assembly, and privacy." The FOC deployed a variety of techniques to forward its foundation principle.

Part of this work was definitional and entailed creating documentary support and research-based backing for significant positions. The Coalition also sought to gain influence by expanding its membership, having grown from an original eleven member states to its present size. It established an annual Internet Freedom Conference and supported working groups on specific aspects of

Internet freedom that include members of civil society, industry representatives, and academics. It helped formulate the Tallinn Recommendations for Freedom Online, to reaffirm a commitment to what would be considered a more robust international norm. It formed a Digital Defenders Partnership (DDP) that would enlarge opportunities to advance the group's transnational agenda. The DDP sought "to keep the Internet open and free from emerging threats," and "to increase and better coordinate emergency support by providing rapid responses to global threats to Internet freedom." This was to be achieved through grants and other support for organizations and individuals working in digital emergency situations such as bloggers and cyber activists who find themselves under attack, human rights defenders, journalists, NGOs, and media organizations. Managed by Hivos, an international NGO based in the Netherlands, the DDP received its financial support from the Netherlands, the United States, the United Kingdom, Estonia, Latvia, the Czech Republic, and Sweden.

Do these efforts make a difference, do they create a constituency for a norm and does strengthening a norm alter domestic arrangements relating to free expression? In 2016, the FOC commissioned an evaluation of its conduct and the extent of its impact. Those queried, including government officials, business representatives, and academics, most frequently cited the FOC's "creation of a space for government coordination and engagement on critical topics with other stakeholders through the working groups" as a success. Other successes cited included the growing number of member states and the opening-up of conversations on critical subjects and raising awareness of "Internet freedom." Failures included the lack of concrete deliverables and the difficulty in pointing to specific impacts the Coalition has had. Respondents cited a lack of clarity on what the Coalition is and what it is trying to achieve while other stakeholder groups were more likely to talk about hypocrisy and questioned whether signing up to the FOC commitments was making any tangible difference in member countries (Morgan 2016).

It is this last point on domestic politics that is central to this chapter, the interplay between supporting strong international norms abroad and affecting the structure of freedom of expression at home. All of this – this competition over international norms and their redefinition – circles back to competing ideas or visions of speech and society within different nation states toward the structure and role of expression on the Internet. What this chapter demonstrates, and the book seeks to confirm, is that underlying debates over domestic laws, transnational arrangements, and international norms are varied deep-seated approaches as to how society is to be organized. The resulting process yields an intense interplay between the global and the local and between defensive and offensive initiatives to affect international norms and domestic practices. How the Internet is perceived and structured globally affects how it is perceived and used locally and, of course, vice versa.

REFERENCES

Abbate, J. 1999. *Inventing the Internet.* Cambridge, MA: The MIT Press.

Alexanyan, K., Barasch, V., Etling, B., Faris, R., Gasser, U., Kelly, J., Palfrey, J., and Roberts, H. 2012. "Exploring Russian cyberspace: Digitally-mediated collective action and the networked public sphere," *The Berkman Center for Internet & Society at Harvard University.* Available at: www.scribd.com/document/248071090/Exploring-Russian-Cyberspace-Digitally-Mediated-Collective-Action-and-the-Networked-Public-Sphere.

China Daily 2011. "The fourth UK-China Internet roundtable." Available at: www.chinadaily.com.cn/china/2011-09/29/content_13821444.htm.

Clinton, H. R. 2010. "Remarks on Internet freedom," US Department of State. Available at: www.state.gov/secretary/20092013clinton/rm/2010/01/135519.htm.

Corbin, K. 2010. "Net censorship central to US foreign policy," Datamation, June 11, 2010. Available at: www.datamation.com/entdev/article.php/3887326/Net-Censorship-Central-to-US-Foreign-Policy.htm.

D'Arcy, J. 1969. "Direct broadcast satellites and the right to communicate," *EBU Review* 118: 14–18.

DeNardis, L. 2014. *The Global War for Internet Governance.* New Haven, CT: Yale University Press.

Doyle, M. 1983. "Kant, liberal legacies, and foreign affairs," *Philosophy & Public Affairs* 12(3): 205–35.

Fisher, D. (1982). The right to communicate. A Status Report. UNESCO, 20(5).

Freedom House 2016. "Reports." Available at: https://freedomhouse.org/reports.

Kopytoff, V. G. 2011. "Sites like Twitter absent from free speech pact," *The New York Times,* March 7, 2011, p. B4.

MacKinnon, R. 2012. *Consent of the Networked: The Worldwide Struggle for Internet Freedom.* New York, NY: Basic Books.

McCarthy, D. R. 2011. "Open networks and the open door: American foreign policy and the narration of the Internet," *Foreign Policy Analysis* 7(1): 89–111.

2015. *Power, Information Technology, and International Relations Theory: The Power and Politics of US Foreign Policy and the Internet.* New York, NY: Palgrave Macmillan.

McIver, Jr., W. J., Birdsall, W. F., and Rasmussen, M. 2003. "The Internet and the right to communicate," *First Monday,* December 1, 2003. Available at: http://firstmonday.org/article/view/1102/1022.

Morgan, S. 2016. "Clarifying goals, revitalizing means: An independent evaluation of the freedom online coalition," *Center for Global Publicaion Studies,* May 2016. Available at: www.global.asc.upenn.edu/publications/clarifying-goals-revitalizing-means-an-independent-evaluation-of-the-freedom-online-coalition/.

Organisation for Economic Co-Operation and Development 2011. "The future of the Internet economy: A statistical profile," *Organisation for Economic Co-Operation and Development,* June 2011. Available at www.oecd.org/internet/ieconomy/48255770.pdf.

People's Republic of China 2010. "The Internet in China," *China.org.cn,* June 8, 2010. Available at: www.china.org.cn/government/whitepaper/node_7093508.htm.

Posner, M. and Harris, L. 2011. "Conversations with America: The state department's Internet freedom strategy," US Department of State. Available at: www.state.gov.j/drl/rls/rm/157089.htm.

Powers, S. M. and Jablonski, M. 2015. *The Real Cyberwar: The Political Economy of Internet Freedom.* Chicago, IL: The University of Illinois Press.

Price, M. E. 2015. *Free Expression, Globalism, and the New Strategic Communication.* New York: Cambridge University Press.

Price, M. and Krug, P. 2000. "The enabling environment for free and independent media," *Cardozo Law School Public Law Research Paper No. 27,* November 14, 2000. Available at: http://papers.ssrn.com/sol3/papers.cfm?abstract_id=245494.

Schmidt, H. A. 2011. "Launching the US international strategy for cyberspace," The White House. Available at: www.humanrights.gov/dyn/launching-the-u.s.-international-strategy-for-cyberspace.

Sidorenko, A. 2010. "Quick overview of Russian blogosphere in 2009–2010," *Global Voices.* Available at: https://globalvoices.org/2010/05/13/quick-overview-of-russian-blogosphere-in-2009–2010/.

2011. "Russian digital dualism: Changing security, manipulative state," Institut Français des Relations Internationales, December 2011. Available at: www.ifri.org/en/publications/enotes/russieneivisions/russian-digital-dualism-changing-society-manipulative-state.

Smith, T. 2007. *A Pact with the Devil: Washington's Bid for World Supremacy and the Betrayal of the American Promise.* London: Routledge.

Thierer, A. and Crews, Jr., C. W. (eds.) 2003. *Who Rules the Net? Internet Governance and Jurisdiction.* Washington, DC: Cato Institute.

Townes, M. 2012. "The Spread of TCP/IP: How the Internet Became the Internet," *Millennium: Journal of International Affairs* 41(1): 43–64.

US Department of State 2015. "Country reports on human rights 2015," US Department of State. Available at: www.state.gov/j/drl/rls/hrrpt/humanrightsreport/index.htm#wrapper.

World Conference on International Telecommunications 2012. "Final acts of the World Conference on International Communications (WCIT-12)," ITU. Available at: www.itu.int/pub/S-CONF-WCIT-2012/en.

Zittrain, J. 2008. *The Future of the Internet and How to Stop It.* New Haven, CT: Yale University Press.

Part II

Dewesternizing Tendencies

4

Confucian Speech and Its Challenge to the Western Theory of Deliberative Democracy

Baogang He

While deliberative politics in contemporary China may seem surprising, no less surprising is the rising influence of Western deliberative theory in Chinese academia.[1] To many, it may be puzzling why theories of deliberative democracy have captured the interest of Chinese intellectuals in a country where the political system is largely authoritarian.

To this end, two main approaches to deliberative democracy in China have emerged. One common approach is to recognize deliberative politics of this kind owing to the influence of Western deliberative *democracy* theories. When distinctive features of deliberation are found in China, the term "deliberative democracy" is used (Leib and He 2006). While such an approach is partially defensible in the sense that Chinese local experiments with public deliberation do indeed exhibit some features of deliberative democracy (Fishkin et al. 2010), this is partially mistaken. The reconstruction of contemporary deliberative practices in terms of the Confucian moral code of speech and the formal institutionalization of speech practices throughout the history of the Chinese imperial states show that these modern practices bear traces of their inheritance. Efforts to understand these practices only through the theoretical lenses of Western deliberative democratic theory will misconstrue what is actually going on, both in the institutional form deliberation takes in contemporary China and the language of deliberation in which both citizens and the Chinese Communist Party (CCP) make sense of why they are appropriate for contemporary China.

The other common approach is to look at China mostly through the eyes of authoritarianism. It is often argued that there is no deliberation, or at best a low level of deliberation, under authoritarianism (Kornreich et al. 2012);

---

[1] To date, more than ten English books on deliberative democracy have been translated into Chinese, with many more planned.

that deliberative democracy can only be developed after the establishment of electoral democracy.[2] This approach is deeply problematic. It closes the door to developing new kinds of knowledge about the unique combination of authoritarianism and deliberation.

Both of these approaches operate within the existing literature on deliberative democracy or liberal democracy. While they "absorb" the new empirical world in their theories, they have unfortunately lost an opportunity to develop a deeper understanding of speech politics.

This chapter offers an alternative interpretation. It proposes a theoretical reconstruction of deliberative culture, exploring the proliferation of contemporary deliberative practices in China, and the CCP's sponsorship of deliberative experiments and institutions, through showing its historical and cultural connections to authoritarianism. Its approach uniquely combines a conceptual refinement of speech or deliberation, an historical-cultural perspective of its indigenous roots and qualities, and linguistic analysis.

The aim is to examine the historical, cultural, linguistic, and moral sources of Confucian speech, a form of authoritarian deliberation, demonstrating its long political life and its problems. The concept of authoritarian deliberation was originally mentioned briefly in a previous work by the author (He 2006, pp. 134–5), and developed further into a theoretical notion in a later piece (He and Warren 2011, pp. 271–3). This chapter consolidates the authoritarian deliberation thesis by tracing its moral codes and language, examining two of its institutional forms and political functions, and drawing on all of these as historical lessons for deliberative theory.

We need to take history and culture seriously, and explore how history and culture impact on the concept and institution of speech. This is because what constitutes speech or deliberation itself is not only highly contested but is to some extent culturally bounded. It is imperative for normative theory to go beyond cultural comfort zones to test normative assumptions in other cultures (Dryzek 2006). Some theorists have paid attention to distinct cultural attributes and influences. Gambetta has hypothesized that deliberative democracy is possible in "analytical" cultures such as those of the UK, but that Italian "indexical" culture inhibits deliberation (Gambetta 1998). Rosenberg makes a thorough examination of cultural differences that have impacted on deliberation in China and the West (Rosenberg 2006). Dryzek calls for a study of the subtlety of different cultural forms in different locations, acknowledging that "deliberation travels to Confucian ... far more easily than do the adversarial

---

[2] For the Chinese debate on the sequence of electoral versus deliberative democracy, see He (2008a, ch. 2).

politics associated with competitive elections or an individualistic conception of human rights" (Dryzek 2009, p. 1396).

Nevertheless, the existing studies and their analyses of deliberative culture have not penetrated into culture deeply enough and have not paid sufficient attention to the history, morality, and language of deliberation. Culture is often glossed over or used in too general a sense, leading to research that either does not take linguistic specificity and cultural complexity seriously or overlooks the history of deliberation in a particular cultural context. Neglecting a close examination of the history, morality, and language of deliberation leads to theoretical superficiality.

This chapter takes history, language, and moral codes together to examine how Confucian culture impacts speech or deliberation and produces the phenomenon of authoritarian deliberation. It conceptualizes and theorizes the historical and living political experience of deliberation as a solid basis for comparative political theory and draws on connections between theoretical ideas as expressed in core texts in an intellectual tradition. It considers the ways in which those ideas can be tracked through the history of political institutions, and the ways in which both indigenous intellectual traditions and historical practice in institutionalized deliberative politics shape and constrain contemporary political ideas and practice.

The chapter also aims to contribute to a comparative understanding of speech, and deliberative institutions and politics. It examines the richness and subtlety of the Chinese conception of speech and its rich institutional practice of deliberation. It also makes an etymological study of the Chinese language to exemplify the development of "rules" of deliberation from ancient through to contemporary times. This adds some depth to the key features of Chinese conceptions of deliberation.

While we look for cultural resources for the development of deliberative democracy in China through tracing ideas and practices in Chinese history (Chen 2006; Min 2009), we also need to ask the opposite question: how Chinese historical practices of speech offer lessons for Western deliberative democracy. A study of the Chinese history of speech offers us a number of critical lessons about a set of problems associated with deliberation.

CHINESE SPEECH: MORAL CODES AND LANGUAGE

The Chinese conception of speech is historically and culturally deep and elaborate, with multifaceted elements. The Confucian *minben* (people-centric) ideal was a political foundation for Confucian speech. The Confucius sage, revered as the ideal personality, ought to be attentive to the opinion of the people, express the voice of the people and serve the people. Even the Chinese word "聖" (sage) literally means that a king should use his mouth and ears wisely when listening and talking.

With regard to the critical question of the proper place of deliberation in political life, Confucianism held a middle position between two other schools. One was the legalist school, which disavowed talk-centric politics in favor of military force and punishment. The other was the school of diplomacy, which, in contrast, specialized in speech, deliberation, and rhetoric but used it strategically to persuade and even deceive others (Lewis 1999). Confucianism advocated a balanced theory of speech: it was thought that a society needed talk-centric politics, but that a pragmatic authoritarian form of discipline or control was also necessary. Only then could Confucian speech have its proper place in moral enterprise and politics.

The concepts of *ren* (仁) (benevolence or humaneness), *li* (礼) (ritual) and *junzi* (君子) (gentleman) were three key terms used frequently in Confucius's original texts. The domination of these terms indicated a political order in which the rule of gentlemen prevailed, the notion of duty was central, moral concerns overrode political bargaining processes, and harmony won over conflict. The practice of *yi* (speech, discussion, or deliberation) was carried out by *junzi* and regulated by the moral principles of *ren* and *li*.

In *The Analects of Confucius,* Confucius stated that "in a world which follows the Way, there is no need for commoners to dispute over politics" ("天下有道，则庶人不议") (Leys 1997, p. 81). Given that the Way had fallen out of favor in Confucius's time, we can and should interpret his statement to mean that people ought to debate and deliberate over how to re-establish the Way. Indeed, there is a strong tradition in China that, when there is a political, economic, and social crisis, public speech or deliberation resurfaces and plays a greater role in reinstating political order and authority.

Certainly, public speech was indispensable. It was a means to check against tyrants, avoid mistakes of political decision, and develop policies in the people's interest. Confucius pointed out the political value of remonstration (a form of official speech):

> Anciently, if the Son of Heaven had seven ministers who would remonstrate with him, although he had not right methods of government, he would not lose his possession of the kingdom; if the prince of a state had five such ministers, though his measures might be equally wrong, he would not lose his state; if a great officer had three, he would not, in a similar case, lose (the headship of) his clan; if an inferior officer had a friend who would remonstrate with him, a good name would not cease to be connected with his

character; and the father who has a son that would remonstrate with him would not sink into the gulf of unrighteous deeds. (Legge 1899, pp. 483–4)

The necessity of remonstration is justified by Confucian scholars' concern with human nature, in particular that of the emperors who would often indulge their power and forget their duty to manage state affairs. It was as easy for emperors to be led astray as it was for ordinary people. In Confucian times, all peoples, including emperors, were perceived as having inherent deficiencies. The misbehavior of emperors was a serious matter and often determined the order or disorder of a state.[3] The conceptual space for *jian* (谏) (remonstrance) therefore opened up a means to achieve the Way (Dao) (Suddath 2006). This was even reflected in the name given to the remonstration office. For example, the office established in 685 AD was called "补阙" (*buque*), which literately meant that its officials needed to correct the wrongdoings of the emperor. Similarly, the term "拾遗" (*shiyi*), the name given to another office, literally meant that its officials needed to remind the emperors what they had forgotten.

Throughout their history, the Chinese have been aware that speech itself does not automatically produce social harmony and that it needs to be regulated. Confucianism had developed a moral regulation regime or set of moral codes for speech, with the aim of avoiding degenerating processes and making speech productive and constructive. There follows a description of different cultural principles and norms regarding deliberation, from ancient to contemporary China.

Normative Ranking

According to Confucian thinking, there are three essential forces: morality, reason, and might (Cheng 2006, pp. 30–1). To persuade people, one must try morality first, reason second, and might last. Morality is normatively higher than reasoning, and reasoning higher than might ("以道服人高于以理服人，以理服人高于以力服人"). In view of this allegiance to morality, there must be minimal reasoning: in Chinese, "*daoli shang shuo de guo qu*" ("道理上说得过去"). Might is acceptable only after reasoning speech has failed, and not before. Or, as Fang Dongmei, a twentieth-century philosopher, configured it: the cultivation of virtue is the most important, cultural refinement the second most important, and laws the least important (Hermann 2007, p. 73).

---

[3] For detailed discussion of these justifications, see Jia (1996, pp. 120–1).

The Principle of Publicity

Confucianism lays down the foundations of private and public interest and the roles of officials and ministers as spokespersons for the people and rulers (Liang 2010). Accordingly, all public discussions are supposed to promote the great *gong* (public). No official matters should be discussed in private (Tan 2011). Deng Xiaoping, as a modern example, famously violated this ancient rule when he deliberated on the policy options towards the students on the June 4th demonstration in the privacy of his home. The "gong" is the principle that regulates the practice of speech or deliberation. Through speech, differences are celebrated, tolerated, and accommodated, finally leading to the realization of the Way. By this, public discussion produces legitimacy. This ideal version of public discussion contrasted with, and was superior to, the legalist school in China and the practice of military leaders, who issued orders and exercised power without public deliberation (Tadashi 2003).

The Subjugation of Self-Interest to Public-Mindedness

This principle was articulated in neo-Confucianism in the Song Dynasty (Cheng 2006, p. 51). It lays down a normative requirement for speech and shapes the ways in which individuals interact with one another. In reasoning speech, people are expected to appeal to the common interest, and then address questions concerning issues such as the distribution of benefits. Purely self-regarding interests are not put on the table, as they should play no part in the consideration of public or shared interests during public speech. In liberal traditions, individuals stand up for their interests and for fairness in the sense that "I have the right to express my own interest against the interest of the majority. I can lay my cards on the table." This seems to be a key advantage of liberal deliberation. By contrast, Chinese communitarian norms promote combined and balanced interests in the following three ways. First, one can talk about one's own interests so long as they align with the interests of others or form a part of collective interests. Second, one must then consider the interests of others in terms of fairness. Third, one must consider overall solutions to conflicts of interest. With limited resources one has to ensure a fair resolution to the dispute at hand. These three normative requirements constitute the Chinese understanding of responsible citizenship in the process of public speech. Ideally speaking, through speech one discovers or constructs a common good, changes one's perception of what constitutes the best interest for oneself and thereby the preference for one's own individual interest, and increases concern for what is most in the public interest (He 2006).

While social behavior in China is manifested in outward displays of moral conduct, moral codes are embedded in Chinese characters. An etymological study of Chinese characters or terms can help to rediscover these hidden moral codes and their meanings. Take "言" (*yan*) for example. Literally meaning "speech," it is a root word (written as "讠" in a simplified form) from which 416 compound words are formed. All component words which use "言" ("讠") are related to speech, the act of speech, literature, and morality. The combination of sound and the root word was accidental in the original formation of words, but takes on its own unique patterns in subsequent development (Yang 2008, p. 386). The ancient Chinese believed that all evil actions are related to speech, which is reflected in word building, for example, "诈" (cheating), "诡" (deceitful), "诱" (lure) and "诬" (falsely accuse). To avoid or minimize speech-related evil behavior, the ancient Chinese realized that the act of speech must be regulated. Several compound words exhibit a great deal of moral effort to regulate and guide speech. "*Yi*" (议) literally means "discuss": the left part refers to "讠" (speech), the right part "义" to "righteousness." In the *Kangxi Dictionary* of 1716, "*yi*" (议) is defined as to discuss and determine propriety for something, or the discussion of moral action made by gentlemen.[4] This definition clearly reveals the original moral meaning of the character, that is, "义" (righteousness) should regulate "讠" or "言" (speech). Both "讨" (*tao*) and "论" "讨"(*lun*) mean "discuss." While the right part "寸" means a unit of length and its extended meaning is rule, "仑" means reason and logic. These two words imply that discussion needs to be guided by rule, reason, and logic. The word "訟" (*song*) means to distinguish indisputably between right and wrong before or by officials; the right part "公" of the word means public or fairness. It implies that publicity and fairness should regulate legal deliberation. The word "评" (*ping*) is to make comment or judgment. The right part "平" means equal, fair, and impartial. It implies that comments and judgments need to be made according to principles of equality, fairness, and impartiality. The moral codes of speech were further reflected in many other Chinese phrases, including: "言责," which meant that the ruler's subject was responsible for offering him advice; "言路," which referred to the channels through which criticisms and suggestions were to be communicated; "言者无罪, 闻者足戒," which meant, rather than blame the speaker, heed his words; and "从谏如流," which meant follow good advice as naturally as a river follows its course.

---

4   The compound words discussed here are onomatopoeic according to Xu (2006). Nevertheless, *Kangxi Zidian* provides a clear moral definition of these words.

Everyday Chinese language also contains many terms and expressions that are in accord with deliberation. The proliferation of this kind of language reveals the existence of a widely accepted social communication system in China to settle disagreement and solve conflicts. In this regard, the term speech or deliberation in China (as elsewhere) is often very closely related to reasonableness and fairness. In vernacular language, many terms express the popularity of deliberation. "*Xieshang*" (协商) or "*shangliang*" (商量) refers to "consult and talk things over." "*Shenyi*" (审议) means examination and discussion. "*Kentan*" (恳谈) is a heart-to-heart talk. When dealing with disagreement and conflict, Chinese people often use terms such as "*bai shishi, jiang daoli*" (摆事实，讲道理), that is, to present the facts and reason things out. In such a process, a popular saying stresses "*baiping*" (摆平) (to treat fairly). If one party feels injustice by the other party, one often appeals to "*shuoli*" (说理), that is, to make an argument. Often, two disputing parties go to see a senior to ask for "*pingli*" (评理), that is, each presents their opinion and argument and then lets the senior figure make a judgment between right and wrong. Chinese people have faith that truth becomes clearer through debate and deliberation: "理越辨越明."

Day-to-day Chinese language exhibits a strong disposition for considered judgment, such as "think three times before taking action" (三思而行) or make a "careful consideration" (深思熟虑). The principle of considered judgment is reflected in one Chinese idiom that "you will be enlightened if you hear all parties or listen to both sides" (兼听则明). The everyday language of the Chinese favors "沟通" (communication) so that one's heart will be at ease, or even-tempered and good-humored (心平气和). Liang Shuming, a renowned Confucian scholar in the 1930s, made this point well: "[w]here can you find reason? You can observe others and think to yourself: when you have a peaceful mind, free from all things in your heart, you can listen to others fully and can communicate well with others without any trouble, it is here that you will find reason" (Liang 1979, p. 125). Here Liang defined reason in communicative terms, and favored substantive reason in rejecting an instrumental form of rationality. Liang formulated this basic idea of communicative rationality much earlier than the contemporary philosopher Habermas.[5]

YUANGUAN: *SPEECH OFFICIALS AND INSTITUTIONS*

In China, consultative and deliberative traditions go back thousands of years. Emperor Yao (2356–255 BC) was said to have abdicated his throne in favor of

---

5 For a comparative study of Liang and Habermas, see He (2008b).

Shun in accordance with the wishes of the people after consulting the opinions of various feudal lords (Hui 2012, p. 60; Karlgren 1950, pp. 1–8). In the Zhou Dynasty, emperors had to consult with officials and peoples regarding foreign invasions, domestic chaos, and the relocation of ancient capital. In a gigantic state such as China, a hierarchical system of authority was employed to govern large areas and populations. The historical evidence suggests that, for more than 90 percent of Chinese history, the Chinese probably governed themselves through a hierarchal system of political organizations and consultative mechanisms. Compared with other governing structures for large areas, the Chinese system was perhaps the most consultative, although it certainly involved an authoritarian version of consultation.

There have been a variety of institutional practices of speech in China. This article will focus on the *yanguan* (speech officials or remonstrating officers) as a state institution. This was not a democratic institution but was highly deliberative in terms of the engagement of debate and reason-based argumentation. This speech institution is selected for its contemporary relevance and historical importance (as it has cemented a deliberative tradition within the long history of the Chinese state).

One great tradition in Chinese history is the practice of "*jian*" (remonstrance) or "*zheng*" (诤) and its political institution, in which officials offer blunt, friendly, sincere, and loyal speech, advice, and criticism. Historic records of dynasties show numerous remonstrations submitted in writing to the emperor as part of an ongoing correspondence within the different administrations (Schaberg 2005, p. 191).

There are five forms of *jian*: correct, humble, loyal, simpleminded, and indirect remonstrance. *Jian* or *zheng* is a kind of critical speech and protest. Such protest, or objection or criticism, presented in China in the form of speech in a court, was based on political loyalty with the aim of correcting mistaken policies and ultimately enhancing authority.

Mencius was somewhat of a maverick as a model *zhengyou*, or "reproving statesman,"[6] in the autocratic or authoritarian system. He candidly expressed a noble spirit, despised bigwigs, was not concerned with celebrated status or power and influence, spurned fine food and the attentions of women, and instead spent his life expounding on and practicing Confucian morality through deliberations with rulers.

---

[6] This might be compared with the Catholic Church's institutionalization of the "devil's advocate" in 1587. From this point of view, the roots of deliberation in the history of Chinese political institutions bear important parallels to the institutionalization of deliberation in the pre-democratic West. See Nemeth et al. (2001).

Once occupying a relatively isolated post in imperial institutions, the "reproving statesman" evolved over time into a network of remonstrating political officials. Remonstrating officials formed a critical mass or community in their own right, adhering to a rule of thumb that forthrightly admonished rulers and encouraged virtuous rule. The historical list of remonstrating heroes, who sacrificed their lives for what they believed, extends back quite some time. We find in its history a strong continuity in the roles played by remonstrators even though there were institutional changes across dynasties. These men knew their place in history; they had a role to play and mission to accomplish, regardless of the consequences. So determined were they to fight unjust policies, they even prepared their own coffins before remonstrating with emperors.

Jian dates as far back as the Eastern Zhou period. During the Spring and Autumn period the famous remonstrations were Shi Jue, Zang Xi, and Ji Liang.[7] In the Han and later dynasties, the institution of "Remonstrant and Consultant" (*jianyi dafu* (谏议大夫)) was created and developed. In the Tang, remonstrating officials were established to admonish the emperor (君) directly; they differed quite significantly from remonstrating officials whose duty was solely to admonish prime ministers and other government officials (臣). The historical differences in the roles and institutions of the remonstrators in the preceding dynasties were later dissolved in the Song. All remonstrating institutions were combined into the *yushitai* (censorate). During the Song period the *yushitai* had become one part of a greater tripartite institution. The military and administration formed the other two. The functioning of central government depended on the positions of remonstrator to the emperor and censors to the officials. One critical question over Confucian constitutionalism is whether the *yushitai* should have been combined as one entity in the Song Dynasty or preserved as two separate entities as in the Tang Dynasty. While the *yushitai* in the Song Dynasty strengthened the remonstrating institutions and its checks on prime-ministerial power, their checks on the emperor's powers were significantly diluted.

Throughout its long history, the art of remonstrating has been governed by a set of rules which are either implicit or explicit by nature. The measure of their success as remonstrators has been accounted for statistically by how many petitions were accepted in respective dynasties, and the failure by death rates of these officials. The *jianyi dafu* in the Tang Dynasty were reasonably successful as remonstrators. They were allowed to see the emperor directly and attend cabinet meetings. In the Tang and Qing Dynasties, remonstrating

---

7   For a detailed discussion, see Schaberg (2005).

officials had a right to see the emperor, who in turn could not refuse to see them. Remonstrating officials generally submitted petition letters to the emperor, who had an obligation to reply and comment. The Ming period was the worst era for remonstrators. In contrast to the Tang and other dynasties, some of them were killed by Ming emperors. One of the chief reasons was the escalation of "party politics" during this historic period. By this account alone, Ming emperors deemed many of the remonstrations by officials to be biased. In the turn of the Qing Dynasty, however, much to the relief of remonstrators, the Kangxi Emperor established a set of rules: emperors could no longer kill remonstrating officials.

In the Tang Dynasty, Emperor Taizong widely consulted with his ministries and established consultative mechanisms. He gave a significant formal role to consultations between highly placed officials and the emperor. Some such officials were morally required to speak the truth to the emperor. The most famous account is Wei Zheng's *Ten Thoughts on Remonstrating with Taizong* (谏太宗十思疏). For example, he remonstrated with Emperor Taizong to be prepared for danger in times of peace, to swear off extravagance in favor of frugality, and to treat subordinates sincerely (Wechsler 1974). Remonstrating officials presented their argument against the policies about punishment, people's livelihood, tax and border control, and importantly against Taizong's lifestyle, such as indulging in music, hunting, and women. Among all thirty-seven remonstrations, Emperor Taizong accepted most, only rejecting a few, amounting to 9 percent. The matters he rejected were related to the change in succession and the expansion of the Tang through warfare (Hu 2005, pp. 208–9).

The success rate of remonstrations varied throughout China's history. An empirical study of seven emperors in the Tang Dynasty found that emperors and empresses adopted 114 remonstrations out of 171, a success rate of 67 percent. (Hu 2005, p. 215). Another study found that 70 percent of remonstrations by 给事中 给 (*geishizhong*) were successful (officially ranking third), 80 percent by 谏议大夫谏 (*jianyi dafu*), ranking fourth, and only 37 percent by 左右补阙拾遗 左 (*zuoyoubuque shiyi*), ranking seventh and eighth (Xie 1992, pp. 47–8). The higher the rank of the remonstrating officers, the higher their rate of remonstrations. In the Ming Dynasty, remonstrating officers were not so lucky; some were ordered to be killed. Emperors had turned down twenty remonstrating petitions and only adopted eight, the success rate being under 30 percent. (Zhang 2000, pp. 168–75).

The *yuanguan* institution did not survive under the communist state. Mao Zedong and the CCP were thought to stand for representing truth, justice, and the people. Given this philosophical underpinning, the remonstrating system was no longer needed. Nevertheless, the great tradition of remonstration never did really end under Mao and has continued in one form or another under successive leaders. Scholars like Liang Shuming and even Mao's generals like Peng Dehui remonstrated with Mao strongly, even though they did not have much luck persuading Mao to change his policies. We have also witnessed the manifestation of a kind of popular remonstration in China in the June 4th movement in 1989 and Charter 08 (Potter 2011). It is not then out of order to propose that China can and indeed perhaps needs to recover its ancient remonstrating institutions. For example, a special remonstrating organization could be set up within the National People's Congress, the People's Political Consultative conference, or the Central Party Discipline Committee. The organization would have the special privilege and duty to remonstrate with the general party secretary, the president of the People's Republic of China, or seven standing Politburo members. This would be one key element of a revived Confucian constitutionalism to supplement the Confucian chamber of scholars advocated by Jiang Qing and Daniel Bell (Qing 2012).

POLITICAL FUNCTIONS OF CONFUCIAN SPEECH

The speech institutions mentioned above are largely designed to improve governance, enhance authority, and generate legitimacy. The political function of speech or deliberation contrasts greatly with the "Western" idealized version of democratic deliberation. While there are many variants to be considered between the speech or deliberative practices of China and the West, the intention here is merely to highlight the different styles of democratic and authoritarian deliberation.

The goal of deliberative democracy in the West is to deepen democracy and to empower citizens. Its normative order is to secure equality and liberty first. Improving governance through well-informed public deliberation is a secondary priority. Democratic deliberation empowers ordinary citizens to influence public policies. There is an elective affinity between deliberation and democracy, in that deliberation emerged primarily from democratic institutions, the traditional structuring of relative equality in these institutions being the incentive behind it. In light of this, deliberation in the West is an attribute of democracy. The normative order and goal of authoritarian deliberation, in contrast, is to improve governance and strengthen authority. Being accountable to public opinion comes after that.

The way in which deliberation in China has legitimized state authority throughout its history has been somewhat of a paradox. The role of remonstrating officials in China's past was to challenge the policies made by emperors directly through strong criticism and protest. However, such remonstrations or acts of speech did not question the legitimacy of the authority of emperors directly, given that the legitimacy of the emperor was taken for granted as the "Son of Heaven" (天命). Re. Remonstrating officials could get around this by interpreting 天命 aas the will of the people, thus requiring emperors to follow the will of the people, and by employing the doctrine of heavenly principles (天理) to to challenge the misbehavior of emperors. They could also appeal to a higher authority in the form of natural disasters. In the event of earthquakes, floods or serious drought, scholar-officials were successfully able to remonstrate with the emperors and push for policy change by presenting disasters as evidence of a warning from heaven. The aim of deliberation was therefore to make a good emperor. Today, we might say that the aim of deliberation is to make the CCP a good ruler. Just as in times past where remonstration enhanced authority and legitimacy by correcting mistakes or the wrongdoings of emperors, so too does deliberation today with the CCP.

Since ancient times, deliberation in China has more or less operated through or manifested itself in processes of political loyalty. Under the remonstrating system, emperors heard competing arguments by remonstrating officials. Those who were best able to demonstrate their loyalty to the emperor won him over and had the greatest influence on his decision-making, even if they were extremely harsh and severe in their criticisms of him. Clearly, it was the authority vested in the emperor and a show of the remonstrator's loyalty that determined policy change.

Today's official system of political consultation and deliberation also emphasizes the necessity and importance of political authority; any understanding of public consultation and deliberation must be compatible with this emphasis. The most important official language or phrase is the "political consultation (or deliberation) system under the leadership of the Party" (党领导下政治协商制度). This concept gives space for deliberative politics. Deliberative fora are deemed necessary in order to develop a people's democracy (人民民主) (人) and to produce good policy. Nevertheless, the concept accentuates the domination of the party, leadership being its core principle. Only under the party's leadership are people allowed to examine and discuss public policies. Public participation with regard to processes of consultation and deliberation must be not only orderly, but also reasonable (引导公众有序、理性地进行参与).

Jane Mansbridge suggests that the underlining difference between the deliberative politics of China and the West lies in the types and styles of resistance. The Western resistance tradition explicitly gave the people the right to resist an unjust ruler and depose him if he was not ruling for the common good. This resistance theory has heavily influenced one major strand of deliberative theory, which renounces ascension to authority and other forms of domination.[8] In contrast, authoritarian deliberation does not support and encourage such forms of popular resistance. Even where Mencius once justified the right of the peasantry to rebel, resistance in Chinese thought has historically been far weaker than in European thought and history. In summary, the *yuanguan* discussed above exhibit features of authoritarian deliberation. The success of the remonstration system depended on whether emperors were willing to accept remonstrations.

LESSONS FOR WESTERN DELIBERATIVE DEMOCRACY

The Chinese history of Confucian speech offers Western deliberative democratic theorists an opportunity to learn several important lessons. The rise and fall of Confucian speech in Chinese history raises a number of questions concerning deliberative politics in general. Today, democratic deliberation faces the challenging question of whether it can be sustained or has a short shelf life as a political phenomenon. Western theoretical discourse on deliberative democracy has after all only been going for a little more than thirty years. While the theories have been rich and sophisticated and provide both theoretical and practical guidelines for improving Chinese deliberative institutions and procedures, we can learn some important lessons from the more than two millennia of history of speech or deliberative practice in China.

There is the question of the effectiveness of public speech or deliberation in relation to governance. The experiment of citizen assembly in Australia, for instance, demonstrates that, when citizens are given the power to control the agenda, they deliberate many issues without a clear focus. This can only lead to ineffective decision-making. In the historical practices of speech or deliberation in China, the Chinese have confronted the difficult problem of division and decision-making; that is, with the understanding that division often still exists after public deliberation, tough decisions are required. Authoritarian deliberation is one such answer to this particular question on the effectiveness of public deliberation; in other words, the government must be involved in deliberative fora in some way if they are to result in effective decision-making. In the end it is the government that makes an authoritative decision. From ancient times to today, all deliberation in China has required an authoritarian

---

[8]   Jane Mansbridge's comment on an early version of this paper presented at Fudan University, May 2010, Shanghai, China.

power to deal with divisions arising from that deliberation. This is the cultural tradition underpinning the contemporary phenomenon of authoritarian deliberation.

There are still more problems associated with the state sponsored speech or deliberative institution. Leib proposed a popular branch of deliberation by ordinary citizens, where citizens were selected through a random process but paid by the state (Leib 2004). Chinese imperial states had been paying officials for their deliberation on public affairs for centuries. In the Tang, remonstrating officers were selected through the examination system to ensure that they were well qualified, with historical knowledge and rhetorical skill (Hu 2005, pp. 240–65). They were even empowered to participate in cabinet meetings or to submit their petitions directly to the emperor. In the Song Dynasty, the remonstrating office was combined with *yushitai*, which supervised prime ministers. This combined institution strengthened the role of remonstration and developed strong checks on emperors.[9] The institution evolved further in Ming, when remonstrating officials were directly related to power politics. However, this caused factions and finally led to the demise of these institutions.

The proper balance between deliberation and authority is a critical issue. On the one hand, as has been seen in the past, too much speech or deliberation (处士横议(处) can lead to empty talk and finally to the collapse of a state. The Qi State (齐国), which had the longest history of deliberation, is one example. During a period of more than a century (374–263 BC) under three rulers, about a thousand scholars were paid to debate state affairs without assuming any single concrete administrative duties (Chen and He 2006, pp. 85–7). However, such an impressive public institution declined over time. In the end, Qi was taken over by Qin (秦国), another powerful state that had developed the military and centralized public administration system that adhered to the legalist school. This shift resulted in the classical Chinese historical lesson that empty talk is likely to destroy a state. Even today, Xi Jinping, the President of China, has stressed the point of doing concrete things rather than engaging in empty talk.

On the other hand, too little deliberation associated with coercion leads to the absence of moral persuasion and legitimacy, and finally shortens the life of any political dynasty. The short political life of Qin (221–207 BC) demonstrated that ruling through control, suppression, and military might was undesirable and politically dangerous. The Han Dynasty learnt this lesson from the Qin and adopted Confucianism as an official doctrine under

---

[9] For a detailed discussion, see Jia (2012, pp. 446–53).

Hanwudi, who incorporated both Confucianism and legalism, as well as both moral persuasion and intellectual deliberation on the one hand, and sophisticated political control in the art of ruling on the other.

An etymological study of Chinese characters of deliberation offers us another important lesson. Currently, deliberative democracy writings largely use the professional language of the academy that is more relevant to theorists than practitioners. "Deliberation" is often discussed in relation to the language of democracy, equality, argumentation, reasoning, and legitimacy. Chinese liberal-minded scholars use Western theories and languages to criticize and even reject the Chinese official use of "deliberation" (Jin and Yao 2007). While professional language is valuable, common use of the Western language of deliberation is likely to reproduce what we already know.

We need to study how other forms of language shape, prescribe, and promote different norms of deliberation in China as well as in other places. To make deliberative democracy a workable enterprise for empowerment requires going beyond professional language to understand how vernacular or even official languages will assist in developing deliberative governance and institutions. A mix of these languages in briefing materials as well as in subsequent reports and writing demonstrates that a synthesizing strategy works,[10] although it does bring some new problems.

Chinese history of Confucian speech highlights the centrality of morality for public speech or deliberation. While both the Chinese and Western conceptions of deliberation emphasize influence through reason-giving, they differ in the place morality has to play in deliberation. Amy Gutman and Dennis Thompson, for example, develop a deliberative approach to addressing the moral disagreement issue (Gutman and Thompson 1996). They perceive deliberation as a normative source of morality; of course they hold the view that the moral principle of freedom and equality is the foundation of deliberative procedure. In China, it is the other way around. Morality plays a greater role. It informs, regulates, and guides Chinese public speech or deliberation. Confucian morality not only offered scholars the intellectual power to resist the wrongdoing of emperors, but also provided practical guidelines. The Chinese conception of speech has developed a list of "moral codes" that regulate it. Morality is seen not as the source of deliberation but is held above it as a guiding principle; deliberation must follow certain moral principles. As discussed before, the *yuanguan* present moral arguments that emperors need to follow.

---

[10] This observation comes from the author's personal involvement in assisting in deliberative polling in Wenling between 2005 and 2013.

A great lesson from the history of Confucian deliberation is that any successful deliberation must be based on pure reasoning on behalf of the greater public, under the Confucian doctrine of "天下为公天下" (the public own everything under heaven). In the West, it is often claimed that party politics and/or factionalism destroys true deliberation. This was also an historical lesson from China. Remonstrating officials were not supposed to seek political power for themselves, rather than present the best argument for policy change. When remonstrating officers in the Ming were factionalized and involved in power politics, this destroyed their credibility and led to a fear of the Wangli emperor who rejected their remonstration (Zhang 2000, p. 174). Today, when politicians or political parties use citizen juries in the United Kingdom or Australia, such public deliberation is likely to suffer a similar credibility problem. To maintain the quality of deliberation, a form of semi-detachment is required.

The Chinese art of remonstration is different from the contemporary two-party system where opposition parties appeal to public reason by sustained, intense and, some might argue, often contrived criticism of the ruling party in their bids to win power. Remonstrating officials by contrast could not usurp let alone entertain such ideas of political power. Theirs was a considerably more modest role: the duty and forte being pure and honest criticism or advice. In the West, this spirit of remonstration is perhaps wanting among political parties in the two-party system. The "two-party" democratic system could be improved with the spirit of something akin to the ancient Chinese style of deliberation. Confucian speech or deliberation could facilitate the development from an adversarial to a deliberative model of governance. Of course, while Confucian speech still has a role to play in politics, it cannot possibly replace the modern two-party system.

CONCLUSION

This chapter has moved beyond existing scholarship on speech or deliberation, and sought to broaden the theory of deliberation by avoiding the reproduction of one specific kind of knowledge and opening up a space for political thinking that cannot be reduced to a Western school of thought. This has been achieved in three ways. First, by stepping outside scholarly or professional language, it has embraced the often-overlooked vernacular language of speech and undertaken an etymological study of Chinese characters. This has revealed a set of hidden moral codes regulating speech. Second, it has discussed multifaceted dimensions of speech in a non-Western society, which are often not a point of consideration in the deliberative theories of the West.

It also confirms the universality of speech or deliberative practice over the theoretical propensity to cultural relativism. Third, in going beyond the usual Western notions of democratic deliberation, this chapter has recognized the persistence of authoritarian deliberation in China throughout its history. The unique phenomenon of authoritarian deliberation is designed to enhance authority and promote unity and the common good. While authority is an expedient means for dealing with governance issues, it can however give too much power to existing power holders and not enough to ordinary citizens, discouraging resistance from within. By contrast, democratic deliberation pays a great deal of attention to citizen empowerment, but may overlook the balance between good governance and authority.[11] Future research could explore more deeply the possibility of a modern transition from authoritarian deliberation to democratic deliberation in China, and the question of whether, or indeed how, deliberative democracy and authoritarian deliberation are creatively but contradictorily mixed in contemporary China.

REFERENCES

Anon (ed.) [undated]. *Kangxi zidian (Kangxi dictionary)*. Hong Kong: Fanshi Tianyige.

Chen, S. 2006. "The native resources of deliberative politics in China," in Leib and He (eds.), *The Search for Deliberative Democracy in China*. New York: Palgrave Macmillan, pp. 161–74.

Chen, S. and He, B. 2006. *Development of Deliberative Democracy: A Collection of the Essays Presented at the International Conference on Deliberative Democracy and Chinese Practice of Participatory and Deliberative Institutions*. Beijing: China's Social Sciences Press.

Cheng, C. 2006. "Toward constructing a dialectics of harmonization: Harmony and conflict," *Journal of Chinese Philosophy* 33: 25–59.

Dryzek, J. 2006. "Deliberative democracy in different places," in Leib and He (eds.), *The Search for Deliberative Democracy in China*. New York: Palgrave Macmillan, pp. 23–36.

2009. "Democratization as deliberative capacity building," *Comparative Political Studies* 42(11): 1379–402.

Fishkin, J., He, B., Ruskin, B., and Siu, A. 2010. "Deliberative democracy in an unlikely place: Deliberative polling in China," *British Journal of Political Science* 40(2): 435–48.

Gambetta, D. 1998. "'Claro!': An essay on discursive machismo," in Elster, J. (ed.), *Deliberative Democracy*. Cambridge: Cambridge University Press.

Gutman, A. and Thompson, D. 1996. *Democracy and Disagreement*. Harvard: Belknap Press.

---

[11] Mark Warren, however, makes an exceptional contribution on this issue (Warren 1996).

He, B. 2006. "Western theories of deliberative democracy and Chinese practice of complex deliberative governance," in Leib and He (eds.), *The Search for Deliberative Democracy in China*. New York: Palgrave Macmillan, pp. 133–48.

2008a. *Deliberative Democracy: Theory, Method and Practice*. Beijing: China's Social Science Publishers.

2008b. *Democratic Theory: Predicament and Transcendence*. Beijing: China's Law Press.

He, B. and Warren, M. 2011. "Authoritarian deliberation: The deliberative turn in Chinese political development," *Perspectives on Politics* 9(2): 269–89.

Hermann, M. 2007. "A critical evaluation of Fang Dongmei's philosophy of comprehensive harmony," *Journal of Chinese Philosophy* 34: 59–97.

Hu, B. 2005. *A Study of Supervising System in Tang Dynasty*. Beijing: Shangwu Publishers.

Hui, V. T. 2012. "Ancient China," in Isakhan, B. and Stockwell, S. (eds.), *The Edinburgh Companion to the History of Democracy*. Edinburgh: Edinburgh University Press.

Jia, Y. 1996. *Supervising System in the Song Dynasty*. Kaifeng: Henan University Press.

2012. *Tangsong shiqi zhongyang zhengzhi zhidu bianqianshi (A Changing History of Central Political Institutions in Tang and Song)*. Beijing: People's Press.

Jin, A., and Yao, C. 2007. "Deliberative democracy should not be misread," *Zhongguo Renmin Zhengxie Lilun Yanjiu Huikan* 3: 26–31.

Karlgren, B. (trans.) 1950. *The Book of Documents*. Goteborg: Elanders Boktryckeri Aktiebolag.

Kornreich, Y., Vertinsky, I., and Potter, P. 2012. "Consultation and deliberation in China: The making of China's health-care reform," *China Journal* 68: 176–203.

Legge, J. (trans.) 1899. *Texts of Confucianism*. Oxford: The Clarendon Press.

Leib, E. 2004. *Deliberative Democracy in America: A Proposal for a Popular Branch of Government*. Pennsylvania: Pennsylvania State University Press.

Leib, E. and He, B. (eds.) 2006. *The Search for Deliberative Democracy in China*. New York: Palgrave.

Lewis, M. E. 1999. "Warring states political history," in Loewe, M. and Shaughnessy, E. L. (eds.), *The Cambridge History of Ancient China: From the Origins of Civilization to 221 BC*. Cambridge: Cambridge University Press, pp. 587–650.

Leys, S. (trans.) 1997. *The Analects of Confucius*. New York: W.W. Norton.

Liang, S. 1979. *Zhonghua wenhua yaoyi (Essentials of Chinese Culture)*. Taipei: Zhengzhong Press.

Liang, T. 2010. "Political thought in early Confucianism," *Frontiers of Philosophy in China* 5: 212–36.

Min, S.-J. 2009. "Deliberation, East meets West: Exploring the cultural dimension of citizen deliberation," *Acta Politica* 44: 439–58.

Nemeth, C., Brown, K., and Rogers, J. 2001. "Devil's advocate versus authentic dissent: Stimulating quantity and quality," *European Journal of Social Psychology* 31(6): 707–20.

Potter, P. B. 2011. "4 June and Charter 08: Approaches to popular remonstrance," *China Information* 25(2): 121–38.

Qing, Q. 2012. *A Confucian Constitutional Order: How China's Ancient Past Can Shape Its Political Future*. Princeton: Princeton University Press.

Rosenberg, S. 2006. "Human nature, communication and culture: Rethinking democratic deliberation in China and the West," in Leib and He (eds.), *The Search for Deliberative Democracy in China*. New York: Palgrave Macmillan, pp. 77–111.

Schaberg, D. 2005. "Playing at critique: Indirect remonstrance and the formation of Shi identity," in Kern, M. (ed.), *Text and Ritual in Early China*. Seattle: The University of Washington Press, pp. 194–218.

Suddath, V. 2006. "Ought we throw the Confucian baby out with the authoritarian bathwater: A critical inquiry into Lu Xun's anti-Confucian identity," in Hershock, P. D. and Ames, R. T. (eds.), *Confucian Cultures of Authority*. New York: State University of New York Press, pp. 222–7.

Tadashi, K. 2003. "The Confucian concept of 'public' and the adoption of deliberative assembly in Japan: Writings of Yokoi Shōnan," *Sungkyun Journal of East Asian Studies* 3(1): 131–50.

Tan, S.-H. 2011. "Confucian resources for experimentation in deliberative democracy," *Social Science Research Network* 1–17. Available at: http://papers.ssrn.com/sol3/papers.cfm?abstract_id=1907492.

Warren, M. 1996. "Deliberative democracy and authority," *American Political Science Review* 90: 46–60.

Wechsler, H. J. 1974. *Mirror to the Son of Heaven: Wei Cheng at the Court of T ang T ai-tsung*. New Haven: Yale University Press, pp. 115–28.

Xie, Y. 1992. *A Study of Central Decision-making in Tang Dynasty*. Taipei: Wenjin Publishers.

Xu, S. 2006. *(110 A.D. – 121 A.D.) Etymological Dictionary*. Beijing: Social Sciences Academic Press.

Yang, G. 2008. *Ci yuan guan nian shi (The Intellectual History of Etymology)*. Chendu: Bashu shushe.

Zhang, Z. 2000. *A Study of Supervising System in Ming Dynasty*. Taipei: Wunan Publishers.

5

From Gandhi to Modi: Institutions and Technologies of Speech and Symbolism in India

William Gould

The use of symbolism in Indian politics has, since at least the early part of the twentieth century, been intimately tied to the project of building a "nation" and how it symbolically evokes different ideas of India's past. Arguably, the vitality of political debate in South Asia, which today manifests itself in the form of the political speech and newspaper media in India, has a deeper heritage going back into some of the ancient and medieval structures of the Indian village governance, and pluralistic debate, of Buddha and Ashoka (Sen 2005). In contemporary times, the requirements of intra-regional mobilization, via unifying symbolism, became a necessary means of ruling or of putting pressure on governments and regimes that sought to control vast, legally differentiated territories. This chapter explores the persistence and changes of speech methods, peculiar to India, in the reworking of mythical, historical, and spatially rooted symbols in Indian politics over the last century. Principally, it looks at a large-scale transition in practices of freedom of speech in India, in which a long-term control of "communal" speech has been inverted to allow India's new regimes to control "anti-Hindu" and "antinational" speech. It goes on to argue that this inversion was made possible for India's governments via the press and its expansion of political debate, as a result of strategies of mobility (the transitional and malleability of symbols in different spaces/histories) and scale (the transformation of common political symbols to different levels of audience and jurisdiction). It goes on to suggest, however, that such changing forms of political speech freedoms and symbolism involved a tension that means that they were never persistent: As ideas moved into different local and linguistic spaces, they were appropriated and transgressed. As a result, state-driven and mainstream symbols of national unity have been challenged by organizations and societies evoking alternative (often low-status) political symbols. And these, too, have been developed in relation to particular ideas of public space.

The extent to which the state has controlled flows of information in India, permitting or restricting freedom of speech in the press and other media, has always existed in balance with movements challenging that control. In other words, the history of speech and its freedoms runs parallel to India's colonial and anticolonial "freedom" struggles in general. There are implications here, too, for how we might view state "power," especially given India's multiple and overlapping regional jurisdictions. As an Indian "Empire" before 1947, it served the interests of colonial rulers to encourage regional differentiation and not least to uphold some of the particular privileges of princely states. This, and Pakistan's eventual creation in 1947, made it all the more important for late colonial and early independent Indian publicists to constantly reiterate the interconnectedness of India's regions, and not just by talking about a single nation. Regimes attempting to inherit political power in the mid-twentieth century aimed to connect India's vast constituencies by employing cultural and historical symbols – these became regions traversed and brought into dialogue via political enactment. This often took place in a quite material and performative way, involving speech tours, demonstrations and ceremonies, meeting and responding to localism, and sometimes being informed by it. Such approaches also mapped well onto the emerging structures of electoral democracy following independence. These means of symbolic communication, precisely because they were spatial, had to be varied and not simply rhetorical. They had to take into account that there were linguistically and culturally varied "publics" in India that built their notions of civic belonging around quite different ideas of the past. However, precisely because such ideas were regionally, culturally and socially circulated, they were often re-formed and transgressed.

Writers on "nationalism" in a range of contexts have argued that one of the key components of national identity is the construction of a shared past, described by one scholar as an "ethno-history" (Smith 1992, p. 58). India is not unlike other nation states in the complexities of its competing community histories, each of which has had an impact on the nature of modern modes of political symbolism. Yet there are, arguably, three unique features to the uses of time, the past and historical memory in India, which have placed religious community at the center of debates about freedoms of speech. First, as a postcolonial state and society, India's historiographies have been shaped, to an extent, by a colonial division of the region's past into "Hindu," "Muslim," and "British" periods, which created the notion of a "spiritual" India, juxtaposed with a materialistic West (Prakash 1999, pp. 384–5). This historiography in turn affected modern (Hindu) Indian intellectuals' periodization choices, which associated the "Hindu" past as one of a "golden age," the medieval

(Muslim) as one of decline and the British colonial era as one of modern renaissance (Guichard 2010, p. 46), although this has been consistently challenged in India's academic mainstream. Second, one of the results of the debate about India's past has been the identification of key moments or dates in the formation of a "secular" united India or a moment of "arrival" for India's major institutions. In this sense, some of the main (and most controversial) historical symbols in recent times relate to India's experience of political independence from colonial rule and its immediate aftermath. Third, the moment of India's independence and state-building opened up the field for other competing symbolic uses of the past that do not fit neatly into the secular-Hindu dichotomy and which build upon variable parochial and social differentiations. Yet the modes of symbolism in this historiography are similar. The most obvious example of this lies in the symbolic uses of the past by Dalit and other low-caste movements and political parties.

All three of these uses of the past have driven forms of political symbolism in India in the last two decades. But, interestingly, around the first two, organizations of ostensibly secular nationalism (principally the Congress) and those of the Hindu right (the BJP) have had much in common, and in fact have competed in their projection of key national symbols. Both organizations have used historical moments of dramatic political transition in India to adapt or transform conventional interpretations of India's past. Recently, for example, the importance of the period leading up to India's first democratic elections in 1952 has been made especially palpable, given the decisive electoral defeat in 2014 of a political dynasty (Congress) that had, with the exception of just a few years, ruled India since 1952, mostly as a single party but also as a dominant partner in coalition. The 2014 election speeches, particularly towards the end of the campaign, illustrated the enormity of 1947–52 for the symbolic construction of state development and national freedom, and the potential desire to "rethink" its significance for a putative new regime. The BJP made as much mileage as possible out of dissatisfaction with the long-standing dynastic politics of the Nehru family. In one of Modi's speeches in Amethi, Uttar Pradesh on May 5, 2014, for example, the sound bites were clear: "India is done with this [Nehru-Gandhi] dynasty. India has had them for over sixty years. It's time for the poor and the dispossessed to rise to the top ... the government of mother and son is about to go, nothing can stop it now."[1] The most direct and salacious attack of all was a poster containing an image of Jawaharlal Nehru and Edwina Mountbatten alongside the words "*Deshi*

---

[1] "Shri Narendra Modi addresses Bharat Vijay rally in Amethi (Uttar Pradesh)," May 5, 2014, *YouTube*: www.youtube.com/watch?v=igcVEqHgTX8.

videshi patni premi" (native foreign-wife-lovers) versus Modi as "*Desh premi*"
(country-lovers), making reference to the alleged love affair between Nehru
and Edwina.[2] Rhetoric about the end of a dynasty automatically evoked the
idea of the end of an era, and movement away from autocracy to democracy, quickly reflecting the idea of the end of princes' rule over most of India
shortly following 1947. Key to Modi's symbolic approach and attack on Nehru
was his connecting himself as directly as possible to the historical drama of
Nehru's conflict with Vallabhai Patel. Again, in the first week of May 2014 in
a speech at Ambedkar Nagar, Modi argued counterfactually that "if Sardar
Patel had become the first prime minister things would have been very different … This family did not do justice with him. I have come from Patel's
state" (DNA 2014). Personal hubris and historical identification also played
their part. One political commentator observed that "[e]verybody knows that
Narendra Modi happens to be the third claimant to Sardar's legacy … L.K.
Advani and Keshubhai Patel, erstwhile chief minister of Gujarat whom Modi
had replaced had also claimed for himself the honorific 'Chote Sardar' [little
Sardar]" (Gatade 2013).

It has long been established that the "Hindu nationalism" of the right in
India borrows or builds its ideology on pre-existing ideas about the nation in
both South Asia and Europe. What is extraordinary about the BJP's appropriation of mainstream Congress nationalism in India, however, is its sim-
ultaneous inversion of modes of speech freedom. From the 1920s, albeit
inconsistently, Indian governments banned or prescribed material considered
politically sensitive or seditious on the one hand, and inciting religious hatred on the other. This was enshrined in the Indian Penal Code (IPC) section
295A (1927), which sought to prevent incitement to religious hatred. There
was an important overlap between these two genres of literature controlled by
the state, however (at least in northern India), in that "communal" rhetoric
became a means to critique the British presence in India, especially via anti-
Muslim statements (Gould 2004). Following India's independence, Nehru's
government attempted to extend and reinforce the proscription of "communal" literature. While Article 19 (1a and 2) of the Indian Constitution posited
"freedom of speech and expression" as a fundamental human right, this liberty could not offend the liberty of others. It could also be subject to restrictions in the interests of decency and morality. Other restrictions, brought into
play under the first amendment in 1951, included security of the state, friendly
relations with other states, contempt of court, defamation and, importantly,

---

[2]   The poster was released by Ashok Chaurasia, who is associated with Modi election campaign-
ing in the city and is convener of the BJP Sahitya Prakashan Prakosth (literature wing).

"public order," implying a "state of tranquility which prevails among members of political society" (Bhatia 2016). These notions of speech freedom were established just following South Asia's most intense ethnic violence (partition) and during the working out of India's caste-based system of affirmative action. As a tenet of India's secular democracy this has meant, in theory, that incitement to communal (and caste) hatred has been intermittently controlled in the press under arguments of public order. Even when such freedoms were made more ambivalent via their suspension during the Emergency of 1974–7, strongly implicit in the notion of "public order" and friendly relations within India's political society was the concept of communal harmony.

Since the 1990s, with the formation of governments of the Hindu right, not only has the entire concept of Indian secularism been questioned, but its basic premises regarding freedoms of speech have also transformed. Some of the main institutions responsible for the generation of anti-Muslim rhetoric (for example, in the early 1990s violence around Ayodhya) had now formed parts of governments at state and (in 1998) central levels. Yet at the same time, in holding power at the center, the BJP still had to create a new political consensus which, in theory at least, has meant the watering-down of hard-line Hindu nationalist ideologies. Compared to Congress then, in both the Gandhian and early postcolonial periods, Narendra Modi's BJP from 2014 was faced with a different set of political challenges that required a delicate and careful selection of historical figures and reference points. In order to map a BJP regime onto the key national symbolic moments of Indian national unity, the party had to overcome charges of being divisive and "communal," especially given the events of the 2002 Muslim pogrom in Gujarat under a Modi-led government. The BJP therefore needed to present a reinterpretation not just of nationalist icons, but a reworking of their symbolic role in Indian history. The symbolic use of Patel amounted to a deliberate appropriation, rather than simply association, with one of Indian nationalism's iconic figures. This was not only the use of a figure who had some sympathies for the Hindu right, but an appropriation that is very specific in its reading of Congress's past: for example, a focus on the personal conflict between Patel and Nehru. It was also a route into the legacies of the other key Gujarati in the nationalist pantheon: M. K. Gandhi. The latter was a ubiquitous user of religious and mythical symbolism in his rhetorical style, which had a deliberately universalizing aim. As a result, it was relatively easy for Modi's team to use historical symbolism to evoke comparisons with the Mahatma. At Faizabad, Uttar Pradesh, as he toured in early May, Modi reportedly stated (in front of a large poster of Ram) that Mahatma Gandhi, when asked how the nation should be, always said there should be Ram Rajya. This idea of Ram Rajya meant there was development for everyone and all were happy.[3] This use of the notion of a mythical Hindu past not only drew lines of comparison to Gandhi's own religious orientation, but also to the symbolic politics of the Congress right, discussed above.

It is not just in the use of Congress's ambiguous past leaders that the Hindu right has profited from older forms of symbolic mobilization. One of the key moments for the rise of the Hindu right in north India in the early 1990s was the use of the Ram Janmabhoomi movement around the Babri Masjid in Ayodhya, to launch a highly performative (and communally destructive) campaign to "rebuild" a temple at the supposed birthplace of Lord Ram. L. K. Advani's *rath yatra* (chariot tour) across India was symbolic politics *par excellence* in its electoral effects. Similarly, bricks for the rebuilding of the temple traversed Hindu communities across and beyond India in a multispatial linking of symbolic forms. But these links between national and local, in the form of theatrical and symbolic political displays, had a longer heritage. The mobilization of sadhus (holy men) at times of large festivals, for example, was a common feature of late-period anticolonial mobilization, and especially that which took place in the years of Congress's mass mobilizations, such as the Civil Disobedience movement of the early 1930s. The Congress and its local cadres in the populous state of Uttar Pradesh also made use of the large interregional religious festivals such as Holi to propagate very specific symbolic messages, which likened struggle against British imperialism with the key battles of Hindu cosmology (Gould 2004, pp. 35–86).

The relationship between Modi's clear Hindu nationalist line and that of an earlier, broader and ostensibly secular form of politics is thus striking and deliberate. It also creates space for, or legitimizes, new kinds of speech censorship that invert proscriptions of incitement to religious hatred to protect a normative majority-Hindu community. There are important historical explanations for this. Section 295A of the IPC was enacted in 1927 in response to the *Rangila Rasul* affair. A booklet of the same title published in that year detailed the marriages and sex life of the Prophet and, although the publication was banned, there was no recourse to prosecution of the publisher. The latter was subsequently murdered in court (see R. Chopra in this volume). Initiated in response to Muslim calls to protect minorities, the colonial government nevertheless maintained an authoritarian control over press freedoms over the last few decades of its government. The core purpose of Section 295A

---

[3] "Lok Sabha election live blog: Narendra Modi addresses rally in Amethi," May 5, 2014, *IBN Live*: http://ibnlive.in.com/news/lok-sabha-election-live-blog-narendra-modi-addresses-rally-in-amethi/469596-37-64.html.

then was to protect important community interest groups whose loyalty to the state was critical. In 1932, a young woman named Rashid Jahan, a member of the CPI(M) and later leader in the Progressive Writer's Association, published a collection of short stories entitled "Angarey" which exposed the sexual hypocrisies of men of religion and Muslim landowners. Threatened with death and disfigurement, Jahan was also faced with the humiliation of her book being banned and confiscated under 295A (Gopal 2007). As we will see below, these long-standing authoritarian instruments of control over freedom of speech, on the one hand, with an association with movements of political freedom, on the other, have allowed organizations of the Hindu right to legitimize forms of speech censorship around the "Hindu" community, but also to associate such controls with national unity and loyalty.

This complicated association however, had to be achieved in the political rhetoric of the regime itself overall, especially via selected references to India's freedom struggle and early postcolonial development. Looking at the 2014 elections, both in the content of the symbolism and the manner of its use, there are processes of convergence between "saffron" representations of the nation, and "secular" Congress-led ones, but only via *particular* kinds of leaders in the past, as well as the specific nature of Congress at the mythical moment of national realization. Significant here, arguably, are ideological ambiguities in Congress's own secularism. The use of Patel, which occasioned an ideological battle between the BJP and Congress, was made possible by the fact that Modi *could* persuasively appropriate the popular symbolic qualities of the "iron man." This was because of more direct links to some of the key Congress Hindu traditionalists of the 1950s, including Rajendra Prasad, K. M. Munshi and P. D. Tandon, as well as Patel. These figures were social conservatives on the Congress right and figures of national importance, supporting, for example, the maintenance of Hindu traditions in social reform (Prasad) and in the protection/promotion of Hindu monuments (Munshi). Purushottam Das Tandon was a champion of the Hindu right in Congress in the 1940s and early 1950s, and was backed by Patel as president of Congress. The late 1940s and 1950s are traditionally viewed as the period when the developmental state was established, Nehru's authority was cemented and Congress's dominance began. There were enough fractures in this narrative however, for the Hindu right to make counter-claims. Modi did not, however, select ideologically obvious figures such as Tandon for his symbolic pastiche, because of the latter's strong association with the region of Uttar Pradesh and ultimately his failure in the contest over the presidency of Congress with Nehru. Instead, it made more sense to highlight his emotional and political patron, Patel, a man who, like

Modi himself, had successfully moved from the politics of Gujarat to the politics of India.

Although not necessarily coordinated in an overall agenda, this was one part of a larger drive by the Modi government to push for a change in India's national iconography, involving the gradual displacement of older icons with newer ones, more conducive to the Hindu right but also with a broad popular appeal. These include the promotion of Deen Dayal Upadhyaya, a political philosopher who is central to the Hindu right but lesser-known in general terms. However, it also involves more famous Hindu revivalists and Congress radicals, such as Sri Aurobindo, Swami Vivekananda, and Syama Prasad Mookerjee. This symbolic strategy has, in turn, allowed some of the lesser-known (but ideologically more significant) historical figures to be feted by associating them with better-known "national" figures. For example, in Modi's maiden speech in the Central Hall of Parliament on May 20, 2014, he promised to celebrate 2015 as Deen Dayal Upadhyaya's centenary year. He then continued to juxtapose Upadhyaya with other more famous social reformers. In his maiden speech in the Lok Sabha (lower house) on June 11, he then declared that "this government's priority is the benefit of the most underprivileged, going by the ideals of Deen Dayal Upadhyaya, Lohia and Gandhi" (Kang 2014). The selection of such historical figures also relates to one of the key socioeconomic tensions within the Hindu right parties: between the lifestyle aspirations of new urban constituencies and the antimodernism of some of the BJP's supporters and associated institutions. In the 1990s this manifested itself in divisions between cultural nationalism and parochialism on the one hand, and a movement towards the free market in the BJP on the other (Hansen 1999). Therefore, symbols of national unity such as Patel are socially acceptable to growing middle-class, urban constituencies. They can also be mixed with more traditional and parochial supporters of the Hindu right via the political thought of Upadhyaya.

Movement between different types of historical figures has fueled BJP iconoclasm in some areas too, especially around Congress's key anniversaries and hagiographies. Most importantly it has allowed the regime to permit authoritarian control of minorities and entire regions who threaten a Hindu majoritarian discourse. October 31, Patel's birthday, has been renamed Unity Day and the celebrations are to be televised by Doordarshan from Patel's home village, Karamsad, Gujarat. This was deliberately designed to eclipse the date's use to commemorate the anniversary of Indira Gandhi's death (Singh 2014). The Modi regime has sought to place its own man, Upadhyaya, at the symbolic center of movements for rural reform and tribal development. It did so by relaunching and renaming an older rural skills program after the ideologue.

Similarly, a decision was made to drop Nehru's name from the Jawaharlal Nehru National Urban Renewal Mission, and there was severe criticism of the change in name of Indira Awaas Yojna, the rural housing scheme, to the National Gramin Awaas Mission (Nagpal 2014). Renaming development and education programs is not simply an exercise in re-signification. It is also a process of establishing a new intellectual and cultural milieu that is *distinctively* Indian by virtue of its historical depth, "prior" to influence from the West. Key here is the idea of India's "ancient" (and therefore "prior" or "superior") culture as a means of rejuvenating the idea of the Indian nation in contemporary India. Two recent events serve as examples. The head of the Indian Council for Historical Research, Professor Y. Sudershan Rao, has as his main agenda a drive to "prove the historicity of the [Indian epics] Mahabharata and Ramayana" (Thapar 2014). In even more bizarre fashion, Anand J. Bodas, who attended the Indian Science Congress, claimed that the first human flight technologies had taken place at the time of the Vedas (Lakshmi 2015). This has been a longer-term approach of the BJP. In the 1980s the party strongly supported the decision by Doordarshan, the Indian television broadcaster, to televise versions of the Mahabharata and Ramayana.

In the context of these symbolic transitions in India's political culture, incitement to religious hatred/offence to religious sentiments has become a technique of authoritarian movements, especially since the new millennium, as they seek to control criticism of this majoritarian vision of India. Two high-profile and internationally significant examples of this are the filing of criminal complaints against the artist Maqbool Fida Husain for paintings depicting the goddesses Durga and Saraswati, which were published in *Vichar Mimansa* – a Hindi magazine – in 1996. Although the Delhi High Court dismissed the complaints of incitement to religious hatred in 2004, the Bajrang Dal attacked the artist's house and an exhibition in the United Kingdom was canceled (Padmanabhan 1998). On February 4, 2014, Wendy Doniger's book *The Hindus: An Alternative History* was withdrawn by Penguin books, following a complaint filed by Dina Nath Batra from the Shiksha Bachao Andolan Samiti organization (see the chapter by R. Chopra in this volume). Crucially, Batra's crusade against what he saw as the misrepresentation of Hindu culture also stemmed back to an earlier 2006 Public Interest litigation against the National Council of Educational Research and Training which made specific complaints about the representation of India's "Hindu" nationalist heroes – including Aurobindo, Tilak, and Lajpat Rai– as "militants."[4] Such actions could be more mundane but no less widespread: in August 2006, two

---

[4] "Lens on Former INCERT boss," *The Telegraph* (Calcutta), June 4, 2015.

religious groups based in Gujarat filed a complaint against a Mumbai fashion designer for "hurting religious sentiments" by selling clothes with prints of Hindu and Jain religious scriptures. In September 2007, after posting an allegedly blasphemous image of the Maratha warrior Chhatrapati Shivaji, BJP workers reported Laxman Kailas, a computer engineer from Pune, who was subsequently arrested.[5] In September 2014, Gujarat police initiated a series of arrests for statements and opinions posted on social media sites such as Facebook.[6]

The larger significance of these controls on freedom of speech, alongside the appropriation of older national symbols, has been the effect on India's multiple regions. This has not always been a stable relationship and in an attempt to broaden out what academics have described as the "saffronization" of education and the media, Hindu nationalists have confronted a range of specific challenges. There are a number of ways in which the inherent authoritarianism of the Hindu right's use of colonial instruments of control has driven anti-insurgency and clampdowns on speech freedoms in the country's peripheries. But as with the symbolism of the Hindu right, these movements, too, have borrowed from older forms of speech control. Most important here has been the recent muzzling of the press in Kashmir following anti-India protests in mid-July 2016. For a number of days, the government, on top of the closing-down of cable TV and private cell phone services, banned all local and regional newspapers. One editor of a principal Kashmir newspaper described the action as an "Information blockade" (Lakshmi 2016). This has extended to digital social media too, with Facebook closing down threads and comments in support of Kashmiri protestors in the summer of 2016. Yet these forms of control have their roots going back at least to the 1970s and 1980s, and arguably to the first India–Pakistan war of 1948, when the role and freedom of journalists in reporting on the state have been routinely restricted. In other words, in regions where the very national project itself is habitually threatened, all national governments have made use of older colonial instruments in controlling speech and the press.

The potential challenge to this new symbolic turn by the Hindu right is that in India such projects circulate through a multitude of regions and languages, and are translated and reconfigured via local, vernacular and culturally specific modes. Moreover, the process after 1947 of renaming India's urban spaces, streets, parks and jurisdictions in a reaction to the colonial past

---

5 *Times of India*, September 2, 2007.
6 *Deshgujarat*, September 27, 2014. Available at: http://deshgujarat.com/2014/09/27/internet-banned-in-vadodara-for-three-days/.

did not just take place in the immediate postcolonial period. It has continued up to the present day in a continual reorientation of India's political icons, which on the one hand connects India's multiple regional histories, and on the other re-interprets religious pluralism. This has assumed regionally specific patterns. The Hindu right, via subsidiary organizations, has promoted seminars and publications to promote "royal" Hindu heroes of the present-day Haryana region, such as Samrat Hem Chandra Vikramaditya (Hemu) who ran campaigns against Mughal India in the mid-sixteenth century. In southern India, it has supported the millennium anniversary celebrations of the Chola ruler, Rajendra Chola, who they claim set up a "Tamil Hindu Empire" and established a university to study the Vedas (Sharma 2014).

Inevitably, arising from these regional projects, certain historical symbols compete against these Hindu majoritarian approaches in a more fundamental way. Most significant since the 1990s across India has been the proliferation of images, monuments and material representations of the iconic Dalit leader of the late colonial period, B. R. Ambedkar. The growing presence of Ambedkar has led to a fundamental transformation in the symbolic landscape of public monuments in states such as Uttar Pradesh, as statuary in particular has been used to mark the key leadership figures of the Dalit movement. These developments arguably represent physical foci for aspirations for democratic government and social mobilization. They also denote a deliberately alternative and "competing" construction of history, which places notions of social justice, reform and majority rule at the center of national and political symbolism. Crucially, as India's first law minister and drafter of the Indian Constitution, Ambedkar has been represented as a figure who handed down constitutional rights to Dalits, as opposed to ancient "Hindu" codes. In other ways, the promotion of Ambedkar symbolism often takes the form of a competitive struggle to occupy space and visual places, as a means of contesting historical control of low-caste spaces by other communities. Opposition to Ambedkar statuary and its associated forms, not least in Tamil Nadu, has taken virulent forms, with the vandalization of statues and other structures (Karthikeyan and Gorringe 2012).

In very direct and material ways, however, a new symbolic consensus surrounding Ambedkar and the rights of Dalits to a different form of freedom of expression has represented mainstream national representations of lower castes as injurious to their rights. On January 26, 2013, at the Jaipur Festival of Literature, the sociologist Ashis Nandy argued that "most corruption" came from lower castes and Dalits, but that this was a necessary condition of their social and political disadvantage. In response, Rajpal Meena, President of the National Union of Backward Classes, filed a First Information Report under sections 506 and 3(1) of the Prevention of Atrocities Act. Mayawati, leader of the Dalit party Bahujan Samaj, called for Nandy's arrest and prosecution (Guru 2013). In its most important manifestations, these challenges have evoked particular kinds of political spaces and places. Dalits and low castes have, since the 1990s, set about to symbolically and materially appropriate social spaces. As we saw above, social spaces historically provided arenas for a range of symbolic mobilizations, particularly in the context of ambiguous political rights. In Tamil Nadu, this has manifest itself in battles between different caste communities around the placing of party political flags in public spaces, extending the reach of the *cheri* (slum) and coming into conflict with both upper-caste parties and the local state. In some cases, posters of Dalit party leaders (for example, Thirumavalavan of the VCK), have been effaced and, in one incident in 1999, smeared with cow dung (Gorringe 2016, p. 172). Since the turn of the millennium there has clearly been a shift in the power of this public symbolism, as the local state has assisted in defending Dalit movements (Gorringe 2016, p. 173). Similar events have taken place in north India. In Uttar Pradesh, such public performances have mimicked official unveiling ceremonies of statues and asserted alternative forms of political authority.

These contestations over space and its symbolism are extremely important in many states of India, given the historical importance of space to signs of social status and power, as we saw earlier in this chapter around symbolic mobilization in Uttar Pradesh. Following independence, not only were definitions of social status represented by the symbolic power of spaces, religious sites and everyday locations. Such connections were also written into India's Constitution. Under Article 15 (2a–b), no Indian Citizen was to be subject to disability, liability, or restriction on grounds of religion, caste, race, sex, or birth, in regard to shops, public restaurants, hotels, places of entertainment, wells, tanks, bathing ghats, or roads. It is this background, along with the rising counter-symbolism of Dalit and Adivasi (tribal) movements that have also bolstered the challenge to mainstream and Hindu nationalist symbols of power. This could also entail the control of landed resources. The website for the Patel Statue of Unity claimed the project would lead to the development of the banks of River Narmada up to Bharuch; development of road, rail, and tourism infrastructure; schools, colleges, and universities for tribal development; the Education Research Centre and Knowledge City; and the Clean Technology Research Park and Agriculture Training Centers. However, being sited on Sadhu-Bet Island, importantly approximately 3.5 km south of the Sardar Sarovar Dam in the Narmada district of Gujarat, this symbolic gigantism marked the state's uniformly tough response to long-term environmental protests against the dam's flooding of farmland and local religious shrines.

Construction of the statue itself involves building a weir, which will flood a number of Tadvi tribal villages and their religious sites (Sadhu Tekri). Protests against this state gigantism and its use of national icons have come, over the medium to longer term, from celebrities, including Arundhati Roy and Aamir Khan, and especially the Narmada Bachao Andolan, an Adivasi movement which has co-opted human rights activists (Fisher 1995, p. 23). In the first week of October 2013, just as Modi's election campaign was building, around 2,000 Adivasis gathered at a village near the statue site to protest against land destined to be acquired for the purposes of "tourism" (Kevadia 2013). At the foundation stone ceremony later in the month, Gujarat state security was increased in anticipation of a large Adivasi black flag protest, against the failure of rehabilitation around the project.

CONCLUSION

Historians interested in mass mobilizations beyond formal institutions, especially those working in the tradition of Subaltern Studies, have emphasized the importance of narrative traditions and figurative speech in South Asia. What the study of political symbolism in a specific locality in this region has traditionally demonstrated is the importance of the interface between symbols that have a national, perhaps even international resonance, and the geographical and cultural margins. Histories of symbolism and rhetoric begin to provide insights into how political symbols are mediated at different spatial, temporal, and discursive levels (Gupta 1995, pp. 395–400). What is most evident when viewed across a broad period of the late colonial period to contemporary times is the persistence of particular methods in the reworking of mythical, historical, and spatially rooted symbols. Public rituals during mass mobilizations were a means of reclaiming control of public spaces in colonial India, and promoting certain forms of intra- or cross-communal visions of the nation. This tradition has stood contemporary regimes in good stead, as they employ culturally "translatable" symbolic tropes to connect India's regions. Arguably, the political requirement to think in spatial terms has allowed technologies of symbolic transmission to develop that are creatively mobile, move between spaces, or appear at different places simultaneously. In this sense, political symbolism has often emerged as a form of mobile theater, exemplified by Nehru's (depicted) election tour over 24,000 miles with nine speeches a day in 1951, or by Modi's 300,000 miles and 3D hologram speech rallies in 1,350 places, which allowed him to deliver speeches in fifty-three locations simultaneously. In 2014, virtual space was also key to the delivery of political symbolism, as the BJP generated 13 million Facebook "likes" and accumulated

3.9 million followers on Twitter, allowing Modi to interact with an estimated 234 million people.

Scale was also important in how particular symbols were selected for particular periods of the past, and in how they were strategically employed both as defined moments and in repeated or routine commemorations. The politics of the iron giant Patel aims to connect the BJP to mainstream anticolonial nationalism, heroic "nation-building" and to convey the importance of a Gujarati figure (whether Patel or Modi) to the national developmental project. This drew on a specific historical reading of India's late colonial and early postcolonial politics, which in turn connects Modi to a range of other national (sometimes Congress Party) figures, particularly those who presented a majoritarian vision of India. It was important for Narendra Modi that these figures should also be associated with historical moments of state transformation (such as in 1947–9) or anticolonial struggle (the late nineteenth century through to the 1920s). This was a deliberate convergence, rooted in a specific postcolonial moment in time, on which a range of symbolic national events and symbolic tropes might draw in the future, using anniversaries and material representations.

The political symbolism currently being employed by the Hindu right in India, then, shares a great deal with much older, Congress-driven forms of national mobilization. As well as employing supposedly unifying national myths and figures themselves, this is also about the method of symbol propagation. The use of different public arenas – festivals, public buildings, or temples – in often quite theatrical ways, for example, to convey political messages across India is common to the late colonial period and contemporary times. At the same time, this convergence between ostensibly secular uses of such symbolism (Congress) and those of the Hindu right, has allowed the latter to effectively invert the politics of speech freedoms. Given the long-term importance of symbols that signify India's histories as either "Hindu" or "Muslim," it is a short step from a largely "secular" consensus around those symbols, to a consensus that valorizes "Hindu" symbols as the essential "national" ones and challenges as potentially "antinational." The older Congress secularism, conveyed in symbolic mobilization, was always (perhaps necessarily) very loose, and contained within it some of the very forms of soft Hindu nationalism that are now championed by the BJP – for example, the politics of Patel himself, or of P. D. Tandon and to some extent M. K. Gandhi. Equally, the Congress's consensus was always potentially about the control of challenges to that consensus and especially those that appeared to undermine national unification, or national-level developmental projects. Armed with colonial controls of speech freedoms, the BJP has effectively inverted the implications of this consensus to champion and protect a high-caste Hindu idea of national culture.

Symbols in speech and performative mobilization however, circulate in cultural territories and temporalities where their meanings can unfold or distort and in this sense they are not easy to control. This is especially the case with historical icons, which embody their own political values and contestable histories. When looked at, for example, in the context of political mobilization in both the 1920s–1940s and the 2010s, forms of symbol "circulation" take place, which disrupt and complicate what Austin (1962, pp. 98–103) described as the "perlocutionary acts" of (political) utterances. We might ask why particular historical symbols are chosen or reignited (or indeed absent) at the times that they are and what happens when their re-emergence takes place in a different temporal context. Gandhi learned to his cost that references to "Ram Rajya," an evocation of older religious symbols that hinted at Tilak and Aurobindo in the first years of the twentieth century, had a deleterious effect in the early 1930s on north Indian Muslim support for Congress. Modi's use of Upadhyaya is legitimized and cushioned by cross-referencing other national figures, but takes place at a time when the notion of the "Gujarat" economic model is still being tested. Equally, any invocation of Ambedkar as an all-India symbol during such ceremonial occasions as Republic Day, in recognition of his constitutional role, has to take into account the different symbolic temporalities invoked around the leader by Dalit parties in Uttar Pradesh and Maharashtra.

Movement into different social and political spaces and places also allows the circulation of symbols to disrupt their original intent. We might describe this as a form of symbolic transgression, to some extent exemplified by the many local and everyday appropriations of Gandhi. Scalar strategies, as for the Congress party in an earlier phase, were absolutely key to Modi for two reasons, relating both to his political past and his economic claims. First, the main attacks against the BJP and Modi in particular were that he was dangerously divisive and autocratic, in the context of the 2002 Gujarat pogrom. He therefore needed to appropriate symbols of unity in his bid for power at the center. Second, he had to attempt to convince constituencies across India that the Gujarat model of development applied across all states but appealed to differences between them. In this sense, his rhetoric of development had to be rooted in the national. Yet, just as this form of symbol selection mobilizes particular margins and regions via its spatial reach, it is vulnerable to a circulating symbolic feedback, which depicts the "iron man" as the representative of unbridled capitalism, Hindu majoritarianism and disregard for the politics of self-determination. This is at the root of the iconoclastic strategies of the Narmada Bachao Andolan. It also characterizes a range of Naxalite groups operating in the red corridor through eastern and central India, who have garnered significant popular support via direct opposition to the larger capital projects of the Indian state and critiques of "high-caste" symbols. The iron Patel then becomes a symbol of gigantism that tramples on environmental rights and those rights seen as marginal to the greater symbolic vision.

REFERENCES

Austin, J. L. 1962. *How to Do Things with Words.* Oxford: Oxford University Press.

Bhatia, G. 2016. *Offend, Shock or Disturb: Free Speech Under the Indian Constitution.* Oxford: Oxford University Press.

DNA India 2014. "Narendra Modi in Amethi: I will come to Amethi again in 2019 and present an account [sic] my work here," *DNA India*, May 5, 2014. Available at: www.dnaindia.com/india/commentary-live-narendra-modi-in-amethi-i-will-come-to-amethi-again-in-2019-and-present-an-account-my-work-here-1985140.

Fisher, W. 1995. *Towards Sustainable Development? Struggling over India's Narmada Dam.* Armonk, New York: M.E. Sharpe.

Gatade, S. 2013. "Statue of unity: How the Varna media is loving it," *Kashmir Times*, December 20, 2013.

Gopal, P. 2007. "A forgotten history," *Outlook*, December 6, 2007. Available at: www .outlookindia.com/website/story/a-forgotten-history/236191.

Gorringe, H. 2016. "Out of the *Cheris*: Dalits Contesting and Creating Public Space in Tamil Nadu," *Space and Culture* 19(2): 164–76.

Gould, W. 2004. *Hindu Nationalism and the Language of Politics in Late Colonial India.* Cambridge: Cambridge University Press.

Guichard, S. 2010. *The Construction of History and Nationalism in India: Textbooks, Controversies and Politics.* London: Routledge.

Gupta, A. 1995. "Blurred boundaries: The discourse of corruption, the culture of politics, and the imagined state," *American Ethnologist* 22(2): 375–402.

Guru, G. 2013. "Freedom of expression and the life of the Dalit Mind," *Economic and Political Weekly* 49(10).

Hansen, T. B. 1999. *The Saffron Wave.* Princeton: Princeton University Press.

Kang, B. 2014. "Who is this man who features in every Modi speech?," *Grist Media*, October 6, 2014. Available at: https://in.news.yahoo.com/who-is-this-man-who-features-in-every-modi-speech-063715210.html.

Karthikeyan, D. and Gorringe, H. 2012. "Rescuing Ambedkar," *Frontline* 29(19): 136–40.

Kevadia, N. 2013. "Tribals protest land acquisition for tourism near Statue of Unity," *Indian Express*, October 3, 2013.

Lakshmi, R. 2015. "Indians invented planes 7,000 years ago – and other startling claims at the Science Congress," *The Washington Post*, January 4, 2015. Available at: www.washingtonpost.com/blogs/worldviews/wp/2015/01/04/indians-invented-planes-7000-years-ago-and-other-startling-claims-at-the-science-congress/.

    2016. "Authorities in Kashmir shut down newspapers in strife-torn Kashmir," *Washington Post*, July 18, 2016. Available at: www.washingtonpost.com/news/worldviews/wp/2016/07/18/modi-government-shuts-down-newspapers-in-strife-torn-kashmir/.

Nagpal, D. 2014. "Narendra Modi government to drop Jawaharlal's name from JNNURM?," *Zeenews*, August 12, 2014. Available at: http://zeenews.india.com/news/nation/narendra-modi-government-to-drop-jawaharlal-nehrus-name-from-jnnurm_954093.html.

Padmanabhan, R. 1998. "Assault on art," *Frontline*, May 9–22, 1998.

Prakash, G. 1999. *Another Reason: Science and the Imagination of Modern India.* Princeton: Princeton University Press.

Sen, A. 2005. The Argumentative Indian: Writings on Indian History, Culture and Identity. Macmillan.

Singh, S. 2014. "Run for unity: PM Modi masterstroke pushes Indira to irrelevance," *Firstpost*, October 31, 2014. Available at: www.firstpost.com/politics/run-unity-modi-masterstroke-pushes-indira-irrelevance-1781041.html.

Smith, A. D. 1992. "National identity and the idea of European unity," *International Affairs* 68(1): 55–76.

Thapar, R. 2014. "History repeats itself," *India Today*, July 11, 2014. Available at: http://indiatoday.intoday.in/story/romila-thapar-smriti-irani-old-history-baiters-of-bjp/1/370799.html.

6

The Making of a Media System in Uganda: A New Vision and a Revolutionary Origin

Nicole Stremlau

Throughout the world, government pronouncements and legislation on the role of speech in society spring often not from international norms and Voltairean aphorisms but from complex histories of origin, particularly histories of national formation. In many places, it is in the harsh experiences of revolutionary warfare and guerrilla movements that leaders are shaped, ideologies hardened, and imaginings of future media systems created. In this chapter I focus on one such origins story, examining the changing approaches to the media within Uganda's political system. Chronicling the roots of popular mobilization and the strategy of persuasion and participation that the National Resistance Movement (NRM) employed during its struggle and early days of its government in the 1980s, the chapter then goes on to explore the tensions between promoting the voices of citizens within the larger promise of ending violence against the backdrop of decades of instability that have plagued Uganda. At the heart of this history is one publication, the *New Vision*, founded in 1986 as the NRM's first postliberation paper and one of the continent's most unusual and interesting experiments in creating a popular government media outlet. By focusing on the *New Vision*, this chapter explores the impact early policies, driven by a unique political ideology, have had on the media system that has developed in postwar Uganda. Ultimately, one might ask whether the struggles for independence, decolonization, and subsequent liberation movements, in Africa produce alternate and useful ideas of the role of speech and society.

When Yoweri Museveni first came to power after years of guerrilla struggle in 1986, he promised a new form of politics rooted in non-sectarianism. Peace and security, Museveni promised, would be the overriding concern. Soon after his inauguration, Museveni argued that "the problem of Africa in general and Uganda in particular is not the people but leaders who want to overstay in power" (Tangri and Mwenda 2010, p. 32). For many observers, these words have sadly carried an unwanted prophetic weight for Museveni's own long future in politics. At different times Museveni has been called a "new leader" representing democratic tendencies tempered by African realities (Connell and Smyth 1998; Ottaway 1999), a neo-populist (Carbone 2005), and, more recently, a competitive authoritarian (Kagoro 2015). Such a range of opinions characterizes the ambiguity inherent in his conception and implementation of one-party politics, a form of politics known to many as the Movement System that has both followed continental trends of allowing political competition and facilitating the ascendance of democracy, while attempting to maintain single-party control.

However, in recent years, there has been a distinctive and unmistakable decline in the values, philosophical approaches, and ideals that once informed the Movement System and were so influential in shaping and defining the media system. New electoral freedoms have been minimal and the NRM has been charged with manipulating polls and imprisoning opposition figures as part of Museveni's quest to remain in power. Yet even today, Uganda possesses a vibrant and diverse, if tempered, media. While journalists do face harassment, there are hundreds of radio stations and dozens of newspapers, with Ugandans having relatively unfettered access to social media. In comparison with many African countries, Ugandans do enjoy a larger degree of media and space for debate.

THE ROOTS OF THE NRM'S IDEOLOGY

The NRM was unusual for a liberation movement in its commitment to non-coercively achieving broad civilian support during the military struggle (Mamdani 1996). This strategy continued to shape government policy after seizing power and influenced political development across the region, including in Rwanda, Ethiopia, and Eritrea. The NRM was formed in 1980 after the then ruling president, Milton Obote (with the support of Tanzanian President and Pan-African liberation leader, Julius Nyerere), claimed to have won highly contested elections.[1] The voting was widely regarded as having been rigged, and most egregiously in the south where Obote, who hailed from the north, had few supporters and many votes. Compelled to act, Museveni and his followers in the newly created opposition group believed that a coup d'état

---

[1] In 1981 when the war began, the NRM was initially known as the Popular Resistance Army (PRA). It did not adopt the name NRM until merging with Yusuf Lule's exiled Uganda Freedom Fighters (UFF). The UFF contributed little more than Lule's name to the struggle as he became the nominal head of the organization, though he passed away during the struggle, formalizing Museveni as the head of the NRM.

would be almost impossible, particularly given the presence of the Tanzanian army overseeing the elections. Thus, they turned to armed struggle, a decision that gave the NRM much of its ideological underpinning. The political thoughts of Che Guevara, Mao Tse-tung, and Lenin were particularly influential, especially in shaping ideas about the role of the "vanguard" in leading the struggle and the stress placed on the political education of the masses and the structure of political mobilization.

Guevara's "foco" theory, which argued that the government's repressive reactions to insurgencies were a critical tool for attracting support from the masses, inspired the NRM's approach to political mobilization (Ngoga 1998). Imbuing greater confidence in the nascent NRM, at the core of foco theory is the belief that in situations where the population is profoundly oppressed, it is not necessary to wait for ideal conditions to launch an insurrection. Instead, a group of revolutionaries can initiate a small-scale guerrilla war that can then act as a "focus" and inspiration for scaling the war up. Roving bands of guerrilla fighters become a key element in creating revolutionary conditions and gaining the support of the broader population. This is a necessarily elitist approach to revolutionary theory as the foco are able to serve as the vanguard, leading the masses in their own struggles without having to actually merge with them.

Following Mao Tse-tung's argument that political education and mobilization was the starting point for any insurgency (Mao 1961), the NRM made political education a central tenet of their doctrine to organize people and establish the structures that could replace the weak state that currently existed. Mao's thought and practice also highlighted the success of groups that had defeated armies that had the advantage of military hardware, a factor that surely resonated with the NRM given Obote's relative strength and the support he drew from regional states. Without an advantage on the field of battle, propaganda was seen by Mao to be at the core of effective education and mobilization (Katzenbach and Hanrahan 1955). The NRM would pay careful attention to these priorities.

Closer to home, the NRM was also heavily influenced in how to structure itself by other liberation movements on the continent, including the Frente de Libertação de Moçambique (FRELIMO), South Africa's African National Congress (ANC), the South West Africa People's Organization (SWAPO) in what is now Namibia, and the Zimbabwe African National Union-Patriotic Front (Zanu-PF). Under Nyerere, Tanzania was something of a sanctuary for these groups and often offered logistical or military support, but it also offered opportunities for exchanging ideas between liberation fronts across Southern, and in the case of Uganda, reaching up into Eastern Africa. It provided a unique opportunity for adapting and teaching liberation theories and experiences about what techniques had been effective. There was, in the words of former Tanzanian president, Benjamin Mkapa (1995–2005), a strategy to:

> give voice to the movements … we would give pages to them. We would interview them, we would reproduce their manifestos, and we would publish their press releases, which would give them a great deal of confidence … and particularly with regards to the radio, they were given special time which was beamed to all Southern Africa, so that helped them to carry the message.[2]

Throughout the guerrilla war, Museveni drew on the teachings and training he received in Tanzania, and it was actually in Tanzania that the precursor to the NRM was established. After going into exile in 1967 and joining Dar-es-Salaam University, where he was active in radical student politics, Museveni made strong links with the Tanzanian government and with other liberation fronts as chair of the University Students African Revolutionary Front, a group of students from around the continent that were advocating anticolonialist and pan-African ideals.

MEDIA, PROPAGANDA, AND THE STRUGGLE

Informed by this range of ideas, from an early stage in the NRM's armed struggle, propaganda was recognized as central for political mobilization and important for garnering mass support for the movement. Political teachings from Mao offered explicit lessons here: "Every large guerrilla unit should have a printing press and mimeograph stone. They must also have paper on which to print propaganda leaflets and notices … in guerrilla areas there should be a printing press or lead-type press." (Mao 1961, p. 61). The NRM acted accordingly, establishing *The Ugandan Resistance News* as a way of publicizing the struggle and explaining the NRM's positions and rationale behind adopting armed struggle.[3] As Eriya Kategaya, who had overall responsibility for publications as coordinator of the External Wing of the National Resistance Army (NRA) during the war, explained, "Maoist movements invest in persuasion, political debate. Guerrilla movements that were supported by Soviets cared more about the military."[4] Given the NRM's lack of arms and independence from Soviet patronage, the efficacy, indeed necessity, of this approach was

---

[2] Interview: Benjamin Mkapa.
[3] Selected excerpts from *Uganda Resistance News* are available in the publication *Mission to Freedom*. NRM SECRETARIAT 1990. *Mission To Freedom*. Kampala: The New Vision.
[4] Interview: Eriya Kategaya.

clear, and the NRM invested heavily in persuading people, even, at times, entering careful dialogue with the people – for, as Kategaya explained, "you can't mobilize support without feedback".[5] Facilitating this approach was a broad camaraderie with the propaganda wings of liberation movements in the region, many of which shared similar ideological grounding and this regional setting was important as many of the NRM's propaganda efforts were best pursued outside of Uganda. Kategaya explains this context and the situation whereby the *Uganda Resistance News* was published outside the country:

> In the beginning, when the NRM was underground we didn't have a clear media strategy or public publicity. The first bulletin issued was in June 1981 just to announce that there is a war. In 1982 a group of NRM leaders went to London where they met Allison Miller from the *Times of London* and gave her an interview about what they were doing, what areas were controlled by the NRM. She was the one to coin the term the "Luwero triangle" and was the first journalist to give the NRM exposure. Soon after, the *Resistance News* was established and published in Nairobi, and smuggled into Uganda. This publication carried a number of articles explaining why they were fighting and the rationale behind their armed struggle.[6]

The *Uganda Resistance News* sought to target both Ugandans and regional and international elites, hoping to establish international support for the movement. A major component of the NRM's propaganda strategy was thus to bring Western journalists to the region. The NRM would contact international journalists it had identified as potentially sympathetic, or, more capaciously, those that might simply be willing to make the trip. Encouraging someone perceived as independent to tell the story of the struggle, it was believed, would lead to greater credibility for the NRM; journalists who visited the bush were seen as a crucial conduit for disseminating information. This wartime strategy later had a major impact on the *New Vision*. At the invitation of the NRM leadership, the founding editor-in-chief of the publication was a British journalist, William Pike, who first engaged with the NRM during his visits to liberated areas in the 1980s while working for a UK magazine. Pike went on to oversee the *New Vision's* development in the role of Managing Director for twenty years.

Invoking ideas of "freedom of expression" was also central to the propaganda messages that the NRM promoted. This was used strategically to differentiate itself from the Obote government but it was also regularly highlighted

---

5   Interview: Kategaya.
6   Interview: Kategaya.

as an integral part of the system they hoped to overturn. Indicating a degree of sincerity, many articles in publications such as *Uganda Resistance News* focused on the extent to which the Obote government was restricting media, highlighting the plight of local journalists who faced censorship and persecution. Such treatment of journalists was often marked as a sign of Obote's weakness, or an indication that the government was unable to engage in critical discussion or cope with unfavorable comments.

THE MOVEMENT SYSTEM IN PRACTICE

NRA troops seized the capital city Kampala on January 26, 1986. Met with a weakened central state after years of conflict, one of the first steps the NRM took in power was to ban the exercise of party politics. This action was taken partly because the leadership feared that even after the extensive propaganda campaigns and efforts to widely mobilize the populace during the war, the NRM was still not fully known across the country and might not win in competitive elections. But this does not explain the decision fully. The NRM also diagnosed party politics as a key source of the divisions in Uganda and that argued that adopting a pluralist democratic model was inappropriate for the current stage of Uganda's development. In the NRM's analysis, political parties in the West functioned to represent the class interests of industrialized societies; in preindustrial Uganda, however, parties may only represent ethnic or religious groups, thereby accentuating divisions.

Eschewing the expectations of the West, the NRM argued that what they termed the Movement System differed from other one-party systems because everyone could participate and elect representatives. The Resistance Councils (RCs), which were started during the war, represented the most important manifestation of this philosophy of power and were a central part of the NRM's strategy to consolidate itself after 1986 and bring peace to the country. The RCs were initially established as rebel support structures during the struggle as a means of directing food and supplies to NRA fighters. As such, the RCs were key to the NRM's strategy of protracted armed struggle but, as the guerrilla war progressed, they also held an important role in the governance of liberated zones. Here the RCs acted to resolve conflicts and adjudicate disputes with leaders that were held accountable via regular elections. RCs were, in essence, the tool through which local communities could govern themselves in the absence of state authorities (Golooba-Mutebi 2004).

Filling a vacuum left by the state and serving the NRA, the RCs were also seen as a way of extending the NRM's agenda of political education and providing a forum for the people to "practice" democracy. Some might view this

cynically and argue the RCs were conceived as a way to keep people sufficiently amused with the pretense of democracy while the leadership indulged
in patronage and authoritarian tendencies. But the RCs were consistent
with the NRM's wider thoughts and complemented the widely held view of
Museveni as "the teacher." RCs were regarded as a "big school" for teaching
appropriate democratic habits. According to the NRM, these habits were not
natural but had to be practiced. As Kategaya elaborates:

> I hope that through the RCs we shall teach our people to accept and handle
> different points of view and even when there are differences to regard each
> other as Ugandans first and foremost. The holding of different views does
> not make you less of a citizen than the other and this has been a problem in
> this country where you find that somebody loses a job because he is reported
> to you as having voted a wrong party. Now what does engineering got to do
> with voting?[7]

The democracy the NRM believed it facilitated through the RCs was more
direct and active than is practiced in most parliamentary democracies where
voters might only engage in politics by casting a vote once every several years
in national elections. Part of the rationale behind the RCs was that Ugandans
would have to be concerned and participate with politics on a quotidian
level, catalyzing an involvement that would strengthen internal security. By
attempting to provide a framework through which conflicts could be resolved
and justice executed, it was the NRM's hope that fewer people would resort
to violence.

With the benefit of hindsight and in recognition of the growing disillusion-
ment with the NRM's political process, the aura and reputation of the RCs
have come under considerable pressure. The Ugandan academic, Frederick
Golooba-Mutebi, describes a process whereby the public meetings that were
at the core of the consultative process began to atrophy due to "participation
fatigue" (2004). In his analysis, the enthusiasm for direct, regular and systematic
engagement in governing processes often became too burdensome. Lethargy
also combined with the inability of the RCs to meet expectations. The RCs
were based on assumptions, theories and expectations about feasibility and the
role of popular participation that simply could not be met in practice. While
in theory the decision-making was transferred from the central government
to the local authorities, this was not always the case in practice. Political hierarchy and power dynamics characterized the relationship between different
governing authorities in many districts. Villagers could be active and knowing

---

[7]   Interview: Kategaya.

players in this process, giving their leaders significant space to govern, despite often expressing dissatisfaction with them (Golooba-Mutebi 2004).

INCLUSIVITY AND THE REBUILDING OF STATE INSTITUTIONS

There have been several distinct periods of governance in Uganda since the NRM came to power in 1986. The first, "the transition period," occurred immediately after the NRM took control and was marked by its efforts to consolidate itself by suspending political parties and prohibiting peaceful assemblies (Legal Notice No. 1, *Uganda Gazette*, 1986). When compared with the rollback of constitutionally limited presidential terms and a more general decline in state recognition of civil and political rights in recent years, it is remarkable to note that the efforts of the NRM to consolidate power in the late 1980s and early 1990s was done in a reasonably benevolent, even almost enlightened way and with significant support from Ugandans. Political parties could continue to exist, but primarily in name only. All political activity was to fall under the Movement System, which aspired to be a broad tent for all voters and candidates. Encapsulating these lofty ambitions, Museveni argued in his January 1986 inauguration speech:

> No one should think that what is happening today is a mere change of guard: it is a fundamental change in the politics of our country. In Africa, we have seen so many changes that change, as such, is nothing short of mere turmoil. We have had one group getting rid of another one, only for it to turn out to be worse than the group it displaced. Please do not count us in that group of people. (Museveni 2000, p. 3)

In this context of securing "fundamental change" the NRM sought not only to say it was different but to clearly demonstrate its difference and as quickly as possible. One means the NRM used to achieve this was to build trust in the government by adopting standards that characterize open societies, respect for human rights, a tolerance of dissent, and the establishment of a rule of law. To outside observers and critics, this was incongruent with the repression simultaneously occurring in Uganda. But the NRM believed these ostensibly liberal measures could not only help to heal a country plagued by years of sectarian violence, but would also lead to a new kind of politics unique from the Western model; a constructive form of autocracy and single-party democracy. The formation of a broad-based and inclusive government would, it was promised, form the basis of the new state.

When a party comes to power by force or fills a vacuum created by the intervention of an external state, there is a tendency for a pervasive and total abandonment of the previous regime as institutions are dissolved, bureaucrats fired, and new constitutions drafted. In contrast to this trend, the first government that the NRM established has been widely credited for its early efforts to promote stability and recognize historical legacies as it carefully balanced the concerns of political and ethnic groups. Many observers, however, are also quick to note that the NRM succeeded in achieving diversity and genuine representation in the body politic only to have it decline over the years, or revert to a "partial reform syndrome," a term used to refer to reform-oriented leaders who embrace the rhetoric but fall back on maintaining their networks of patronage and political elites to retain control (Van de Walle 1999).

It is right that the NRM's early successes should not blind us to criticism. Northerners have been marginalized in political life and this is a widely cited factor that has been driving the war in northern Uganda for decades (Allen 2006) but there have been unprecedented efforts to be inclusive. Made up of thirty-two positions, the NRM's first cabinet contained ten members from the Democratic Party (DP), the leader of the Conservative Party, a former prime minister of Baganda, Moses Ali (formerly a minister in Idi Amin's government), and members of the Uganda's People's Congress (Tripp 2010, pp. 48–9). These were not just headline appointments. Lower down the state apparatus, the NRM was careful not to exacerbate political factions by dismissing civil servants who had served under previous governments. These decisions bore witness to the instinct of the NRM to reform rather than dismantle the state apparatus. The NRM believed that the problems with government institutions were principally rooted in corrupt individuals and ineffective political supervision, rather than the size or inherent inefficiency of the government, the latter position put forth at the time by the donor community and international financial institutions in the age of structural adjustment (Brett 1994).

The retention of civil servants proved important and contributed to the general feeling that Museveni was indeed bringing the peace and security he promised. Former Minister of Information, Nsaba Buturo, noted that in the Ministry of Information:

> This government didn't go about dismissing those they thought were unfriendly. Those who wanted to continue working could. If you are to get stability you don't interfere … Stability can only be when you carry-on with everyone so there have not really been arrests either. [Uganda] has a turbulent past so achieving stability only happens when you involve everyone.[8]

---

[8] Interview: Nsaba Buturo.

Speaking in a similar fashion, Kategaya recalled that in the immediate after-math of the NRM coming to power, there was a feeling that the NRM needed to reverse the trend of Uganda's political history where "one group comes and sweeps everyone out" and to instead "let everyone settle down, not feel harassed" because we wanted to "show that we are a new group with different thinking."[9]

The inclusivity approach of these years had a significant impact on how the NRM dealt with the media during the transition period. As the NRA troops descended on Kampala in 1986, the NRA seized control of the government radio, Radio Uganda, in a highly symbolic projection of power. The day after taking control of the capital, Museveni used the radio to appeal for calm and to outline his plans for stabilizing and ruling the country. Significantly, the medium that carried his voice to a population largely cut off from each other, as telephone lines and other infrastructure were damaged in the war, was eyed quickly for reform. Reflecting the broader strategy adopted toward govern-ment institutions, Museveni decided not to disband Radio Uganda (a deci-sion also made with respect to notoriously dull government newspaper, the *Uganda Times*). As Jack Turyamwijuka, Head of Radio Uganda during the transition from Obote to Museveni, noted:

> No one was fired when the Movement came to power ... People were civil servants but now they are independently recruited. For our editorial policy, having the other independent radio stations makes little point in restricting government radio because if you don't say it, others will. Radio Uganda now has a board of directors. Most are former civil servants but there are business people as well ... No one was sacked during the transition. Civil servants were not affected by change of power.[10]

But if old institutions were allowed to continue, new ones were also created. The *New Vision*, the important media new start of the newly empowered gov-ernment, embodied this dual imperative of promoting change and stability. In establishing the *New Vision*, the NRA hired some of the journalists from the recently collapsed *Uganda Times*. But incorporating the *Uganda Times'* journalists was difficult because, as James Tumusiime pointed out:

> Most of the journalists were used to propaganda and advancing a particular cause. They couldn't imagine they could write openly... The nucleus team going to run the paper was far from cohesive. A climate of suspicion hung over the paper as old political beliefs simmered below the surface. Many of

---

[9] Interview: Kategaya.
[10] Interview: Jack Turyamwijuka.

the recruits who came in from outside thought that those they found there were moles of the old regime. This kept the latter on the defensive.[11]

While the newsroom was often a tense place as a consequence, this policy of inclusion provided a valuable opportunity to create consensus. On both sides, journalists held different perspectives on the recent changes in Uganda and yet in the process of working together the journalists had to reconcile certain historical and contemporary interpretations of events to report on the new directions Uganda was heading. Gradually, a new team was built, journalists were trained and the *New Vision* was able to carve out its own independent direction.

This inclusionary process, well witnessed in the establishment of the *New Vision*, has been an important component of successful nation-building and the policy's success can be contrasted with actions in Ethiopia following the fall of Mengistu in 1991. Here, former Ministry of Information officials under the Derg were forced to resign, creating a pool of disgruntled people who channeled their bitterness and opposition to the government into private papers.[12] In Uganda, by deciding to keep former Amin and Obote-era journalists as part of the system, the number of old journalists seeking employment in opposition spaces was much reduced and further meant those remaining in their jobs were less likely to be deeply opposed to Museveni's changes as they had vested interests in the new system.

A NEW NEWSPAPER FOR A NEW COUNTRY

Beyond meeting the inclusivity agenda, the *New Vision* newspaper further captured the practical implementation of how the NRM's political ideology impacted and shaped the early development of the media sector. Unprecedented in its scope and intentions to be both readable and independent,[13] the *New Vision* became arguably the most ambitious government newspaper experiment on the continent. The paper, which emerged from a cabinet meeting in the early days of the NRM, was a manifestation of the NRM's belief that it was bringing a fundamental change or a "new vision" not

---

[11]   Interview: James Tumusiime.
[12]   The broader lessons of reconciliation and incorporation within these institutions are evident and have most recently been demonstrated in Iraq, where the US occupying forces made the grave error of dismantling the Iraqi army only to have them re-emerge unemployed as various insurgencies.
[13]   The editorial policy was established by a legal statute that specifically stated that the paper should be national and publish criticism of the government without being an institutional opponent of the government. See www.newvision.co.ug/V/.

only to Uganda, but also to the African continent. As William Pike noted, "I think it was part of the whole concept of fundamental change, that you could have an [independent] media, including a government newspaper, because after all, the BBC's independent, so why shouldn't an African newspaper be independent?"[14]

Unique in the continent at the time in that it was staffed by an eclectic mix of people rather than ideologues, and granted a large degree of freedom, the *New Vision*'s development can again be traced back to the formative experiences during guerrilla war. The *New Vision* reflected the ideology and vision of the type of debate, including the RCs and policies of constructive criticism that the NRM believed could contribute to single-party democracy. It was, as Pike continued, an extension of the rallies or parades during the struggle where:

> the soldiers were allowed to criticise the officers, as long as it's done openly in good faith ... And the rule was that you would never get in trouble as a soldier for practicing the principle of constructive criticism. So really the newspaper was an extension of that ... They came out, they were a guerrilla army but as a guerrilla army they'd supported free speech, constructive criticism and that kind of thing so they wanted that to continue in the newspaper.[15]

This approach to "positive" or constructive criticism was reiterated widely. An early edition of *New Vision* quoted Minister of Information and Broadcasting, Mr. Abu Mayanja, as saying:

> The newspaper should not censor any honest opinion but that instead it should encourage debate on matters like security, economy, politicisation and other issues which affect all Ugandans ... Ugandans who have strong cases to argue ... use the newspaper for that purpose ... no single individual or group has all the answers to our problems ... let us encourage positive criticism because we as a government are not enemies of the people. (*New Vision* 1986b, p. 1)

Grand in design and carefully justified, the beginnings of *New Vision* were, however, humble; the offices were made up of a few desks with some Russian computers, one telephone line and there was no money to pursue stories. Indicative of the working conditions in these early days, only one copy of the first *New Vision* is known to exist, which is held in the Corporation's

---

[14] Interview: William Pike.
[15] Interview: Pike.

library but contains a fascinating section of text. The first editorial, entitled "We Will Contribute to This Change," set the agenda of the paper, declaring that:

> "New Vision" has been chosen as the name of the paper at this point in time because our motherland has undergone a fundamental change following over two decades of brutal regimes, economic stagnation and social and political upheavals as well as corruption, inefficiency and neglect in the highest reaches of administration … At this time when we enter the threshold of renewed hope, the *New Vision* will count on the good will of all Ugandans in its contribution towards national unity, reconciliation and patriotism. Since the main problems which beset us in the past were man-made, it should not take us too long to solve them if we adhere to the NRM political programme. Indeed this may well be the last chance in a lifetime for every mature Ugandan to contribute to our nation's stability, development and prosperity. (*New Vision* 1986a, p. 4)

The editorial continued by turning to ideas of human rights and freedoms and arguing that while it is important for an "individual to exercise his human rights in a free and peaceful atmosphere" it must be done "without losing sight of his obligations to ensure that freedom is not lost again" (*New Vision* 1986). Confident in explaining the limitations of liberal principles for Uganda's present situation, the first issue of the *New Vision* also explained other NRM decisions to the public, including its ban on political party activities such as the issuance of press and public statements, the wearing of party political colors, and displaying party flags and other symbols. Here it argued that these actions were necessary to create a grace period in which the government could develop a government of national unity. In defending these positions, early issues of the *New Vision* came close to acting as a propaganda mouthpiece for the government but remained able to present itself as a fresh start. The editors did not have to struggle with reforming a large bureaucracy such as Radio Uganda or Uganda Television and as a self-accounting and profit-oriented company it acted as a completely local and self-sustaining initiative.

Throughout its history the *New Vision* demonstrated an ability and freedom to criticize the government within certain bounds. This continues today, although the degree to which the *New Vision* is independent from government influences remains debatable and is contested by many, including journalists that work there. The paper is often accused of being a government mouthpiece, not least by the political opposition and other business competitors such as the *Monitor*. David Mukholi, former managing editor of *Sunday Vision*, for example, argues that "total independence [of the paper] would be far fetched"[16] and most people agree that there are a few areas that journalists fear to tread, including Museveni's personal life (especially stories relating to his wife), and military activities, particularly relating to the war in the north of the country and the Ugandan army's involvement in the Democratic Republic of Congo.

The paper has, however, had a tremendous impact on developing the media industry, playing an important part in the institutionalization of the media. Somewhat paradoxically, this institutionalization has encouraged other media outlets to be more independent from government than they otherwise might have been. Soon after *New Vision* was founded, the private newspaper *Monitor* was launched in 1992 by a liberal group of journalists, several of whom had just left the private *Weekly Topic* out of frustration with the extent to which that paper had begun to align itself with the NRM. This alignment occurred following government efforts to co-opt both current and potential critics by giving *Weekly Topic* journalists prominent government positions, a decision that blunted the paper's ability to criticize the NRM. Ironically, this meant *New Vision* now had more freedom to cover news than *Weekly Topic*.[17]

The launch of the *Monitor*, a paper that was likely to be more critical of the government than *New Vision* became a strategic opportunity for the *New Vision*. Its editors actually supported the *Monitor*'s first print runs, providing them with financial credit. In many respects, it may seem counter-intuitive that the leading paper would hamper its own development by assisting what was likely to become its most significant competitor. However, founding journalist of *Monitor*, Charles Onyango-Obbo, explained the careful strategy behind this move. The *New Vision*, he argued:

> wanted a strong independent political newspaper because that determined his face. So long as there was a newspaper that was more critical of the government than the *New Vision* then he could write without pressure, but as soon as there was no other newspaper then he would become [pressured]. He needed … a newspaper that was critical of the government in order that he could place himself in the center position.[18]

While there was little indication that *Monitor* was going to become a stridently oppositional paper, *Monitor* journalists were not afraid to criticize NRM's policies. For Pike, this meant that *Monitor* could help his

[16] Interview: David Mukholi.
[17] Interview: Charles Onyango-Obbo.
[18] Interview: Onyango-Obbo.

publication as it gifted *New Vision* a distinct space. The *Monitor's* position would allow *New Vision* to take the middle ground and participate and cover certain issues and debates raised by *Monitor* that *New Vision* might not otherwise be able to address due to government pressure.

Both newspapers were thus launched with strong founding principles – *New Vision* to communicate the NRM's vision and *Monitor* to closely hold the NRM to account – but profitability increasingly moved to the fore, changing the papers in significant but different ways. The *New Vision* has been an important source of income for the government. While the government now owns 53 percent of the company's shares after selling to institutional and individual investors, the company is listed among the top ten companies on the Uganda Securities Exchange. More recently, the style and management of *Monitor* has been deeply affected by the buy-in of the Aga Khan and its incorporation into the Nation Media Group. As the group has been the market leader among private media, this has affected the development of the entire media sector. The Aga Khan, the title of the Imam or leader of the Niziri Ismailis, has been a major investor across Eastern Africa and founded the Nation Media Group in 1959. This body has grown into the largest private media house in the region, with offices in Kenya and Tanzania as well as Uganda. Change came as the Aga Khan sought to protect his investments by reducing risk, which encouraged *Monitor* to move to a more centrist position. While in the early years the *Monitor* reflected the tenacity and views of the first editorial team, the majority of the founding journalists were eventually pushed out and replaced, lending the publication a more corporate approach.

THE IMPACT OF THE NRM'S EARLY MEDIA POLICIES ON THE DEVELOPMENT OF UGANDA'S MEDIA SYSTEM

Uganda's media has been under increasing pressure from politicians to rein in criticism, particularly during major political events. There was, for example, a blockade on all social media during the February 2016 elections and a subsequent shutdown during May that year when President Museveni was sworn back into office. Facebook, Twitter, and WhatsApp were the main targets and were made inaccessible to all Ugandans, apart from those that had downloaded Virtual Private Network applications. The Ugandan Communications Commission (UCC) justified these shutdowns on the basis of the need to preserve "security," "public order," and "safety" (*Daily Monitor* 2016). During the elections Museveni explained the closure of social media by arguing that "some people misuse those pathways. You know how they use them – telling lies. If you want a right, use it properly" (BBC 2016). Mirroring trends elsewhere in the world, Museveni and his government has exhibited a clear apprehension about the potential for new platforms to be a site for coordinating demonstrations or for the exhibition of public difference with government on reporting election results, aiding election monitors, and potentially delegitimating the government's characterization of results. Cloaked with only a thin veneer of reality, the inauguration shutdown was justified as "a measure to limit the possibility of terrorists' taking advantage" of the presence of foreign leaders in the country (*Insider* 2016). This measure extended to a directive that banned live coverage of the "defiance campaign," a series of protests coordinated by the opposition party, Forum for Democratic Change (FDC). The FDC was using weekly public prayer rallies and demonstrations to express concerns about the election process and demanding an independent audit of the results. Any media houses covering the FDC campaign were threatened by the UCC with the loss of their broadcast licenses (*Global Voices* 2016).

This repressive approach towards the media in recent years, and social media in particular, is evidence of the NRM's changing strategy when it comes to advancing their interests, and Museveni's interests in particular. The NRM, long accused of shutting down media and arresting journalists, tended to do so in a targeted way, playing out almost as a personal struggle with the particular journalist or outlet being targeted. Recent moves are more encompassing, though, and signal increasingly autocratic tendencies. This may be understood as a response to the shifting structure and increasing decentralization of media across the country. For much of the 1990s, government policy toward the media was forged from a simple compound; the relationship between print media and the government effectively stood for the relationship between media and the government. Since then, media outlets have proliferated, especially on the electronic side, with recent surveys suggesting that there are 292 government and private FM radio stations (Ugandan Communications Committee 2015, p. 11), many of which broadcasting in languages other than English and specifically targeting rural communities. Alongside social media, radio has increasingly become the medium through which Ugandans engage with politics, launching the careers and aiding the ambition of a host of local politicians and businessmen eager to further their interests.

With more bodies to take aim at, and voices to disagree with, the decentralization and proliferation of media outlets can make it difficult to determine what is government policy or NRM strategy, and what is an action taken by a local politician to use the media for their own ends. For example, during the recent 2016 elections, many of the controversies with radio stations suspending their employees for hosting opposition figures, or shutting off the transmitters mid-interview, involved stations that were owned by local politicians from the NRM (Human Rights Watch 2016). Different characterizations of these conflicts reflect tensions between what the journalists or radio hosts see as the objectives and role of their programs and the intentions of owners to use it for their political projects. In this increasingly polyphonic space, it would thus be a mistake to understand the contemporary harsh relationship between the government and media as simply the reaction of an "autocratic" president. As this chapter has argued, the NRM has a long record of adopting tactics and strategies to consolidate power. Some of these have become worn over time but many have continued. Legal maneuvering, the co-option of critics and efforts at persuasion, all seen over the past twenty-five years, persists. What, however, has declined is the "vision" that the *New Vision* and NRM so boldly emphasized. As Uganda increasingly became a major security player in the region, providing troops to the conflict in Somalia, for example, the NRM also abandoned much of the political ideology that shaped the struggle and early days of government outlined in this chapter. The passion and clarity of these ideas have dimmed; but the legacy of the institutions that the NRM put in place in the late 1980s and early 1990s, and the culture of engagement, including legal negotiation, that emerged during this period has continued to undergird Uganda's media system.

REFERENCES

Allen, T. 2006. *Trial Justice: The ICC and the LRA*. London: Zed.

BBC 2016. "Uganda election: Facebook and Whatsapp blocked," February 18, 2016. Available at: www.bbc.co.uk/news/world-africa-35601220.

Brett, E. A. 1994. "Rebuilding organisation capacity in Uganda under the national resistance movement," *The Journal of Modern African Studies* 32(1): 53–80.

Carbone, G. 2005. "'Populism' visits Africa: The case of Yoweri Museveni and no-party democracy in Uganda," *Crisis States Programme, London School of Economics, Working Papers Series No. 1*. Available at: www.files.ethz.ch/isn/57583/wp73.pdf.

Connell, D. and Smyth, F. 1998. "Africa's new bloc," *Foreign Affairs*. Available at: www.foreignaffairs.com/articles/africa/1998-03-01/africas-new-bloc.

Daily Monitor 2016. "UCC shutdown of social media backfires," Available at: www.monitor.co.ug/Elections/UCC-shutdown-of-social-media-backfires/-/2787154/3083658/-/ax1g1h/-/index.html.

Global Voices 2016. "Uganda's defiance campaign will not be televised,". Available at: https://globalvoices.org/2016/05/10/ugandas-defiance-campaign-will-not-be-televised/.

Golooba-Mutebi, F. 2004. "Reassessing popular participation in Uganda," *Public Administration and Development* 24(4): 289–304.

Human Rights Watch 2016. "'Keep the people uninformed': Pre-election threats to free expression and association in Uganda," *Human Rights Watch*. Available at:

www.hrw.org/report/2016/01/11/keep-people-uninformed/pre-election-threats-free-expression-and-association-uganda.

Insider 2016. "Gov't restores social media after imprisoning Besigye for treason," Available at: www.theinsider.ug/govt-restores-social-media-after-imprisoning-besigye-for-treason/#.WElDAccw2f4.

Kagoro, J. 2015. "Competitive authoritarianism in Uganda: The not so hidden hand of the military," *Zeitschrift für Vergleichende Politikwissenschaft* 11(1): 155–72.

Katzenbach, E. L. and Hanrahan, G. 1955. "The revolutionary struggle of Mao Tse-tung," *Political Science Quarterly* 70: 321–40.

Mamdani, M. 1996. *Citizen and Subject: Decentralized Despotism and the Legacy of Late Colonialism.* Princeton, NJ: Princeton University Press.

Mao, T. 1961. *On Guerrilla Warfare.* Translated from Chinese by S. B. Griffin. New York, NY: Praeger.

Museveni, Y. K. 2000. *What Is Africa's Problem?* Minneapolis, MN: University of Minnesota Press.

New Vision 1986a. "We will contribute to this change," March 19, 1986, p. 4.

1986b. "Vision role spelt out," April 9, 1986, pp. 1 and 8.

Ngoga, P. 1998. "Uganda: The national resistance army," in C. Clapham (ed.) *African Guerrillas.* Oxford: James Currey.

Ottaway, M. 1999. *Africa's New Leaders: Democracy or State Reconstruction?* Washington, DC: Carnegie Endowment for International Peace.

Tangri, R. and Mwenda, A. M. 2010. "President Museveni and the politics of presidential tenure in Uganda," *Journal of Contemporary African Studies,* 28(1): 31–49.

Tripp, A. M. 2010. *Museveni's Uganda: Paradoxes of Power in a Hybrid Regime.* Boulder, CA: Lynne Rienner Publishers.

Ugandan Communications Commission 2015. "Post, broadcasting and telecommunications market and industry report," Available at: www.ucc.co.ug/files/downloads/Q3-Market%20Report%20%20for%20Third%20Quarter%20-%20July-September%202015.pdf.

Van de Walle, N. 1999. "Economic Reform in a Democratizing Africa," *Comparative Politics* 32(1): 21–41.

7

Neoliberal "Good Governance" in Lieu of Rights: Lee Kuan Yew's Singapore Experiment

Cherian George

When Lee Kuan Yew died in March 2015 at the age of ninety-one, the outpouring of emotion in his country was only to be expected. Lee had been the giant of Singaporean nation-building throughout the lives of most of its citizens. What may have been more surprising even to patriotic Singaporeans, let alone the country's critics, was the superlative praise heaped on him by leaders and commentators all over the world, including in the liberal democratic West, whose finger-pointing he had so scornfully rebuffed throughout his career. US President Barack Obama called him "a true giant of history" and "a devoted public servant" from whom world leaders had sought "advice on governance and development" (White House 2015). Former British Prime Minister Tony Blair said Lee "was the first to understand that modern politics was about effective Government not old-fashioned ideology" (Office of Tony Blair 2015). Roger Cohen (2015) opined in the *New York Times* that "the 20th century produced few greater statesmen and perhaps no greater pragmatist."

The praise was largely due to Singapore's undeniable success in raising the standard of living of its citizens to First World levels in the space of a generation. It is not just an economic powerhouse; it is also exceptional in managing to stave off financial corruption and in providing quality housing, education and healthcare for the vast majority of its people. The fulsome praise may also have been a reflection of the uncertainty and doubt prevailing within the democratic world. Long gone is the triumphalism that bloomed at the end of the Cold War. Since then, the West has been forced to look inward, at the limitless and destructive greed of its richest, as well as the limited impact it has had on the lives of its poorest. It has become harder to hold as a self-evident truth that other countries would capitulate to the waves of democracy or, even more disconcertingly, that they would necessarily be worse off if they refused to conform to liberal democratic norms. Accordingly, the January 2016 issue of the *Journal of Democracy* was devoted to the question of whether democracy is in decline. The questions posed in this very volume are themselves an indicator of the current intellectual mood: they probably would not have been asked with such open-minded humility twenty years ago.

If, for whatever reason, the time has come for social scientists to look anew at non-Western societies, Singapore is certainly an important case to consider. It is a state that lustily internalized the Western model of economic development. It did not go the way of socialism or communism, nor did it opt for the isolationism of Bhutan or Burma. Government leaders embraced the so-called Washington Consensus (of macroeconomic stability and integration with the global economy) long before it had a name. Further, it eventually beat many Western countries at their own game, creating an economy that was more globally competitive in attracting high-quality investments. It did so without accepting modernization theory at its unreconstructed crudest: that advanced industrial status comes hand-in-hand with full-blown democracy (Lipset 1959). As a result, Singapore is an extreme outlier on the development-democracy grid. It is among the world's ten most developed countries (according to the United Nations' inequality-adjusted Human Development Index) (UN Development Programme 2014) and the only one not rated 1 in Freedom House's freedom rating: it scores a middling 4. In press freedom, with 0 for the most free and 100 for the least free, Freedom House gives rich countries scores of between 10 and 30, while Singapore gets 67; it is the only developed country rated "not free" (Freedom House 2015a; Freedom House 2015b). No other First-World country has a discretionary licensing system for newspapers and magazines: in Singapore, government permission is required to publish one and it can be banned with the stroke of a pen. Singapore refuses even to give lip service to freedom of expression as a human right: it is one of the handful of countries that have not signed the International Covenant on Civil and Political Rights.

This is not the place to explain this paradox, although some clues should emerge in the course of this chapter. Instead, in keeping with the thrust of this volume, the following pages will try to crystallize the thinking behind Singapore's approach to speech. The most commonly heard theory is that Singapore represents some sort of "Asian" way, informed by Confucian values. Lee Kuan Yew said it himself, so it is not surprising that this interpretation has caught on (Barr 2012; Zakaria 1994). This chapter will suggest that the Asian values argument was largely a convenient post-hoc justification, rather than a conviction that actually drove policy. Instead, the central motivating idea was that an achievement-oriented government needs more room for maneuver than a free press and free speech would allow. This belief has remained a constant, long after Singapore overcame its most pressing development challenges decades ago. The Internet has complicated the application of the government's principles for media management, opening up a space for precisely the kind of political contestation that Lee had succeeded in squeezing out for more than two decades. The government swiftly embraced new technology as essential economic infrastructure and was prepared to promote its growth, even at the expense of some control over speech. However, as we shall see, the government never reformed its core convictions about the proper relationship between speech and society. It has tried to find ways to reconcile its belief in the value of a dominant, hegemonic executive with Internet policies that allow most speech to take place outside its control. It has not been entirely successful in having its cake and eating it. However, on the other hand, one cannot say that it has failed. The combination of a dominant state and a pervasive Internet has not been as contradictory as had been assumed by those who believed that the World Wide Web was inherently and exclusively libertarian.

Before proceeding along this line of inquiry, we should clear the clutter that has been laid in our way by the Asian Values debate. The argument was that the Singapore model was in tune with cultural values that emphasized community, harmony, consensus, and respect for authority. In contrast, Western liberal values stressed individualism, contention, and the need to challenge authority. Western governments, media, and human rights groups were urged to consider these deep cultural differences before lecturing Asian societies about their divergences from liberal democratic norms (Kausikan 1998; Zakaria 1994). The Asian Values perspective has influenced several scholarly studies of the region's media in general, and Singapore's in particular (see, for example, Christians et al. 2009; Massey and Chang 2002; Xu 2005). However, the theory that Asian Values underlie Singapore's approach is contradicted by history. It fails to account for the fact that such cultural justifications were not emphasized when Lee's approach to speech was being articulated and institutionalized in the 1970s. They also receded after 2000. The Asian Values justification is best understood as a construct developed for geopolitical reasons within the specific historical circumstances of the 1990s. It was largely a reaction to the perception that the United States, having seen off the Soviet Union, was intent on exporting democracy to Asia, possibly with destabilizing results. The "Singapore School" countered that Asian democracies had their own norms, more suited to their history and culture; the rapid economic growth in these countries showed that their norms should not be treated as inferior to Western values (George 1994). However, by the 2000s, the argument had run out of steam. First, the Asian financial crisis, starting in 1997, melted its materialist justification. Then, Singapore found former allies in the Asian Values debate embracing global democratic norms. Its giant neighbor, Indonesia, ousted President Suharto and his authoritarian regime and embarked on decisive and dramatic democratization. The East Asian polities of South Korea and Taiwan deepened their commitments to democracy. In 2003, the Taiwanese government even set up a Foundation for Democracy, modeled on the US National Endowment for Democracy, to promote democracy in Asia (not "Asian-style" democracy, it should be stressed). South Korea and Taiwan also have much stronger Confucian credentials than Singapore, which is not geographically part of Greater China and has a population that is 25 percent non-Chinese. For such reasons, the Confucian argument lost credibility and largely disappeared from Lee's rhetoric (Barr 2012). Subsequent rationalizations of the Singapore media system returned to the core principles that had been articulated in the early 1970s.

THE HERITAGE OF HELSINKI

Lee Kuan Yew's seminal statement on media freedom was delivered to the General Assembly of the International Press Institute (IPI) in Helsinki, Finland in June 1971. The previous month, he had sensationally shut down two daily newspapers and arrested the chief editor and top executives of a third. IPI members called for his invitation to be withdrawn, but the organization decided that it would be a good idea for Lee to come and account for his actions before 300 editors from around the world. Barely six years had passed since Singapore had become an independent republic and its reputation among Western investors was far more tenuous than it is now. Lee seized the opportunity to explain his position, the essence of which would be repeated in the coming decades. Describing the circumstances of a small, young nation, at risk of being pulled apart by ethnic forces and external threats, he concluded:

> In such a situation, freedom of the press, freedom of the news media, must be subordinated to the overriding needs of the integrity of Singapore, and to the primacy of purpose of an elected government. The government has taken, and will from time to time have to take, firm measures, to ensure that, despite divisive forces of different cultural values and life styles, there is enough unity of purpose to carry the people of Singapore forward to higher standards of life, without which the mass media cannot thrive. (Lee 1971, p. 13)

In this pithy quote, Lee encapsulates three key points. First, there is the idea of putting free speech in its proper place: not negating it entirely, but preventing it from getting in the way of the job that an elected government needs to do. Second, media cannot be allowed to pull the country apart: social cohesion is required if people are to improve their lives. Third, commercial media have a vested interest in the success of the government's pro-development policies.

In his Helsinki address and several other speeches, interviews and writings over the following decades, Lee elaborated on his defense of the Singaporean approach. His view was echoed by other officials, who today continue to justify Singapore's exceptionalism in much the same terms. Lee and his People's Action Party (PAP) rejected the idea of a universally applicable human rights standard for speech, a principle that would later apply to the Internet. Instead, they said that each country would have to decide its political formula for itself. "What we have argued consistently is that diversity is an empirical fact – countries have different histories, cultures, values, and problems – and thus each nation must find its own best social and political arrangements by means of a pragmatic and continuous process of experimentation," said senior official Bilahari Kausikan (1998). Critics dispensing prescriptions from outside do not have to live with the consequences. In contrast, the Singaporean government bears responsibility for the country's survival; its judgments should be seen in that context. The same principle of governmental responsibility is used to relegate media freedom to a position that is "subordinate … to the primacy of purpose of an elected government," as Lee put it in Helsinki.

The press, Lee argued, is an unelected institution that is ultimately accountable only to its owners. As such, it has no moral authority to challenge the government on equal terms, contrary to the Fourth Estate role that liberal democracy gives it. Lee's distrust of the media probably had much to do with the fact that they had been unsympathetic to his party during its years in opposition. When the PAP came to power in 1959, the press was slow to support Lee's nation-building agenda. Journalists could not predict that they were witnessing the arrival of a nationalist movement that would dominate Singapore for decades to come. In many countries, the press played a major role alongside independence movements and would be rewarded with a permanent place at the high table of political institutions. In Singapore, Lee never got over the feeling that he succeeded despite the press, not because of it. Elaborating on his principles, Singapore's second prime minister, Goh Chok Tong, told journalists that it was all right "to probe, to ask the inconvenient question, to report fully and fairly what is going on … [b]ut the concept of the press being all powerful and having the last word smuggles in the power that ordinary citizens do not bestow on them" (Goh 1995a, p. 4).

Lee's model, it should be noted, recognizes that democratic elections are the ultimate source of legitimacy: it is because the Singapore government is elected that it can claim authority over the press. This is a thin version of democratic legitimacy. In liberal democratic theory, the government's legitimacy derives not just from periodic elections, but also from the ongoing, permanent state of freedom that all citizens possess to express dissenting views. Only if all are given the unconstrained opportunity to voice their interests, woo supporters, and deliberate their choices can they be expected to accept peacefully those decisions that may go against them (Barendt 2005; Dworkin 1999). Singapore's model replaces this procedural test with performance legitimacy: people can simply judge the government by its results. "While democracy and human rights are worthwhile ideas, we should be clear that the real objective is good government," Lee said (Han et al. 1998, p. 381). PAP leaders have defined "good government" in different ways, but their emphasis is mainly on material progress and social order. Lee has described good government as one that is "honest, effective and efficient in protecting its people, and allowing opportunities for all to advance themselves in a stable and orderly society, where they can live a good life and raise their children to do better than themselves" (Han et al. 1998, p. 380).

Although the PAP recognizes the people's will as the ultimate source of its legitimacy, it is not in favor of the people's intrusive participation in governmental decision-making. Its elitist model of democracy entails citizens voting freely in competitive elections, but then allowing the winning party to govern decisively, with minimal interference from lobby groups, protest movements and a populist press. In its view, a responsible and responsive government rules with the consent of the public and in the public interest, but without being a slave to public opinion. Many national challenges can be addressed only by a strong leadership able to push through the occasional unpopular decision. Short-term public opinion can obstruct good government, which requires a long-term orientation. "If Singaporeans do not have an appreciation of the big picture, the challenges they face, the realistic alternatives, the level of public debate falls, populism prevails, and the difficult decisions will never get taken," said Goh (1995a, p. 4). "This is why, in Singapore, the government acts more like a trustee ... As a custodian of the public's welfare, it exercises independent judgment on what is in the long-term economic interests of the people and acts on that basis," (Goh 1995b, p. 5). The implications for the press are clear: the media's primary role is not to champion public opinion but to educate the public. This does not mean that they must be pro-PAP. Rather, their mission is to get Singaporeans to understand policy choices and the constraints on their society. According to Lee, "[t]he mass media can help to present Singapore's problems simply and clearly and then explain how if they support certain programmes and policies these problems can be solved" (Lee 1971, p. 6).

As for how to produce good government, Lee was certain that the quality of leaders is the critical factor. Sound institutions and correct processes
are pointless if the wrong people are in charge, he believed. Therefore, the
PAP government tries to induct public servants of "high competence and high
integrity" (Lee 1996, p. 34). While would-be leaders must expose themselves
to electoral competition, they should be shielded from the most destructive
aspects of competitive politics, such as personal attacks and invasions of privacy. These would deter able individuals from public service and erode a good
government's authority. "If you make a personal attack of fact against a person's reputation, for example by alleging that he is corrupt, or that he is a liar,
or that he embezzled State funds, then you should be prepared to prove it in
court," said law minister K. Shanmugam (2010), defending Singapore's strict
defamation laws. "We do not believe that public discourse should degenerate
to a base level, by allowing untrue personal attacks. We would like to keep
political debate focused on issues" (Shanmugam 2010).

Instead of acting as an adversarial watchdog, the media should instead help
perpetuate the "virtuous cycle of good government, constructive journalism,
cohesive society and strong, stable and prosperous Singapore" (Goh 1995a,
p. 4). Thus, PAP evaluates press freedom and democracy in largely instrumental terms: what these can do for Singaporeans' material well-being and security. It concludes that, since the country has done well for so long by blazing its
own trail, it would be unnecessary and even risky to change course to follow
countries that may be less successful than Singapore and that are certainly
very different. Freedom of expression is treated by PAP as a self-centered value
in tension with societal interests. PAP does not deny the universal appeal of
this freedom. "I believe that most people, regardless of race, religion or culture will want to live in societies which promote individual liberty and freedom, including the right of free speech," said Shanmugam (2010). However,
this individual longing is treated as a luxury that Singapore cannot afford.

This would not be an unusual argument coming from Third World countries: it is in line with the "development journalism" model, in which the
media is a partner of government in lifting societies out of poverty (Book 2009;
Romano 2005). Singapore, of course, is not a poor country. However, PAP
ideology positions Singapore in a permanent state of vulnerability that will
not be overcome by economic advancement (Barr and Skrbiš 2008; Khong
1995). From this perspective, the country will never be ready for the political
freedoms that liberal democracies enjoy. The city-state's vulnerability is said to
arise from unique and immutable geographical and social realities. The country is one of the world's tiniest by land area: it is slightly smaller than New York
City's five boroughs, for example. Its population of under six million means

that, if it were a city in China, it would not even be among the largest ten. Its hinterland lies outside its national borders, making it vulnerable to strains in relations with its neighbors. Culturally, it is the only majority-Chinese country in Southeast Asia. Its two closest neighbors, Malaysia and Indonesia, are majority-Muslim and have a history of discrimination against, and outright persecution of, their Chinese minorities. Internally, PAP views Singapore as a society riven by ethnic divides. The memory of communal riots in the 1950s and 1960s continues to be invoked as a warning of what could happen without a vigilant and strong government.

The ideology of unique vulnerability has grown increasingly important as a justification for PAP's illiberal policies. With more basic needs having been met, policy debates now deal with matters on which there is a wider spectrum of demands (Low and Vadaketh 2014). The political culture has become more contentious: it has become more difficult to persuade highly educated and well-traveled Singaporeans that the government always knows best and that they should defer to its judgment. In this context, the national sense of exceptional vulnerability has become the most reliable justification for dampening public discourse. Nevertheless, vulnerability is not an indisputably unique condition of Singapore. In an open global economy, being small is not necessarily a liability, for example. World rankings for economic competitiveness consistently place small countries among the highest: Switzerland, Sweden, Finland, and Denmark, along with Singapore, all have populations of under ten million (Schwab 2014). Relations within the Association of Southeast Asian Nations have been peaceful and stable since the 1970s. Further, Singapore's decades-old experience with communal violence is not particularly bloody by twentieth-century standards. Singapore's exceptionalism has therefore had to be consciously cultivated by Lee and other PAP leaders, through books, speeches, documentaries, and school curricula. Asked what the country needed to survive, Lee (1996, p. 34) said, "[T]he people must be aware of its fundamental vulnerabilities, and willing to pull together to face challenges."

DISRUPTION FROM THE INTERNET

The international human rights approach treats freedom of speech and of the press as the default position, with state restrictions required to pass strict tests. Lee Kuan Yew's philosophy of executive dominance, like other authoritarian systems, turned the democratic norm on its head. Government permission is required to publish newspapers and magazines, run broadcast stations, stage plays, or organize public rallies and other events (George 2012). There is no tradition of independent public regulators applying transparent, clearly defined, and content-neutral criteria when issuing licenses for any of these activities. Instead, regulators' decisions involve wide discretion and are subject to direction by the executive branch. Newspaper publishing permits, for example, can be revoked at any time by order of the information minister. The law does not require the minister to give reasons, nor provide for an appeal process. It is important to recognize that, although some elements in the PAP philosophy sound reasonable, the laws and policies that arise from it are hardly proportionate to PAP's stated nation-building goals. For example, public interest in preventing ethnic riots does not require government to have the power to ban a newspaper before it prints its first issue. The PAP's skeptical view of public opinion and its misgivings about people's participation in the affairs of state is shared by respectable strands of Western political theory, such as the democratic elitism of Samuel Huntington (1996), Joseph Schumpeter (1942) and Walter Lippmann (1925), who would have no trouble accepting the need for elite institutions that are insulated from the masses. However, elitist theories of democracy would still require that these institutions are themselves open, competitive and subject to strict checks and balances. The PAP model rejects this in favor of centralized and monopolistic power.

The Internet's arrival in the mid-1990s represented a radical disruption, in that it was Singapore's first (and remains the only) medium for mass communication that is not subject to a system of prior censorship (George 2006). No permission is required to publish anything on the Internet. Of course, one could still be punished after publication, but the absence of prior restraint was significantly new nonetheless. Singaporeans have taken to this new freedom with a vengeance. They have been able to publish views strongly critical of the government. Over time, this has resulted in a palpable change in the political culture. There is far less deference towards government leaders and much more open criticism and even contempt (George 2010). This may be one reason why PAP has virtually stopped claiming that the relationship between rulers and the ruled is shaped by Confucian norms. When it said so in the 1980s and 1990s, the claim was supported by the observed reality of a quiescent public sphere, since disrespectful views were shut out by media gatekeepers and confined to private spaces. By the 2000s, Confucianist deference hardly described what Singaporeans were experiencing on online fora.

Despite knowing the political risks, the government allowed public access to the Internet in the mid-1990s and enthusiastically rolled out the infrastructure required to put Singapore at the technological cutting edge (George 2006). Long before the World Wide Web, Singapore had harnessed computerization and information technology as key components of global competitiveness. Its technocratic political leaders had no trouble recognizing the economic value of the Internet. This trumped all political misgivings. By 2014, 95 percent of homes and businesses were connected to a fiber-based next-generation nation-wide broadband network; 82 percent of households had Internet access in 2014. Smartphone penetration reached 85 percent. A national wireless network offers free public access (Freedom House 2015c).

At the dawn of the World Wide Web, the government was anxious to demonstrate to technology investors that it understood this new medium. Pressured by early adopters attuned to the Internet's libertarian zeitgeist, it promised in 1996 not to block or filter any political content; a symbolic list of only 100 sites, mainly pornographic, is blocked to signpost societal values as a sop to the social conservatives (Yip 2013). Remarkably, it has kept that promise, even as it refused to liberalize laws instituting prior censorship of print and broadcast media. Singapore thus operated a dual regulatory regime for the media, with one set of rules for traditional platforms and another, overlapping, but only partly, for the Internet. It is important to note that, even as it permitted this opening-up of political discourse in practice, at no point did PAP make any philosophical concession to liberal values. On the contrary, it took pains to establish the principle that the Internet in Singapore was fully under its jurisdiction. Under the 1996 amendments to the Broadcasting Act, it declared all websites hosted in Singapore to be automatically licensed as a category. Although they did not have to apply for individual permits and could publish without prior restraint, the "class license" meant that this freedom was not theirs as a right.

Predictably, the dual regulatory regime was strained by digital convergence. With large traditional media companies increasingly going online and online-only organizations growing in reach and capability, it was clear that content regulations would have to be increasingly platform-neutral. Some argued for harmonization in a liberal direction: print and broadcast media should be allowed the freedoms of online media. Instead, since around 2010, PAP has taken steps to rein in online media. However, it did not attempt anything as massive as China's "great firewall." Instead, its interventions have been more surgical, in line with its approach to censorship that has been called "calibrated coercion" (George 2012). PAP understood that it is neither possible nor necessary to micro-manage political discourse by preventing most individuals from engaging in what one might call the "retail" exchange of information and ideas. Instead, the focus is on more "wholesale" dissent. Political scientists have observed that public opinion as such need not be threatening to centralized authority (Przeworski 1991). It is only when public opinion is organized and channeled into action that it develops power. Appreciating this, PAP was content to target dissent at the point where it left the online sphere and materialized in the real world as, for example, political rallies. In the offline world, the government had no shortage of instruments to apply, such as restrictions on assembly and political funding, as well as a tight grip on institutions such as trade unions, universities and professional groups.

MANAGING OPENNESS

The idea that Singapore had to be porous to ideas as a result of the openness of its economy was not new. A few years before the public was given access to the Internet, the government had recited the same line with regard to cable and satellite television. Explaining to conservatives why Singapore had to allow foreign channels, policy-makers said that the financial and business community would lose out if they did not have access to live coverage of market-moving events via twenty-four-hour news channels such as CNN and the BBC World Service. Lee Kuan Yew echoed this argument in a 1998 speech. "As an international trading centre, our economy is fuelled by information. Our financial markets cannot be a nano-second behind London, New York or Tokyo," he said. This being the reality, "we cannot stop reports which are disagreeable to us." He added, "[g]overnments that try to fight the new technology will lose" (Lee 1998). The roots of such thinking go back to Lee's 1971 speech. Isolationism was not a realistic option for Singapore, he said, because "in practice, new countries, particularly the smaller ones, cannot altogether insulate themselves from outside news and views" (Lee 1971, p. 2). Lee (1988) later reminded critics that he had personally appealed for the BBC World Service to keep its FM transmission station in Singapore as a service to Singaporeans when the British military pulled out in 1971. While firmly resisting the liberal route, Lee also did not consider the closed authoritarian model to be attractive, a fact that is usually overlooked in analyses of his approach. He told his audience in Helsinki:

> Some governments like China, or the Soviet Union in pre-Khrushchev days, effectively sealed off their people from the outside world. Then the world is what the rulers say it is. And the rulers are unchanging for long years. But there is a heavy price to be paid for such isolation. The incessant exhortation to progress, the constant stress on conformity in ideology, ideas and action, they lead to drab uniformity. (Lee 1971, pp. 2–3)

Singapore's outstanding economic record, compared with closed societies and even with liberal democracies, shows that, whatever the faults of PAP's approach to speech, being unresponsive to the needs of markets is certainly not one of them. Although critics usually portray PAP as single-mindedly focused on political dominance, its policies show a clear willingness to moderate its demand for control if the economy requires it. What then needs to be explained is how PAP managed to balance the two, maintaining its dominant-party model even as it encouraged the development of a vibrant and open economy. The simple answer is that Lee Kuan Yew never saw it as a total contradiction. The informational needs of the market are not identical to those of a democratic polity. Understanding this distinction, the government was able to build a system with a high level of economic transparency but a low level of political transparency. Investors would be able to operate in a predictable environment with clear, business-friendly rules, while political entrepreneurs faced constant uncertainty and the constant threat of arbitrary reaction (Rodan 2004).

In line with critical approaches to media studies, Lee seemed to understand, at least a decade before other authoritarian leaders, that market dynamics could work to the advantage of concentrated political power. This is why Singapore bucked the trend of undemocratic regimes that chose to nationalize the press either directly or via proxies. Lee realized that the government did not have to own the media in order to tame it; private owners could do the job for it. They would, uncoerced, realize that radical journalism was not be in their commercial interests, as long as the country was being ruled by a pro-growth government that was creating a larger middle class and boosting business activity, thus adding to commercial media's subscription and advertising revenues. Thus, Lee understood neoliberalism before it had a name. He knew that profit-oriented media would align themselves with a government intent "to carry the people of Singapore forward to higher standards of life, without which the mass media cannot thrive", as Lee put it in his Helsinki speech (Lee 1971, p. 13).

This insight materialized in a newspaper policy of startling genius. Three years after his Helsinki speech, Lee rolled out the Newspaper and Printing Presses Act of 1974, a regulatory regime that PAP has not needed to change in more than forty years (George 2012). The new law counter-intuitively intensified the profit orientation of newspaper companies by requiring them to be listed on the stock exchange, with strict caps on shareholdings, so ownership had to be spread thinly. In effect, this outlawed family-owned newspapers and media barons, who (as the history of newspapers in Singapore and elsewhere had demonstrated to Lee) were prone to use their titles to pursue ideological causes even at the expense of the financial bottom-line. To guarantee that newspapers would not become rogue, the government was empowered to nominate "management share" holders with 200 times the voting rights of ordinary shareholders. Management shares were allocated mainly to financial institutions with a strong preference for political stability. The licensing system inherited from the British colonial government was retained, protecting incumbents from competition and allowing them to enjoy monopoly profits. Lee Kuan Yew took a direct interest in the financial health of the media. Up until 1971, the Chinese-language media, under headstrong owners, had borne the brunt of his repression. However, after he had neutered them, he intervened to ensure that Chinese newspapers, which were in decline due to the greater use of English, were placed on a firm financial footing. He forced a merger of the Chinese papers with the highly profitable English newspaper group. When Lee said sarcastically that freedom of the press in the West was little more than the freedom of media owners to profit from it, he did not mean to separate them from their gains. He granted them this freedom to excess, the better to divert them from their democratic mission. Thanks to Lee's clear understanding of the political economy of news production, Singapore Press Holdings, the country's dominant newspaper group, became one of the most profitable newspaper publishers in the world and, because of rather than in spite of this, also among the politically most conservative.

Although the Internet was a major disruption to the PAP approach, some of its governing principles remained relevant and resilient. It continued to believe that the main challenge was posed not by profit-oriented media but by politically motivated ones. Prior to its crackdown in 1971, these came in the form of newspapers owned by individual and family businesses with strong community affiliations. From 2010, the government saw the potential threat coming from donor-funded online news start-ups, replicating the success of Malaysiakini across the border in Malaysia. Malaysiakini, set up in 1999, had received funding from the likes of the Open Society Foundations. It grew to become one of the most critical and influential news sources in the country. Singapore had several amateur individual and group blogs generating regular commentary, but no professional site like Malaysiakini, with the capacity to conduct daily news reporting that would challenge the pro-government mainstream media's take on events.

It seemed only a matter of time before a Singapore start-up followed in Malaysiakini's footsteps. The government pre-empted this by targeting promising political websites for special regulatory attention. It banned them from receiving foreign grants and loans. It initially used the Political Donations Act to accomplish this, but in 2013 it included these restrictions in a new registration system for news start-ups (Freedom House 2014). Thus, while it continued to resist blocking and filtering as a means of restricting political discourse online, it drew from Lee Kuan Yew's forty-year-old insight that media could be diverted from pursuing a radical direction through financial carrots and sticks.

Meanwhile, larger news sites, such as Yahoo! News and the online platforms of national news organizations, were removed from the class license and subjected to individual licensing. They were required to agree to a notice-and-take-down regime and to post a compliance bond of S$50,000 (US$40,000). Since these sites answered to managements that already co-operated with government, the new licensing system made no noticeable difference to their content. However, it placed beyond doubt PAP's intent to harmonize online and offline regulation in a conservative direction wherever possible.

Lee's approach would have failed if his intent had been to keep Singapore frozen in time. He understood clearly that the only way for Singapore to make a living, as a small island state strategically located on the main shipping route between the Pacific and Indian Oceans, had always been and would always be as a trading and commercial hub. His success was in understanding the late twentieth-century game of global capitalism before most leaders, and ensuring that Singapore played it very well. This required an almost obsessive commitment to adapting infrastructure, laws and human capital to each new demand posed by the global economy. Guided by a capable and clean government, Singapore was able to transform itself from a low-cost manufacturing center to a diversified high-value economy that included financial services and creative industries. The country therefore does not fit the stereotype of regimes that brazenly restrict speech. Most of them to do so to conceal incompetence and corruption, and to avoid responding to the material needs of their citizens. Lee Kuan Yew's approach to speech was integral to his consuming desire for concentrated power, but the goal was not to capture the state for private gain. It was to clear the decks for a "developmental state", the term David Harvey (2005) uses to describe a Singapore-style variant of the neoliberal state, with a more active role for the public sector and state planning.

The formula is certainly not failsafe. In particular, it remains to be seen whether a governing elite that has insulated itself so effectively from criticism and competition can maintain its high standards of probity and performance (Low and Vadaketh 2014). However, the fact that it has lasted so long, and with strong public support, demands that we consider seriously the questions it poses for the analysis of speech and society. We might start by noting, with Amartya Sen (1999), that democratic freedoms have intrinsic, constructive and instrumental value. What PAP appears to have achieved quite successfully is to make the instrumental justification almost redundant, by providing Singaporeans with highly responsive, capable, and virtually corruption-free governance. As the country developed and Singaporeans hankered for a post-material First World lifestyle, the government allowed the flowering of leisure and entertainment options (Tan 2007). Since these desired ends of livelihood and lifestyle are already being achieved, democracy loses value as a means to that end. As for Sen's "constructive" argument, this refers to how publics are formed through deliberation. It is through open public discourse that citizens practice the negotiation and conciliation that is central to public life. PAP has de-emphasized this form of horizontal deliberation and instead engaged in top-down nation-building. As for its intrinsic value (democratic freedom for its own sake, as part of what makes humans whole) this is something that Lee's ideology has no answer for. His justification for government controls is mainly instrumental and partly constructivist. They ignore the human desire to speak up and be counted as members of society.

The empirical reality, though, seems to be that most people everywhere are moved to demand free speech and democracy mainly for their instrumental value. Their intrinsic worth may be part of the rhetoric of change, but the driving force tends to come from material conditions of deprivation and extreme injustice. As Karl Marx understood, revolution is driven by material contradictions, not the dialectics of ideas. Ultimately, what is exceptional about the Lee Kuan Yew model is not its ideological foundations but its uniquely effective implementation. Through its practice of government, PAP has consistently found a political sweet spot, such that political protest is far less than what can be found either in liberal democracies or in more authoritarian societies. It dispenses enough repression to increase the cost of dissenting speech, but also reduces the incentive to pay that cost, by giving people enough personal autonomy and social justice. As a result, Singaporeans are neither sufficiently empowered nor sufficiently victimized to join the global chorus for free speech and democracy.

REFERENCES

Barendt, E. 2005. *Freedom of Speech*. Oxford: Oxford University Press.
Barr, M. D. 2012. *Cultural Politics and Asian Values*. Abingdon: Routledge.
Barr, M. D. and Skrbiš, Z. 2008. *Constructing Singapore: Elitism, Ethnicity and the Nation-Building Project*. Copenhagen: NIAS Press.
Book, C. L. 2009. "Development journalism," in Sterling, C. H. (ed.), *Encyclopedia of Journalism*. Thousand Oaks, CA: Sage, pp. 401–7.
Christians, C. G., Glasser, T. L., McQuail, D., Nordenstreng, K. and White, R. A. 2009. *Normative Theories of the Media: Journalism in Democratic Societies*. Urbana and Chicago: University of Illinois Press.
Cohen, R. 2015. "Can-do Lee Kuan Yew," *The New York Times*, March 23, 2015. Available at: www.nytimes.com/2015/03/24/opinion/roger-cohen-can-do-lee-kuan-yew.html.
Dworkin, R. 1999. *Freedom's Law: The Moral Reading of the American Constitution*. Oxford: Oxford University Press.

Freedom House 2014. "Freedom on the net 2014: Singapore," Available at: https://freedomhouse.org/report/freedom-net/2014/singapore.

 2015a. "Freedom in the world 2015," Available at: https://freedomhouse.org/report/freedom-world/freedom-world-2015#.VvpmqnmZ-mw.

 2015b. "Freedom of the press 2015," Available at: https://freedomhouse.org/report/freedom-press/freedom-press-2015#.Vvpm7HmZ-mw.

 2015c. "Freedom on the net 2015: Singapore," Available at: https://freedomhouse.org/report/freedom-net/2015/singapore.

George, C. 1994. "The West gets testy over 'Singapore school of thought'," *The Straits Times*, October 15, 1994, p. 30.

 2006. *Contentious Journalism and the Internet: Towards Democratic Discourse in Malaysia and Singapore*. Singapore and Seattle: National University of Singapore Press and University of Washington Press.

 2010. "Control-shift: The internet and political change in Singapore," in Chong, T. (ed.), *Management of Success: Singapore Reassessed*. Singapore: Institute of Southeast Asian Studies, pp. 257–71.

 2012. *Freedom from the Press: Journalism and State Power in Singapore*. Singapore: National University of Singapore Press.

Goh, C. T. 1995a. "How the press can best serve Singapore," *The Sunday Times*, Sunday Review, July 16, 1995, pp. 1, 4.

 1995b. "Government as trustee: The role of government in the east Asian miracle", *The Sunday Times*, Sunday Review, September 24, 1995, pp. 1, 4–5.

Han, F. K., Fernandez, W. and Tan, S. 1998. *Lee Kuan Yew: The Man and his Ideas*. Singapore: Times Editions.

Harvey, D. 2005. *A Brief History of Neoliberalism*. Oxford: Oxford University Press.

Huntington, S. P. 1996. *Political Order in Changing Societies*. New Haven: Yale University Press.

Kausikan, B. 1998. "The 'Asian values' debate: A view from Singapore," in Diamond, L. and Plattner, M. F. (eds.), *Democracy in East Asia*. Baltimore: Johns Hopkins University Press, pp. 17–27.

Khong, C.-O. 1995. "Singapore: Political legitimacy through managing conformity," in Alagappa, M. (ed.), *Political Legitimacy in Southeast Asia: The Quest for Moral Authority*. Stanford: Stanford University Press, pp. 108–35.

Lee, K. Y. 1971. "The mass media and new countries" (address to the General Assembly of the International Press Institute, Helsinki, June 9, 1971. Available at: http://www.nas.gov.sg/archivesonline/data/pdfdoc/lky19710609a.pdf/.

 1988. Speech to the American Society of Newspaper Editors, Washington, DC, April 14, 1988. Available at: http://www.nas.gov.sg/archivesonline/data/pdfdoc/lky19880414a.pdf.

 1996. "Singapore can survive if two preconditions are met," *The Straits Times*, June 8, 1996, p. 34.

 1998. Speech at the Asian Media Conference, Los Angeles, October 29, 1998. Available at: www.nas.gov.sg/archivesonline/speeches/view-html?filename=1998103002.htm.

Lippmann, W. 1925. *The Phantom Public*. New York: New York University Press.

Lipset, S. M. 1959. "Some social requisites of democracy," *American Political Science Review* 53: 69–105.

Low, D. and Vadaketh, S. T. 2014. *Hard Choices: Challenging the Singapore Consensus*. Singapore: NUS Press.

Massey, B. L. and Chang, L.-J. A. 2002. "Locating Asian values in Asian journalism: A content analysis of web newspapers," *Journal of Communication* 52(4): 987–1004.

Office of Tony Blair 2015. "Tony Blair pays tribute to Lee Kuan Yew," March 22, 2015. Available at: www.tonyblairoffice.org/news/entry/tony-blair-pays-tribute-to-lee-kuan-yew/.

Przeworski, A. 1991. *Democracy and the Market: Political and Economic Reforms in Eastern Europe and Latin America*. Cambridge: Cambridge University Press.

Rodan, G. 2004. *Transparency and Authoritarian Rule in Southeast Asia New: Singapore and Malaysia*. London/New York: RoutledgeCurzon.

Romano, A. 2005. "Asian journalism: News, development and the tides of liberalization and technology," in Bromley, M. and Romano, A. (eds.), *Journalism and Democracy in Asia*. Abingdon: Routledge, pp. 1–14.

Schumpeter, J. A. 1942. *Capitalism, Socialism and Democracy*. New York: Harper & Row.

Schwab, K. (ed.) 2014. "The global competitiveness report 2014–2015," World Economic Forum. Available at: www3.weforum.org/docs/WEF_GlobalCompetitivenessReport_2014-15.pdf.

Sen, A. K. 1999. "Democracy as a universal value," *Journal of Democracy* 10(3): 3–17.

Shanmugam, K. 2010. "Report fully and fairly, but remember this ain't America," Speech at the inaugural forum of A Free Press for a Global Society, Columbia University, New York, November 4, 2010. Available at: http://blog.freedomfromthepress.info/2010/11/06/shanmugam-to-the-press-report-fully-and-fairly-but-remember-this-aint-america/.

Tan, K. P. (ed.) 2007. *Renaissance Singapore? Economy, Culture, and Politics*. Singapore: NUS Press.

United Nations Development Programme 2014. "Table 3: Inequality-adjusted human development index," Available at: http://hdr.undp.org/en/content/table-3-inequality-adjusted-human-development-index.

White House, The 2015. "Statement by the president on the death of Lee Kuan Yew," March 22, 2015. Available at: www.whitehouse.gov/the-press-office/2015/03/22/statement-president-death-lee-kuan-yew.

Xu, X. 2005. *Demystifying Asian Values in Journalism*. Singapore: Marshall Cavendish.

Yip, Y. H. J. 2013. "Internet regulation: A myth in Singapore?," *The Singapore Law Review*, November 30, 2013.

Zakaria, F. 1994. "A conversation with Lee Kuan Yew," *Foreign Affairs*, March/April 1994. Available at: www.foreignaffairs.com/articles/asia/1994-03-01/conversation-lee-kuan-yew.

8

Atatürk and Contemporary Speech Lessons from the Late Ottoman and Early Republican Era

Altug Akin

In recent decades, discussions in Turkey regarding limitations on speech and the press have intensified, attracting widespread global attention. From frequent bans on online communication platforms including Twitter, Facebook, and YouTube, to the seemingly arbitrary imprisonment of journalists with opposition views, regulation of speech during the rule of the Justice and Development Party (AKP) since 2002 has been highly contentious. This chapter aims to put debate on these practices into an historical perspective, by focusing on the era of the foundation of modern Turkey, namely the late Ottoman and early Republican period, which stretched roughly between 1830 and 1945. It argues that it is in this period that significant fields of contemporary Turkey, such as politics, education, and the legal system, emerged, leaving an enduring legacy, in the context of which contemporary policies must be understood.

This earlier era is associated with one of the most significant political characters in Turkey's history, Mustafa Kemal Atatürk (1881–1938), who played a momentous role in the transition from the Ottoman order to modern Turkey. In his single-minded efforts to realize his utopia, a modern, secular republic being part of the Western world, Atatürk brought about a drastic reshaping of Turkish society, and neither Turkey nor the Muslim world will ever be the same again (Hanioğlu 2011, p. 232). Although Mustafa Kemal was evidently not the sole factor that made the transformation of Turkish society possible, he was a radical and authoritative figure who marked the process with his own stamp. It is therefore important to examine his approach to speech as a sociopolitical phenomenon and its regulation, in order to understand the foundational framework in which speech has been handled in the Turkish context. His stamp is central to a consideration of tendencies in speech and society in Turkey.

Accordingly, after summarizing Atatürk's views on the issue of speech, its role and regulation, this chapter presents the context of the late Ottoman and early Republican era that heralded his approach, in order to uncover his inspirations and their underlying dynamics.

MUSTAFA KEMAL ATATÜRK'S THINKING ON SPEECH: ROLES, MISSION, AND REGULATION OF THE PRESS

Mustafa Kemal, an inspired leader rather than an academic, committed little to paper on the subject of speech, its social meaning or regulation. Nevertheless, some attempt can be made to piece together his thoughts on this issue – thoughts that were expressed at different times, in diverse contexts, but that might lead to a coherent philosophy. For example, one of Atatürk's speeches from 1924, barely five months after the Turkish Republic was established, illustrates the core of his thinking about speech and the press at the time:

> I would like to reemphasize the great duty of the press in public life, political life and the progress of the Republic. There is no need to mention how delicate a situation it is to make good use of wide and absolute freedom of the press. Beyond all kinds of legal reservations, a man of letters should have the solemn obligation to regard and respect science, requirements of the day and his own political considerations as well as the rights of the citizens and the esteemed interests of the country, which are beyond all private considerations. And it is this obligation that may ensure public order. Even if there should be failures and faults on this path, the effective instruments to remedy these faults will not be as in olden days, certain institutions that take the press under control. Quite the contrary, the means of removing troubles, born out of the freedom of the press, shall be the freedom of the press itself.[1]

This quotation, where Atatürk's philosophy about speech begins to crystallize, can be studied in three layers: the tasks, mission, and regulation of the press. The press, in this emerging theory, has significant *tasks* (regarding and respecting science, journalists' own political considerations, rights of citizens, and, most importantly, interests of the country) that serve the *mission* of "ensuring public order." Echoing this understanding that attaches public duties to the press, Atatürk had earlier stated that:

> The press is the common voice of a nation. In the illumination and enlightenment of a nation, in furnishing a nation with the intellectual nourishment it needs, in short, in ensuring that the nation, the sole target of which is

[1] Atatürk's speech on March 1, 1924.

to achieve happiness, walks on a joint path, the press constitutes a force, a school, a guide for such nation.[2]

Similarly, in 1923 he emphasized the watchdog role of the press: "[j]ournalists should do necessary reporting when they witness and uncover actions against the law and interests of the public"(Arsan 1997b, p. 55). In 1924, highlighting the public tasks as opposed to private interest, Atatürk declared that "[t]he influence that newspapers with particular intentions may have on the majority of the people, just like in any other country, is not in favor of these papers" (Arsan 1997b, p. 110).

Due to these public tasks and the mission Atatürk identified for the press, he believed that it had to be *regulated*, though in ways dissimilar to regulation during the Ottoman era. On freedom of the press, he stated that the "[p]ress, for no reason, can be held under domination and influence" (Arsan 1997c, p. 88) and "[j]ournalists should write sincerely what they see, what they think, what they know" ("Bir aylık dünya sçu'unu" Aylık 1929, p. 4791). The press lacked such a notion in the Ottoman past; therefore, Atatürk claimed, regulation was necessary. Such regulation would be in accordance with the Republic's principles represented by the Grand National Assembly and, as he asserted in 1925, when the principle of press freedom would not suffice to solve the troubles stemming from itself, use of other means would be justified:

> If those fundamental principles, established within the guiding and mature understanding of the Grand Assembly, suggesting that troubles stemming from the freedom of the press may only be resolved by way of freedom of the press, enable those who are far from virtue, which is the spirit of the Republic, to act as plunderers within the press; if the ill-omened affects of the ideas of those deceptive and seductive individuals give rise to the death of innocent citizens, working on their farms or to the loss of their homes and finally if these deceptive individuals make recourse to the waste type of brigandage and find the opportunity to make use of special favors or laws, then it will be without doubt inevitable that the Grand National Assembly stretches out its taming and punishing arms, in order to interfere and warn ... Only the Republic can rear the press with the mentality and morality of the Republic. On one hand, the men and papers of the past era, which are impossible to be corrected, appear in the minds of the nation, while on the other hand, a clean and prosperous field of the Republican press is expanding and rising. It will be only the press in this mentality, which will facilitate and motivate our great and noble nation's novel work and civil life.[3]

---

[2] Atatürk's speech on March 1, 1922.
[3] Atatürk's speech on November 1, 1925.

These declarations represent, in a nutshell, a utilitarian understanding of speech that primarily serves the public interest and must be carefully regulated by "modern" means. In practice, throughout the two decades after the establishment of Turkish Republic in 1923, the regulation dimension of the press in particular, and speech in general, followed a course that demonstrated the complications behind this understanding of Mustafa Kemal. As it turned out, the political context of the Republic was far from being tolerant to voices and tendencies different from those of the official ideological position. For instance, shortly after Atatürk's declaration mentioned above, "the means of removing troubles, born out of the freedom of the press, shall be the freedom of the press itself," the infamous Law of Maintenance of Order (*Takrir-i Sükun*) was promulgated in 1925, originally as a response to the first massive ethnic insurrection in the eastern provinces (Tunçay 1981, p. 27) with religious undertones. Almost all press and mass-communication channels outside of the official ideology were silenced, regardless of their conservative, liberal or progressive leanings (Gevgilili 1990, p. 125). A year after the order came into effect, Mustafa Kemal stated that "in the face of maltreatments and abuses, the law certainly did not condition freedom of opinion and of the press, aiming to preserve welfare and security, as well as defending and affirming the revolution vital for the nation."[4] Under press laws issued in 1931 and in place until 1945, newspapers were heavily controlled under a single-party regime, as were other forms of speech deemed threatening to the Republic.

SPEECH AND ITS REGULATION IN THE LATE OTTOMAN PERIOD (1830S–1923)

What was the context that made Atatürk's thinking and practices about speech and its regulation possible? The Turkish modernist movement, which he epitomized, had its roots in pre-republican Turkish history going back, in a significant way, at least a century. Therefore, despite the radical changes that it brought about, the Turkish transformation led by Atatürk did not represent a sharp break from the Ottoman past but, in significant respects, its reformed continuation. The ideas he espoused, including those with regard to speech, press, and regulation, had been widely discussed in detail long before the republican reforms, and were in many ways not novelties originated by the founder of the Republic. Furthermore, the ideas embraced by Atatürk had flourished in the context of the dynamics of nineteenth-century Ottoman society, which was the period of grand transformation. As a response to the

---

4 Atatürk's speech on November 1, 1926.

Empire's decline from being a vast power in the region for four centuries, extending from Persian Gulf to North Africa and Central Europe, the nineteenth century was marked with Ottoman government attempts to modernize in social, political, economic, and military spheres. Social communication and speech were among the fields in which major transformations would take place, including the birth of public opinion and print media.

ROLE AND REGULATION OF SPEECH BEFORE THE PRESS ERA

Until the second half of the nineteenth century, public debate on contentious political and social issues largely existed underground and often included hearsay and slander (Mardin 1987, p. 13) through different public spaces, Ottoman coffeehouses (*kahvehane*) being the most prominent. Coffeehouses fulfilled the function of a two-way route of communication where decisions of the authorities were passed to the public "to be reflected upon and deliberated on the one hand and through which the reactions and opinions of the community might be conveyed to authorities on the other" (Işın 2001, p. 32). For communication scholar Serdar Öztürk (2005a), the emergence and popularity of Ottoman coffeehouses and hearsay as forms of almost uncontrollable media of the common people, were two components of early public opinion in Ottoman society, where literacy levels were low and the hierarchical structure of society was stark. For instance, Öztürk argues (2005b) that the tradition of Ottoman puppet theatre (*karagöz*), mostly performed in these coffee houses, served as a forum for the criticism of government officials. European observers visiting Istanbul in the nineteenth century were struck by the practice; Méry stated in 1855 that "*Karagöz* was a daily newspaper, without security, without stamp, without a responsible editor, a terrible newspaper because it cannot write, it talks and sings in front of its numerous subscribers" (Méry 1855, pp. 358–9).[5]

In another Ottoman theatrical form, *ortaoyunu*, an early one-man stand-up show composed of humorous storytelling and occasionally covert or indirect criticism of those in power, was perceived akin to *karagöz* by a French observer who stated that, in Constantinople and other major Middle Eastern cities, performers of *ortaoyunu* played almost the same role as newspapers, in telling stories with political content (quoted in Georgeon 1999, p. 50). Hearsay and other forms of oral communications noted above served as the most dominant

---

[5] Quoted in Kömeçoğlu, Uğur 2001. "Historical and sociological approach to public space: The case of Islamic coffeehouses in Turkey" (unpublished PhD dissertation, Boğaziçi University), p. 94.

form of media until the introduction of the first daily newspaper in Turkish in 1831.

Because of their popularity, Ottoman rulers and the governing bureaucracy developed several mechanisms to regulate these public spaces, where absolute power of the monarch could potentially be subverted if not challenged through forms of uncontrolled speech. An essential principle of early modern governments, including the Ottoman Empire, that informed the relationship between the ruling elite and its subjects was that politics were the prerogative of the ruler and consequently popular utterances regarding politics were forbidden by law. Accordingly, the Ottoman state vigilantly monitored public places for "seditious" political conversations and punished subversive rumor-mongers prior to the mid-nineteenth century, especially in times of political crisis. For the government, popular opinions were perceived as noise that had to be supervised, controlled, prevented, and, if disturbing enough, silenced (Kırlı 2009, p. 183).

Wholesale banning of the coffeehouses was the harshest prevention mechanism deployed by Ottoman rulers. For example, the janissary coffeehouses established in the seventeenth century, which had a radical and subversive aura, were seen as centers of revolt and were banned in 1826 for provoking an ethic of rebellion under the rubric of "state talk" (*devlet sohbeti*), an inseparable part of the political opposition represented by the janissary corps.[6] Almost all social anger triggered by rumors of corruption and bad administration was first expressed here, and occasionally the seeds of insurgence against the palace were sown in the coffeehouses. In fact, "more than one coup d'état has been launched from, or at least plotted in a coffeehouse" (Hattox 1996, p. 102). Thus, the Ottoman government did not hesitate to ban these sites, although bans rarely worked as most of the coffeehouses went underground. Instead of banning, other, more efficient mechanisms were found to keep coffeehouses under control and surveillance (Işın 2001, p. 29). These included using religious rulings to prohibit particular themes from being touched upon during theatrical performances (*fetvas*) in coffeehouses (Kırlı 2000, p. 181), direct government warnings (Öztürk 2005b, p. 298), and placing spies at the nerve centers of the city. Throughout the eighteenth and early nineteenth century, spies closely monitored coffeehouses and other public places to prevent insolent talk and punish seditious gossipmongers. In 1809, for instance, a woman informer had a group of women discussing state affairs in a bathhouse arrested and imprisoned (Kırlı 2009, p. 184).

---

[6] Idem, pp. 45–6.

The introduction of print media, particularly newspapers as a modern and institutionalized form of speech, came to Ottoman society at a time when a new form of political power was being shaped in response to "the new demands of modernity" in many parts of the world (Kırlı 2009, p. 195). The Ottoman state's response to this new political order, officially known as *Tanzimat*, took the form of a massive reform program in the legal, economic, and administrative spheres, initiated by Sultan Mahmud II (1789–1839) in 1839. Such extensive reforms of the state's operations did transform the way speech as a social phenomenon was perceived and, accordingly, regulated. Surveillance by spying, for instance, began to be carried out in a more systematic way, by incorporating local people as "unofficial" spies and, most importantly, adopting a different rationale. Instead of subduing the populace by persecuting "seditious" words, the new purpose was to investigate public moods and opinions, which was the "discovery of the public opinion," not to denounce it (Kırlı 2009, p. 185), but to govern or control it in a modern fashion. The launch of the newspaper by the Ottoman state was an attempt to influence newly discovered public opinion and its constituting component, speech.

"MODERNIZATION" OF SPEECH: PUBLIC OPINION AND NEWSPAPERS

In his efforts to further his reforms, Sultan Mahmud II saw the necessity of securing the support and cooperation of his people (Yalman 1914, p. 27) and one of the most important steps he took in this direction was the founding of the newspaper *Takvim-i Vekayi* (*The Calendar of Events*) in 1831, the first newspaper in the Turkish language published in Istanbul. The paper also emerged as a counterattack to rebellious Governor Mehmed Âli Pasha's newspaper *Vekayi-i Misriye* (*Egyptian Affairs*) that had been established in 1828 in Egypt. Once the loyal governor of a lucrative Egyptian province, Mehmed Âli Pasha, rebelled and posed a substantial challenge to the Empire. *Takvim-i Vekayi* began to serve as a new front in the war between the sultan and his governor (Kırlı 2009, p. 189), precisely in the battle over public opinion. The leading article in the first issue, explaining the newspaper's raison d'être, reveals that the purpose of the paper has much to do with this battle:

> If daily events are not made public at the time of their occurrence, and their true nature is not disclosed, the people are apt to interpret governmental acts in ways that are not even dreamed of or imagined by the authors. Human nature is always inclined to attack or criticize everything, the character or truth of which it does not know. In order to check the attacks and

misunderstandings and to give people peace of mind, and satisfaction, it
is necessary to make them acquainted with the real nature of the events.
(Yalman 1914, p. 30)

The editorial clearly presents from the outset the Ottoman government's
understanding of the newspaper as a tool to influence emerging public opinion, although public opinion (*efkâr-ı umume*) as a concept did not emerge
in Ottoman society before 1860. This conception of the first official newspaper's origins, from 1830s onwards, constituting the public and its opinion
as a source of authority, were processes intimately linked with the changing
"governmentality" (Foucault 1991; Dean 1999) of the Ottoman state, processes
by which the population became the primary target to be acted upon (Kırlı
2009, p. 180). While "the public" and public opinion emerged as a legitimate
force in the business of governance, this major transformation brought along
the constitution of the people as political subjects, as well as the birth of institutional practices through which people raised their voices.

In this period, between roughly 1840 and 1860, "Ottoman print capitalism"
emerged and the consequences proved nearly revolutionary, in both the short
and long term (Findley 2010, p. 103).

Among the mid-term consequences was the formation of a generation of
rebellious "Young Turks" around the turn of the twentieth century, including
Mustafa Kemal Atatürk. A short-term consequence was the start of unofficial
journalism, commonly accepted as the real beginning of Turkish journalism,
with the launch of *Tercuman-ı Ahval* (*Interpreter of Events*) in 1861, to be followed by a number of dailies and periodicals, including those taking positions
on current affairs as well as criticizing the government. By the mid-1860s the
antigovernment attitude of the press was clear, as was the government's attitude towards the press. The first comprehensive press law was issued by the
government in 1864, an adaptation of Napoleon III's strict French press law of
1851, to be followed by the infamous press ordinance of Âli Pasha in 1867 that
closed numerous publications as well as banning several renowned journalists
writing for opposition newspapers. As a prominent member of the Ottoman
administration of the era, Âli Pasha is known for his argument, "I would not
consider telling the weaknesses of the state to the nation to qualify as patriotic conduct" (İskit 1943, p. 25), in order to justify the "first institutionalized
form of press censorship" (Kocabaşoğlu 1997, p. 37). In response, a number
of journalists left for abroad to continue writing critically in opposition to the
government, while in Ottoman territories numerous humorous and satirical publications became popular for waging subtle, indirect criticism of the
Ottoman elite. Both Âli Pasha's antipatriotism accusation designed to silence

dissident speech and the search by such voices for other means to further their criticism would be among the defining characteristics of the following century-and-a-half, up until today.

The second phase of press development in the Ottoman Empire, 1870–1908, was characterized by the growing influence of newspapers both among the populace and in government circles (Karpat 1964, p. 263), as well as harsher measures to control the press. In 1876, a two-chamber Ottoman Parliament was established following street demonstrations against Sultan Abdulaziz (1861–76) and his descent from the throne, which marked the beginning of the First Constitutional Era (*Meşrutiyet*). The new Emperor Abdulhamid II (1876–1908) was clearly aware of the public influence of the newspapers. Accordingly, he first nurtured friendly relations with journalists to keep them on his side, yet gradually abolished the freedom of the press, believing that most journalists were republicans at heart (Karpat 1964, p. 264). After two years he adjourned the Parliament and waged a war on a critical press which had gained a brief period of freedom. The humorous newspaper *Hayal* (*Illusion*) of Teodor Kasab, for instance, was closed down because of a cartoon representing a man with tied hands and feet with a caption taken from the new constitution "the press is free within legal limits" (Kocabaşoğlu 1997, p. 38). As the satirist mocked, although it was purported that the press was free under the law, the limits posed on nonconforming voices would practically disable them. Following the bans, the number of newspapers fell dramatically; the surviving papers were institutionally censored more rigidly than ever before, opposition journalists were forbidden from practicing journalism, and their books were banned.

Namık Kemal (1840–88) was among the people whose books were banned under Abdulhamid II's regime. He had been a significant figure among the founders of the Young Ottoman Society, the first modern-style opposition movement among Ottoman intellectuals (Findley 2010, p. 104), which fought for a representative and constitutional government in the 1860s. Upon his return home after four years of opposition press activity abroad, Namık Kemal emerged as the model and example for Turkish journalists of the era. He was revered by Young Ottomans as the "liberty-writer" or symbol of struggle against the absolutist Ottoman regime. The next generation of dissidents organized themselves under the rubric of the Young Turks, reflecting an ideological shift from Ottoman nationalism to Turkish nationalism. Their goals were not only to overthrow the oppressive regime of Abdulhamid II, but also to adhere to a representative government path defended by Namık Kemal. Mustafa Kemal Atatürk was among the followers of Namık Kemal from his youth and, as stated by Deringil (1993, p. 170), one can trace the "shadow of Namık Kemal" in the utterances and policies of the early Republican cadres, Mustafa Kemal being the most obvious example.[7]

INFLUENCES ON ATATÜRK'S THINKING ABOUT SPEECH AND ITS REGULATION

Changes in social communications in the Ottoman Empire of the nineteenth century played an important part in the process of modernization and the concomitant growth of a feeling (first of Ottoman, then of Turkish) national consciousness (Mardin 1961, p. 250). The gradually increasing influence and popularity of the press were among the important drivers of this process. As it was the Ottoman government itself that had introduced modern media in order to enhance its own authority and sympathy for its policies, it opposed all attempts to use them for different purposes. Yet, newspapers, satirical magazines and other forms of speech were appropriated by diverse actors with critical opinions about the government, as well as about how the Empire should be saved. Even though, as Deringil argues, the state power attempted to curtail a whole new generation's access to potentially subversive literature, such as that of the writers of the Enlightenment, it proved to be impossible and with every day that passed more young minds became fired by Voltaire and Rousseau (Deringil 1993, pp. 167–8). Young Mustafa Kemal Atatürk was a member of this generation. His attitudes and policies were shaped to a large degree by the ideas he encountered and the experiences he underwent as an activist in the Young Turks movement.

Young Turks were, thus, the products of a restricted yet intellectually formative era of speech in the late nineteenth century. As they developed their ideas and beliefs via the publications of the time, they used the press efficiently as the major tool to spread their opinions about saving the Empire, before their ascent to power in 1909. After the declaration of the Second Constitutional Era (*Meşrutiyet*) in 1908, diverse ideas were defended in these publications, including positivism and nationalism, pro-Islamism, Western-liberalism, and social democracy (Karpat 1964, p. 267), and an atmosphere of diverse voices flourished in Ottoman society, though only for a short while. As Karpat argues, under the Young Turks the press became directly associated with the emerging political parties and with a rather well-defined view of the nascent centralized

---

[7]   In addition to the opinions he would inherit from Namık Kemal, Mustafa Kemal inherited his second name, "Kemal", from him. His mathematics teacher, also named Mustafa, asked his attentive student to add a second name in order to avoid confusion and proposed Kemal, meaning "maturity" or "perfection." As it was also the name of Namık Kemal, Mustafa gladly accepted (Hanioğlu 2011, p. 23).

national state. In 1912 their rule became intolerant to opposition. The Union and Progress government of Young Turks instituted a press law, inspired again by the French Press Law of 1881, where the very function of the press, it was held, imposed obligations on it, and these obligations had to be defined by the government. The brutal silencing of journalists, including with bullets, became an unfortunate and persisting component of Turkish press history, paralleling the period of a fierce ideological battle over the future of the crumbling Empire. Still, the Young Turks era had served, as Karpat argues, as a period of political training and experience when liberal ideas, borrowed from the West, were debated, tried, and, for the most part, found unworkable. With the Balkan War in 1913 ending in the loss of territories, there was a reaction against the West and an infusion of Turkish nationalism, which became the main theme in the modern-minded press (Karpat 1964, p. 269), found reflection with many of its readers and impressed Mustafa Kemal himself.

Mustafa Kemal, as an activist in the Young Turks movement, stood out as an intractable opponent of the personality cult surrounding Sultan Abdulhamid. In a sign of growing opposition to the sultan, many students at the imperial colleges (a hybrid of classical Ottoman education and modern French schooling) demonstrated an increasing aversion to any expression of loyalty to him (Hanioğlu 2011, p. 39). Despite the moral disgust for the regime, however, the initial aims of the Ottoman officer corps, including Mustafa Kemal, were not revolutionary or destructive. Unlike contemporary revolutionaries elsewhere, such as the Bolsheviks, they felt a stubborn loyalty to the state and, accordingly, their main goal was to revive the ailing Empire and save it from collapse. According to Deringil, this was among the traits that are common both to Mustafa Kemal and Namık Kemal, as both ultimately sought "to be useful to the state."

Ideological linkages between them went further than this: Namık Kemal saw the French Declaration of the Rights of Men and the Citizen as the "dawning of truth." Deep belief in "progress" came down to the Republic via the bridge of the Young Turks. Namık Kemal's belief in the "innate ability of man to progress" was very much a theme of republican ideology, to be established by Mustafa Kemal in 1923 (Deringil 1993, pp. 183–4).

Namık Kemal produced a "political philosophy" (Mardin 1962, p. 286), in which reconciliation between the West and East was sought via a return to the essence of Islamic law, *şeriat*, to be reconciled with French revolutionary ideology as expressed by Rousseau and Voltaire. Central to Namık Kemal's thinking was the concept of *meşveret*, or consultation, which he along with other young Ottoman thinkers saw to be a notion correspondent to "representative government" as opposed to an absolute monarchy. In this framework,

Namık Kemal advocated that "[t]he right of sovereignty belongs to all" and that a legitimate government consisting of a group of "specialists" would be assigned to the task of ruling in the name of the "people" according to the precepts of "an absolute normative force" (Deringil 1993, p. 172).

As stated by Deringil, these ideas found a distinct echo in Mustafa Kemal's often-repeated declaration that "sovereignty belongs unconditionally to the nation," yet with a critical difference. The normative force would become secular principles, with the religious component of Namık Kemal's ideological framework rejected absolutely. As Hanioğlu presents it in *An Intellectual Biography* (2011), Atatürk's upbringing in Salonica and his education at secular institutions undoubtedly made him receptive to criticism directed against the religious establishment. During his education at the Royal Military Academy, he read the work of a chief idol of Young Turks, German physiologist Ludwig Bucher's *Kraft und Stoff (Force and matter)*, as well as works of other materialists like Baron d'Holbach and Voltaire, and evolutionists such as H. G. Wells (Hanioğlu 2011, pp. 52–3). One of his most well-known aphorisms, "[t]he most truthful guide in life is science," reveals a worldview that ascribed an overarching role to the secular in every aspect of human life. "Seeking a guide other than science," he avowed, making an indirect allusion to religion, "is thoughtless, prevarication, and ignorance" (Arsan 1997b, p. 202). As Hanioğlu argues, an overwhelming number of his generation were disciples of a peculiar mid-nineteenth century German philosophy known as *Vulgarmaterialismus*: a version of the doctrine of materialism, fusing popular notions of materialism, scientism, and Darwinism into a simple creed that upheld the role of science in society (Hanioğlu 2011, p. 67). Sharing this, Mustafa Kemal departed from Namık Kemal's proposal to reconcile Western principles with Islam.

This basic difference aside, with regard to the conceptualization of public opinion, press, and its regulation, Mustafa Kemal seems to have been deeply influenced by Namık Kemal. Namık Kemal's most mature activity as a journalist and a political thinker started with the publication of *Ibret (Lesson)* in 1872, where he embraced the duty of "giving the public information, about political matters and the progress of civilization" (Karpat 1964, p. 260). Public opinion, in Namık Kemal's view, consisted in political morality, or the sum total of feelings for freedom, justice, and country, among all members of the national community. According to him, it was every person's privilege to have thoughts and ideas, and to express them (Karpat 1964, p. 261). Namık Kemal was also among the earliest to recognize the connection between the press and nation-building. Convinced that journalism constituted an almost sacred duty with regard to the fatherland (*vatan*), he attributed the Ottoman Empire's "backwardness" relative to Europe to its lack of a newspaper press until the

1860s. In keeping up with European theories, Namık Kemal believed that the primary value of the press lay in the constant opportunity to repeat ideas, influence public morals and values, and imbue readers with a love of their country (Brockett 2011, p. 9).

Having suffered from the sanctions of Ottoman governments for his opinions and writings, Namık Kemal naturally defended freedom of the press. Yet, as stated by Cemil Koçak (2009 p. 247–8), according to Namık Kemal, the press warranted this freedom only insofar as it was useful. Due to the direct link established in his thinking between the freedom and utility of the press, the limitations of such freedom would be apparent when usefulness of the press is under question. The influence of Namık Kemal's views on Mustafa Kemal's thinking and policies about speech and society was fundamental. Speech seen as the "voice of the nation" became a legitimization mechanism of the actions Mustafa Kemal would take as both a military commander and political leader. The National Independence movement he led in 1919 was legitimized by the newspapers initiated by the movement in the face of the Ottoman government's resistance. The names of the official papers chosen by Mustafa Kemal for the national movement clearly reflect this anticipated role: *Hakimiyet-i Milliye* (*National Sovereignty*) and *İrade-i Milliye* (*National Will*). He embraced a populism in which these papers purported to speak for the people. These papers were instrumental in spreading the opinions of the independence movement against the views of newspapers aligning with the government. This battle for winning the hearts and minds of Ottoman society was waged via other forms of speech as well, including, as before, the sacred rulings (*fetwas*) issued by religious authorities.

These roles attached to speech during Mustafa Kemal's military career would shape his approach and practices once he won the war in 1922, established the Republic in 1923 and began his grand program of transformation. The press would now claim to be speaking for the people of the new Republic and at the same time would be instrumental in spreading the ideologies justifying Atatürk's policies. The populism of the Independence War period would transform into state-sponsored populism during the Republican era, and the press would be instrumental in legitimizing the radical reform program, including abolishing the Caliphate (1924) and changing the Arabic script to Latin script (1928). Opposition voices, particularly with religious or ethnic undertones, would not be tolerated, as he believed that revolutionary aspects of his reform program would naturally upset those who were against the unity of the secular Republic. The press, he believed, should "build a steel fortress, a fortress of opinion and ideology protecting the Republic. And it is the Republic's right to ask this role from the press" (Arsan 1997b, p. 171). Mustafa Kemal's archetype was France's Third Republic (1870–1940), which he viewed as a genuine republic and the most successful regime in the history of human-kind. Following its example, justifying the limitation of freedom of speech for the sake of the Republic was therefore comprehensible. Like Jean-Jacques Rousseau, he considered the principal aim of a republic not to assure individ-ual liberty but to give expression to the "general will" and, like Machiavelli, he thought that a true republic should pursue national strength even at the expense of individual freedom (Hanioğlu 2011).

Until the beginning of the multiparty era in 1945, when speech organized in the form of political parties and press gained unprecedented freedom, Atatürk's views, embodied in his Republican People's Party (RPP) shaped the ways in which speech would be regulated in his utilitarian perspective. On the one hand this would involve brief periods when limitations on freedom of speech were expanded, such as 1923–5, 1929–31, and 1939–45. On the other hand, the overall of logic of the single-party era (1925–45) was using forms of speech to unite the nation in accordance with Republican reforms. In addition to "traditional methods," such as banning opposition voices, other more "con-temporary and productive" methods (Kocabaşoğlu 1997, p. 55) were deployed. These included establishing patronage relations with press bosses, extending the RPP's presence in social life via highly controlled spaces of speech, such as people's houses (*halkevleri*) (Karpat 1974), the Public Orators Organisation (*Halk Hatipleri Teşkilatı*) (Uzun 2010), and People's Tribune (*Halk Kürsüsü*) (Bolat 2007), and refashioning existing mechanisms to survey public opin-ion, such as a "demands system" of petitioning (Akin 2007) and "party inspec-tion tours." All in all, as Mete Tunçay suggests, the difference between the Ottoman and Republican eras was that, in the former, the press refrained from what the government disdained, while in the latter period, it affirma-tively published what the state desired (Tunçay 1987, p. 48). Thus, channels and spaces of speech were regulated in more versatile ways by the Republican regime, a strategy that worked until the beginning of the multiparty era. With political liberalization in 1945, first print and then political parties became platforms of expression for suppressed perspectives of different sorts, including those against Kemalist principles. The first opposition party to RPP rule, the Democrat Party, built its election campaign in 1946 on the claim of represent-ing the nation whose voice has not been heard until then, embodied with their slogan: "[e]nough! The nation has the say" ("Yeter! Söz milletin").

CONCLUSION

This chapter has sought to explain facets of Turkish ideas of the role of speech in the structuring of society. Mustafa Kemal Atatürk's thinking on speech and its regulation are presented from a historical perspective, because of the pivotal role that Mustafa Kemal Atatürk played in the formulation of speech and press policies in modern Turkish history. Andrew Mango writes of Atatürk's practical experience as a military commander, the opposition he confronted from defenders of the Ottoman dynasty, the threat that the spreading communist and fascist ideologies in Europe and Asia posed to his leadership, and his knowledge of the severity of physical destruction throughout his nation (Mango 2002, pp. 361–6). Equally relevant was his record as a disciple of Western Enlightenment ideals interpreted in the late Ottoman context. Mustafa Kemal adopted a centralized approach to constructing the Turkish Republic, where opposition voices would be permitted only as long as they were deemed "useful" or supportive for his political program, the ultimate goal of which was to establish and protect the Republic he envisioned. The chapter demonstrates how current policies have roots, not only in Atatürk's approaches but in those Ottoman times.

In 2015, a popular trade book was published in Turkey on the history of journalism, entitled *From Palace to Palace: Tales of Turkish Journalism*. The title of the book refers to the introduction of the first newspaper by the Ottoman Palace, by the Sultan himself in 1831, and the current alarming situation of freedom of the press in Turkey. According to its author, repression of press freedom by President Recep Tayyip Erdoğan who also resides in a palace, White Palace (*Ak Saray*), illustrates an unfortunate continuity in this almost two-century-long trajectory of the press in Turkey (Alan 2015).

How do the period of Atatürk's rule and his policies regarding speech and its regulation fit in this journey from one palace to the other? One possibility is to consider Atatürk's era as a radical, libertarian break from the Ottoman Palace's strict limitations on speech, since Atatürk himself was a devoted Republican opposed to the absolute monarchy of Ottoman rule. The second way to answer the question is that, with regard to freedom of speech, Atatürk's period presented a significant difference neither from the rule of the Ottoman regime, nor from what followed afterwards until today, including the current AKP rule under President Erdoğan.

The first approach, the idea of rupture, is countered in this chapter by showing that in many ways Atatürk's understanding was shaped by the prevalent debates that took place in the late Ottoman era. Despite his radical Republican overtones, Atatürk's approach to speech and its limits was, to a large extent, a revamped or "modern" version of the mindset of late Ottoman governments. The second approach, that Atatürk's period was essentially continuous and consonant with what preceded and followed it, is similarly inaccurate. Even the minimal gains regarding freedom of speech as a result of regime change towards a republic from a monarchy are sufficient to qualify this transition as "progressive," despite significant deficiencies of the Republican era. During almost a century between Mustafa Kemal's rule and AKP rule, although far from perfection in many respects (Akin 2011), Turkey has become a multiparty democracy, a signatory of international laws protecting the rights of speech and expression, while journalism has developed professional standards and other forms of public discourse have become common features of Turkish democracy.

Despite the transformations they brought along, Atatürk and successive Turkish governments inherited the utilitarian logic of speech from the Ottoman era, and applied it according to their own definitions of its utility. Atatürk's support for speech that primarily served to protect the new regime led to its careful regulation by modern means. This has been transformed into successive governmental approaches, in which some governments restrict speech very much in their own interest of retaining power outweighing the public interest. Some governments have resorted to archaic methods of regulating speech, such as imprisoning if not killing "dissident" public figures. Yet, the utilitarian understanding of speech has been a lasting legacy and current problems about limitation of speech in digital platforms can best be understood in this context.

As veteran Internet scholar Akgül has written, Internet censorship in Turkey has rested mainly on two pillars: preventing "undesired" political messages and fighting pornography (Akgül and Kırlıdoğ 2015). Turkey is no exception in the latter area; with regard to political messages, the scope of attacks on the "existing social system" is becoming increasingly vague. The ruling AKP and President Erdoğan are fervently seeking to transform the country into what the president calls the "New Turkey" (Akgül and Kırlıdoğ 2015). AKP's idea of a "New Turkey," conservative and neo-liberal, embracing its Sunni-Muslim identity, becomes a Neo-Ottoman regional power. This vision carries with it a particular definition of utility, with regard to speech, as well as its regulation with many other measures.[8] It casts a broad net as to what is unwanted and unconstructive.

A symbolic case is the recent limitation on Twitter, the most commonly used communication platform, particularly during the Gezi events between May and June 2013. Against the backdrop of widespread complaints about the direct and indirect control of mass media by the government, Twitter's

---

[8] Tim Arango's article, entitled "Islamist websites in Turkey manage to evade strict internet censorship," focuses on the religious sensibilities of the AKP and its difference from earlier governments: "Turkey was no paragon of free speech under its old secular and nationalist system, although, then, the frequent offense was to insult notions of 'Turkishness.' Now the government focuses on speech it deems insulting to Islam or the president, or that promotes atheism." (Arango 2015).

significance increased further following the appearance of corruption-related material on a microblogging site about President Erdoğan and his four cabinet ministers. In response, Erdoğan first labeled Twitter "a menace to society," then vowed to eradicate it, and the same day Twitter was blocked without a court order. Another method, milder than the wholesale banning of Twitter, has been the "removal request" ultimatums issued to Twitter by the government. According to Twitter's own statistics covering the period July 2014–July 2015, requests from Turkey are higher than the aggregate requests from all other countries (Twitter 2015). Furthermore, Internet usage is controlled at the access point: Internet cafes are subject to stringent regulations, which extend beyond limits defined by the law (Akgül and Kırlıdoğ 2015).

The case of Twitter dramatically recalls the regulation of speech in the prepress period of the Ottoman Empire. Then the coffeehouses, as the most significant spaces for speech, were banned, monitored by spies, and seditious themes were prohibited by religious or legal rulings. Since then, as presented in this chapter, the utilitarian logic of understanding speech has been inherited, while definitions of utility have changed as have the methods to set the limits of speech, in accordance with the priorities of successive governments. Likewise, throughout the same trajectory, the ensuing struggle to advance freedom of speech in Turkey has become part of the fight for democracy generally. Current problems, and their solutions, can be better understood through the debates and influences of the earlier transition and the special framing of the role of the press in that key period.

REFERENCES

Akgül, M. and Kırlıdoğ, M. 2015. "Internet censorship in Turkey," June 3, 2015, *Internet Policy Review*. Available at: http://policyreview.info/articles/analysis/internet-censorship-turkey.

Akin, A. 2011. "Desarrollo de los medios en Turquía: Cuando se abre la caja mágica de Pandora" ("Development of media in Turkey: Once Pandora's box is open"), *Infoamérica–Iberoamerican Communication Review* (Special issue: The Emerging Nations' Media Systems) 6: 97–114.

Akin, Y. 2007. "Reconsidering state, party, and society in early republican Turkey," *International Journal of Middle East Studies* 39: 435–57.

Alan, Ü. 2015. *Saraydan saraya: Türkiye'de gazetecilik masali (From Palace to Palace: Tales of Turkish Journalism)*. Istanbul: Can.

Arango, T. 2015. "Islamist websites in Turkey manage to evade strict internet censorship," *New York Times*. March 13, 2015. Available at: www.nytimes.com/2015/03/14/world/europe/islamist-websites-in-turkey-manage-to-evade-strict-internet-censorship.html?_r=0.

Arsan, N. 1997a. *Atatürk'ün söylev ve demeçleri (Atatürk's Speeches and Statements)*, 5th ed., vol. 1, Atatürk Araştırma Merkezi: Ankara.

1997b. *Atatürk'ün söylev ve demeçleri (Atatürk's Speeches and Statements)*, 5th ed., vol. 2, Atatürk Araştırma Merkezi: Ankara.

1997c. *Atatürk'ün söylev ve demeçleri (Atatürk's Speeches and Statements)*, 5th ed., vol. 3, Atatürk Araştırma Merkezi: Ankara.

"Bir aylık dünya şu'unu: Reisicümhur Hz. Ankara'dan, İstanbul'a gitmek üzre, hareket ettiler" ("Monthly news: President departed from Ankara to Istanbul") 1929. *Ayın Tarihi (Month's History)* 20(65): 4790–3.

Bolat, B. S. 2007. *Milli bayram olgusu ve Türkiye'de yapılan Cumhuriyet Bayramı kutlamaları (1923–1960) (Notion of National Festival and Republic Festival Celebrations in Turkey (1923–1960))* (Unpublished PhD thesis, Hacettepe University, Ankara).

Brockett, G. D. 2011. *How Happy to Call Oneself a Turk: Provincial Newspapers and the Negotiation of a Muslim National Identity*. Austin: University of Texas Press.

Dean, M. 1999. *Governmentality: Power and Rule in Modern Society*. London: Sage.

Deringil, S. 1993. "The Ottoman origins of Kemalist nationalism: Namık Kemal to Mustafa Kemal," *European History Quarterly* 23(2): 66–91.

Findley, C. 2010. *Turkey, Islam, Nationalism, and Modernity*. New Haven: Yale University Press.

Foucault, M. 1991. "Governmentality," in Burchell, G., Gordon, C., and Miller, P. (eds.), *The Foucault Effect: Studies in Governmentality*. Chicago: The University of Chicago Press, pp. 87–104.

Georgeon, F. 1999. "Osmanlı İmparatorluğu'nun Son Döneminde İstanbul Kahvehaneleri" ("Coffeehouses in Istanbul during the late Ottoman period"), in Desmet-Grégoire, H. and François, G. (eds.), *Doğu'da Kahve ve Kahvehaneler (Coffee and Coffeehouses in the East)* Ankara: Yapı Kredi, pp. 43–85.

Gevgilili, A. 1990. *Türkiye'de yenileşme düşüncesi: Sivil toplum, basın ve Atatürk (Modernization Thought in Turkey: Civil Society, Press and Atatürk)*. Istanbul: Bağlam.

Hattox, R. S. 1996. *Coffee and Coffeehouses: The Origins of a Social Beverage in the Medieval Near East*. Seattle and London: University of Washington Press.

Hanioğlu, M. Ş. 2011. *Atatürk: An Intellectual Biography*. Princeton and Oxford: Princeton University Press.

Işın, E. 2001. "A social history of coffee and coffeehouses," in Özpalabıyıklar, S. (ed.), *Coffee: Pleasures Hidden in a Bean*. Istanbul: Yapı Kredi Yayınları, pp. 10–43.

İskit, R. S. 1943. *Türkiye'de matbuat idareleri ve politikaları (Press Administrations and Policies in Turkey)*. Istanbul: Tan.

Karpat, K. H. 1964. "Turkey: Mass media," in Ward, R. and Rustow, D. A. (eds.), *Political modernization in Japan and Turkey*. Princeton University Press: Princeton, pp. 255–82.

1974. "The impact of the People's Houses on the development of communication in Turkey: 1931–1951," *Die Welt des Islams* 15(1–4): 69–84.

Kırlı, C. 2000. *The Struggle Over the Space: Coffeehouses of Ottoman İstanbul, 1780–1845* (Unpublished PhD thesis, SUNY, Binghamton).

2009. "Surveillance and constituting the public in the Ottoman Empire," in Shami, S. (ed.),*Publics, Politics and Participation: Locating the Public Sphere in the*

Middle East and North Africa. New York: Social Science Research Council, pp. 177–203.

Kocabaşoğlu, U. 1997. *İki arada bir derede: İmlaya gelmez tarih yazıları (Historic Writings that Cannot be Regulated)*. Ankara: İmge Yayınları.

Koçak, C. 2009. "Namık Kemal," in Bora, T. and Gültekingil, M. (eds.), *Modern Türkiye'de siyasi düşünce (Political Thought in Modern Turkey)*, vol. 1., 9th ed., Istanbul: İletişim, pp. 244–9.

Mango, A. 2002. *Ataturk: The Biography of the Founder of Modern Turkey*. Woodstock, New York: Overlook Press.

Mardin, Ş. 1961. "A note on the early phase in the modernization of communication in Turkey," *Comparative Studies in Society and History* April: 250–71.

1962. *The Genesis of Young Ottoman Thought*. Princeton: Princeton University Press.

1987. "Türk toplumunu inceleme aracı olarak 'sivil toplum' (Civil society as a tool to investigate Turkish society)," *Defter* 2: 7–16.

Méry, P.-A. 1855. *Constantinople et la Mer Noire (Constantinople and the Black Sea)*. Paris: Leprieur Editeur.

Öztürk, S. 2005a. "Osmanlı İmparatorluğu'nda kamusal alanın dinamikleri (Dynamics of civil society in the Ottoman Empire)," *İletişim, Gazi Üniversitesi İletişim Fakültesi Yayını* 21: 95–124.

2005b. "Karagöz co-opted: Turkish shadow theatre of the early Republic (1923–1945)," *Asian Theatre Journal* 29(2): 292–312.

Tunçay, M. 1981. *Türkiye Cumhuriyeti'nde tek-parti yönetimi'nin kurulması (1923–1931) (Establishment of Single-Party Regime in Turkey)*. Istanbul: Yurt.

1987. "Tek Parti Döneminde Basın (Press in the single-party era)," *Tarih ve Toplum* 7(37): 48–9.

Twitter 2015. "Transparency report," Available at: https://transparency.twitter.com/removal-requests/2014/jul-dec.

Uzun, H. 2010 "Bir Propaganda Aracı Olarak Cumhuriyet Halk Fırkası Halk Hatipleri Teşkilâtı (Republican People's Party's public orators organization as a propaganda tool)," *Cumhuriyet Tarihi Araştırmaları Dergisi* 11: 85–118.

Yalman, A. E. 1914. *The Development of Modern Turkey as Measured by Its Press*. New York: Columbia University.

9

Jewish Law and Ethics in the Digital Era

Yoel Cohen

Speech, language, and communication play a central role in Judaism. As an ethical religion, Judaism regulates not only man's relationship with God but also with his fellow man. Judaism does not preach asceticism or social isolation, but encourages social participation. The Jewish *Weltanschauung* (philosophy of life) is that Man should use his free choice to raise his stature to emulate the characteristics of the Infinite God. The process of so doing can be said to yield a "Jewish" theory of the functions of speech in society. By Jewish theory and Jewish law, I refer primarily to dominant religious traditions as they have evolved over centuries, recognizing that there are increasingly plural perspectives with different claims to legitimacy.

A theory of communication and society draws upon the Five Books of Moses, or *Torah*, which contains 613 positive or negative commandments. True, the Bible is multifaceted and is also a source of information about the growth of the Israelite people from the days of the Patriarchs, the 210-year-long slavery in Egypt, the forty-year-long travels in the Sinai desert to the Land of Canaan, as well as a chronicle of such media events as the exodus from Egypt and the giving of the Ten Commandments at Mount Sinai. However, the covenant between God and the Israelites appears paramount. Drawing upon the covenant made between God and the Patriarchs and Moses, Judaism provides an important ethical dimension; the commandments aim to establish a society that was just by the standards of the day and distinctive in its service of God. The covenant promised the Israelites that they would be God's chosen ones if they observed God's commandments. The most famous are those in the Decalogue, or Ten Commandments, which include such fundamental rules of ethical conduct as those prohibiting murder, theft, adultery, and idol worship, as well other commands like observing the Sabbath day of rest. Judaism's view of speech and communication, as I relate it here, draws upon edicts which originate in the Bible and have been subject to interpretation and extrapolation in the *Talmud* and to codification in books of Jewish law (*Halakhah*). Given that the *Torah*, the Prophets, later Jewish law works like the *Mishnah* and *Talmud*, and codifiers such as Maimonides necessarily predated the mass-media age, it is necessary, in determining Judaism's view of mass media, to locate points of contacts between Judaism and social communication. With the exception of the seven so-called Noahide Laws (including those prohibiting murder, theft, and adultery, and requiring the recognition of the monotheistic God), other commands, including Jewish laws on speech, are not imposed upon the Gentile. Nevertheless, in regulating conduct among people, Judaism is a source of norms of behavior, including about speech, for mankind as a whole (Cohen 2001; Cohen 2006).

Judaism's view of speech has a number of levels. First and foremost, communication is the most basic ingredient of God's revelation to humanity. Communication is no less than the sum total of divine effects in the finite world. Hebrew becomes a holy language, not only with a set of symbols to communicate between a sender and receiver but itself enjoying the power of creation; witness the Creation in the first chapter of the Book of Genesis, in which the various stages of the Creation were effected by divine commands (Gross 2008; Wolpe 1992). Another illustration of the centrality of speech is that in the *Vidduy* prayer or Confession in the Yom Kippur prayer services, over a quarter of the Jew's confession relates to the abuse of speech. Given all this, it is incumbent upon the Jew that speech should be performed in a dignified manner, free of violence, threats, or nonpeaceful statements.

A number of stages of speech and communication may be delineated. There is the question of information and the right to privacy. Whether information is in written, oral, or visual form, Judaism offers guidance. For example, for visual information there is the principle of *hezek reyah*, which prohibits public disclosure about the private realm. A related question concerns publishing information which is not correct or is slanderous (Falk 1999). While there is no all-embracing Jewish view of accurate information, it is alluded to by Jewish sources at certain levels of human behavior. So long as the communicator's purpose is not to deceive (*gneivat daat*), they have not committed a transgression. Publishing information which is inaccurate about a person, institution, or corporation has to be corrected. Damages may be received.

The age of digital media has intensified a tension in Judaism between free speech and privacy. The global village, or superhighway of information, is but one further breach in the wall that Judaism has sought to construct over thousands of years to protect and nourish an ethical society. Judaism constructs significant standards governing speech among Jews. Judaism, therefore, offers perspectives about the threats to cohesiveness, secrecy, and privacy characterized by the age of computers and the Internet. Judaism's discussion of speech goes beyond the question of privacy and related matters. Much of the discourse emphasizes that the content of a message should not be damaging or slanderous. However, it does not evaluate whether the overall presentation of facts paints an accurate and objective record of an event, short of demanding that the communicator does not possess bad intentions. With regard to the separate question of accuracy in pictorial images there appears to be less rigorous supervision in Judaism of the visual image because pictures are susceptible to more diverse interpretations than words. As a result, numerous images are sometimes constructed of the same event with different meanings.

Against the background of the digital age, this chapter discusses the application of Jewish rules of conduct of speech to questions regarding theology, and how different communities have interpreted these rulings in practice from day to day. Under the former it discusses the importance in Judaism of accuracy in journalism and advertising, the Jewish view of the principle of the right to know, the Jewish law of copyright, and Jewish thinking about privacy and data protection, and social networking.

ACCURACY IN SPEECH

At its most basic, Judaism's view of speech emphasizes the need for accuracy and intellectual honesty. Information reported in the media has to be accurate to avoid the audience being deceived. The question of complete and honest reporting is referred to in the Bible. Reflecting that truth is regarded as a foundation of the world, the Book of Proverbs (12.19) reads: "[t]ruthful lips shall be established forever, but a lying tongue is only for a moment." So important is truth, that lying is tantamount to idol worship. For example, the sin of the biblical spies was that they colored with their own opinions the report of their mission to spy out the Promised Land (Liebes 1994).

The requirement for accuracy is problematic when a news organization, under tight deadlines, faces news sources which do not wish to give their account of events. The provision of information about events and societies, which contributes to understanding and conflict reduction, while not generally identified as a peculiarly religious goal, is endorsed by Judaism. The sin of the misreporting by ten out of the twelve spies about the Promised Land was not only that they added their own ideological views to their factual report. In addition, according to the Bible commentator Abarbanel, instead of reporting back directly to Moses, they went public with their report to all the Israelites, generating public pressure against Moses. "The communicator should not possess any bad intentions to distort" (Book of Numbers, Chapter 13).

The problem of deception is acute in advertising, where customers can be persuaded to buy a product which they would not otherwise buy if they knew all the facts. Judaism therefore places limitations on modern advertising (Cohen 2012b). While advertising plays a positive role in providing customers with information regarding different brands of products, there are moral limits to what may or may not be done. Drawing upon the biblical verse, "[i]n selling ... do not be distortionate" (Leviticus 25:17), Judaism prohibits the trader from creating a false impression (*genevat daat*) when promoting his products. A trader is required to divulge to a prospective customer all defects in his product. A trader is also permitted to draw the buyer's attention to the good features of a product he is marketing as long as these are accurate. Levine (1981) argues that, while goodwill drawn as a result of the product quality or good service is positively regarded in Judaism, goodwill obtained deceptively through actively creating a false impression is forbidden. However, a trader is not obliged to correct an erroneous impression that is the result of self-deception. Showing the defects of an opponent's products is forbidden (as distinct from pointing out the positive aspects of one's own products) and is tantamount to slander and falsehood.

SOCIAL GOSSIP

Privacy appears to have a privileged status in Jewish thought. Judaism values the right of privacy above the public's right to know, in contrast to some developments in Western societies that give the public's right to know greater weighting over the right to privacy. Tents during the Israelites' forty-year wanderings in the Sinai desert did not face one another, for reasons of modesty and privacy. This impressed even the Gentile prophet Balaam in the Balak story in the Book of Numbers. In a famous edict, Rabbenu Gershom imposed a prohibition not to read a letter addressed to another (Halachically Speaking 5:17). Finklestein (1924) says that this edict was developed in the Middle Ages when letters were transported by personal messengers; the edict was intended to deter these carriers from reading the contents of messages.

One's property includes information about oneself. The right to privacy covers information that is not publicly known about a person. According to Talmudic sources, under the principle of *hezek reyah*, it is forbidden to look into the yard of the neighbor. In discussing the concept of *hezek reyah'*, or causing damage by prying into somebody's home, the *Talmud* says that in, for example, a courtyard between two dwellings, there is a religious obligation to construct a fence between the two to ensure the privacy of each. In a spirited discussion, Babylonian Talmud Tractate *Baba Bathra* (2a) in the *Talmud* discusses whether a neighbor is required to share the expense of building the fence. Privacy is a prerequisite in relationships between two people, including sharing or not sharing private emotions and thoughts. The characteristic of a monotheistic God of being unknown, except by his deeds and actions, is arguably a clue to the right of man, who, by virtue of being created in God's image, also has aspects unknown except to him or herself alone.

Notwithstanding the importance which Judaism gives to privacy, there is no Jewish law of privacy per se. Some scholars claim that such a concept exists in Judaism. Rakover (a former Israeli government Jewish law advisor) and some other scholars identified with the Jewish law movement (which seeks to imprint modern Israeli law with features of ancient Jewish law) argue that various religious laws allude to an underlying theme in Judaism for the right to privacy (Rakover 2006). However, others argue that Judaism lacks a fully fledged principle of human dignity, from which a rule of privacy might be extrapolated.

In his tome *Hofetz Hayyim*, Israel Meir Kagan (1877) presented a sophisticated system for regulating speech. A key law deals with the divulging of previously unknown information. Leviticus (19:16), in warning against not being "a talebearer among your people, or standing idly by the blood of your neighbor," imposes substantial limits on the passage of undisclosed, or private, information. The rabbis have divided types of information into a number of categories. Most severe has been divulging secret information to the wider public with the intention or effect of damaging somebody's reputation (*loshon hara* (evil gossip)). When Miriam spoke ill of Moses for "the Cushan woman he married," she was smitten with leprosy (Deuteronomy, ch. 12). Also forbidden, but with lesser severity, is the disclosure of even positive information about somebody (*rehilut*).

With the growth of print, the Jewish laws of speech became transformed from oral speech to written text. What began with *loshon hara* as rules of interpersonal communication became applied to mass-communication channels like publishing. However, the growing number of books in the fifteenth and sixteenth centuries, the appearance of the Gutenberg printing press in 1450 and the spread of printing throughout most of Europe, and the rise of the press in Europe in the seventeenth and eighteenth centuries challenged Judaism's limits on speech. The rise of democracy in the Western world that legitimized free speech, including the unlimited transfer of information, went further.

These restrictions in Judaism profoundly affect the disclosure of previously unpublished information. A journalist, for example, draws much of his information from sources who disclose selectively, often in order to weaken a political opponent. Reflecting that the very verse from Leviticus noted above prohibiting gossip also contains a prohibition against "spilling blood" has led some commentators to equate evil gossip with "murder" or character assassination (for example, Passamaneck 1976). However, once the information is known to three people, publication is no longer forbidden, and it becomes permissible to hear it. As the Babylonian Talmudic Tractate *Erachin* (16a) notes, once information is known to three people, it is the same as announcing it to the world. Information, therefore, takes on a relative value. The source and his informant have carried out a most heinous act in making the information public, but that same information may be heard by other people. Yet there are even rabbis who disagree and do not allow publication of information already known to three persons.

In Judaism an individual's principal duty is to know and understand Jewish knowledge, i.e., the *Torah*, and there is an obligation to make that knowledge available. In addition, a person should have access to national laws and information that, if kept secret, would cause damage to someone. Western concepts of freedom of expression encourage the wide publication and circulation of knowledge, with limited exceptions. In Jewish law, there is then this large middle category of information between that which is banned and that which there is a duty to know. This "middle category," central to the Enlightenment, is not seen as of vital importance to be known. Judaism does not acknowledge an automatic right to this middle category of information. Thus, Judaism distinguishes between the large flow of otherwise-interesting information disclosed by the media that does not come under this category, disclosure of which it prohibits, and the much smaller category of information of social value. So serious is the prohibition of *loshon hara* that even gossip between husband and wife is frowned upon. Even though there should be no secrets between man and wife, this positive command of disclosures with social value should not be carried out at the expense of a transgression being committed (Contemporary American Reform Responsa (CCAR) 1990).

A major innovation of Judaism in the field of religion and mass-media behavior concerns limits on the divulging of previously unknown information. These Jewish principles would have influence far beyond Jews, because deeply embedded principles in Islam of honor and family fealty, introduced by Muhammed, are, it is argued, a direct influence of Judaism. In building his new religion in the seventh century, Muhammed was influenced by the Bible, partly in the hope, not often successful, of converting local Jews living in the region of Medina to his new religion.

The tension and conflict between the right to know and the right to privacy have moved in favor of the right to know. However, legal frameworks in different countries have over the years taken steps against excesses in the right to know. Libel and slander laws were introduced to protect the reputation of an individual tarnished in print or orally. With the rise of the Internet and computers, the challenges for Jewish religious laws about speech have moved far beyond what they were before. Judaism does not offer a single unified view on *loshon hara*, or interpersonal communication. Indeed, some rabbis have debated how the reality of modern democracy may be reconciled with the ancient principles of *loshon hara*. The hardline position of the *Hofetz Hayyim* may be contrasted with that of Rabbi Abraham Kook, the influential chief rabbi during the British mandate in Palestine, who recognized that mass media were part and parcel of the modern state (Chwat 1995). Azariah Ariel (2001) postulated the concept of "evil gossip by consensus," in which holders of, or candidates for, public office today understand that, as politicians, they will be under the glare of public attention and scrutiny.

Judaism is not against public scrutiny of elected officials. In stating "do not stand by the blood," the Biblical verse may also be interpreted as a religious obligation to correct misdemeanors in the Jewish state. That the same verse, in prohibiting the disclosure of secret information, continues "do not stand idly by the blood of your neighbor," suggesting that, if somebody hears of information such as corruption committed by a government minister or official, he has an obligation to take steps to rectify the situation. The Bible, therefore, acknowledges the Fourth Estate, or societal watchdog, role fulfilled by the media. Social dangers, such as radiation or pedophilia, should be brought to public attention. While not generally identified as a peculiarly religious goal, Judaism endorses the provision of information about events and societies, which contributes to understanding and reduces conflict. After the Israelites entered the Promised Land they each became socially responsible for the sins of others. While this raises other questions of individual liberties, the idea of collective responsibility does allude to how social evils are to be corrected. Judaism, therefore, is dualistic. Even *loshon hara* is not an absolute value, but is conditional upon the no-less-important obligation "not to stand by bloodshed" or a social danger.

One example involves the not-infrequent disclosures of information regarding corruption or sexual improprieties committed by rabbis. Rabbis set high standards of moral conduct and such disclosures defame the religion and even God (*hilul Hashem*). Over the years, rabbis have generally favored cover-up rather than disclosure, even if it may be in the public interest for people to know. To be true, the question of embarrassing media revelations concerning rabbis may be distinguished between disclosure in the secular media and in the community's religious media. Wide differences are found among rabbis from different religious streams. For example, Haredi rabbis strongly oppose that revelations should be published in any media form. Even most modern Orthodox rabbis also oppose this, but less so than their Haredi colleagues. Yet, the Bible itself was not averse to publishing details of the sins of the righteous as a means towards moral teaching. Miriam's sin of speaking ill of Moses for "the Cushan woman he married" was followed by her becoming smitten with leprosy (Deuteronomy 12); and Moses's sin in striking the rock to draw water instead of speaking to it was punished by his not entering the Promised Land. In contrast to Orthodox rabbis, rabbis belonging to the Reform and Conservative streams are more inclined to agree that scandals involving rabbis should be reported by the general media.

The question of whistleblowing has been the subject of more than a few responsa by rabbis. Recent questions include the case of a rabbi who was informed about a murder suspect but sworn to secrecy not to pass details of the suspect's name to the authorities (Freehof 1969). Another question is whether one is obligated to pass information of others in criminal matters in which one is involved oneself, particularly if it could bring about plea-bargaining and release (CARR 1983). Does an obligation regarding whistleblowing only concern a Jewish court or also a Gentile court, where when one might be damned by the community as an "informer?" (Shohet 1974). Is registering a convert in a community's public registry an invasion of her privacy? (CARR 1984). If a woman is terminally ill, should that information be passed to her prospective husband, to avoid transgressing the biblical command of not "placing a stumbling block before the blind?" (CARR 1986). In one case where hospital patients were accidentally given transfusions with blood containing HIV, should the information be withheld from the patients, possibly avoiding hysteria and the endangerment of their mental state, or do the patients possess a right to be fully informed regarding their medical situation, if only to monitor it? (Plaut and Washofsky 1997).

Yet even media exposure of public officials is not unconditional, but focuses on their public work and not their private lives. An example is the case of Barack Obama, who, in 2008, while a US presidential candidate, visited the Middle East during his electioneering campaign and placed a message, as many do, in the Kotel, the Western Wall in Jerusalem. Its contents were subsequently disclosed by the *Maariv* newspaper after a yeshiva student removed the message from the Wall and gave it to one of the paper's reporters. It read, "Lord – protect my family and me. Forgive my sins, and help me guard against pride and despair. Give me the wisdom, to do what is right and just. And, make me an instrument of your will." The rabbi of the Western Wall, Rabbi Shmuel Rabinowitz, described as "sacrilegious the removal of the note. Notes placed in the Kotel are between the person and his Maker. Heaven forbid that one should read them or use them." Before the Israeli attorney-general could decide whether or not to open a police investigation, the yeshiva student returned the prayer note to the Kotel. For *Maariv*, it was newsworthy because it was interesting. Was *Maariv*'s disclosure an infringement of Obama's privacy? Some might argue that there is a public interest in disclosing Obama's private beliefs. After all, the American public arguably has a right to know what influences an American presidential candidate, including the nature of his religious beliefs.

If *tikun olam* or social correction can be achieved by going to the appropriate authorities, discreetly, rather than to the media, leading to less-discriminate exposure, that is to be preferred. Where this is not possible, such as when even the state authorities themselves are corrupt, media exposure should be used to bring public pressure on the authorities. Disclosure of information requires that the facts need to be correct and that the deed is indeed illegal. Sometimes it is ambiguous whether the deed is indeed wrong. Rumors are not enough. The discloser has to know firsthand about the crime. Under Jewish law, the reporter has to attach his name to the claim and cannot disclose behind an unattributable leak. If the danger to the public is so great, it should be reported in the media in a manner in which it is unequivocally qualified as "according to rumors" and not as if it is proven information. Over time, repeated rumors may be perceived as general knowledge and the tendency, then, might be to overlook the weakness in sourcing. This continues to be a problem in Jewish law.

SOCIAL NETWORKING

Jewish speech ethics have found new areas of heightened relevance with the arrival of social media. In one sense, social networking has the potential to play an important goal in building relationships between individuals. It contributes to communication, and peace and harmony, including dialogue (which has to be preferred as a form of communication over violent means of conflict resolution), and could arguably be a channel for strengthening family ties, notably between children and parents, and friends. It therefore clearly fulfils a Jewish goal as a communication channel.

However, social networking also revisits Jewish legal questions concerning speech and the right to know, and speech and modesty, as well as raising important Jewish educational and pedagogic issues. In encouraging the free passage of information about people networked, it involves the exposure of details about an individual to numerous, indeed innumerable, "friends," with the individual having little or no control over the reach of that information. In so doing, it challenges key Jewish principles about the right to privacy. And it certainly provides a new framework with a different balance of exposures that has an impact on the development of education and sense of self and community.

Until the latter half of the first decade of this century and the growth of social media sites, mass media were assumed to be operated by journalists who were generally aware of the limitations of writing, including the laws of libel and slander. With the broader public less skilled in the dos and don'ts of communication, social media altered the expectation of professionalism regarding the standard of communication. Social media can more readily lead to abuse or the infraction of norms.

With the goal of encouraging usage, Facebook encourages exposure, a sense of competition and social ambition, as well as a need for self-aggrandizement, such as placing photographs of oneself on the Internet. This contrasts with such valued Jewish goals as righteousness and modesty. Indeed, in the analyses of potential impact, some religious leaders contend that social networking may result in a person's social image being changed and distorted as a result of disappointment, and may lead to depression and even instances of suicide. Social networking challenges the Haredi rules of conduct, partly by facilitating informal relationships between men and women (Lev-On and Ben-Shahar 2009).

In conventional off-line social relationships, whether for example in the family, club, place of work, or synagogue, each social setting has a certain uniqueness, in that it is understood that certain types of information are shared or not disclosed. In a media age, these distinctions are difficult to maintain; social media underscores and magnifies this incapacity to self-regulate. Haredi rabbis perceive the growth of blogs and social media as a challenge to the undisputed authority of the rabbi. In the Hassidic Haredi community, for example, the custom is to see the *admor* (head of the court) as not only providing religious law rulings, like the Lithuanian Haredim, but also acting as a family counselor-cum-psychologist, proffering advice across a myriad of questions such as whom to marry, where to live or where to work. Social media challenge this rabbinical supervision of the flow of information. "The development of Facebook is a tragedy. It is not possible that the Haredi community – trained from a young age towards the separation between men and women – should have a mixed social network," said Rabbi Mordechai Blau of the so-called Committee for the Purity and Sanctity of the Camp. One leading Haredi body, Agudath Israel of America, for example, held a special session at its annual convention in 2006, entitled "Have bloggers declared open season on *Torah* authority?" One speaker declared blogs to be "actors in the tradition of Korah, the Saducees and the Enlightenment Movement in the 18th century" (Deen 2014). As with earlier Internet battles, the chances of rabbinical bans against Facebook being wholly accepted throughout the community were limited. Instead, the matter lay with grassroots Facebook users to develop their own Haredi Facebook code of networking.

In contrast to the Haredim, modern Orthodoxy, in recognizing that social networking is a feature of the twenty-first century, favors developing tools for a more controlled participation in social networking. It is, they argue, a modern reality where even discussions about Judaism take place. They may be as concerned as Haredi rabbis about how social media might facilitate improper relationships between men and women. However, social media offers the modern Orthodox rabbi a creative way to reach thousands of people, in a way that would not have been possible in the pre-Internet era, including sharing thoughts with congregants – not only with those who come to synagogue but also those who seek to share "virtually" their thoughts and beliefs online. Rabbis in the Jewish Diaspora have used networking sites like Facebook as tools for pastoral work. This is less true of Orthodox rabbis within Israel.

One modern Orthodox educator, Yona Goodman (2012), proposed handling social networking both through tactical or technological means and through strategic means. In the case of the former, he proposed that limiting the use of Facebook to youths aged thirteen and over be enforced by families in practice, with hours fixed daily or weekly, and that parents monitor their children's activities remotely. In terms of strategy, Goodman adopted a media literacy approach, namely to educate children to be selective about with whom they network, only networking with people with whom they are acquainted, only networking with members of their own sex and only posting photos of themselves if they will not object to them being shared more widely.

COPYRIGHT AND DATA PRIVACY

The protection of information is recognized by Judaism, and intellectual property is to be protected no less than physical property. Material, such as a book or song, which is the exclusive property of one person, may not be copied without the owner's permission. While copyright ownership cannot be claimed over news coverage of events which are publicly known, investigative journalism in which one news organization is the exclusive source of information may claim exclusivity. "News borrowing" of information in the latter category is, therefore, only permitted where permission has been obtained. One exception in copyright is the *Torah*, because it is not regarded as the property of one person.

Copying tapes and video cassettes is regarded by most rabbis as stealing, regardless of whether or not there will be a loss and even if the copy is for educational purposes. Rabbis are inclined to prohibit copying computer software both because that would deprive the owners, who have invested large sums in its production, of their livelihood, as well as because it infringes the laws of the state (*dina d'malhuta dina*). Further, all rabbis forbid copies of software to be made for commercial use, and some rabbis forbid copying even if it is only for personal use, because otherwise the person would buy additional copies. However, some allow a back-up copy for personal use only.

Many people regard downloading and copying texts as acceptable practice, particularly in light of a basic principle in Jewish law that, once an owner has given up possession of an object that has gone missing and has no expectation of it being returned, the object does not have to be returned. Yet most rabbis from different Jewish religious streams (Leff 2007) agree that, while information technology has become more sophisticated, the ethical issues that led to the creation of copyright laws remain the same. Whether it is respect for the "laws of the state" or Jewish religious law itself, the rights of authors and publishers need to be respected. One Orthodox rabbi, Nahum Weisfish (2010), distinguishes between profit-oriented matter, where the author or creator will feel a loss if not reimbursed for his creative property, and not-for-profit material. In the former, he argues, copying creative work is tantamount to theft, according to most authorities on Jewish law (*Halakhah*), while a minority of rabbis see it as theft only if the owner specifically stipulates a prohibition on duplication. In the case of nonprofit material, it is permissible to reproduce material if it is clear that the creator would not object. However, it is forbidden to alter material even for noncommercial purposes, since it is assumed that the creator will object.

The question of copyright has been readdressed in the digital age where so much has been placed on the Internet, with the focus on questions of data protection and privacy. Eighty-eight percent of Americans polled in 1998 thought that their privacy was threatened, in contrast to only 34 percent when polled in 1970.[1] While it is true that the debate about privacy and computers has not been influenced by rabbis in the main, it does reflect the tension between openness and privacy in Judaism in its uphill and foundering battle

---

[1] National Association of Attorneys General Annual Conference, June 2000, Seattle, Washington.

to maintain the Jewish principle of the superiority of the right to privacy over the principle of the right to know.

Given the ability to gather information (even basic consumer data resulting from monitoring or surveillance of a person's computer usage) or to construct a profile of a person's use, the problems of privacy in the age of computers and the Internet have assumed greater importance. The use, and sale, of information about a person's predilections should, according to Jewish sources, not be used without the person's knowledge and consent. Some companies today acknowledge the right of the computer surfer to indicate on his computer that information about his surfing behavior should not be gathered. Moreover, according to some rabbis, a person should be able to see whether information is held about him or her and to correct it (Dorff and Spitz 2001).

The religious commandment against *loshon hara* and the Jewish principle of privacy become intermingled in the computer age. The question of surveillance by a state of its citizens and even of noncitizens was raised because of the surveillance activities of the US National Security Agency in order to locate terrorists. This entailed massive surveillance of audio, video, e-mail, and documents held by Internet service providers. One Conservative rabbi, David Golinkin, justified this because "it might have prevented the death of almost 3,000 people on 9/11. If electronic surveillance saves lives, I believe that Jewish law would sanction such surveillance. After all, Judaism allows, indeed requires, that this information in such a case be passed to the authorities" (Golinkin 2013, p. 3). Yet, Judaism clearly doesn't permit total surveillance of individuals or allow for the information to be used for other reasons.

Meir has argued that *loshon hara* is not just passing information to somebody, but also the mere gathering of the information itself. Given the prohibition of *hezek reyah*, or looking into one's neighbor's property, Meir argues that engaging in a web search that discloses private information not available from a casual Googling is religiously questionable (Meir 2014, p. 35). The intermingling of the laws of privacy and of *loshon hara* appears to confirm the view discussed above that the various related laws of speech show the respect which Judaism gives to the privacy of the individual.

One solution would be to redefine the very discussion of privacy. In preserving the Jewish ideal of privacy in the age of digital media, one way is to refocus contemporary debate about the threat to privacy upon the individual. There is a need to give greater emphasis to human dignity, including the right to privacy. Washofsky, advancing the Reform school of Progressive Halakhah, proposes that "man shows restraint before he shares his life with the virtual universe – to consider the potential outcome of one's actions before one posts, uploads text or tweet" (Washofsky 2014, p. 120). Releasing oneself more from

"Big Brother" and from data control, to an obligation on the individual to take personal responsibility, is not dissimilar to the original biblical injunction for Jews: to build the ideal community in the image of God.

SOCIO-RELIGIOUS CONTROL OF INFORMATION

Given the free flow of information that characterizes the modern state of Israel, it is instructive to examine how different communities in Israel today view speech, communication, and the transfer of information. One only needs to divide any discussion between the ultra-Orthodox (some 10 percent of the Israeli Jewish population) and the modern Orthodox, or *dati leumi*, population (15 percent of the population). While the Reform and Conservative Jewish communities number some 70 percent of the US Jewish population of 6.7 million, these remain very small in Israel, even though they do offer alternative theological views. The 75 percent in Israel not belonging formally to the Orthodox in Israel may be divided between 40 percent who define themselves as "secular" and 35 percent as "traditional" or selective in religious observance. (The last category, "traditional," has been broken down further by the Central Bureau of Statistics, Jerusalem between traditional Jews who are closer to the religious, and those who feel closer to the secular.)

The threat to religious identity encouraged ultra-Orthodox Jews to build cultural ghettos around themselves. Haredi rabbis have over more than a hundred years given religious rulings against exposure of their followers to the media, regarded as a threat to the family values in the *Torah*. From the appearance of newspapers in the nineteenth century, through to the development of radio and television, and latterly video, computers, and Internet and cellphones, Haredi rabbis have enacted such decrees. When Israel Television was established in 1968, Haredi rabbis banned their followers from watching television because its content was considered morally inappropriate. While entertainment per se is not invalidated, the Haredi perspective is nevertheless critical of it, regarding it more as an avoidance of higher activities such as religious study. The bans on television and secular newspapers were the most successful of the bans. An earlier ban on radio, based on the prohibition against hearing *loshon hara* as well as the importance of modesty, was less widely observed because Israel's ongoing security problems made listening necessary. When video cameras were produced, which many Haredi families used to record family celebrations, no rabbinical ban was introduced initially because usage could be controlled. After it was discovered that entertainment videos could be seen on computers or cameras, video cameras were banned as well (Cohen 2012a).

Tensions regarding access to information peaked with the creation of the Internet. Haredi rabbis took a similar approach toward the Internet as they had taken to earlier media forms, but the existence of, for example, pornographic websites was seen as a greater threat than that from all earlier media forms. Haredi rabbis had established a committee on communication affairs which, over the years, discussed the ramifications for their community of the computer. Initially, in 2000, the committee imposed a ban on the computer itself but, in recognition of its role in e-mail communication and *Torah*-related programs, it retracted, and the debate switched to the question of the Internet, given its accessibility to sex-related sites (Cohen 2011). Broadly, three approaches could be identified in the discussions of those Haredi rabbis who did not ban the Internet in its entirety or computers themselves. According to one, albeit lenient, approach, access is given to all Internet sites except those sites known specifically to have problematic content. According to a stricter approach, the content of all sites had to be examined. A disc comprising some 3,000 approved sites was prepared by one Haredi body. A third approach recognized that different people have different Internet requirements: a businessman will need access to different sites than those required by, for example, a school principal. Accordingly, each person would submit the sites for which they require access to a Haredi computer-screening committee, to seek approval for the contents of each site. This third approach has an inbuilt contradiction. Moreover, different approaches within the Haredi world mean that some Haredi sub-communities are stricter than others; thus, Haredim of one community may find themselves given access to sites which are not approved by the rabbis of other Haredi sub-communities.

The invention of the Internet poses myriad dilemmas for the Haredim. The centrality of the Internet in twenty-first-century life has left these rabbis in a major quandary in dealing with dangers posed by the Internet. Some Haredi rabbinical fora distinguish between prohibiting the use of the Internet at home and allowing Haredi businesses to be linked to it. By only allowing the Internet for businesses, the intention is to stop children from surfing the web at home. Parallel to these rabbinical discussions there have been a number of commercial attempts by Haredi entrepreneurs to create computer filtering programs. One early attempt, "Torahnet," undertook to process requests for clearance to websites within twenty-four hours.

Like traditional media, the Internet widens the marketplace of religious ideas, weakens rabbinical hierarchies and threatens religious loyalties. If religion in traditional societies was based upon authority vested in religious bodies, in complex industrial societies there is increased emphasis upon personal choice in moral and religious matters, with religious and spiritual issues increasingly mediated through print and electronic technologies. Haredi control over media is threatened from within the Haredi community with the growth of Haredi news websites. A handful of Haredi news websites operate independently from rabbinical supervision. These include *B'Hadrei Haredim* and *Ladaat*. While there are no pictures of women, and there is clearly awareness of the acceptable social limits within the Haredi religio-cultural ghetto, the sites do not subject themselves to the rabbinical censors. These censors, in the case of the Haredi daily press, inspect newspaper copy on a nightly basis. The independent Haredi websites followed the earlier phenomenon since the 1980s of Haredi weekly magazines like *Mishpacha*, *Bakhilla*, and *Shaa Tova*, which have not received the institutional approval of the Haredi rabbis. Like the weeklies, the news sites print uncensored information about the political infighting within different sections of the Haredi world, such as between rival Hassidic courts. At times, the information appears to transgress the prohibitions of *loshon hara*. These are fora for expressing criticism, sometimes vehemently, of the positions and behavior of Haredi leaders.

In contrast to Haredi rabbis, other religious Jews did not see that their religious values were threatened by the media, but have sought to reconcile and integrate modernity with religious life. Modern Orthodox Jews participate at all levels, including engaging in university study. For those living in Israel, the state entity should be run along democratic lines as long as this does not clash with Jewish law. The rabbis of the modern Orthodox (*dati leumi*) stream have not issued legal rulings against exposure to newspapers, radio, and television, reflecting their broader philosophy of seeking to create a synthesis between Judaism and modernity. Use of the Internet has been a subject of debate within the modern Orthodox community as well, though in ways that seek to reconcile modernity with Jewish values. Given the existence of much pornographic material on the Internet, they, no less than the Haredim, have been faced with the question of whether to compromise their open culture view. Three approaches have evolved towards the Internet inside the modern religious community. The most traditional view concerns increasing media literacy, depending on the believing Jew having the self-discipline and maturity not to enter forbidden websites. A more cautious view involves external means of self-discipline: parental supervision of controlled access through filtering processes. The most extreme position, identified with a stricter community within the modern Orthodox entitled "Haredi leumi," requires banning the Internet in its entirety (Cohen 2013).

CONCLUSION

As an ethical system seeking to elevate Man created in God's image, Judaism is concerned first and foremost with the need for social correction. Clearly, Judaism would prefer its watchdog role to function away from the glare of the cameras, such as reporting confidentially to a parliamentary committee. Judaism does favor bringing social misdemeanor to the attention of the police. However, if the police or civil authorities are so corrupt that they fail to deal with social misdemeanors, then a citizen has a social and moral obligation to encourage correction, including by going to the media. The problem arises in Jewish law when the media perceives exposure of a social misdemeanor more as a competitive scoop or as an ambitious reporter ingratiating himself with editors, rather than as a noble act of good citizenry.

The ultra-Orthodox Haredi stream, feeling threatened and alienated by Israel's secular Western-style media, has erected its own cultural barriers and produces its own alternative media. The dilemmas regarding speech ethics for Judaism have peaked regarding the flow of information characterizing social networks. True, not all Orthodox rabbis invalidate the substantial so-called middle category of information in the public sphere or, at least, do not appear to invalidate it en masse. However, the pre-eminent influence which the *Hofetz Hayyim* enjoys in any discussion on Jewish speech ethics must raise certain doubts as to what extent Jewish media ethics on speech share common ground with Western media ethics. Certainly, questions addressed by the *Hofetz Hayyim* become even more relevant in the digital media age. Kagan, the author of *Hofetz Hayyim*, was writing in the nineteenth century when Europe had an ideological political press and the newspapers enjoyed free rein to attack political opponents. Were he alive today, one speculates whether Kagan would have dealt differently with speech in the digital age. Moreover, the information age in general and the Internet in particular are characterized by a superhighway of information and images. Overall, images, information and impressions go far beyond questions of what should or should not be in the public sector. Jewish speech and communication ethics do not offer a sophisticated view regarding the Internet. If Judaism does have guidelines about information comprising text, it has even less to say about the accuracy with which pictures and images represent reality.

REFERENCES

Ariel, A. 2001. "Loshon HaRah B'Maarrerkhet Tzibori Democrati" ("Evil gossip in the public democratic framework"), *Tzohar* (6) Lod.

Chwat, A. I. 1995. *Itonim V'Hadashot Mitzva O Isur (Newspapers & News: Religious Obligation or Prohibition)*. Elkana: T'lalei Orot.

Cohen, Y. 2001. "Mass media in the Jewish tradition," in Stout, D. and Buddenbaum, J. (eds.), *Religion & Popular Culture: Studies on the Interaction of Worldviews*. Ames: Iowa State University Press, pp. 95–108.

2006. "Communication in Jewish perspective," in Eilers, F.-J. (ed.), *Social Communication in Religious Traditions of Asia*. Manila: Logos (Divine Word) Publications, pp. 111–24.

2011. "Haredim and the internet: A hate-love affair," in Bailey, M. and Redden, G. (eds.), *Mediating Faiths: Religion and Socio-Cultural Change in the Twenty-First Century*. Aldershot: Ashgate, pp. 63–74.

2012a. *God, Jews & the Media: Religion & Israel's Media*. New York and London: Routledge.

2012b. "God, religion & advertising: A hard sell," in Hetsroni, A. (ed.), *Advertising & Reality: A Global Study of Representation and Content*. London and New York: Continuum, pp. 73–90.

2013. "Awkward encounters: Orthodox Jewry and the internet," in Ahlback, T. (ed.), *Digital Religion*. Abo/Turku, Finland: The Donner Institute for Research in Religious and Cultural History, Abo Akademi University, pp. 42–54.

Contemporary American Reform Responsa (February 1983). "Informing others in criminal matters."

Contemporary American Reform Responsa (February 1984). "Privacy of a convert."

Contemporary American Reform Responsa (November 1986). "Confidential information."

Contemporary American Reform Responsa (1990). "Gossip between husband and wife."

Deen, S. 2014. "Online and unabashed: Orthodox Rabbis and scholars take to the internet," *Tablet*, April 11, 2014. Available at : http://Tabletmag.com/jewish-life-and-religion/168520/orthodox-rabbis-Internet?print=1.

Dorff, E. N. and Spitz, E. K. 2001. *Computer Privacy and the Modern Workplace*. New York: Rabbinical Assembly, HM 331:1.

Falk, E. 1999. "Jewish laws of speech: Toward multicultural rhetoric," *The Howard Journal of Communications* 10 (1): 15–28.

Finklestein, L. 1924. *Jewish Self-Government in the Middle Ages*. New York: JTS Publications.

Freehof, S. B. 1969. "Secrets of the 'confessional'," *Current Reform Responsa*. Hebrew College Press.

Golinkin, D. 2013. "Does Jewish law permit internet surveillance?" *Responsa in a Moment* 7(8): 1–3.

Goodman, Y. 2012. "Edan Ha-Facebook" ("The age of Facebook: Parental power and the educational challenge in religious Zionism"), in Rachimi, M. (ed.), *HaMishpacha B'Ayin Hasaara* (Emdah Annual Research volume). Elkana: Orot Academic Educational College, pp. 109–42.

Gross, B. 2008. *The Holy Tongue & How it Changed the Course of History*. New York: Devora Publishing.

Leff, B. 2007. *Intellectual Property: Can You Steal It If You Can't Touch It?* New York: Rabbinical Assembly, HM 203:1.

Levine, A. 1981. "Advertising and promotional activities as regulated in Jewish law," *Journal of Halacha and Contemporary Society* 1(2): 5–37.

Lev-On, A. and Ben-Shahar, R. N. 2009. "Forum MiShelohem: Emdot B'Yahas L'Internet B'kerev Ha-Golshot B'Forumim Sgurim Ha-Myuodim Lnashim Haredit" ("A forum of their own: Views about the internet among Ultra-Orthodox women who browse designated closed fora"), (Hebrew transliterated title) (4).

Liebes, T. 1994. "Crimes of reporting: The unhappy end of a fact-finding mission in the Bible," *Journal of Narrative and Life History* 43(1–2): 135–50.

Meir, A. 2014. "Internet privacy in Halachah," *Jewish Action* (Winter): pp. 34–5.

Passamaneck, S. M. 1976. "The Talmudic concept of defamation," in Fuss, A. M. (ed.), *Studies in Jurisprudence*, vol. IV. New York: Hermon Press.

Plaut, W. G. and Washofsky, M. (eds.) 1997. *Teshuvah in the Nineties: Reform Judaism's Answers to Today's Dilemmas*. New York: CCAR Press.

Rakover, N. 2006. *Ha-Hagana al Tzinut Ha-Prat (Protection of Privacy in Jewish Law)*. Jerusalem: Jewish Legal Heritage Society.

Shohet, D. M. 1974. *The Jewish Court in the Middle Ages*. New York: Hermon Press.

Washofsky, M. 2014. "Internet, privacy, and progressive Halakhah," in Walter, J. (ed.), *The Internet Revolution and Jewish Law*. Pittsburgh: Solomon B. Freehof Institute of Progressive Halakhah.

Weisfish, N. M. 2010. *Copyright in Jewish Law*. Jerusalem/New York: Feldheim.

Wolpe, D. J. 1992. *In Speech & in Silence*. New York: Henry Holt.

Part III

The West as Progenitor and Modifier
of Concepts of Free Expression

10

Where Should Speech Be Free? Placing Liberal Theories of Free Speech in a Wider Context

Richard Danbury

INTRODUCTION

This chapter advances a modest case for the universality of free speech, in that it argues that many of the justifications for free speech offered in the liberal tradition[1] are convincing beyond such a context. It is intended as a contribution to the literature that wrestles with the problem that human rights in general (and free speech in particular) are expressed in international human rights documents as being universal, but can be challenged as being culturally specific.[2] It does this by drawing attention to, and applying, some elements of free-speech theories from the liberal tradition that do not rely for their persuasive force on the assumptions inherent to liberalism.

The case is worth advancing for at least four reasons. First, discussions about free speech and related questions in liberal democracies that frequently invoke references to democracy and the values of liberalism can lead to a relativist assumption that liberal arguments that defend free speech are more limited than is appropriate. In particular, an assumption can arise that theories offered within the liberal democratic tradition have force only in political environments where the values axiomatic to liberal democracy are afforded a theoretical precedence.

Second, and related to the first point, placing liberal theories of free speech in a wider context draws attention to the fact that arguments that exist for free speech can be severed from debates about wider aspects of political philosophy. This is important, as it can be helpful to

---

[1] By this is meant the tradition of political thought that holds values such as liberty, equality, and autonomy to be of cardinal importance, and the system of administration for which justification is sought by reference to these values. Examples of discussions that relate free speech to liberalism and democracy are discussed below.

[2] The point is discussed in, for example, Donnelly (2013, part II).

distinguish the case for free speech in, for example, China[3] or Saudi Arabia as supplementary to and distinct from more political arguments about liberalism and democracy.

Third, the fact that the free-speech theories described can be somewhat disengaged from their political context is of importance in a world of Internet communication where, given the prevalence, immediacy, and internationality of such communication, questions of the relativity of freedom of speech become acute. Words uttered in one country can now be distributed and readily accessible worldwide, which can lead to a more acute clash of doctrinal and normative traditions as to whether such words should be permitted or restricted than was experienced in the past. One country's free speech, for example, can be another's hate speech. How should one resolve the dilemma that this presents? Some arguments that seek to explain the benefits from permitting free speech rely on liberal foundations; Mackinnon (2012), for example, advances a compelling case on such a basis. However, this chapter explains why such arguments are not the only ways that a case for free speech can be made.

The fourth reason why the viability of non-liberal democratic free-speech theories is significant is that they provide an approach that can be overlooked to resolving dilemmas related to speech within liberal democracies.

An example of one way the analysis in this chapter can be useful can be demonstrated by considering the debate about the so-called "right to be forgotten," which has been spurred by the European Court of Justice's 2014 decision in *Google Spain* v. *AEPD*. This case is discussed in more detail below,[4] but essentially turned on whether Google should be compelled to remove certain private data from its search index. Normative arguments in favor of such a course of action can be advanced on the grounds that certain private data published by Google should be delisted because their presence in Google's index can amount to an affront to the dignity and autonomy of individuals, which are core liberal values. Conversely, the purported right can be challenged on the basis that wide publication of information is necessary in a democracy. Both arguments are appropriate, but this chapter argues that it would be a mistake to think that arguments about this issue, and other subjects related to freedom of speech, need to rely on fundamental liberal values such as dignity and

---

[3]   The argument in this chapter has been developed from observations by Hartmann in his introduction to the first edition of Weisenhaus (2007), which is discussed below. It is also consistent with, but complementary to, the analysis developed in Tong (2011), discussed below in the text to note 16.

[4]   *Google Spain CL* v. *AEPD* C-131/12. See the text to note 21.

autonomy, or the operation of a democracy. There are a significant number of free-speech theories within the liberal tradition that do not.[5]

To describe these, this chapter does not rely on the common taxonomies of free-speech theories developed by Schauer (1982) and Barendt (2007) amongst others because, while eminently useful, they can obscure the ways that such free-speech theories can work. The chapter describes two such mechanisms: the first relating to common psychological reactions to speech and censorship, and the second resting on assumptions about the efficient operation of administrative structures.

This introduction began by calling this a "modest case," because its ambit is curtailed. This is because, after advancing the case for the universality of free speech, it is necessary to balance the chapter by recognizing a relativist argument against universality. Even within the liberal tradition, there is a limit to the extent to which democratic arguments support universalist conclusions about appropriateness of particular instances of speech. The way the notion of freedom of speech is applied in America, for example, is not necessarily the way the notion should be applied in other countries. It is quite appropriate for the bar in relation to Nazi speech, say, to be set differently in a country that did not experience the tyranny of the Third Reich, from where it is set in a country that labored under it. It may be that speech should be free everywhere, but that does not mean that all instances of speech should be free everywhere: the principle may be valid, but the application of the principle should vary. Differences in history, politics, and sociology are crucial.

VARIETIES OF LIBERAL THEORIES OF FREE SPEECH

The idea that speech and expression[6] should be free has a remarkable force in many Western societies, but explaining why speech should be free is difficult. Indeed, Joseph Raz, a prominent contemporary liberal theorist, famously called freedom of speech a "liberal puzzle" (Raz 1991). Consequently, it is not surprising that there have been many attempts within the liberal tradition to explain why it should be free and what it means for it to be free.[7]

---

[5] There are also free-speech arguments that arise outside the liberal tradition. For example, Tong (2011), discussed in the text to note 16, sets out an account that is based on Confucianism.

[6] While the distinctions between speech and expression, and between speech and press freedoms, are important in some contexts, they are not so important in the current discussion as to require explicit distinction. This chapter uses the general term "freedom of speech" unless the context requires otherwise.

[7] Summaries of these theories can be found in Schauer (1982) and Barendt (2007). Moreover, this chapter describes theories advanced by Meiklejohn, Dworkin, Scanlon, Milton, Raz, Blasi, and Bentham.

Part of the difficulty arises from the nature of free-speech theories themselves, in that they seek to address a wide set of questions. These include,
but are not limited to, identifying what freedom of speech is, and working
out why it should be a right. In relation to the first, pertinent questions
include: why speech, as opposed to other activities, should be marked out
for special treatment; what it means for speech to be "free," and in particular
why one should protect speech that one knows or believes to be harmful; and
what the boundaries are between speech that is protected and other activities. Once one has considered the ambit of freedom of speech, there are
further dilemmas to do with what is a "right," why freedom of speech should
be considered to be one, and what this entails. For example, should this
right have legal, moral, or other force, and how should one resolve dilemmas that arise when protected speech conflicts with other desired ends, such
as the security of a state, the privacy and honor of individuals, or the social
and moral imperative to inhibit crime? Finally, for Raz a core puzzle is
why such high importance is frequently placed on free speech when many
people do not value their own individual right particularly highly, particularly in comparison with other interests, such as having employment or "not
running a risk of having an accident when driving along public roads" (Raz
1991, p. 303).

Some take the view that there is one or a few prime theories that justify freedom of speech,[8] others that there are a multitude of theories that complement
each other or, as Lichtenberg has said, "plurality is not necessarily miscellany"
(Lichtenberg 1990, p. 106). It is an assumption of this chapter that the latter
position is correct, but there is insufficient space to argue the point. Hence the
argument proposed here should be seen in the context of the view that theories of free speech interlock, support, or undermine each other, and are related
to a network of other principles that need to be examined when determining
why in general speech might be free, and why a particular instance of speech
should be protected or restricted.

As has been mentioned, the theories that have been proposed to answer
these questions have been classified in a variety of ways. One significant classification distinguishes between consequentialist and deontological theories.
The former seeks to explain why speech should be free by virtue of its immediate or ultimate consequences, and in general terms hold that speech should
be afforded protection because such protection brings about a better state
of affairs than the inhibition of speech. Meiklejohn, for example, essentially

---

[8]   Baker, for example, argues for the primacy of self-expressive liberty as a rationale for free
      speech (Baker 1989).

suggests that freedom of speech is justified as it brings about the free flow of information necessary in a democracy, whereby the self-governing electorate can make informed decisions as to how the state is run (Meiklejohn 1961). Permitting speech to be relatively unrestricted is defensible even if the speech at issue is harmful, relates false information or is motivated by ill will, as the consequences to democracy that will flow from permitting such speech will be better than those that accrue from restricting it.

Deontological theories do not rely on tracking through the consequences of speech to make the case for protecting the activity, but rather look at other rationales. These are various, but are frequently based on structures and logic. Hence, for example, deontological arguments can look at profound political and moral values held to be true, and deduce that freedom of speech follows as a consequence of holding these values. Scanlon proposes a theory along these lines, holding individual autonomy to be a prime value and deducing from this the existence of limits to the extent of which some speech can be appropriately inhibited or prevented (Scanlon 1972).

Other deontological theories focus more on particular political systems and hold that inherent to particular systems are certain axioms. The existence of these axioms leads to the protection of speech, not because of the consequences of so doing, but because such protection is a necessary consequence of holding a prior position. Hence Dworkin derives a right to free speech from the view that equality is axiomatic to a state run along democratic lines. As equality is inherent to the concept of a democracy, freedom of speech should be respected as it is a manifestation of equality: there should be equal respect paid to utterances of those who live in a democracy, as this is part of what it means to treat people equally (Dworkin 1986).

This short and incomplete survey highlights the point that many prominent speech theories rely on the existence or recognition of a set of political structures and political values to be persuasive. This is true both of consequentialist and deontological theories, as the three examples sketched out above show. In the examples given, each theory relies on democracy. It is worth stressing that "democracy" here does not merely connote a set of political structures, as the term can also mean a set of political values, as Dworkin observed (Dworkin 1986, pp. 15–19). Meiklejohn's theory is persuasive within a system administered by democratic structures, and where there is a belief that the people are self-governing and ruled through representatives. Scanlon's is persuasive where individual autonomy is considered to be a prime political value, which is frequently a tenet of liberal democratic thought. Dworkin's account works where the political structures that operate are a version of democracy that holds equality to be an axiomatic value.

This emphasis on liberalism and democracy tends to support a relativist view of free speech that suggests that, generally speaking, free-speech theories are only or mainly applicable to societies that share these assumptions, and so only work in liberal democracies or in political systems that share their values and structures. To counter such a view, it is valuable to emphasize the theories of free speech propounded within the liberal tradition that may have persuasive force in other contexts. Indeed, such an emphasis is also valuable to highlight the importance of such theories, which is sometimes overlooked, in resolving dilemmas that arise within liberal democracies.

This can be done by considering four free-speech theories; all are consequentialist theories, but deontological theories might also make the point. Two theories are primarily based on psychological traits, the other two primarily on political structures of administration. These theories have been chosen because they contrast well with each other, utilizing differing routes and positing differing mechanisms to arrive at a case for protecting speech, mechanisms that it is plausible to assert are present in societies that challenge, at least to some extent, the values of liberal democracy. The survey is brief, illustrative, and not comprehensive, as the intention is to show the viability and applicability of these non-democratic free-speech theories, not to address all the various questions required of a free-speech theory, some of which were set out at the beginning of this chapter.

TWO PSYCHOLOGICAL CONSEQUENTIALIST THEORIES

The first rationale for freedom of speech comes from Milton, the English poet, and the second from the contemporary liberal theorist Raz. Both are consequentialist theories that operate because of psychological characteristics common to many people, but differ in respect of the characteristics on which they rely.

Censorship and Curiosity

To begin with Milton, his famous *Areopagitica*, written in the seventeenth century, is an extended account of why printing should be unlicensed (Milton 1918). While very much a document of its time (Milton limits the tolerance that he would afford to "popery" (Milton 1918, p. 60)), it contains in condensed form many of the arguments that have subsequently been advanced as to why speech should be free. Some of these do not require liberal or democratic presumptions to have persuasive force, and have a remarkable resonance today.

One argument of particular resonance relates to the unintended consequences of restricting speech. It relies on a common psychological reaction, namely that things that are hidden invoke curiosity. Milton, citing Sir Francis Bacon, puts the point this way: "suppressing sects and schisms ... raises them and invests them with a reputation ... a forbidden writing is thought to be a certain spark of truth that flies up in the faces of them who seek to tread it out" (Milton 1918, p. 43). Given the curiosity that frequently arises when a person is told not to listen to a particular instance of speech, attempts at suppression will frequently fail. Indeed, not only will they fail, but they may well lead to exactly the opposite result from that intended by the putative suppressor, by advertising the information and drawing people's attention to it. This is because attempts at the suppression of information frequently garland speech with an allure, or even provoke outright resistance and defiance amongst those from whom it is attempted to withhold information, which advertises the speech.

The reason that this argument resonates is because Milton's case bears a striking resemblance to a contemporary argument against suppression of information on the Internet called the "Streisand effect." This effect, named after the singer Barbra Streisand, was identified after Streisand attempted to restrict viewing of an aerial photo of her house that had been placed online. Ironically, this action led to a vast increase in the number of times the photograph was viewed (Nabi 2014). The attempt at suppression of the photograph inspired curiosity amongst people, which led to an unintended consequence at odds with the intention of the putative suppressor of the information, very much in the way described by Milton.

Now, this argument against suppression is limited. One limitation is that it would be naïve to assume that complete suppression is impossible; indeed, there are too many occasions throughout human history where information has effectively been completely suppressed. Examples may not be required to illustrate this simple point but, if they are, they can be found in many jurisdictions where injunctions prevent the reporting of particular facts of court cases: such information is effectively suppressed. Where suppression is effective, then there will be no allure and no curiosity, and the attempt at suppression will lead to the consequences desired by the suppressor, not those that are undesired.

That said, it is clear that this case for freedom of speech, albeit limited, does not depend for its persuasive force on liberal assumptions or democratic structures. This is because it rests on the particular characteristic of human curiosity and how it is piqued by attempts at suppression. It is a plausible claim that this characteristic is likely to be relatively widespread, although clearly not universal. Wherever it is found, this is an argument that is likely to be persuasive as to why suppression of speech might be ill-advised, even for those who think the speech in question is wrong or may be harmful. It is, in other words, a theory that applies in countries and contexts outside the liberal tradition.

Some support for this view can be found from the fact that the argument has been advanced in different societies and contexts. It seems to have been recognized, for example, in Roman times. Clearly there is a close association with classical politics and liberalism, so the inferences to be drawn from this should not be overstated. But Lange (1975) cites the Roman historian Tacitus as describing a similar consequence of an act of censorship. It seems that he is referring to Tacitus's account of what happened when Emperor Nero banned the works of Cremutius Cordus. Despite Cordus's books being burned, interest was maintained in his works, which led Tacitus to observe, "one is … inclined to laugh at the stupidity of men who suppose that the despotism of the present can actually efface the remembrances of the next generation. On the contrary, the persecution of genius fosters its influence" (Tacitus 1876, p. 4.23).[9] The same might also plausibly be said of the persecution of stupidity.

Validation and Alienation

A second psychological consequentialist theory emerges from recognizing one further difficulty with the Miltonian argument. This difficulty arises because of the assumption in Milton's theory that it is a common psychological reaction to suppression to seek to find out what was suppressed. Some, it is reasonable to observe, do not react in this way. Recognizing that this is so leads to the argument, or to be more exact the pair of arguments, advanced by Raz, of why one should not to suppress speech is based on the observation that some people feel alienated, not intrigued, by the suppression of speech.

Raz's account (Raz 1991) starts with the observation that it is generally very much in the interests of individuals to feel a part of, and included in, a wider society. He notes the importance of public forms of communication in creating such a sense of inclusion, and cites as an example the portrayal of life in a television sitcom. He observes that the portrayal of a particular form of life in such an act of public expression can validate that form of life, familiarize the public with it, and reassure the many who share the characteristics

---

[9] Lange (1975, p. 93) goes on to quote a summary of Tacitus: "so long as the possession of these writings was attended by danger, they were eagerly sought and read; when there was no longer any difficulty in securing them, they fell into oblivion."

portrayed that they are not alone. This validation helps people who live the form of life portrayed to identify with and assimilate in a society, and presents the form of life portrayed as a valid way of living. Not only is this of benefit to such individuals, but such validation can also be of benefit to others who live in the society. It is, in other words, a public good because individuals do not need to have their life portrayed to receive a benefit, as the benefits from inclusion accrue to anyone living in a cohesive society with which people feel they can identify. One example of a form of life to which this argument relates is homosexuality, the portrayal of which in public discourse can validate, reassure, and bind gay people into a society. This provides a benefit, whether one is gay or straight.

Conversely, Raz argues, when a portrayal of a particular form of life is suppressed, it amounts to an official condemnation of that way of life. This is an insult not only to those who have had their speech curtailed, but also to those whose lives are not represented. Further, because Raz holds that every content-based suppression amounts to official condemnation of a way of life through being criminalized or censored, there is harm in such an act to the common interest of all in that society. It is because these arguments, which Raz terms the validation and censorship arguments, have consequences beyond those felt by the particular individuals affected by validation and censorship that there is a cogent reason to resist suppressing speech and expression. To do so brings about detrimental consequences to society as a whole.

It is beyond the scope of this chapter to investigate Raz's arguments in detail, but one point should be covered. This is the fact that Raz does not advance these arguments as the sole case for free speech, but presents them to be combined with the other rationales that explain why restricting speech can be wrong. In particular, in response to the criticism that his theories do not answer the question of why one should protect bad speech, Raz observes that for such an account one should pay regard to some of the other principled arguments for free speech beyond this theory, which his theory is intended to supplement.[10] This is important, because it draws attention to the fact that Raz sees his free-speech arguments very much as part of a wider set of liberal arguments about the nature of society and individuals. Indeed, he conceives his discussion about free speech as part of a wider political philosophy of liberal perfectionism: the notion that states should encourage individuals to develop and live a good life, in Aristotelian terms. That presents difficulties for the present purposes because this chapter aims to show how

---

[10] Examples of such theories include those canvassed in this chapter.

some free-speech theories can apply beyond liberal societies, and it appears that Raz's do not.

However, the problems are not insurmountable; even though Raz sees his arguments as fitting into a wider liberal scheme, some central mechanisms of his free-speech argument do not rest on wider liberal theories. Rather, they rest on two presumptions: one about human psychology, that people frequently feel validated by public speech and alienated by its suppression; and the other about the benefits that accrue to all from being able to affiliate to one's society. To the extent that these are perceived to be present (in the case of the psychological assumption) and valuable (relating to the social and political assumption), then his argument against restricting speech can have force outside liberalism.

The latter point is somewhat more controversial than the former, and hence requires further comment. This is because, to some who do not hold liberal views, social affiliation may not have much value: a theocratic state, for example, might pay greater heed to the precepts of a revealed religion than to the benefits that accrue to society from individuals having a sense of belonging. In such a context, the Razian argument would not have much force, because according to such a worldview, even if a public good arises from avoiding alienation or encouraging validation, that benefit may not be considered to be particularly important. Therefore, is it not true that this argument is confined to those who see tolerance and social affiliation as of central importance in a political scheme or, in other words, to those who are likely to adhere to this aspect of liberalism? The answer is "not necessarily." After all, all that is required for this facet of Raz's theory to be convincing is to accept that there is a benefit to all in a society, deriving from individuals feeling affiliated to the group in which they live. One does also need to have views characteristic of liberalism and democracy about the primacy of autonomy, equality, or democratic representation to agree that there are beneficial consequences that can flow from individuals feeling closely affiliated to the group in which they live. If this assumption about the importance of social affiliation can be valid outside liberal democracies, then this freedom-of-speech theory can be applicable in such contexts.

Together, the two psychological free-speech arguments described, Milton's and Raz's, provide different but complementary accounts as to why speech should be free. They are limited and not comprehensive theories, and their boundaries have not been mapped; questions, for example, as to their scope and strength have not been addressed. However, what is clear is that the assumptions on which they rest are not solely liberal or democratic assumptions, and hence they have applicability beyond liberal societies.

TWO POLITICAL CONSEQUENTIALIST THEORIES

The second set of free-speech theories contrast with the psychological accounts and relate to the structures of the administration of a state. The first can be associated with the contemporary American theorist Blasi, the second with the eighteenth-century British philosopher Bentham. They have a common theme, in that they hold that free speech is valuable in ensuring that administration is appropriately limited, efficient, noncorrupt, and fair, but they operate in subtly different ways. Despite the fact that they have been propounded from within the liberal tradition, both are applicable outside it.

What is required for these theories to apply is not that liberal democratic values and structures are recognized, but rather that there is an aspiration in a society that there should be an efficient, effective, non-corrupt, and controlled administration, whether public or private. Clearly these requirements are not evident in every context and every state, but, equally clearly, they are present even in states where the public only has a limited hold over the authorities. What is required, in other words, is a belief in the need for an administration to be well-run, not a belief that it is legitimate according to liberal democratic norms.

Policing of Power

Blasi, to begin with, defends free speech on the grounds that it can restrain power (Blasi 1977). This is brought about, Blasi holds, because permitting speech to be relatively unrestricted facilitates the investigation, discovery, and communication of information about the use, and in particular the abuse, of power. The mechanism can be seen at work in many cases both in the past and, in recent times, arguably at least, in the speech containing the revelations linked to Edward Snowden and Julian Assange. In the way sketched out by Blasi's theory, such speech uncovered at least some excesses of governmental action, about which the public was not aware.[11]

Some aspects of Blasi's theory make it particularly relevant in an age of Internet communication. This is because he identifies certain contingent factors about modern government, which mean that this function of speech has

---

[11] A classic example is the Pentagon Papers reporting of *The New York Times* and others, which led to *New York Times Co. v. United States*, 403 U.S. 713 (1971). More contemporary and international examples include United Kingdom's Channel 4 *Dispatches* program, *Sri Lanka's Killing Fields*, first broadcast in 2011.

becomes more important the bigger and more complex that governments and the communication environment have become.

> The inevitable size and complexity of modern government is related to another premise that underlies my understanding of the contemporary significance of the checking value. This is the need for well organized, well-financed, professional critics to serve as a counterforce to government – critics capable of acquiring enough information to pass judgment on the actions of government, and also capable of disseminating their information and judgments to the general public. (Blasi 1977, p. 541)

It is evident from this excerpt that Blasi's account is particularly applicable to the institutional press, and indeed it arguably provides the basis of an account as to why institutional journalists merit special treatment. However, to be persuasive, Blasi's idea does not necessarily have to be so confined, because the Internet has greatly widened people's ability to investigate and report on power. Such action is no longer confined, to the extent that it was in the past, to people affiliated to organs of institutional journalism. The Bellingcat website provides a notable example.[12] Indeed, this phenomenon has spurred scholars such as Dutton to argue that the traditional Fourth Estate[13] function of the media can be supplemented by a Fifth Estate of networked individuals performing similar functions (Dutton 2008). Blasi's justification for free speech can therefore be seen potentially to be widely applicable in an online world. Moreover, it is not a phenomenon confined to online communication in liberal democratic countries, as even official Chinese information channels praise the ability of speech on Chinese social media to combat corruption (China.org.cn, 2013; Xinhua agency, 2013).[14]

Does one have to be a liberal democrat to find Blasi convincing? Two factors that arise from Blasi's own account of his theory would suggest one would have to be, but both are superficial. The first is that Blasi locates his theory very much in American jurisprudence, describing it as the checking value of the First Amendment and characterizing it as an interpretation of a rationale behind the First Amendment to the US Constitution. However, it is of wider application. This is because it draws on the idea that speech can police the

---

[12] www.bellingcat.com.
[13] Other accounts agree with Dutton's proposal, notably Benkler's idea that there is a "networked public sphere" (Benkler 2006, ch. 7).
[14] Conversations with Chinese journalists indicate that the benefits perceived by those governing China to pertain from investigations to uncover corruption are likely to tail off the closer an investigation comes to the central administration: "beating flies and leaving tigers," in the words of Tong (2011, p. 28).

misuse of power (corruption, misfeasance, inefficiency, and the like) and this may be true outside the United States as much as it is within. Indeed, even in a country such as the United Kingdom that has a political rather than a legal constitution, the function of free speech in policing executive action may be all the more important than in a country like the United States where this task is primarily undertaken, in theory at least, by the judiciary. Similarly, the theory has force in many countries with legal constitutions but relatively ineffective judiciaries, which may include non-liberal democratic countries, where the executive is not sufficiently overseen and official bodies do not work adequately to keep the executive under appropriate control.[15]

The second concern about the wider applicability of Blasi's theory is that Blasi conceives his idea as grounded in the context of American democracy, and indeed relies on this for a deeper rationale for the legitimacy of this function of speech. He conceives democracy as a means of self-government, and free speech as a means of curtailing the power of the state so that the autonomy of the self-governing individuals who constitute the state is preserved. Clearly, therefore, Blasi's account is firmly situated within liberalism. But again, as was the case with the psychological theories, elements of Blasi's theory remain convincing even without this conceptual architecture. What are required are two beliefs that do not rely on the tenets of liberalism. The first is a belief that a state is better if it is non-corrupt, efficient and the like, and the second that freedom of speech can facilitate the discovering of abuses of power. Neither of these is linked to the structures of liberal thought and, where they are granted, Blasi's theory provides a rationale for permitting speech to be free without relying on presumptions of liberalism.

In practice, does this amount to a case that these theories of free speech have persuasive force, stripped of this aspect of their liberal democratic assumptions? Taking China as an example, it seems that it does. Zhou Yuezhi argued as long ago as 2000 that the Communist Party used investigative journalists to investigate corruption in local bureaucracy, which appears to engage the "policing of power" rationale for speech, in a non-liberal democratic context (Zhou 2000). Admittedly, Zhou indicated that the picture is somewhat complicated by the fact that the intention behind official endorsement of an investigation may have been prompted as much by the desire to control local administrators as by the curtailment of bad administration. Nevertheless, a more thorough grounding of these free-speech activities in a non-liberal democratic tradition is advanced by Jingrong Tong, who places

---

[15] This is not to suggest that liberal-democratic countries necessarily provide sufficient oversight of executive bodies.

investigative journalism (to which these theories of free speech have a particular affinity) in a Chinese philosophical context. Tong identifies this activity as consonant with, and indeed situated in, Confucianism, late Qing liberalism and Communist Maoism (Tong 2011, pp. 15–27).[16] She puts the point this way: "Confucian authoritarian regimes need intellectuals ... to provide criticism to improve the regime at the same time as comprising with and belonging to the system" (Tong 2011, p. 23).[17] Further, that the intention is "to reveal the problems and pitfalls within society in order to correct them, rather than challenging the prevailing political system and overthrowing the ruling Party completely" (Tong 2011, p. 29). It should be emphasized that it is not necessary to take a view on the merits or otherwise of overthrowing the ruling party, to see that this analysis shows how liberal theories of free speech, that defend it as being beneficial because it amounts to a force for the policing of power, can be applied outside a liberal political context.

Inhibiting Misfeasance

The second political free-speech theory is similar to Blasi's in that it deals with policing abuses of power. However, in this case, instead of investigating and uncovering such action, the suggestion is that freedom of speech inhibits misfeasance. This theory is prominent within the English legal system and derives from the writings of Jeremy Bentham. Indeed, one of the cornerstones of the British conception of open justice is this passage, which is frequently referred to in English case law: "[w]here there is no publicity there is no justice. Publicity is the very soul of justice. It is the keenest spur to exertion, and surest of all guards against improbity. It keeps the judge himself while trying under trial" (Bentham 1789, p. 316).

The idea here is that the presence of relatively free speech can act as a force for good by preventing misdeeds. This is one reason why there is a presumption in English courts that trials will be conducted in public and will be reportable;[18] moreover, there are concrete examples of the principle in action in wider spheres than the merely legal. In one famous incident, government minutes were ultimately made public, recording the decision of a British civil servant not to cover up evidence in a high-profile trial. The evidence was embarrassing to the government, and it was the existence of free speech and

---

[16] Tong distinguishes Qing liberalism from Western liberalism (Tong 2011, p. 22).

[17] Nevertheless, Tong concedes that "the adversarial relationship that Chinese investigative journalism has with the ruling Party is not fundamentally thorough" (Tong 2011, p. 27).

[18] However, there are numerous exceptions to this general rule.

active journalists exercising this right that prevented the civil servant advising that the material be withheld from the trial court. The civil servant wrote that his decision not to cover up was motivated by apprehension that "the informa- tion ... may well appear across the front of the tabloid press."[19]

Moreover, and perhaps more relevant to the current argument, this prin- ciple has also been recognized as apposite in other countries. It is an influen- tial doctrine throughout the common law world and, significantly, has been recognized as applicable in relation to Hong Kong, in the context of which Hartmann J observed that a free press (and thereby free speech) is "as import- ant as an independent judiciary. For how can a judiciary remain independent unless its actions are themselves subject to scrutiny?" (Weisenhaus 2007, p. x). This is significant because one can see that this argument potentially applies as much to mainland China, and elsewhere, as it does to Hong Kong.

Again, it should be noted, as it has been in relation to the other free-speech theories described here, that there are limitations to this case for speech. Jaconelli holds, for example, in relation to the operation of Bentham's prin- ciple in court, that publicity is not a significant operating factor in keeping judges on the straight-and-narrow, but a more weighty pressure is the opin- ion of their judicial peers (Jaconelli 2002). Moreover, in other situations Bentham's case can plausibly be turned on its head, and it can be asserted that publicity is as much a chill on free speech as it is a lubricant, as forthright discussions normally held behind closed doors may be impeded if they are made public. One may not want to speak freely if one's words will be recorded and published. And this is not to mention the potentially distorting effect of publicity on speech. This leads to the risk, while not strictly to do with free- dom of speech, that some politicians may become more demagogic in front of a microphone or a camera than when they are talking in private.

However, these concerns, and similar arguments that can be mounted against this case for free speech, do not impede the point being advanced. Whatever its limitations, the argument remains a persuasive rationale for free speech, so long as it is accepted that there can be a benefit in publicity. For it is not only in liberal democratic societies that publicity may impede bad behav- ior, because it is not only in liberal democratic societies that shame, guilt, and being ostracized can arise from one's misdeeds becoming widely known.[20] To

---

[19] The letter contained evidence pertinent to what became called the Matrix Churchill trial, a 1992 prosecution of businessmen for exporting arms to Iraq. The businessmen's defense was that they had acted with governmental authority. Quoted by Bowers (2007, §1.20).

[20] It is difficult to provide an example of this having occurred, as it necessitates proving that something did not happen, or was inhibited, as a result of the existence of publicity. The example in note 19 only came to light because of a judicial inquiry.

put the point in the famous words of the American jurist Brandeis (who was applying the point in a non-legal context, advocating the benefits of publicity in what we now call the financial services industry): "[s]unlight is said to be the best of disinfectants; electric light the most efficient policeman" (Brandeis 1914, p. 92).

PAYING MORE REGARD TO THESE THEORIES WITHIN LIBERAL SOCIETIES

It will be remembered that, as well as seeking to argue for the greater application of these theories beyond the context of liberal democracies, this chapter also seeks to argue that greater regard should be paid to these theories when considering some issues of free speech within them. This will be briefly illustrated, first with regard to the psychological theories described and then the political theories.

Psychological Theories and the "Right to be Forgotten"

The relevance of the psychological theories can be demonstrated by referring to Google and what has become known as the "right to be forgotten." This "right" is a shorthand term for the consequences of the European Court of Justice's decision in *Google Spain* v. *AEPD*. By applying data protection law, the court in this case indicated that certain items of personal data should be removed from Google's indexing of the web. Is this an appropriate restriction on Google's freedom to speak and the public to know?[21] Arguments rage over the question, many relying on the democratic theories of speech, which operate by discerning damaging consequences for democracy that may arise from exercising the right.

However, both Milton and Raz's theories, among others, also have an application here. Milton's theory applies, particularly in its modern variant of the Streisand effect, because the removal of such a fact may prompt people to become suspicious, about the de-indexed fact and what it entails, and encourage them to conduct greater research. De-indexing may therefore have the unintended consequence of highlighting the information that such an act seeks to obscure. Additionally, the removal of the fact may incur suspicion about the fact of removal itself and the rationales for undertaking this course

---

[21] Article 10 of the European Convention on Human Rights includes a right to receive, as well as impart, ideas, although there is disagreement as to the existence and nature of a "right to know."

of action. Raz's validation and censorship arguments may apply where links to material that could validate people's lives are removed from search engines. It is feasible, for example, that the de-indexing of a shameful episode from the past of a prominent figure may inhibit the ability of a young person, who has committed a similar crime, to recognize the possibility that they too can reform and be rehabilitated into society.

Of course, these factors are not determinative and, despite them, it may still be appropriate to recognize a right to be forgotten and compel Google to de-index search results. However, due regard should be paid to the theories described above in debates such as this, and care needs to be taken to avoid focusing solely on the liberal democratic arguments for speech.

Political Theories and Media Plurality

A similar point can be made with respect to the political theories for free speech. To illustrate this, one can look at contemporary discussions around issues of media plurality, particularly the issue of anti-concentration laws, prohibiting media owners from possessing too many news outlets. Other areas of concern include the extent to which it is appropriate to mandate that certain news outlets must carry, or offer, particular content. Such interventions in the media market are contentious and require justification in response to those who consider them to be inappropriate. In defending them, recourse can be made to democracy theories, which is entirely appropriate. However, in doing so there is a risk that the sorts of free-speech arguments described in this chapter may be overlooked.[22]

To give a particular example, one issue of debate is the extent to which local reporting should be mandated, and indeed perhaps subsidized by the government, given that in many countries it is not commercially viable to provide extensive local reporting. In justifying the direct or indirect subsidization of this activity, recourse is frequently made to arguments related to democratic arguments for free speech. These emphasize, in a way set out by Meiklejohn, issues concerning the accountability of elected officials to the electorate and the need to inform people of what is happening in their local administration.

There is no doubt that there is a place for such arguments, but there are difficulties in mounting such a case. Perhaps the most significant is that it is plausible to assume that many local people are not particularly interested in

---

[22] This is not to say that scholars have not recognized the existence of such arguments, as is demonstrated by Hitchens (2006, ch. 2). The point, however, is that their implications have not been fully examined.

the day-to-day events of their local administration. Indeed, this is evidenced at least in part by the inability of news organizations to make money from gathering and selling this news. Moreover, even if the gathering of the material were subsidized, there are still significant concerns about whether it would be consumed by the local electorate. It appears likely, particularly in countries such as the United Kingdom, that news relating to local democracy is not something people readily consume. Further, if people do not wish to become informed to the extent that Meiklejohn assumes they will, democratic arguments of his stripe have only limited persuasive force and any case for subsidizing local news-gathering will be weakened.

However, this is where there is merit in considering separately the type of arguments described above. In particular, the Benthamite argument is effective in supporting the case for subsidizing local news-gathering. This is because it is not particularly relevant for the argument to work whether or not the local electorate actually read the local news that has been gathered by virtue of a subsidy. Instead the argument works by recognizing that the mere fact of there being a reporter is likely to inhibit misfeasance in local administration. Evidently, there is a link to the Meiklejohnian democratic argument, in that, where such misfeasance is discovered and reported, the local electorate will be informed, but it has a distinct viability. This is because, to be effective, it does not require, as does the democratic argument, anyone to read the news; it is effective by the mere fact that there is a news-gatherer observing and recording who acts as an inhibitor. By invoking the prospect of shame and guilt, and indeed being ostracized, the Benthamite theory operates by virtue of the state of mind of the local administrator who might be tempted to act in an inappropriate way. This distinct mechanism, therefore, means it should be considered separately when evaluating the propriety of subsiding local news-gathering, and failure to do so is an omission.

CONCLUSION

This chapter has sought to show how free-speech arguments from the liberal tradition may have a wider application beyond their conceptual home in liberalism and affect a wider range of societies than is sometimes recognized. However, having advanced a universalist position in relation to free speech, it is useful to conclude the account with some relativist observations. This is because some free-speech arguments are less universal than they seem, as they can lead to certain speech being appropriately unrestricted in one liberal democratic country, but appropriately restricted in another comparable state.

To some this may seem somewhat self-evident, but to others it may not. Bollinger, for example, avers that it is good to "encourage the development of a free press around the world, to achieve in this century on a global stage what the United States created on a national stage in the twentieth century" (Bollinger 2010, p. 131). To an extent this is uncontroversial, if it is in general terms asserting that there are sufficient benefits from having a free press to justify exporting the concept; nevertheless, further discussion is clearly needed as to what these benefits are and how they arise. (Indeed, this chapter advances certain reasons in support of such a claim.) However, if Bollinger is advocating exporting the US model of freedom of speech and the press, much greater diffidence is required.

This is not least because exhortation of the benefits of US freedom of speech needs to be tempered with sufficient recognition that the version of free speech and the press found in America is something of an outlier internationally. Indeed, as Schauer explains, this is true both in substantive and methodological terms (Schauer 2005). Some speech acts are protected in the United States that would not be protected in many other countries, such as instances of hate speech and extreme political speech, and the means of free-speech adjudication in the United States is not widespread beyond its borders.

However, there are also more substantive reasons to be wary of the proposal to export a First Amendment approach to free speech. Schauer suggests a number of reasons for this, when explaining the divergence that exists between the United States and other countries. He suggests that America's approach has been the result of (amongst other things) a particular distrust of the government, a preference for liberty over equality (there being frequently a patent tension between the two) and the "seeming absoluteness" of the First Amendment, as drafted. Now these qualities may support the First Amendment approach to free speech within the United States, but their relative absence in other countries undermines the case that it is appropriate for others to follow the US example.

Indeed, in more general terms, it seems evident that appropriate application of free-speech arguments depends greatly on the social and political context and history of the country in which they are being evaluated. This creates a great impediment for the export of the US approach to free speech in particular, but also to the internationalization of free-speech law and policy in general. For example, it *might* be considered appropriate in the United States to permit Nazis to march through a Jewish area, on the strength of the idea that one must protect even harmful speech to have a coherent concept of freedom of speech,[23] but completely inappropriate to permit such an act in

---

[23] *National Socialist Party of America v. Skokie*, 432 U.S. 43 (1977).

Germany given Germany's experience of Nazism in the twentieth century. Freedom of speech and the press may be a virtue, but that does not mean that the American model is the embodiment of virtue or that such freedoms elsewhere should follow its model.

It is important to emphasize that this is not essentially a point about the differences of free-speech theories per se: the theories of Meiklejohn, Dworkin, Scanlon, Milton, Raz, Blasi, and Bentham may be as persuasive in the United States as in Germany. However, even when they are, there are likely to remain differences as to how they are applied, even in comparable countries that share common presumptions about significant political values and operate under generally similar political structures. This is the result of crucial differences of history, sociology, and politics. Hence, even in the age of the Internet, when there is a case for a more universalist recognition of the merits of freedom of speech, precipitated by widespread international communication (a view that this chapter has sought to assist by drawing attention to the fact that some free-speech arguments can be decoupled from liberalism and democracy), caution must remain about the extent to which the application of liberal theories of freedom of speech should be seen as universal.

REFERENCES

Baker, C. E. 1989. *Human Liberty and Freedom of Speech*. Oxford/New York: Oxford University Press.

Barendt, E. 2007. *Freedom of Speech*. Oxford/New York: Oxford University Press.

Benkler, Y. 2006. *The Wealth of Networks: How Social Production Transforms Markets and Freedom*. New Haven: Yale University Press.

Bentham, J. 1789. "Draught of a new plan for the organisation of judicial establishment in France," in Bowring, J. (ed.) 1843, *The Works of Jeremy Bentham with an Outline of His Opinions on the Principal Subjects Discussed in His Works*, Vol. 4. Edinburgh: W. Tait, pp. 285–406.

Blasi, V. 1977. "The checking value in First Amendment theory," *Law & Social Inquiry* 2: 521–649.

Bollinger, L. C. 2010. *Uninhibited, Robust, and Wide Open: A Free Press for a New Century*. New York/Oxford: Oxford University Press.

Bowers, J. 2007. *Whistleblowing: Law and Practice*. Oxford: Oxford University Press.

Brandeis, L. D. 1914. *Other People's Money, and How the Bankers Use It*. New York: Frederick A Stokes Company.

China.org.cn 2013. "Weibo: An eye on corruption," March 11, 2013. Available at: www.china.org.cn/china/NPC_CPPCC_2013/2013-03/11/content_28201650.htm.

Donnelly, J. 2013. *Universal Human Rights in Theory and Practice*. Ithaca, NY: Cornell University Press.

Dutton, W. H. 2008. "The Fifth Estate emerging through the network of networks," *Prometheus* 27: 1–15.

Dworkin, R. 1986. *A Matter of Principle*. Oxford: Clarendon Press.

Hitchens, L. 2006. *Broadcasting Pluralism and Diversity: A Comparative Study of Policy and Regulation*. Oxford: Hart Publishing.

Jaconelli, J. 2002. *Open Justice: A Critique of the Public Trial*. Oxford: Oxford University Press.

Lange, D. 1975. "The speech and press clauses," *UCLA Law Review* 23: 77–119.

Lichtenberg, J. 1990. "Foundations and limits of freedom of the press," in Lichtenberg, J. (ed.),*Democracy and the Mass Media*. Cambridge: Cambridge University Press, pp. 102–35.

Mackinnon, R. 2012. *Consent of the Networked*. New York: Basic Books.

Meiklejohn, A. 1961. "The First Amendment is an absolute," *Supreme Court Review* 1961 1961: 245–66.

Milton, J. 1918. *Areopagitica, with a Commentary by Sir Richard Jebb*. Cambridge: Cambridge University Press.

Nabi, Z. 2014. "Resistance censorship is futile," *First Monday* 19: 11. Available at: http://firstmonday.org/article/view/5525/4155.

Raz, J. 1991. "Free expression and personal identification," *Oxford Journal of Legal Studies* 11: 303–24.

Scanlon, T. 1972. "A theory of freedom of expression," *Philosophy & Public Affairs* 1: 204–26.

Schauer, F. 1982. *Free Speech: A Philosophical Enquiry*. Cambridge: Cambridge University Press.

    2005. "The exceptional First Amendment," in Ignatieff, M. (ed.), *American Exceptionalism and Human Rights*. Princeton/Oxford: Princeton University Press, pp. 29–56.

Tacitus, 1876. *Annals of Tacitus*. London: Macmillan.

Tong, J. 2011. *Investigative Journalism in China: Journalism, Power, and Society*. London: Continuum.

Weisenhaus, D. 2007. *Hong Kong Media Law*. Hong Kong: Hong Kong University Press.

Xinhua Agency 2013. "New media major outlet for exposing corruption," June 25, 2013. Available at: http://en.people.cn/90882/8298919.html.

Zhou, Y. 2000. "Watchdogs on party leashes? Contexts and implications of investigative journalism in post-Deng China," *Journalism Studies* 1: 577–97.

11

The History, Philosophy, and Law of Free Expression in the United States: Implications for the Digital Age

Stephen M. Feldman

The meaning of free expression in the United States has varied through the nation's history. Nowadays, many Americans view the First Amendment protection of free speech and press as a constitutional lodestar (White 1996). Numerous US Supreme Court justices and legal scholars have proclaimed that democracy cannot exist without robust free expression. Yet, American conceptions of democracy changed in the 1920s and 1930s. That change, from republican to pluralist democracy, engendered a significant transformation to a more protective free-expression legal doctrine (Feldman 2008).

Even during the pluralist democratic era, however, the American record regarding free speech and writing remained uneven. To understand free expression in the United States, one must appreciate not only legal doctrine but also the existence of two competing traditions: those of dissent and of suppression. The tradition of dissent embodies the American ethos of speaking one's mind without fear of government punishment. For instance, while a well-developed theory or legal doctrine of free expression did not yet exist in the 1790s, a robust de facto liberty existed. Yet, alongside this tradition, one must acknowledge the countervailing and equally powerful tradition of suppression. Whereas many Americans have reasonably expected to speak their minds without penalty, many (and often the same) Americans have simultaneously suppressed social and cultural outsiders, whether based on race, religion, or otherwise. Suppression has operated through both official (legal) and unofficial (extralegal) mechanisms. Mob violence, tar-and-feathering, and chasing outsiders from town have been common means of suppressing those who seem to diverge too far from the mainstream. Both traditions, dissent and suppression, reach back to the nation's beginnings. During the Revolution, Patriots enjoyed a full sense of free expression; in fact, American newspapers were filled with tributes to the glories of a free press (Levy 1985). Yet, those same Americans were quick to suppress the views of Tories who wanted to voice their support for the British. At the direction of the Continental Congress, numerous towns even created committees of observation or inspection that monitored the output of suspected Tory printers with the ominous vigor of an Orwellian Big Brother (Siebert 1920; Van Tyne 1902).

When it comes to free expression, legal doctrine is important, but it is not everything. As a general matter, legal doctrine harmonized more closely with the tradition of suppression during the era of republican democracy, while it shifted closer to the tradition of dissent during the era of pluralist democracy (starting in the 1930s). Nevertheless, in the course of both the republican and pluralist democratic regimes, both traditions have contributed to the experience and understanding of free expression (Feldman 2008). The degree of free expression at any particular time, for any particular group of Americans, depends greatly on the contemporary political and cultural alignments.

This chapter traces the history, philosophy, and law of free expression in the United States. It concludes by exploring the implications of that background for free-expression issues related to digital technology, particularly in relation to open Internet access. On February 4, 2015, the chair of the Federal Communications Commission (FCC) proposed new rules that would require open Internet access or, as it is commonly called, net neutrality. The FCC soon adopted the proposed rules. Net neutrality requires that all Internet users have open and unrestricted access to the Internet. Internet service providers (ISPs) will be forced to provide all customers with an equal service. Net neutrality, therefore, prevents ISPs, including multinational corporations such as Verizon, Comcast, and AT&T, from charging customers extra for a faster service. The ISP trade groups and lobbying associations have already initiated multiple lawsuits challenging the new FCC rules. At some point, the courts, and probably the Supreme Court, will need to decide whether these rules violate the First Amendment.

THE FRAMING, BILL OF RIGHTS, AND EARLY DOCTRINAL DEVELOPMENTS

The delegates to the Constitutional Convention in 1787 devoted little energy to questions of free expression. The overwhelming majority of delegates believed a Bill of Rights, including express protection for either free speech or a free press, was unnecessary. Once the convention delegates had completed their work though, the national debate over ratification began. While the Anti-Federalist opponents of the Constitution voiced numerous objections to the proposed document, their overriding concern was the continuing viability of state sovereignty vis-à-vis the enhanced sovereign power of the national

government (Maier 2010). These opponents realized, however, that their concerns might garner the most popular traction if they stressed the lack of a Bill
of Rights, which, for many, was also a genuine concern. If the Constitution
would vest enormous power in the national government, as the Anti-Federalists
feared, then the government would be empowered to trample upon many
essential individual rights and liberties. A Bill of Rights, the Anti-Federalists
therefore argued, was essential to protect those rights and liberties and to prevent government tyranny (Storing 1981). The Anti-Federalists repeatedly ham-
mered on this supposed defect in the proposed Constitution and, in doing so,
stressed that freedom of the press, in particular, was unprotected.

Ultimately, in 1788, the states ratified the Constitution, which came into
effect in 1789. Ratification came, however, only after James Madison and
other Federalist leaders committed to adding a Bill of Rights; as a member of
the first House of Representatives, Madison introduced to the first Congress a
draft Bill of Rights on June 8, 1789. Madison's initial draft became all-important
because Congress devoted little time and energy to the substance of the various provisions. Many members of Congress believed a Bill of Rights was relatively inconsequential. They viewed it as an unnecessary redundancy: a Bill of
Rights would reiterate what was already understood, that the national government lacked the power to infringe on individual rights and liberties, such as
freedom of the press. For many Federalists, the Bill of Rights remained little
more than a political bone that they were tossing to the Anti-Federalists, who
then, it was hoped, would quietly lie down. When Madison initially presented
his first draft, numerous representatives, Federalists and Anti-Federalists alike,
opined that Congress needed to remain focused on more important matters. Benjamin Goodhue of Massachusetts observed that "the present time
[was] premature [for considering a Bill of Rights]; inasmuch as we have other
business before us, which is incomplete, but essential to the public interest"
(Kurland and Lerner 1987, p. 21). Eventually though, Congress approved a
Bill of Rights, which was ratified in 1791 by the requisite number of states. The
First Amendment states: "Congress shall make no law ... abridging the freedom of speech, or of the press."

The lack of extensive congressional discussion about the substantive meanings of a free press and free speech underscores that the First Amendment did
not elucidate the law of free expression. As of 1791, most Americans believed
they had a right to speak their mind, in accord with the tradition of dissent,
but they would not have articulated this right in precise legal terms (Feldman
2008, pp. 3, 69, and 83). Lawyers would have assumed that legal rights to
free expression still, for the most part, tracked the common law. Madison suggested as much when he stated during the congressional debates over the

Bill of Rights that he sought to enumerate "simple, acknowledged principles" (Kurland and Lerner 1987, p. 203). The main parameters of the common law of free expression had been long established. As stated by William Blackstone in his *Commentaries on the Laws of England*, published in the 1760s, the crux of free expression was a prohibition on prior restraints:

> The liberty of the press is indeed essential to the nature of a free state: but this consists in laying no *previous* restraints upon publications, and not in freedom from censure for criminal matter when published. Every freeman has an undoubted right to lay what sentiments he pleases before the public: to forbid this, is to destroy the freedom of the press: but if he publishes what is improper, mischievous, or illegal, he must take the consequence of his own temerity. (Blackstone 1771–2, pp. 151–2)[1]

Even before the Constitution was implemented in 1789, Americans generally followed this common-law doctrine. In 1788, Chief Justice Thomas McKean of Pennsylvania called the ban on prior restraints the "true liberty of the press" (*Respublica* v. *Oswald*, 1 Dall. 319 (Pa. 1788)). Thus, at a minimum, the First Amendment constitutionalized the prohibition of prior restraints but, beyond this, the precise legal meanings of free speech and free press remained unclear. In particular, whether the national government had the power to punish seditious libel, that is, criticisms of government officials and policies, was ambiguous.

This lack of clarity would contribute to controversy during the 1790s. Early in that decade, political disputes became so ferocious that the Federalists, recently united in support of constitutional ratification, were rent apart into two opposed "proto-parties," the Republicans and the Federalists (Sharp 1993, pp. 8–9). Divergent visions of national power, citizenship, and commercial development emerged. Most notably, James Madison and Thomas Jefferson articulated the Republican vision, based on Virginia's (southern) agrarianism, while Alexander Hamilton, a New Yorker, enunciated the Federalist vision, based on the northeast's mercantilism and incipient industrialism. Both sides believed they represented the common good, but they could not reach consensus. Instead, their conflicts became so intense that each side accused the other of seditious and even treasonous activities. Throughout the decade, Federalists controlled most government offices and debated among themselves whether to seek criminal punishment for Republicans who had allegedly uttered seditious statements. At the time, most Americans, Federalists and Republicans alike, would have agreed that the state governments retained the power to

---

[1] Emphasis in original.

punish seditious libel, but a national power to act similarly was on a less clear footing. Regardless, among Federalists themselves, the disputes over sedition usually focused on the political costs and benefits of prosecutions, not on the legality or constitutionality of such actions. In effect, Federalists recognized the strength of the American tradition of dissent. While the law might permit federal prosecutions, Federalists realized that the tradition of dissent suggested caution before taking such action (Feldman 2008, pp. 70–100).

By 1798, however, the politics had shifted sufficiently that the Federalist-controlled Congress passed the Sedition Act. Still mindful of the tradition of dissent, the Federalists enacted the most liberal seditious libel statute then imaginable. Even so, Federalists also seemed cognizant of the tradition of suppression. Many Federalists could remember how, during the American Revolution, Patriots harassed and banished Tories for speaking their minds. Now, Federalist mobs repeatedly threatened and attacked Republicans, including Congressmen and newspaper editors. When Sedition Act prosecutions began, some Republicans responded by invoking the First Amendment. These invocations led Republicans to elaborate increasingly complex definitions of free expression, but the Republicans' main critique of the Sedition Act was a jurisdictional (or federalism) argument: that the states but not the national government had the power to punish seditious libel.

During this crisis, the Supreme Court never ruled on the constitutionality of the Sedition Act. In fact, it avoided free-expression issues for more than a century after the adoption of the First Amendment. In *Barron v. Baltimore*, 32 U.S. 243 (1833) and *Permoli v. New Orleans*, 44 U.S. 589 (1845), the pre-Civil War court held that Bill of Rights guarantees, including those of the First Amendment, applied only against the national government. Consequently, when state and local governments regulated speech and writing during the antebellum period, lower courts developed the relevant legal doctrine in accord with state constitutions and the structures of republican democratic government. Under republican democracy, virtuous citizens and officials ostensibly pursued the common good. Courts, therefore, reviewed government actions to ensure that they promoted the common good rather than partial or private interests. Consistent with this general practice of republican democratic judicial review, courts articulated a "bad-tendency" test to delineate the scope of free expression. The government could not impose prior restraints on expression, but could impose criminal penalties for speech or writing that had bad tendencies or likely harmful consequences, in contravention of the common good.

During the nineteenth century, many free-expression disputes arose outside the courts and thus, frequently, the traditions of dissent and suppression mattered more than legal doctrine. Once abolitionism began to spread in the 1830s, slavery and abolition became the flashpoints that sparked the greatest controversies of the pre-Civil War period.[2] Initially, abolitionists sought to persuade whites, including southern slaveholders, to support abolition because it was right from a moral, religious, and legal standpoint. As abolitionists quickly discovered though, the nobility of this approach matched only its ineffectiveness in generating a mass movement. Even so, pro-slavery advocates often reacted violently to abolitionist messages. For instance, anti-abolitionists repeatedly destroyed abolitionist printing presses and, when such tactics failed to silence the abolitionist printers, more violent threats and actions, including murder, were implemented. However, once anti-abolitionists began violently to suppress abolitionist messages, abolitionists were able to chart a convergence of interests among themselves, other whites, and slaves. Abolitionists could now argue that slaveholders and their cohorts not only sought to deny liberty to black slaves but also to free whites. In this context, the reality of the law of free expression mattered little; what mattered was that an increasing percentage of northern whites began to perceive that the "slave power" purposefully denied whites their rights and liberties so as to protect the slaveholders' interests (Stewart 1976, p. 84). With this perception of slave power, whites could be encouraged to support abolition not merely because it was right, a claim from which abolitionists never wavered, but also because abolition was in the interest of free whites (Feldman 2008, pp. 121–42).

THE UNITED STATES SUPREME COURT AND WORLD WAR I

When the Supreme Court first began to decide issues related to free expression, around the turn of the twentieth century, the justices followed the legal doctrine as it had developed in state courts during the nineteenth century. Prior restraints were prohibited, but the government could punish speech with bad tendencies, because doing so would promote the common good (*Patterson v. Colorado*, 205 U.S. 454, 462 (1907)). However, even the proscription of prior restraints was sometimes more rhetorical than real. The Supreme Court, for instance, consistently upheld labor injunctions, enjoining union leaders' and members' expressive activities such as picketing, without acknowledging that such injunctions might be categorized as impermissible prior restraints.

Soon after Congress declared war against Germany in April 1917, President Woodrow Wilson encouraged Congress to enact the Espionage Act, which proscribed obstructing the draft or causing or attempting to cause insubordination

[2]   The American Civil War lasted from 1861 to 1865.

or disloyalty within the military. Less than one year later, Congress over-whelmingly passed an amendment, the Sedition Act of 1918, which clarified the congressional desire to suppress protests against the draft and war. The Department of Justice vigorously enforced both statutes. The first Espionage/Sedition Act cases to reach the Supreme Court were not argued until January 1919, after hostilities had ended. In the first, *Schenck v. United States*, 249 U.S. 47 (1919), the general secretary of the Socialist party and an Executive Board member were convicted for printing several thousand copies of a leaflet and mailing it to draft-eligible men. The leaflet advocated the repeal of the draft law and argued that conscription violated the Thirteenth Amendment's proscription of slavery. Justice Oliver Wendell Holmes, Jr., wrote an opinion for a unanimous court upholding the convictions. In response to the defend-ants' argument that the First Amendment protected their expression, Holmes articulated a doctrinal test: "[t]he question in every case is whether the words used are used in such circumstances and are of such a nature as to create a clear and present danger that they will bring about the substantive evils that Congress has a right to prevent" (*Schenck v. United States*, p. 52). While Holmes's "clear and present danger" terminology was novel (and apparently derived from his book, *The Common Law*), his application of the test dem-onstrated that he did not intend to articulate a new standard for delineating the scope of free expression. For Holmes, clear and present danger meant bad tendency. The First Amendment proscribed prior restraints but otherwise allowed the government to punish any speech or writing that would contra-vene the common good.

One week later, the court unanimously upheld convictions in two more Espionage Act cases: *Frohwerk v. United States*, 249 U.S. 204 (1919) and *Debs v. United States*, 249 U.S. 211 (1919). Writing the court's opinions in both cases, Holmes followed bad-tendency doctrinal principles while disregarding his clear and present danger terminology. This first set of World War I cases reveals that all of the justices, including Holmes, considered free expression to be an individual liberty like any other under republican democracy, sub-ordinate to government actions furthering the common good. The govern-ment could punish any speech or writing that impeded the national war effort because such expression would be deemed harmful or with bad tendencies. Eight months later, the court decided its next Espionage Act case, *Abrams v. United States*, 250 U.S. 616 (1919). The defendants had been convicted for printing and distributing leaflets that criticized President Wilson's leadership during the war. Affirming the convictions, the court brushed aside the defend-ants' First Amendment arguments by reasoning that *Schenck* and *Frohwerk* controlled. Surprisingly, Holmes and Justice Louis Brandeis dissented, with

Brandeis joining Holmes's opinion. Holmes asserted the correctness of the court's previous decisions in *Schenck*, *Frohwerk*, and *Debs*, and then reiterated his "clear and present danger" phrasing from *Schenck*. Now though, Holmes imbued this phrase with new vigor; it no longer equated with the bad-tendency test. In applying the clear and present danger test, Holmes stressed that Abrams and his codefendants were "poor and puny anonymities," their writings were insignificant and the government should not have prosecuted (*Abrams v. United States*, p. 629). "[N]obody can suppose that the surreptitious publishing of a silly leaflet by an unknown man, without more, would present any immediate danger that its opinions would hinder the success of the government arms or have any appreciable tendency to do so" (*Abrams v. United States*, p. 628). The government, in short, had not proven clear and present danger.

Holmes continued by reasoning that a philosophical rationale, the search for truth, justified an expansive concept of free expression under the First Amendment. While Holmes did not acknowledge his intellectual forebears, John Milton had first articulated this rationale in 1644 during the English Civil War. "Let [truth] and falsehood grapple," Milton wrote, "[and] who ever knew truth put to the worse, in a free and open encounter" (Milton 1644). In the nineteenth century, John Stuart Mill reiterated the search for truth rationale and, more recently, an American constitutional scholar, Zechariah Chafee, has done the same (Chafee 1919, pp. 957–9; Mill 1956, pp. 21–7). Holmes explained the societal search for truth as follows:

> [W]hen men have realized that time has upset many fighting faiths, they may come to believe even more than they believe the very foundations of their own conduct that the ultimate good desired is better reached by free trade in ideas – that the best test of truth is the power of the thought to get itself accepted in the competition of the market, and that truth is the only ground upon which their wishes safely can be carried out. (Abrams v. United States, p. 630)

Holmes linked the search for truth rationale with the clear and present danger test. "[W]e should be eternally vigilant against attempts to check the expression of opinions that we loathe and believe to be fraught with death," he warned, "unless they so imminently threaten immediate interference with the lawful and pressing purposes of the law that an immediate check is required to save the country" (*Abrams v. United States*, p. 630). In other words, the government should allow speech and writing to flow into a marketplace of ideas. From this free exchange of ideas, the truth will emerge. Harmful ideas must be met with better ideas – counterspeech – rather than with force or suppression.

The only ideas (speech and writing) that should be restricted are those that would inhibit the further exchange of ideas, namely those that would engender a clear and present (or imminent) danger of unlawful or harmful conduct.

DEMOCRACY AND FREE EXPRESSION TRANSFORMED

During the 1920s, the Supreme Court continued to interpret the First Amendment narrowly, in accord with republican democratic principles. Holmes and Brandeis often dissented while relying on the clear and present danger test, as distinct from the bad-tendency test. During World War I and a subsequent Red Scare period (1919–20), numerous states passed criminal syndicalism statutes (laws that prohibited violence or advocacy of violence as a means of accomplishing political change) and challenges to convictions under these laws began to reach the court in the mid-1920s. The court upheld one such conviction in *Whitney v. California*, 274 U.S. 357 (1927). California had convicted Charlotte Whitney, a member of the Communist Labor Party, for organizing and belonging to an organization advocating criminal syndicalism, even though Whitney personally sought peaceful political change. Brandeis, joined by Holmes, wrote a separate opinion that functioned as a dissent, although technically it concurred in the judgment (Whitney could not rely on free-expression issues on appeal to the Supreme Court because she had not adequately raised them first in the trial court). Brandeis acknowledged that the parameters of the clear and present danger test remained obscure, so he articulated three philosophical rationales to explain the test and its protection of speech and writing: philosophical justifications that theorists would develop (and modify) over the following decades into the primary rationales for an expansive interpretation of the First Amendment. First, Brandeis reiterated the search for truth or marketplace rationale, emphasizing that counterspeech "affords ordinarily adequate protection against the dissemination of noxious doctrine" (*Whitney v. California*, p. 375). Second, he linked free expression to democratic government, though he did not argue that freedom to express one's opinion on political issues is a prerequisite to full democratic participation. Rather, consistent with republican democracy, he maintained "that public discussion is a political duty" and that free discussion of "supposed grievances and proposed remedies" nurtures stable government (*Whitney v. California*, p. 375). Brandeis implied that, through public discussion of political issues, the citizenry discerns the public good and discourages government corruption. Third, Brandeis alluded to the inherent value of individual liberty: the founders "valued liberty both as an end and as a means"

(*Whitney* v. *California*, p. 375). Free expression was not only a means to truth or free government, it was valuable in and of itself.

These three philosophical rationales, particularly the search for truth and democratic governance rationales, elucidated the clear and present danger test. "[N]o danger flowing from speech can be deemed clear and present, unless the incidence of the evil apprehended is so imminent that it may befall before there is opportunity for full discussion," Brandeis wrote (*Whitney* v. *California*, p. 377). "If there be time to expose through discussion the falsehood and fallacies, to avert the evil by the processes of education, the remedy to be applied is more speech, not enforced silence" (*Whitney* v. *California*, p. 377). The only expression that should be punished is that which would likely engender an imminent (or "present") danger of unlawful or harmful conduct and would therefore preclude any further discussion or exchange of ideas. Meanwhile, for expression to constitute a "clear" danger, Brandeis explained that it must generate a probability of "serious evil" or injury (*Whitney* v. *California*, p. 376). Because free expression is so significant to republican democratic government, punishment "would be inappropriate as the means for averting a relatively trivial harm to society" (*Whitney* v. *California*, p. 377).

In 1931, the court decided its first two cases validating free expression claims (*Stromberg* v. *California*, 283 U.S. 359 (1931) and *Near* v. *Minnesota*, 283 U.S. 697 (1931)). At this point, the justices still conceptualized free expression within the structures of republican democracy. Yet, by the late 1920s and early to mid-1930s, republican democracy was crumbling and the practices of pluralist democracy were crystallizing under the pressures of industrialization, immigration, and urbanization. In the republican system, an alleged lack of civic virtue could preclude one from participating in democratic processes. On this ground, the exclusion of African Americans, Irish-Catholic immigrants and other peripheral groups had supposedly been justified during long stretches of American history. Under pluralist democracy, however, one did not need to demonstrate civic virtue to qualify as a participant. During the 1930s, many ethnic and immigrant urbanites who had previously been discouraged from partaking in national politics became voters and actively cast their support for the New Deal[3] and its broad social programs. Moreover, pluralist democracy acknowledged that politics was about the pursuit of self-interest. Interest group efforts to satisfy preexisting values and desires became normal and legitimate. Government goals could no longer be condemned as

---

[3] The New Deal was a political program of the 1930s in which the national government primarily attempted to end the Great Depression and to protect Americans from economic deprivations.

contravening the common good; all such substantive goals were determined through interest group bargaining and coalition-building. Ultimately then, pluralist democracy was defined through processes that ensured full and fair participation, including the assertion of one's interests and values, especially in the legislative arena.

Starting in 1937, the court accepted the structures of pluralist democracy and, in doing so, the justices rendered judicial review problematic. Previously, courts had used their power to enforce basic republican democratic principles: upholding government actions that promoted the common good and invalidating actions that furthered partial or private interests. With the repudiation of republican democracy, the purpose of judicial review became obscure but, over time, the Supreme Court developed new doctrines to implement its power. In the context of free expression, the change began with *Herndon* v. *Lowry*, decided on April 26, 1937. The court reversed Georgia's conviction of Angelo Herndon, a black Communist Party organizer who had attempted to persuade other individuals, mostly African Americans, to join the party. Justice Owen Roberts's confusing majority opinion rested on multiple grounds, yet it nonetheless marked a significant doctrinal turn. Roberts invoked the clear and present danger test while repudiating the bad-tendency test, and also created a presumption favoring the protection of expression. While the precise meaning of the clear and present danger test remained ambiguous, Roberts unquestionably interpreted it to be more rigorous and speech-protective than the bad-tendency test. Roberts's conception of clear and present danger, in other words, echoed Holmes's dissent in *Abrams* and Brandeis's concurrence in *Whitney*. After *Herndon*, in a phenomenal string of cases from 1938 to 1940, the court upheld one free-expression claim after another (for example, *Cantwell* v. *Connecticut*, 310 U.S. 296 (1940) and *Hague* v. *Committee for Industrial Organization*, 307 U.S. 496 (1939)).

IS FREE EXPRESSION A CONSTITUTIONAL LODESTAR?

After 1937, the Supreme Court elaborated and primarily relied on Brandeis's three theoretical rationales to justify the new expansive protection of free expression. The justices persistently reiterated the search for truth rationale. In *Chaplinsky* v. *New Hampshire*, 315 U.S. 568, 572 (1942), the court reasoned that certain types of speech, particularly so-called fighting words, "those which by their very utterance inflict injury or tend to incite an immediate breach of the peace," do not deserve constitutional protection because "such utterances are no essential part of any exposition of ideas," and thus do not contribute to the discovery of "truth." The justices have continued to invoke the search for truth rationale ever since. In *Red Lion Broadcasting* v. *FCC*, 395 U.S. 367, 390 (1969), a unanimous court wrote that "[i]t is the purpose of the First Amendment to preserve an uninhibited marketplace of ideas in which truth will ultimately prevail."

The justices also relied increasingly on a democratic- or self-governance rationale that they shaped to harmonize with the emergent pluralist democracy. Pluralist democratic government depended on adherence to certain governmental processes, and no liberty seemed more central to those governmental processes than free expression. Free speech and writing allowed diverse groups and individuals to contribute their views in the pluralist political arena. If government officials interfered with the pluralist process, if they dictated or controlled public debates, then they would skew the democratic outcomes and undermine the consent of the governed. No less so than voting, free expression was a prerequisite for pluralist democracy. The court, when discussing free expression in *Thornhill* v. *Alabama*, 310 U.S. 88, 96 (1940), emphasized that government cannot be allowed to "diminish the effective exercise of rights so necessary to the maintenance of democratic institutions." In *West Virginia State Board of Education* v. *Barnette*, 319 U.S. 624, 641–2 (1943), the court reasoned: "[w]e set up government by consent of the governed, and the Bill of Rights denies those in power any legal opportunity to coerce that consent. Authority here is to be controlled by public opinion, not public opinion by authority."

During the post–World War II era, scholars developed a self-fulfillment rationale that the justices soon began to invoke. Thomas Emerson began with "the widely accepted premise of Western thought that the proper end of man is the realization of his character and potentialities as a human being" (Emerson 1963, p. 879). From this premise, Emerson reasoned that "every man – in the development of his own personality – has the right to form his own beliefs and opinions," as well as "the right to express these beliefs and opinions" (Emerson 1963, p. 879). When understood in this manner, free expression allows the individual "to realize his potentiality as a human being" (Emerson 1963, p. 879). In *Hurley* v. *Irish-American Gay, Lesbian and Bisexual Group of Boston*, 515 U.S. 557, 573 (1995), Justice David Souter described "the fundamental rule of protection under the First Amendment [to be] that a speaker has the autonomy to choose the content of his own message." Partly because the self-fulfillment rationale is not instrumental (it values expression as an end in itself rather than as a means to other ends, such as truth), it justifies an expansive concept of free expression. As Thurgood Marshall phrased it in his concurrence in *Procunier* v. *Martinez*, 416 U.S. 396, 427 (1974), free expression "serves ... the needs of ... the human spirit – a spirit that demands self-expression."

In conjunction with these three philosophical rationales, the court developed two overarching doctrines that it used to adjudicate free-expression disputes: the two-level approach and a balancing test. Under the two-level approach, the First Amendment fully protects speech and writing unless the expression falls into a low-value category, in which case the expression is unprotected. In *Chaplinsky* v. *New Hampshire*, the court identified (at 571–2) several low-value categories: "[t]here are certain well-defined and narrowly limited classes of speech, the prevention and punishment of which has never been thought to raise any Constitutional problem. These include the lewd and obscene, the profane, the libelous, and the insulting or 'fighting' words." If the court designated disputed speech to be, for example, obscene, then the government could punish the speaker; the First Amendment did not shield the expression. The court's two-level approach to free expression can be contentious in two ways. The court's initial designation of expression as a low-value category (or not) can provoke vigorous disagreement; the court often invokes a theoretical rationale such as self-governance to justify its categorization. Once the court has defined a low-value category, the identification of specific materials as within that category can then generate disputes. Most justices have long agreed that obscenity should be a low-value category, but for decades, until *Miller* v. *California*, 413 U.S. 15 (1973), they were unable to converge on a single doctrinal test for identifying materials as obscene.

The predominant alternative to the two-level doctrine has been the balancing test, which became especially common in disputes involving time, place, and manner, rather than content-based restrictions on expression. In one time, place, and manner case, *Martin* v. *Struthers*, 319 U.S. 141 (1943), the court held that the defendant's conviction for distributing leaflets door-to-door violated free expression. "We are faced in the instant case with the necessity of weighing the conflicting interests of the appellant in the civil [free-speech] rights she claims," explained the majority opinion, "as well as the right of the individual householder to determine whether he is willing to receive her message, against the interest of the community which by this ordinance offers to protect the interests of all of its citizens, whether particular citizens want that protection or not" (*Martin* v. *Struthers*, p. 143). While the court in *Martin* suggested that it weighed the various interests evenhandedly, it often skewed the balance against the government to create, in effect, a presumption favoring the protection of speech and writing. In *Schneider* v. *New Jersey*, 308 U.S. 147, 161 (1939), the court distinguished free-expression-balancing cases from others: "[m]ere legislative preferences or beliefs respecting matters of public convenience may well support regulation directed at other personal activities, but be insufficient to justify such as diminishes the exercise of rights so vital to the maintenance of democratic institutions." In numerous cases, the court translated this skewed balancing test into the clear and present danger standard. For example, when the court weighed competing interests in *Thornhill* v. *Alabama*, 310 U.S. 88, 105 (1940), it focused on whether the statutorily proscribed behavior created a "clear and present danger of destruction of life or property." To be sure, the clear and present danger test was chameleon-like: its meaning varied over time, depending on the political circumstances. However, in *Thornhill* and similar cases from that era, the clear and present danger test strongly protected speech and writing. "What finally emerges from the 'clear and present danger' cases," explained the court in *Bridges* v. *California*, 314 U.S. 252, 263 (1941), "is a working principle that the substantive evil must be extremely serious and the degree of imminence extremely high before utterances can be punished."

Pursuant to the two overarching doctrines (the two-level approach and the balancing test) and the three philosophical rationales (search for truth, self-governance, and self-fulfillment) the court often treated free expression as a constitutional lodestar. From the mid-1960s to the early 1970s in particular, the court decided numerous landmark cases that emphasized the preeminence of the First Amendment. For instance, *New York Times* v. *Sullivan*, 376 U.S. 254 (1964) asked whether the First Amendment protected the press from civil libel actions brought by government officials. *The New York Times* had published a full-page advertisement that solicited support for the civil rights movement, criticized the police commissioner of Montgomery, Alabama, but contained several minor factual errors. The police commissioner successfully brought a civil action in the state courts for defamation. The court had previously recognized defamation as a low-value category, yet this case resembled a criminal prosecution for seditious libel: the government, through the institution of the state courts, sought to punish the press for criticizing a public official, the police commissioner. Reversing the state court's decision, a unanimous Supreme Court alluded to both the self-governance and search for truth rationales. [W]e consider this case against the background of a profound national commitment to the principle that debate on public issues should be uninhibited, robust, and wide-open, and that it may well include vehement, caustic, and sometimes unpleasantly sharp attacks on government and public officials (*New York Times* v. *Sullivan*, p. 270). After deeming government prosecution of seditious libel unconstitutional, the court reasoned that, if a state could not constitutionally punish criticisms of government policies and officials through a criminal prosecution, then it should not be able to impose punishment through a civil defamation action. Instead, a "public official" can recover "damages for a defamatory falsehood relating to his official conduct" only if "he proves that the statement was made with 'actual malice' – that is, with knowledge that it was false or with reckless disregard of whether it was false or not" (*New York Times* v. *Sullivan*, p. 279–80).

In recent years, the Supreme Court has combined the two-level and balancing doctrines in cases that involve content-based restrictions on expression. In these cases, the court generally begins with a presumption in favor of protecting speech and writing. It then asks whether the expression falls into a low value and therefore constitutionally unprotected category. Even if the expression is not low value, however, the First Amendment does not necessarily protect it. The court now affords the government an opportunity to show that the expression should nonetheless be unprotected. To make this showing, the government must satisfy strict scrutiny, a type of balancing test strongly skewed against the government. To satisfy strict scrutiny, the government must demonstrate that its action (the regulation or punishment of expression) is narrowly tailored to achieve a compelling government interest (*Turner Broadcast System* v. *FCC*, 512 U.S. 622 (1994)). In theory at least, the strict scrutiny doctrine continues the strong judicial protection of speech and writing, because the government can rarely satisfy its requirements.

Nevertheless, throughout the pluralist democratic era, the court has not consistently protected free expression despite the many encomiums to its lodestar status. During a post–World War II Red Scare, for instance, the federal government convicted eleven leaders of the Communist Party of the United States (CPUSA) for conspiring both to organize the CPUSA and to advocate for the violent overthrow of the government, though the prosecution proved only that the defendants taught Marxist-Leninist doctrine. The court upheld the convictions in *Dennis* v. *United States*, 341 U.S. 494 (1951), with Chief Justice Fred Vinson writing a plurality opinion. If the justices had applied the clear and present danger test as it had recently been understood, then the expression would have been constitutionally protected because the danger was not imminent. Teaching abstract doctrine is unlikely to produce immediate revolution or other criminal action. This judicial result, however, would have contravened the current political and public desire to root out Communism. Vinson, therefore, followed a reformulated clear and present danger test: "[i]n each case [courts] must ask whether the gravity of the 'evil,' discounted by its improbability, justifies such invasion of free speech as is necessary to avoid the danger" (*Dennis* v. *United States*, p. 510). In this particular case, the advocated evil (the violent overthrow of the government) was so grave as to overcome its improbability. Clear and present danger "cannot mean that before the Government may act, it must wait until the putsch is about to be executed, the plans have been laid and the signal is awaited" (*Dennis* v. *United States*, p. 509). The court's decision prompted the government to begin arresting and indicting CPUSA members en masse.

Overall, despite the strength of the tradition of dissent under pluralist democracy, "the outliers in American politics were more often than not the victims than the beneficiaries" of the court's free-expression decisions (Graber 2002, p. 310). Even though the 1960s was one of the court's most speech-protective eras, the court refused to recognize a constitutional right to protest during that decade, though such political expression resonated with the self-governance rationale. In *Adderley* v. *Florida*, 385 U.S. 39 (1966), 200 college students marched from their school to a jail to protest against the earlier arrest of other students for protesting against racial segregation. The court upheld the protesters' convictions for trespassing on jail premises. The majority reasoned that the state could apply its general law proscribing trespass because of the protesters' conduct, regardless of their message. Justice William Douglas dissented, emphasizing that in protest cases the government always claimed to apply some general criminal law proscribing trespass, breach of the peace or the like, and the government always claimed that the message was irrelevant to the prosecution. Given the political nature of the defendants' expression in *Adderley*, moreover, the jailhouse appeared to be the perfect location for the protest. Not only do members of peripheral groups often find their expression unprotected, as in *Adderley*, they also often find themselves the targets of expression that the court deems constitutionally protected. For example, in *Brandenburg* v. *Ohio*, 395 U.S. 444 (1969), the court dramatically expanded First Amendment protection for expression encouraging unlawful conduct, particularly subversive advocacy. Yet the *Brandenburg* decision protected the expression of a Ku Klux Klan leader, who had directed malicious hate speech against racial and religious minorities.

IMPLICATIONS FOR THE DIGITAL AGE

The digital age has not only radically transformed technology and social life, but has also ushered in new and momentous free-expression issues. One of the most important issues is open Internet access. In a speech on Internet freedom, delivered in January 2010, then secretary of state Hillary Rodham Clinton advocated for a

> [F]reedom to connect – the idea that governments should not prevent people from connecting to the internet, to websites, or to each other. The freedom

to connect is like the freedom of assembly in cyber space. It allows individuals to get online, come together, and hopefully cooperate in the name of progress. Once you're on the internet, you don't need to be a tycoon or a rock star to have a huge impact on society. (Clinton 2010)

Clinton was primarily concerned with government restrictions on Internet access but, in the Internet age, private actors, particularly corporations, have the power and the incentive to impose restrictions. ISPs, such as the multinational corporations Verizon, Comcast, and AT&T, are in business to maximize profits. One way for them to increase profits is by discriminating among their customers. If allowed, ISPs can create fast and slow lanes of Internet access. The ISPs could then discriminate among customers based on their willingness to pay for a faster service. Customers unwilling or unable to pay a premium would be relegated to the slow lane of Internet access. Customers paying the premium would slide into the fast lane. Corporate customers, such as Netflix, which rely on ISPs to provide access to their end users, would effectively be forced to pay for fast-lane access. On November 10, 2014, President Barack Obama recommended that the FCC impose net neutrality, which would require ISPs to provide all customers with an equal service. ISPs would not be allowed to discriminate based on willingness to pay a premium. They would not be able to block or slow down online services or specific applications. On February 4, 2015, Tom Wheeler, the chair of the FCC, proposed new rules that would mandate an open Internet, which the FCC soon adopted. Almost immediately, ISPs, trade groups and lobbying associations began filing lawsuits challenging the agency rules on multiple grounds related to statutory construction and administrative procedures. However, at some point ISPs will likely challenge the net neutrality rules as violating their First Amendment rights to free expression. The ISPs will claim that they have a constitutional right to transfer or not transfer any information they desire and at any speed they desire.

The constitutional values at stake in a First Amendment battle over net neutrality would be complex. On the one hand, the corporate ISPs would be invoking free-speech rights. On the other hand, if the FCC did not mandate net neutrality, then ISPs' individual and corporate customers would find their Internet access restricted or blocked, unless they were able and willing to pay a premium to their ISP. Therefore, but for net neutrality, ISPs would be able to restrict the communicative capabilities of individual and corporate Internet users. Even so, Internet users cannot claim that the ISPs are violating their constitutional rights, because the First Amendment applies only against the government, not against non-government entities (such as a corporate ISP). In this situation then, the government (i.e., the FCC) must act, by mandating net neutrality in order to protect free-speech values. Without government regulation, ISPs will be able to restrict Internet users' freedom to communicate.

If the Supreme Court were to decide the constitutionality of the net neutrality rules, what would be the likely result? The histories of the philosophical rationales and the court's free-expression doctrines and decisions highlight a key insight: the concept of free expression in the United States is far from static. It changes in response to political and social forces, particularly as they are manifested in the traditions of dissent and suppression. Thus, it is difficult to predict how the court will ultimately respond to digital-age free-expression issues. Indeed, a new philosophical rationale might emerge precisely because of the changes wrought by digital technology. Yet, recent history provides some clues about the court's likely direction.

If outliers often lose free-expression cases, even during the pluralist democratic era, the wealthy and powerful often win. This maxim, that the "haves" typically come out ahead (Galanter 1974), fairly summarizes the court's recent free-expression decisions under Chief Justice John Roberts, who was appointed in 2005. In fact, empirical studies show that the Roberts court is the most pro-business Supreme Court since World War II; five of the current justices rank among the top ten justices most favorable to business during that time (Epstein et al., 2013). For instance, during the years before Roberts's appointment, the court had vacillated over the degree to which the government could regulate corporate campaign spending, but the Roberts court ended the uncertainty. *Citizens United v. Federal Election Commission*, 558 U.S. 310 (2010) invalidated provisions of the Bipartisan Campaign Reform Act of 2002, which maintained limits on corporate spending for political campaign advertisements. The majority opinion began by reiterating two foundational premises pronounced in prior decisions: that spending on political campaigns constitutes speech; and that free-speech protections extend to corporations. The court then emphasized two of the philosophical rationales. In the societal search for truth, the court explained, the First Amendment protects the flow of ideas in a "general public dialogue" (*Citizens United v. FEC*, p. 341). The court especially stressed the self-governance rationale. "Speech is an essential mechanism of democracy," the court explained; "[t]he right of citizens to inquire, to hear, to speak, and to use information to reach consensus is a precondition to enlightened self-government and a necessary means to protect it" (*Citizens United v. FEC*, p. 339). Even so, the court acknowledged that the government can prevent corruption or the appearance of corruption in democratic politics. Yet, the court so severely narrowed the definition of corruption that any evidence (of corruption) was rendered practically irrelevant. According to the court in *Citizens United*, only a direct contribution to a candidate or officeholder can constitute corruption or its appearance. Independent expenditure, even on behalf of a specific candidate or officeholder, cannot do so. Apparently, the government can never justify its regulation of expenditure, whether by corporations or others. Ultimately then, *Citizens United* amounted to a judicial proclamation that corporations and other wealthy entities and individuals can spend unlimited sums in their efforts to determine elections and government policies. In the democratic sphere, wealth and corporate power are now unfettered.

The Roberts court does not always demonstrate such respect for free expression as a constitutional lodestar. On the contrary, the court has eroded some of the protections articulated in the landmark decisions of the late 1960s, particularly in cases where the First Amendment claimant does not wield significant wealth and power. For instance, *Morse* v. *Frederick*, 551 U.S. 393 (2007) limited students' rights of free speech, while *Garcetti* v. *Ceballos*, 547 U.S. 410 (2006) diminished government employees' rights. However, corporations continue to achieve wins, including in the as-yet-few decisions involving free expression and digital technology or data. In *Brown* v. *Entertainment Merchants Association*, 131 S. Ct. 2729 (2011), a state law prohibited "the sale or rental of 'violent video games' to minors." Video games, the court began, are a form of expression within the compass of the First Amendment and are, therefore, presumptively protected. Moreover, even violent games do not fall into a low-value category, such as obscenity or fighting words. However, could the government satisfy strict scrutiny? While protecting children from portrayals of violence might be a compelling state interest, the court concluded that the regulation in this case was not narrowly tailored to achieve that end. The regulation of video games was, for instance, under-inclusive because it still allowed children to be exposed to depictions of violence in sources other than video games. *Sorrell* v. *IMS Health Inc.*, 131 S. Ct. 2653 (2011) involved the control and use of data. When pharmacies process prescriptions, they routinely record information such as the prescribing doctor, the patient, and the dosage. Data-mining businesses, like IMS Health Inc., buy this information, analyze it and sell or lease their reports to pharmaceutical manufacturers. When armed with this information, pharmaceutical salespersons are able to market their drugs more effectively to doctors. Vermont enacted a law to prevent pharmacies from selling this information. The legislature had two primary purposes: to protect the privacy of patients and doctors; and to improve public health by, for example, encouraging doctors to prescribe drugs in patients' best interests rather than because of effective pharmaceutical marketing. Justice Stephen Breyer's dissent, joined by two other justices, characterized the statute as a police power regulation of the economic marketplace that did not trigger free-speech concerns (*Sorrell v. IMS Health Inc.*, p. 2673). The court's conservative majority disagreed. It reasoned that the statute raised an unusual commercial speech issue. Commercial speech cases typically involve advertising and, as the court admitted, the statute in *Sorrell* did not restrict advertising per se. Yet, the court reasoned that the First Amendment not only applied but also required "heightened judicial scrutiny," a standard more rigorous than the balancing test ordinarily applied in commercial speech cases (*Sorrell v. IMS Health Inc.*, p. 2663).

These decisions, when combined with the Roberts court's generally solicitous attitude toward corporations, do not bode well for net neutrality, if that issue were to reach the court. If a corporate ISP were to claim that the net neutrality rules violate the First Amendment, the court would likely side with the corporation and invalidate the federal rule. The conservative justices would reason as follows. First, corporations enjoy First Amendment free-speech rights. Second, free expression is a constitutional lodestar. Third, the government must therefore satisfy the strict scrutiny standard. Finally, the government cannot satisfy this rigorous judicial standard. Consequently, corporate ISPs would be able to maximize profits, while their customers would be forced either to pay a premium or to suffer inferior or limited Internet access.

To be sure, the Roberts court can surprise in free-expression cases. The justices sometimes emphasize the philosophical rationales, but not always. The justices might effectively declare in one case that free speech is a constitutional lodestar, then uphold a restriction on expression in the next. The Roberts court, however, has shown a strong and consistent propensity for protecting wealth and corporate activity. Thus, if multinational corporate ISPs were to invoke free expression in a challenge to net neutrality rules, the court would likely interpret the First Amendment to favor the corporations. Ironically, such a court decision would diminish the communicative freedom of many Internet users.

REFERENCES

Blackstone, W. 1771–2. *Commentaries on the Laws of England*. Philadelphia: Robert Bell.

Chafee, Z. 1919. "Freedom of speech in war time," *Harvard Law Review* 32: 932–73.

Clinton, H. R. 2010. "Remarks on Internet Freedom," speech delivered to Newseum, Washington, DC, January 21, 2010.

Emerson, T. I. 1963. "Toward a general theory of the First Amendment," *Yale Law Journal* 72: 877–956.

Epstein, L., Landes, W. M., and Posner, R. A. 2013. "How business fares in the Supreme Court," *Minnesota Law Review* 97: 1431–73.

Feldman, S. M. 2008. *Free Expression and Democracy in America: A History*. Chicago: University of Chicago Press.

Galanter, M. 1974. "Why the 'haves' come out ahead: Speculations on the limits of legal change," *Law and Society Review* 9: 95–151.

Graber, M. A. 2002. "Constitutional politics and constitutional theory: A misunderstood and neglected relationship," *Law and Social Inquiry* 27: 309–38.

Kurland, P. B. and Lerner, R. (eds.) 1987. *The Founders' Constitution*. Chicago: University of Chicago Press.

Levy, L. W. 1985. *Emergence of a Free Press*. New York: Oxford University Press.

Maier, P. 2010. *Ratification: The People Debate the Constitution, 1787–1788*. New York: Simon & Schuster.

Mill, J. S. 1956. *On Liberty*. New York: Liberal Arts Press.

Milton, J. 1644. *Areopagitica: A speech of Mr. John Milton for the liberty of unlicensed printing to the Parliament of England*. Available at: www.constitution.org/milton/areopagitica.htm.

Sharp, J. R. 1993. *American Politics in the Early Republic: The New Nation in Crisis*. New Haven: Yale University Press.

Siebert, W. H. 1920. *The Loyalists of Pennsylvania*. Columbus: The University at Columbus.

Stewart, J. B. 1976. *Holy Warriors: The Abolitionists and American Slavery*. New York: Hill and Wang.

Storing, H. J. 1981. *What the Anti-Federalists Were For*. Chicago: University of Chicago Press.

Van Tyne, C. H. 1902. *The Loyalists in the American Revolution*. New York: The Macmillan Company.

White, G. E. 1996. "The First Amendment comes of age: The emergence of free speech in twentieth-century America," *Michigan Law Review* 95: 299–392.

12

The Evolution of a Russian Concept of Free Speech

Elena Sherstoboeva

INTRODUCTION

Without examining the historic evolution of free speech in any specific context, one can neither understand its current meaning nor predict its future development. In Russia, freedom of speech only emerged as a legal concept in 1990 on the eve of the collapse of the USSR. While the public had considerable hopes, in those halcyon days, for generating an open society free from censorship or state pressure, those hopes soon dissolved. Perhaps history now sheds light on why that was the case. In the last few years, scholars and experts have noted increasing attempts by the Russian government to intensify control over speech, particularly online speech. This poses several questions, which this chapter will try to answer:[1] Why is this happening? What is the real meaning of the concept of free speech in Russia? How has it been impacted by Soviet ideology and legislation? How has the Russian concept of free speech been affected by international standards?[2]

The chapter begins with an analysis of the Soviet perspective on speech and the press, particularly how Marxism-Leninism and the Soviet Constitutions

[1] This chapter draws on research from the project "Russian media markets between modernization and conservatism: social meanings, managerial disruptions and regulation," carried out within the framework of the Basic Research Program at the National Research University Higher School of Economics (HSE) in 2016.

[2] In this chapter, the term "international standards" refers to the documents of the United Nations (UN), the Organization for Security and Cooperation in Europe (OSCE), as well as of the Council of Europe. Russia participates in these organizations and has ratified their most important documents, which have established foundations for the freedom of speech. "International standards" encompasses not only conventional documents, such as the Universal Declaration of Human Rights (UDHR), the International Covenant on Civil and Political Rights (ICCPR), and the European Convention on Human Rights (ECHR), but also international case law, such as European Court of Human Rights (ECtHR) case law, as well as recommendations interpreting the conventional norms on free speech.

shaped the concept, and then proceeds to examine *glasnost*. The chapter then studies concepts related to speech in legislation concerning mass media, followed by the modern Russian constitutional concept of free speech, showing how it has been interpreted and implemented in legislation as well as in the practice of the highest Russian courts.

THE SOVIET PERSPECTIVE ON FREE SPEECH

Marxism-Leninism is a key theory underpinning the Soviet perspective on speech and the press in the construction of society. It was recognized as the party's leading ideology in the USSR's 1936 Constitution and proclaimed as the country's official ideology in the next USSR Constitution of 1977. It should be noted, however, that Karl Marx was not a Russian author, he was not thinking of Russia when he elaborated his theories and he did not even play a role in the Russian revolutions, unlike Vladimir Lenin. Marxism-Leninism was developed by Lenin to represent his understanding of Marx's ideas.

Marxist-Leninist Perspectives on Free Speech

Marx challenged the liberal approach to freedom of the press on the grounds that it led to commercialization. He suggested that freedom of the press was the highest human value. According to Marx, freedom of the press should not be a "privilege of particular persons" because it is a "privilege of people's spirit" (Marx 1842, p. 55). Therefore, the press should not be grasped by the establishment or commercialized. Marx claimed that "the main freedom of the press is not to be a business:" a writer should make money in order to exist or write, but not write and exist in order to make money (Marx 1842, p. 76). Marx valued press freedom per se and stressed its significance for human self-recognition as well as for intellectual development. For Marx, one could not realize other human freedoms without press freedom, because all democratic freedoms are interconnected.

He rejected any censorial laws as mere punishment for opinions, since no law can actually eliminate them. Furthermore, Marx considered censorship as unnatural and harmful: a censored press, he said, is a "deformity of non-freedom, is a civilizational monster" (Marx 1842, p. 58). Marx refuted arguments that the press needs restrictions in order to prevent its abuses because any media can abuse its power but censorship is an ineffective and harmful remedy from such abuses. He also questioned the competence of censors. As a journalist, Marx also defended authors' anonymity, which, he stated, facilitates greater freedom and impartiality of both author and audience because the personality of the author can impact the audience's judgment (Marx 1843).

Marx believed that, being a separate branch of social control, the press should be absolutely free and independent from the authorities. He also claimed that, in order to solve vital problems, both governments and people needed a "certain third element" an independent press, "with a citizen's head and a civic heart" (Marx 1843, p. 206). A free press is beneficial for governments and people because it highlights peoples' needs to the state authorities, while censorship "kills governmental spirit" (Marx 1842, p. 69). He believed that censorship forces people to consider free (uncensored) works as illegal. Therefore, people become accustomed to thinking that "free" means illegal and that exercising freedom shows disregard for the law.

For Marx, the only acceptable limitation was free criticism generated by the press itself. On equal rights, Marx suggested that people and governments should criticize each other's principles and requirements (Marx 1842). While rejecting the idea of censorial law, Marx nevertheless proclaimed the need to adopt a press law. According to Marx, a press law is a legal acknowledgment of a free press, while the lack of such a law exempts the press from legally acknowledged freedoms.

Lenin often called himself a journalist or a writer. Like Marx, Lenin was initially a proponent of the idea of fully free press and speech (Lenin 1905) and countered bourgeois freedom with "real" proletarian freedom driven by the idea of socialism rather than by profit. For Lenin, "free" meant to be free of capitalist power, of "careerism," as well as of "bourgeois and anarchical individualism" (Lenin 1905, p. 100). He argued that the freedom of the bourgeois intellectual is hypocritical because it is "dependent on moneybags" (Lenin 1905, p. 104). The bourgeois concept of freedom of the press, from Lenin's viewpoint, simply meant the freedom to bribe newspapers, buy writers and frame "public opinion" in favor of the bourgeois class (Lenin 1921).

The 1917 revolution made Lenin reconsider his support for absolute press freedom. In 1921, he wrote that "we do not believe in 'absolutes'" (Lenin 1921, p. 78) and he questioned: "[w]hich press freedom? For *whom*? For *which* class?" (Lenin 1921, p. 78). Lenin justified press restrictions with the need to combat powerful bourgeois enemies, who "besieged" speech in Soviet Russia. Absolute press freedom could serve as a bourgeois weapon against communism. From Lenin's perspective, the Party's insufficiencies could be eliminated by "proletarian and Party measures" rather than by bourgeois freedoms.

Unlike Marx, Lenin did not acknowledge the value of press freedom for its own sake. Lenin stated that the press had to serve as a tool for socialist construction and to be a collective propagandist, agitator, and organizer. The press, according to Lenin, had to follow several interconnected principles, among which the most important were *partiinost, ideinost,* and *narodnost.*

Partiinost meant that literature and press should become part of the activities of the Bolshevik Party, a forerunner of the Communist Party of the Soviet Union. Newspapers had to become the Party's organs, and writers had to join the Party in order to create new literature promoting the Party's policies (Lenin 1905). According to the principle of *ideinost,* the press had to disseminate the Bolshevik Party's ideas.

Narodnost meant that the press must be created for the masses and by the masses. After the 1917 Revolution, Lenin wanted to ensure the "active participation" of the masses in building the national economy and so claimed that the main task of the press during transition from capitalism to communism is to educate the masses especially on issues of national economy" (Lenin 1918). Calling for the press to reveal defects in the economy and to report about the best practices in all spheres of a new life, Lenin introduced the principle of *glasnost* (openness) and accountability in production and distribution. However, Lenin wanted the press to interpret facts and events in the light of the Party's policies and refrain from extensive debates on political issues. Therefore, the principle of *partiinost* remained the main principle determining speech and press policies.

Soviet Regulation of Speech

While Marx was merely an observer and critic, Lenin illustrated his theories with pervasive action, which was sweeping and revolutionary in its impact. He could demonstrate and structure the role the press and speech should play. The first Soviet press law, the 1917 Decree on the Press of the Council of People's Commissars of the Russian Soviet Federative Socialist Republic, caused the shutdown of ninety-two newspapers and triggered the "Bolshevization" of the press (McNair 1991). The decree was announced as a temporary measure, but it endured and remained in place until 1990.

In realizing Lenin's perspective, the Russian Constitution (1918) and the Soviet Constitutions of 1924 and 1936 ostensibly guaranteed freedom of speech and of the press but, as a matter of theory, only to the laboring class. The USSR's ratification in 1973[3] of the International Covenant on Civil and Political Rights (ICCPR) caused Lenin's concept of "proletarian" free speech to be reconsidered. The USSR's new 1977 Constitution

[3] The ICCPR was ratified by the Decree of the Presidium of the Supreme Soviet of the USSR on September 18, 1973.

proclaimed freedom of speech and of the press for all citizens, echoing the formal ICCPR commitments. Nevertheless, both constitutions granted these freedoms with the aim of developing socialism and understood them merely in the context of a state duty to provide certain equipment and other conditions. In other words, these freedoms constituted no rights for either the laboring class or citizens in general. Along with Lenin and contrary to Marx, the constitutions only valued free speech and a free press within the goals of the Soviet regime.

The USSR's ratification of the ICCPR also led to the drafting of a proposed press statute in 1976, but it was not adopted. The draft would have banned censorship and granted some version of press freedom more generally. Press freedom was understood in the draft to be the right freely to express opinions and receive information of interest to citizens on all issues of state, social, and cultural life, but only to the extent that it did not contradict the aims of the socialist state. In general, the USSR's membership of the UN and ratification of the ICCPR had no effect on the regulation of speech in the USSR, being aimed purely at external propaganda.

Concept of Glasnost

Another perspective on free speech was formed in the USSR during the *perestroika* (restructuring) period (1985–90), in which *glasnost* became a central idea developed by Mikhail Gorbachev, then general secretary of the Communist Party of the Soviet Union. Like Lenin, Gorbachev initially promoted the idea of *glasnost* to involve people in solving the problems related to the national economy. The core of *glasnost* was to allow access to information, as Baturin (2006) notes, but that access was mainly to ensure a measure of control by working people over the execution of the Party's decisions. Gorbachev believed that access to information would make people more informed and more socially active, with the result that they would work more effectively.

However, in 1987, Gorbachev's concepts soon started to differ significantly from Lenin's. In the course of the January Central Committee Plenum of the Communist Party of the Soviet Union, Gorbachev announced comprehensive reforms for the democratization of the Soviet economy, society and international policy. *Glasnost* became the central tenet of the reforms, and Gorbachev gradually expanded the boundaries, allowing access and criticism. In particular he claimed: "[i]n Soviet society, there should not be any zones closed to criticism. This is entirely related to the media" (Gorbachev 1987). Gorbachev also called for criticism of the Soviet past, particularly Stalinism, in order "to move forward."

Nevertheless, along with the Marxist-Leninist perspective, *glasnost* contradicted the bourgeois concept of free speech. Gorbachev claimed that *glasnost* was a broader concept than free speech and included not only "the right of citizens to express opinions openly on political and social issues" but also "the duties of the Party and state bodies to be open when making decisions, to respond to criticism and to pay attention to recommendations" (cited in Richter 2007, p. 40).

The main document of that period was the 1988 resolution on *glasnost*.[4] It proclaimed the need to create a constitutional basis for the right to information. It also outlined acceptable limitations to *glasnost*,[5] which look similar to the limitations on freedom of expression established in the ICCPR. The resolution assigned journalism to be a tool of "public control," comprehensively highlighting the activities of the Party and state as well as nongovernmental organizations, so that Soviet readers would be aware of these activities, and could criticize them and create their own initiatives. The resolution even attempted to elaborate on the notion of "public interest" by proclaiming citizens' rights to receive information "on any issue of social life" and to conduct open and free discussions on "any issue of public importance," largely developing provisions of the 1976 draft press statute.

However, *glasnost* was not a right but a privilege (Fedotov 2002). Both criticism and access were meted out in small doses and used to justify the "correctness" of state policy. In practice, journalists were legally powerless: while they were very influential, they had no rights or freedoms and could not establish media enterprises. Because the USSR was part of the Commission on Security and Cooperation in Europe (now the OSCE) and political leaders wanted to show some adherence to the commission's principles,[6] a new press statute was included in the agenda in 1986. However, it was more a matter of political image than a demonstration of real convictions. As Fedotov (2002) notes, the new draft was even more conservative than the 1976 draft and was ultimately not adopted. At that time, words significantly differed from reality.

---

[4] Adopted at the XIX All-Union Party's conference on July 1, 1988.

[5] The resolution called for a ban on any use of *glasnost* to the detriment of the state and public interest, of society and human rights, to advocate war, violence, racism, or national and religious intolerance, or for the dissemination of pornography, as well as any subversive manipulation of *glasnost* itself. It also sought to establish responsibility for the violation of citizens' rights and damage to public order, security, public health, or morality.

[6] Fedotov (2002) suggests that the OSCE meeting in Vienna in 1986 was of particular importance. The USSR signed the concluding document of that meeting, adopted on January 15, 1989.

Nevertheless, the policy of *glasnost* opened space for the flow of information. As Brown (2007) suggests, by 1987 free speech had become nearly unlimited. When journalists moved on from "socialistic pluralism of opinions" to real free speech, public opinion "obediently followed journalists" (Fedotov 2002, p. 28). *Glasnost* crystallized demands for the adoption of a press statute to legitimize the new status quo.

THE POST-SOVIET PERSPECTIVE ON FREE SPEECH

Freedom of Speech in Media Statutes

The 1990 USSR Law on Press and Other Mass Media (Press Statute) was adopted in the last throes of the Soviet period. It was not Soviet in spirit and drastically altered the Soviet legal concept of free speech and free press. For the first time in the USSR, formal censorship was officially banned. In theory, free expression was guaranteed to all citizens without any reservations or reference to socialism. Soviet citizens were granted limited rights to establish media outlets, and journalists obtained a wide range of rights and freedoms within press organizations, including in selecting the editor.

The Press Statute had as its underlying conception a unique blend of Soviet and emerging European perspectives. Media would be registered with a state body and professionalism was something that could be regulated. Because of its scope the statute only affected professional journalism. It defined free speech and free press as the right to express opinions, and to seek, select, receive, and disseminate information as well as ideas in any form including in the media. The same definition conceptualized both freedom of speech and freedom of the press, but in a way that limited rights of free speech, reducing them merely to a press freedom and virtually transforming free speech into the journalists' right. Citizens' right to access information could be realized only through the media, as provided by the statute.

The 1990 USSR statute was, to a large degree, a declaration, but it caused the legal destruction of the state monopoly over the media, as well as the rapid development of private news outlets. After the ban on the Soviet Communist Party in 1991, the Party's own press ceased to exist and there were thousands of examples of journalists transforming the party's news outlets into private ownership (Richter 1995). This formed a new model for journalism: journalists then considered themselves to be a "fourth power" (Zassoursky 2006).

The Russian Statute on Mass Media (Mass Media Statute) was adopted on December 27, 1991. In two months, it replaced the USSR Press Statute and remains in force today. The statute sought to transform declarations in the

Press Statute into efficient legal mechanisms. For instance, it defined censorship by banning preliminary as well as punitive censorship[7] and prohibiting the creation or funding of censoring bodies as had existed in Soviet times. The statute also created some unique legal mechanisms to ensure editorial independence not only from government, but also from boards of directors or arbitrary action by the publisher. Interestingly, instead of the concept of a free press, it introduced a new concept, the freedom of mass information, later guaranteed in the Russian Constitution.

The freedom of mass information[8] is a unique post-Soviet concept, which looks beyond press freedom. The freedom of mass information is not only the right of media outlets or professional journalists. It is also the right of every single individual to seek, receive, produce, and disseminate mass information to undetermined receivers, as well as the right to employ technical equipment. It is clear that the importance of the freedom of mass information goes beyond the time this freedom was created, because it can now be seen as a fundamental instrument to protect online modalities of journalism beyond the traditional concept of media or press freedom. However, the Mass Media Statute considers the freedom of mass information to be a negative freedom, thus negating its positive influence (Richter 2011).

The Mass Media Statute contains inadequate provisions to protect the media from interference by major economic players, such as emerging oligarchs, most likely because such a problem had not existed in Soviet times nor in the early 1990s when Russian journalism is sometimes said to have experienced its "golden age." Additionally, the statute retained the procedures of state outlet registration and media closure established by the USSR Press Statute as a result of a compromise between new and old political forces.

Nevertheless, the Mass Media Statute formed essential frameworks for further development of the Russian communication policy, as Price noted (1995). Price hoped that the imperfections of the Mass Media Statute could be ironed out in future applications but acknowledged that this would require appropriate institutions to interpret and adjust the statute to "pluralistic goals" (Price 1995, p. 806).

---

[7] According to Article 3 of the Mass Media Statute, "censorship" means two actions: requesting editorial offices to allow pre-approval of information or materials (except in cases when a requesting person is the author or an interviewee); or banning the dissemination of all or any parts of any information or materials.

[8] The Mass Media Statute defines the freedom of mass information as the right: to seek, receive, produce, and disseminate mass information; to establish mass-media outlets and to own, use, and dispose of them; and to make, acquire, keep, and employ technical facilities and raw and other materials meant for the production and distribution of mass-media content.

A Constitutional Concept of Freedom of Speech

The need for a new constitution was universally understood by 1992, as underscored by the political confrontation between the Russian Parliament and its then president, Boris Yeltsin. The competing factions had developed their own separate drafts for the constitution: the draft of the Constitutional Commission (debated in 1990–3) and the Presidential draft (debated in 1993). The latter became the basis for the new constitution and was debated by the new deliberative body, the Constitutional Conference, called by Yeltsin.

The approach to free speech in both drafts was similar, differing only in structure and terminology. The participants at the Constitutional Conference saw freedom of speech as an abstract, Western value that would be a prerequisite for any democratic state. Censorship was a natural taboo, and participants at the conference unanimously rejected the proposal to exclude the ban on censorship from the draft. In 1992, Russia had already expressed its intention to enter the Council of Europe, which would impact the constitutional provisions. During the debates, the participants attempted to rely upon international documents to show their adherence to new Western democratic values, but they sometimes lacked knowledge of international standards. In the course of the debates at the Constitutional Conference, provisions from both proposed drafts were incorporated in the article on free speech of the Russian Constitution.

The Russian Constitution was adopted by a national referendum on December 12, 1993. Article 29[9] develops and enshrines at the constitutional level the perspective on free speech elaborated by the mass-media statutes of 1990–1. At the same time, the constitutional concept of free speech is broader. It includes several elements: freedom of thought and speech; freedom of opinion; the right to access information; and freedom of mass information. A specific limitation excluding hate speech from protection is also based on provisions of this statute, which banned various abuses of the freedom of mass information, including hate speech, in its Article 4.

---

[9] Article 29 of the Russian Constitution guarantees free speech in the following way: "1. Everyone is guaranteed the freedom of thought and speech. 2. Propaganda or agitation exciting social, racial, national or religious hatred and strife is not permitted. Propaganda of social, racial, national, religious or linguistic superiority is banned. 3. No-one may be compelled to express his or her opinions and convictions or to renounce them. 4. Everyone has the right freely to seek, receive, pass on, produce and disseminate information by any lawful means. A list of information comprising state secrets is determined by federal law. 5. The freedom of mass information is guaranteed. Censorship is banned."

Because the constitution neither defines the freedom of speech nor its elements, Russian scholars argue about their precise meanings. Despite various interpretations, scholars tend to consider Article 29 in the light of international standards or Western constitutional norms. Baglay (2004) stresses that Russian free speech is akin to other free-speech concepts found in all democratic constitutions.

Indeed, the Russian constitutional concept of free speech is almost identical to the one declared in international documents, such as Article 19 of the UDHR, Article 19 of the ICCPR, and Article 10 of the ECHR.[10] Along with international standards, the constitution does not consider free speech to be an absolute freedom. According to Article 55(3) of the constitution, it can be limited "by federal law and to such an extent as is necessary for the protection of the fundamental principles of the constitutional system, morality, health, the rights and lawful interests of other people, for ensuring defense of the country, and security of the State."

Such an approach is similar to the so-called three-part test[11] in Article 19(3) of the ICCPR and Article 10(2) of the ECHR. The limitation on the freedom of speech in Russia in a state of emergency (Article 56 of the constitution) also correlates with international standards, in particular Article 15 of the ECHR. Another limitation excluding hate speech from protection in Article 29(2) of the Russian Constitution may have a connection with Article 20(2) of the ICCPR, as well as with Articles 10(2) and 14 of the ECHR. Even a vague ban on inciting "social hatred" might have been interpreted in the light of international standards as protecting minorities.

However, scholars assess the ramifications of the "universality" of constitutional norms differently. Pastukhov (2008) argues that the Russian Constitution should not be a "universal cloak." Universality causes indeterminacy of the Russian Constitution, which may explain why Russia's "democratic" theories

[10] The UDHR, Article 19 guarantees everyone the right to freedom of opinion and expression and states that "this right includes the freedom to hold opinions without interference and to seek, receive and impart information and ideas through any media and regardless of frontiers." The ICCPR, Article 19 provides that the right to freedom of expression "shall include the freedom to seek, receive and impart information and ideas of all kinds, regardless of frontiers, either orally, in writing, in print, in the form of art, or through any other chosen media." The ECHR, Article 10 states that the right to freedom of expression includes "freedom to hold opinion and to receive and impart information and ideas without interference by a public authority and regardless of frontiers."

[11] This test implies that: limitations must be *provided by law*; there must be a *legitimate aim* for limitations; limitations of the freedom of expression must be *necessary* in a democratic society, meaning that, in the absence of a strong social need, limitations must not be imposed. The Russian Constitution does not establish this third criterion, but agrees to apply it by ratifying the documents mentioned above.

of information rights have become "formulae for authoritarian rather than popular control" (Foster 2002, p. 107). At the same time, Balkin sees no problem with the application of abstract or vague constitutional norms because "we must apply them to our own circumstances in our own time" (2011, p. 3). Thus, they can be adjusted better to the needs of modern society by means of prompt and proper interpretation of constitutional norms, although that depends on the integrity of the courts.

The onset of institutionalization in Russia coincided with a bitter political conflict and significant economic challenges. In this very early stage of construction, journalists were not used to having freedoms. In a free environment, they felt more like activists in their treatment of news. They were not impartial or objective, and they were almost doing politics rather than journalism. Although, in 1994–5, the state nearly lost financial and ideological control over the flow of information, free speech was realized more as a free-for-all including bootlegging, payola, and yellow journalism, instead of a free flow of information. Facing new financial challenges caused by the market economy, many journalists began to abuse their power.

Legal rules soon became unnecessary. Between 1996 and 2000, free speech mainly served as a weapon in the "information wars" of the Russian tycoons. By 1996, they had taken control over the media, leaving the Russian media politicized while politics were "mediatized" (Kachkaeva 2006). Yeltsin and his team considered Russia's entrance to the Council of Europe (CoE) on the eve of the presidential elections in 1996 only in a political sense, as Bowring suggests (Bowring 1996). Ratification of the ECHR in 1998 could not impact the concept of free speech at that time.

Journalism became a tool for manipulation and propaganda, just as Marx and Lenin had predicted. This model of journalism is termed "authoritarian and corporatist" (Zassoursky 2006). Propaganda came roaring back and political journalism gradually transformed into "PR-nalism." Tabloid journalism flourished. All this shaped a social demand for censorship. Efimova stated (2000) that the "ultra-naïve" and "ortho-liberal" approach of pure free speech was not very appropriate for regulating the media.

Free Speech Under Putin

In 2000, a new perspective on freedom of speech was put forward and remains in place today. On September 9, 2000, Vladimir Putin, the newly elected Russian president, approved the Doctrine of Information Security of the Russian Federation, which established the main trajectory for legal developments on freedom of speech. Reminiscent of Lenin's argument against unlimited free speech in order to combat internal and external enemies of the Soviet ideology, the doctrine states that Russian "national" interests, which are in fact the interests of the political establishment, require protection from "internal and external informational threats."

As analysis of the doctrine has shown, these threats come from private media disseminating political dissent and from various foreign and international organizations, which may also support this dissent by various means. Fedotov (2001) argues that private media are, according to the doctrine, the prime threat to the safety of information in Russia, rather than hackers or terrorists. The doctrine states that the media particularly threaten Russians by "restricting their freedom of thought" and propagating moral values alien to Russian society.

According to the doctrine, various foreign and international organizations, including criminal and terrorist groups, act against Russian "national interests" with the aim of intentionally weakening the state's influence on Russian society and of reinforcing Russia's "dependence" on foreign sources of information for their "spiritual, economic, and political spheres of a social life." Like Lenin's writing, this document is intended to protect official ideology and, for that, it applies rhetoric that significantly resembles that of Lenin. However, unlike Gorbachev, the modern Russian political leadership has never directly referred to Lenin's writing in order to justify new policy, in order to avoid negatively impacting Russia's democratic image.

Although the constitutional provisions on free speech remain the same, in reality the concept of free speech has been significantly transformed by the doctrine. This includes consolidation of the state-owned media and making laws on freedom of speech a tool for "neutralizing" information that the Russian political establishment deems threatening. Consequently, speech requires constant limitation through legislation. While the doctrine is not a legally binding document, its perspective has gradually been implemented in Russia, thus providing several directions for legislation limiting free speech.

In the 2000s, this gave rise to antiextremist legislation, which emerged under the pretext of combating terrorism. The Russian legal concept of extremism is unique, presenting an entire mechanism for suppressing freedom of speech and covering "almost all forms of political dissent" (Richter 2012, p. 290). Several CoE documents requested that Russia reconsider the concept of extremism. Among these are the Opinion of the European Commission for Democracy through Law (better known as the Venice Commission, which is the CoE's advisory body of experts on legislation) and reports about Russia by the European Commission Against Racism and Intolerance. However, all the documents have thus far been ignored. Furthermore, this antiextremist mechanism has been significantly advanced and constantly adjusted to the regime's goals. For instance, it has also been recently applied to a ban on discussions about the annexation of the Crimean peninsula.

After 2000, the new state media policy led to a decline in the authority of the media and caused a "state-controlled model" of the media in Russia (Zassoursky 2006). Starting between 2000 and 2003, Putin managed to wrest control over the traditional media from the major tycoons. To curb media freedom, the state developed a "paternalistic" policy implying a great dependence of the media on the state, primarily financial (Eriomin 2011). The entire legal structure of state support for the independent press was abolished. Subsovereign entities were virtually deprived of the opportunity to pass their own mass-media legislation. Several laws constrained the establishment of outlets for foreign companies or Russian companies with foreign stakeholders. All national television stations became directly or indirectly state-owned, including the Russian public service television founded in 2012.

Rapid growth in laws restricting online speech has been observed since the 2011–12 Russian mass-protest movement, in which the Internet played a significant role. Since then, the Russian regime has seen the Internet as a threat to its "national interests" or, as Asmolov argues, the Internet plays the role, alongside the USA, of Russia's external enemy (Asmolov 2015), which may explain attempts by the Russian state to establish a national intranet in Russia. The Internet is particularly threatening to Russian "national interests" because it helps to disseminate political dissent coming from within Russia as well as from abroad.

This may also explain why Russian legislation abounds in regulations controlling the online activities of global companies and users, while it lacks regulation specifically protecting online speech or the Internet itself. According to Russian legislation, popular blogs having more than 3,000 visitors per day, as well as social media and messaging services, must be registered with the Russian state watchdog agency, Roskomnadzor, which also blacklists websites. Social media and messaging services must store users' correspondence for six months and provide state bodies with that correspondence upon request. Popular bloggers are obliged to perform journalistic duties without having the relevant rights and their identities cannot be anonymous. Personal data relating to Russian citizens must be stored within the Russian territory; access may be blocked to foreign websites that contain personal data of Russian citizens. According to Russian legislation on the right to be forgotten, search engines are obliged to delete any outdated information, even information in the public interest.

This concept of speech in society gives much attention to the individual sphere of the Russian people in novel ways: protection of the national interest engages ideas of "spiritual renewal" and "patriotism." Therefore, since 2010, Russia has widely regulated morality. This includes a ban on propaganda for "untraditional" sexual relationships, a ban on obscene language in media, blogs or films, as well as during any live shows. After a landmark case on the musical band "Pussy Riot," Russia also criminalized insulting religious feelings.

Against the backdrop of sanctions and decline of the Russian national currency after the annexation of Crimea in 2014, maintenance of the media assets became costly. To keep control over public opinion, the government had to provide new privileges in the media sector to loyal business people and corporations and to state-run media organizations. The combination of commercial and political rationales instigated new limitations to foreign media ownership. They caused the new wave of media redistribution in favor of loyal structures which considerably changed the media market in Russia.

It seems, however, that many Russians support strict speech regulation. A 2010 questionnaire conducted by the Russian sociological company, VTSIOM, showed that more than half of Russians (58 percent) support the need for censorship because the mass media is "oversaturated" by violence, vulgarity and misinformation" (Fedorov 2010). More recent research by the Center for Global Communication Studies at the University of Pennsylvania, and the Russian Public Opinion Research Center (2015) has indicated that nearly half of Russians support online censorship. These results may provide evidence of an extreme level of self-censorship or great public support for Russia's policy on speech and the press.

On December 6, 2016, Putin's decree approved the new Doctrine of Information Security of the Russian Federation, which develops the main provisions of the 2000 Doctrine but the new narratives seem to get even closer to the Marxist-Leninist's stances and to the Soviet policy in the period of the Cold War. The Doctrine claims that "several countries" use information technologies to destabilize the political and social situation in Russia and to undermine its national sovereignty "in military purposes." With this aim, such countries exploit various individuals, religious, ethnic, and human rights organizations, as well as hackers, as the document says. It also claims that such countries discriminate the image of the Russian media abroad, interfere with Russian journalism, and exert "information influence" to the Russian population to "blur traditional Russian spiritual and moral values." Among the main measure of resistance, the Doctrine proposes further advances in the country's militarization and protection of state secrecy, national regulation of the Internet, the education of Russians as to the spiritual sphere as well as promotion of the Russian vision in the international arena.

RUSSIAN JUDICIAL DOCTRINE ON THE FREEDOM OF SPEECH

Russia is not a common law country, but the examination of court practice is, nevertheless, very important to determine how concepts of rights and free speech are interpreted or implemented. Of particular interest is the practice of the Russian Constitutional Court, which is authorized to verify the constitutionality of laws and instigate the abolition of unconstitutional laws. Recently, Russian law authorized the Russian Constitutional Court with the power to challenge any document of any international body. This step is unprecedented anywhere in the world.

The practice of the Russian Supreme Court is also significant because it may offer examples of law enforcement and clarify abstract or vague provisions for the lower courts, on which its decisions are legally binding.

Krug's (2008) analysis of the highest Russian courts' practice in relation to Article 29 of the constitution (on free speech) indicated "a normative paradox." The highest courts often failed to apply Article 29 in cases requiring its application. For instance, important decisions regarding the closure of federal television stations NTV and TV-6 were treated purely as business disputes.[12] Krug noted that, even though the courts mentioned Article 29, they neither interpreted it nor established any consistent doctrine regarding it. At the same time, Krug highlighted some positive developments in the practice of the Russian Supreme Court concerning free speech and forecasted that ECtHR case law could positively impact Russian jurisprudence in the future.

The author's analysis[13] of the practice of the highest Russian courts regarding Article 29 over the last decade has revealed several changes in the trends highlighted by Krug. This has shown that the courts always engage Article 29, as well as international standards, in cases concerning free speech. However, the resulting outcomes for the Russian right to free speech differ between the two highest courts.

---

[12] Resolution of the Constitutional Court of the Russian Federation on the case of the constitutionality test of Article 35 of the Federal Statute on Joint-Stock Companies; Articles 61 and 99 of the Civil Code of the Russian Federation; Article 31 of the Tax Code of the Russian Federation; and Article 14 of the Arbitral Procedural Code of the Russian Federation in response to complaints of a citizen, A. B. Borisov, and companies Media-Most and Moscow Independent Broadcasting Corporation (Moscow, July 18, 2003).

[13] This analysis was undertaken for the author's PhD thesis.

For the Constitutional Court, the application of the constitution and international standards is often just a formality. For instance, in 2013, the court rejected a complaint by a citizen, Kochemarov,[14] who complained about the ambiguity of the antiextremist law. The court claimed that the challenged provisions were constitutional because they merely elaborated the constitutional ban on propaganda exciting hatred, enmity, and supremacy. The court claimed that the laws on extremism complied fully with international standards, despite calls from several CoE bodies to reformulate them.

Furthermore, the Constitutional Court tends to apply international standards to justify the legitimacy of new and excessive restrictions on freedom of speech, and such justification is often inconsistent and open to question. For instance, in its 2011 decision on the complaints of Kondratijeva and Mumolin,[15] the court misinterpreted the ECtHR case law in claiming that public service requires "loyalty and restraint." It thus justified the constitutionality of laws preventing officials from criticizing the bodies in which they work, contradicting ECtHR case law. In 2014, the court invoked the UN and CoE conventions to justify the constitutionality of the ban against propaganda for "untraditional" sexual relationships among minors.[16] No reference was made to the landmark ECtHR decision of February 9, 2012, *Vejdeland and Others v. Sweden*, banning homophobic speech.

On the other hand, the Russian Supreme Court tends to engage Article 29 and international standards to shape its free-speech doctrine so that lower courts can establish a balance between the protection of free speech, and other rights and legitimate interests. Over the last decade, this court has issued several specific decrees of its plenum[17] on various free-speech issues, such as

[14] Resolution of the Constitutional Court of the Russian Federation on the admissibility of the complaint of citizen, V. S. Kochemarov, complaining about the violation of his constitutional rights by Article 1, paras. 1 and 3 and Article 13, para. 3 of the Federal Statute of the Russian Federation on Counteraction of Extremism Activity (Saint-Petersburg, July 2, 2013).

[15] Resolution of the Constitutional Court of the Russian Federation on the case of the constitutionality test of Article 17, para. 1(10) of the Federal Statute on the State Civil Service and of Article 201 of the Statute of the Russian Federation on the Police in response to complaints by two citizens, L. N. Kondratijeva and A. N. Mumolin (Saint-Petersburg, June 30, 2011).

[16] Resolution of the Constitutional Court of the Russian Federation on the case of the constitutionality test of Article 6.21 part 1 of the Russian Code of Administrative Offences in response to complaints of citizens, N. A. Alexeev, Y. N. Yevtushenko and D. A. Isakov (Saint-Petersburg, September 23, 2014).

[17] The Plenum is a body of the Supreme Court, comprising all its judges, which has the aim of ensuring a proper and unified application of laws by various courts as well as explaining and interpreting laws by issuing decrees.

defamation (2005), extremism (2011), elections (2011), terrorism (2012), and the Mass Media Statute (2010).

The decree on the Mass Media Statute[18] is of specific importance because it not only addresses media freedom but also contributes several significant developments for free speech, thus showing that freedom of mass information goes beyond media freedom. Referring to international standards, the decree states that the freedoms of expression and of mass information comprise fundamentals for the development of modern society. Therefore, their limitations cannot be arbitrary and must only be aimed at protecting rights and interests which are critical for the development of a democratic country. The decree also tried to define the concepts of public interest as well as of the freedom to access the Internet. It also refers to several critical media issues, such as censorship, editorial independence, self-regulation, journalistic access to information, and media outlet registration (see Richter 2015).

The Supreme Court seems to be the only shield protecting speech in Russia. In the Pussy Riot case, the Supreme Court found mistakes and sent the case back for reconsideration, which resulted in a reduction in the defendants' sentence. In 2014, the court protected Rosbalt, an online news media outlet, from revocation of its registration certificate for the publication of links to videos containing obscene language. The Supreme Court found the punishment significantly disproportionate.

However, it is complicated for the Russian Supreme Court to stand alone against current policy for speech and the media. Unlike the Constitutional Court, it has no authority to bring about repeals or revisions of repressive laws. Moreover, lower courts can ignore or misinterpret its rulings.

CONCLUSION

Overall, politics has been the main driver of the free-speech debates in Russia and, more generally, for determining the role and boundaries of speech and press in society. Political regime-change has always triggered reconsideration of the Russian concept of free speech and each political administration has employed the concept as a tool to serve its political goals.

The Russian concept of speech and media regulation has become extremely polarized, as reflected by two divergent bursts in the laws regulating speech: in the early 1990s and since 2000 until now, and these periods

---

[18] The decree of the Plenum of the Supreme Court of the Russian Federation on the Practice of Application by Courts of the Mass Media Statute (June 15, 2010).

in Russian history are extremely different from one another. On the one hand, the Russian legal concept of free speech contains some rules (formed in 1991–3), that provide even greater freedoms and rights than those that are typically provided in Western countries. On the other, some rules explicitly legitimize censoring practices (formed during Putin's rulings). What is observed since 2000 can be characterized as a kind of "rollback" – to the practices and rhetoric of Soviet times, to censorship, and to state control over speech.

In other words, the Russian concept of free speech reflects the clash of two legal paradigms. The first one is the "pro-Western" concept, ultra-liberal and driven by escapism from the Soviet past (1990–3). The framers of this concept tried to stick to international standards and Western concepts, as they understood them.

The other paradigm (2000–present) embraces a somewhat "pro" or rather a "re-Soviet" attitude, which is really a rollback to the "anti-Western" stance, driven by a need to legitimize censoring practices in order to regain state control over the flow of information.

The analysis of judicial practices by the two high Russian courts has also demonstrated a clash of the two paradigms with regard to speech regulation. While the Supreme Court sticks to the pro-Western patterns, the Constitutional Court's practice tends to express the re-Soviet paradigm. This makes the Constitutional provisions on free speech legally powerless. Although they were drafted in line with the pro-Western paradigm, the Constitutional Court tries to reinterpret them in the light of the pro-Soviet paradigm, subverting them substantially.

Despite their different vectors, these two legal paradigms are both inconsistent and even largely unrealistic and unattainable. The "pro-Western" concept has been naïve or abstract and neither was properly institutionalized nor implemented. As for the "re-Soviet" model, it must remain dormant for a while first. If it were fully implemented right now, it might result in the immediate shutdown of the Internet in Russia, which would be extremely undesirable for the regime economically. Therefore, censoring legislation has been enforced very selectively, so far, and has been very targeted, just as it was in Soviet times.

Both legal paradigms try to use the international standards as a tool for their regimes: the "pro-Western" model – for the integration of post-Soviet countries into the Western world as well as for internal propaganda of Yeltsin's regime, while the "pro-" or "re-Soviet" model uses international standards for the legitimization of restrictions on freedom of speech.

REFERENCES

Asmolov, G. (interviewed by G. Nejaskin) 2015. "Internet, kak i SShA, nachal vypol-njat' rol' vneshnego vraga (The internet, like the USA, has started to play the role of an external enemy)," *Slon*, August 12, 2015. Available at: https://slon.ru/posts/54906.

Baglay, M. 2004. *Konstitucionnoe Pravo Rossijskoj Federacii (The Constitutional Law of the Russian Federation)*. Moscow: Norma.

Balkin, J. 2011. *Living Originalism*. Cambridge, MA: Harvard University Press.

Baturin, Y. 2006. "Neokonchennaja istorija glasnosti (Unfinished story of glasnost)," in Zassoursky, Y. and Olga, Z. (eds.), *Glasnost i zhurnalistika: 1985–2005*. Moscow: Gorbachev-Fund, Faculty of Journalism of Moscow State University, pp. 14–29.

Bowring, B.1996. "Vstuplenie Rossii v Sovet Evropy i zashhita prav cheloveka: Vser'joz li vypolnjajutsja objazatel'stva?" ("Russia's entry to the Council of Europe and the protection of human rights: Are obligations really being performed?"). Available at: www.hrights.ru/text/b10/Chapter5.htm.

Brown, A. 2007. *Seven Years that Changed the World: Perestroika in Perspective*. Oxford: Oxford University Press.

Center for Global Communication Studies, University of Pennsylvania and Russian Public Opinion Research Center 2015. "Benchmarking public demand: Russia's appetite for internet control." Available at: www.global.asc.upenn .edu/publications/benchmarking-public-demand-russias-appetite-for-internet-control/.

Efimova, L. 2000. "Publichno-pravovye osnovy gosudarstvennogo regulirovanija tel-evidenija i radioveshhanija v. Rossijskoj Federacii" ("Public-law foundations of the state regulation of TV and radio broadcasting in the Russian Federation"), (*Kandidat nauk* (Candidate of Science) dissertation, Presidential Academy of Public Administration, Moscow).

Eriomin, A. 2011. "Gosudarstvennaja politika Rossijskoj Federacii po formirovaniju otrasli SMI" ("State policy of the Russian Federation on the formation of the media industry"), (*Kandidat nauk* (Candidate of Science) dissertation, Moscow State University, Moscow).

Fedorov, V. 2010. "Svobody ne hvataet no cenzura nuzhna" ("There is a lack of free-dom but censorship is needed"), *VTSIOM*. Available at: http://wciom.ru/index .php?id=266&uid=13779.

Fedotov, M. 2001. "Rossijskoe Pravo Massovoj Informacii na Fone Obshheevropejskih Standartov: Kontrasty i Polutona" ("Russian Law on Mass Information against the Background of the Common-European Standards: Contrasts and Nuances"), *Konstitucionnoe Pravo: Vostochnoevropejskoe Obozrenie (Constitutional Law: Eastern European Review)*, 3(36): 105–8.

2002. *Pravovye osnovy zhurnalistiki (Legal Basics of Journalism)*. Moscow: Vlados.

Foster, F. H. 2002. "Information and the problem of democracy: The Russian experi-ence," in Price, M., Richter, A., and Yu, P. K. (eds.), *Russian Media Law and Policy in the Yeltsin Decade: Essays and Documents*. The Hague: Kluwer Law International, Vol. 1, pp. 95–118.

Gorbachev, M. (1987). *O Perestrojke i Kadrovoj Politike Partii (On Perestroika and Personnel Policy of the Party)*. Report at the Plenum of the Central Committee of the Communist Party, January 27. Available at: www.constitution20.ru/ckeditor_assets/attachments/50/1987_01_27_gorbachev_o_perestr_i_kadr.pdf.

Kachkaeva, A. 2006. "Transformacija Rossijskogo televidenija" ("The transformation of Russian television"), in Zassoursky, Y. (ed.), *Sredstva massovoj informacii Rossii*. Moscow: Aspect Press Ltd, pp. 298–321.

Krug, P. 2008. "Press freedom in Russia: Does the constitution matter?," in Smith, G. B. and Sharlet, R. S. (eds), *Law in Eastern Europe. Volume 58: Russia and its Constitution: Promise and Political Reality*. Leiden: Koninklijke Brill NV, pp. 79–103

Lenin, V. 1905. "Partijnaja organizacija i partijnaja literatura" ("The party's organization and party's literature"), in Lenin 1968, Vol. 12, pp. 99–105.

1918. "Pervonachal'nyj variant stat'i ocherednye zadachi Sovetskoj vlasti" ("The original version of the article 'Immediate tasks of the Soviet power'"), in Lenin 1968, Vol. 36, pp. 127–64.

1921. "Pis'mo G. Mjasnikovu" ("The letter to G. Mjasnikov"), in Lenin 1968, Vol. 44, pp. 78–83.

1968. *Polnoe Sobranie Sochinenij (Complete Works)*. Moscow: Izdatel'stvo Politicheskoj Literatury. Available at: http://vkpb.ru/images/pdf/Lenin_pss/tom12.pdf.

Marx, K. 1842. "Debaty o svobode pechati i ob opublikovanii protokolov Soslovnogo Sobranija" ("Debates on freedom of the press and publication of the proceedings of the Assembly of the Estates"), in Marx and Engels 1955, Vol. 1, pp. 30–84.

1843. "Opravdanie Mozel'skogo korrespondenta" ("Justification of Mozel's correspondent"), in Marx and Engels 1955, Vol. 1, pp. 187–217.

McNair, B. 1991. *Glasnost, Perestroika and the Soviet Media*. London: Routledge.

Pastukhov, V. 2008. "Vtoroe dyhanie Russkogo konstitucionalizma" ("The second breath of Russian constitutionalism"), *Sravnitelnoe Konstitucionnoe Obozrenije* 2(63): 4–10.

Price, M. 1995. "Law, force and the Russian media," *Cardozo Arts & Entertainment Law Journal* 13: 795–846.

Richter, A. 1995. "The Russian press after perestroika," *Canadian Journal of Communication*. Available at: http://cjc-online.ca/index.php/journal/article/view/842/748.

2007. "Svoboda massovoj informacii v Postsovetskih gosudarstvah: Regulirovanie i samoregulirovanie zhurnalistiki v uslovijah perehodnogo perioda" ("The freedom of mass information in the post-Soviet states: Regulation and self-regulation under conditions of transitionary period"), (doctoral dissertation, Moscow State University, Moscow).

2011. "The post-Soviet media and communication policy landscape: The case of Russia," in Mansell, R. and Raboy, M. (eds.), *The Handbook of Global Media and Communication Policy*. Oxford: Wiley-Blackwell, pp. 192–209.

2012. "Freedom of mass information in the post-Soviet countries: Two models of regulation," in Gross, P. and Jakubowicz, K. (eds.), *Media Transformations in the Post-Communist World: Eastern Europe's Tortured Path to Change*. Plymouth: Lexington Books, pp. 155–232.

2015. "Russia's Supreme Court as media freedom protector," in Molnar, P. (ed.), *Free Speech and Censorship Around the Globe*. Budapest: Central European University Press, pp. 273–98.

Zassoursky, Y. 2006. "Tendencii funkcionirovanija SMI v sovremennoj strukture Rossijskogo obshhestva" ("Trends in functioning of the mass media in the modern structure of Russian society"), in Zassoursky, Y. (ed.), *Sredstva Massovoj Informacii Rossii*. Moscow: Aspect Press Ltd, pp. 3–50.

Part IV

Technologies and Ideologies in Turbulent Times

13

Free Speech, Traditional Values, and Hinduism in the Internet Age

Rohit Chopra

Voices are being silenced. Publishers are more frightened to publish ... The chilling effect of violence is very real and it is growing in this country. (Salman Rushdie)[1]

INTRODUCTION

This chapter examines the relationship between free speech, traditional values, and Hinduism in the digital age, with a focus on Hindu intolerance toward perceived attacks on Hindu values, culture, and faith. The author understands Hinduism broadly as a religious and cultural framework, focusing on the actions of groups that define and view themselves as Hindu. Beginning with an overview of the landscape of free speech in India, the chapter examines the relationship between Hindu speech, tradition, and religion with reference to four frames: ideas of freedom in Hindu texts; the colonial-era classification of Indians as constituted primarily by religious communities; the distinctive character of the secularism of the Indian state; and the impact of globalization and the Internet on Indian audiences across the globe. The focus is on how the relationship between Hindu speech, tradition, and religion is shaped by the politics of visibility, in which the public control of speech is seen as essential to the affirmation of Hindu identity by members and gatekeepers of the community. The chapter concludes with a brief reflection on recent developments in the arena of free speech, such as the accelerated corporatization of Indian media and initiatives by the Indian state to circumscribe speech on the Internet and in the media more widely. It shows that the practices opposing free speech displayed by self-professed ideologues of Hindu nationalism also hold wider legitimacy in Indian society.

---

[1] Speech at *India Today*, Conclave, 2012. The full speech is available at: http://conclave.intoday .in/conclave2012/speechtranscript.php?id=3429&issueid=38.

The definition of Hindus in this chapter includes but is not limited to those who espouse allegiance to the ideology of "Hindutva" or "Hinduness." This term refers to the core theory of Hindu nationalism. Articulated by V. D. Savarkar in a text initially published in 1923, the ideology of Hindutva defines the Indian nation as a fundamentally Hindu cultural entity. In Savarkar's definition, Hinduness encompassed more than religion in a narrow sense; it served as the fundamental ground of Indian identity (Savarkar 1969, pp. 3–4). According to the logic of Hindutva, Indian Muslims and Christians were followers of alien faiths who needed to acknowledge the foundational cultural identity of the Hindu motherland to qualify to be authentically Indian (Khilnani 1999, p. 161; Neufeldt 2003, p. 138; Vanaik 1997, p. 151).

The related term "Hindu nationalism" is best seen as describing a political project, which, as Christopher Jaffrelot notes, "took concrete shape in the 1920s," even if it drew on historical antecedents from the previous century (Jaffrelot 2007, p. 3). Jaffrelot calls it ethnic nationalism because its characteristics echo "many other European nationalisms based on religious identity, a common language, or even racial feeling" (Jaffrelot 2007, p. 5). However, it may be viewed somewhat more generally as a cultural nationalist project, in keeping with the movement's own insistence on Hindu culture as its basis. In political terms, "Hindu nationalism runs parallel to the dominant political tradition of the Congress Party, which Gandhi transformed into a mass organization in the 1920s" (Jaffrelot 2007, p. 3). Opposed to the Gandhian conception of India in the era of anticolonial resistance (Jaffrelot 2007, p. 4), Hindu nationalism has, since 1947, pitted itself against the secular nationalism of the independent Indian state. And especially since the 1990s, the Hindu nationalist movement has garnered increasing prominence in Indian social and political life. On December 6, 1992, a mob of Hindu nationalists destroyed a mosque, the Babri Masjid, in the Indian city of Ayodhya. It has been a longstanding claim of the movement that the mosque had been built by Babar, the first Mughal emperor of India, at the site of the birthplace of the Hindu deity, Lord Ram. The event, a turning point in the political history of the nation, led to religious rioting in several cities across India, fraying interfaith relations and dealing a severe blow to India's self-conception as a pluralistic, multi-religious society.

Hindu nationalism encompasses a broad range of religious, cultural, and political organizations, including the Rashtriya Swayamsevak Sangh (which forms the backbone of the movement), the Bharatiya Janata Party (the political party that spearheads the current Indian coalition government), the Vishwa Hindu Parishad, and the Hindu Mahasabha. That Hindu nationalism has succeeded in gaining widespread legitimacy, even as it has sought to remake itself in a more pragmatic vein, is borne out by the fact that the BJP-led alliance swept to power with an overwhelming majority in the 2014 national elections. The coalition secured 336 seats out of a total of 543 in the Lok Sabha or the lower house of the Indian Parliament, of which the BJP itself secured a remarkable 282. More recently, adherents of Hindu nationalism have begun using the term "Indian Right" to describe their sympathies with the project. This trend reflects the adoption of a US-style rhetoric and vocabulary of politics, in which the term "Right" is sought to be redefined primarily as a descriptive term akin to the American term "conservative."

FREE SPEECH IN INDIA TODAY: A BRIEF OVERVIEW

The world of public discourse in India today is characterized by astonishing diversity, fascinating changes and obvious as well as unexpected contradictions. India's booming media industry includes a large number of news channels in numerous languages, responding to Indians' seemingly insatiable appetite for news. The Internet and mobile space have generated many interesting initiatives, from comedy troupes like All India Bakchod to ventures such as *Scroll, Daily O*, and the *Wire*. India's Hindi-language film industry, or Bollywood, now boasts slick production values and a professionalized production paradigm. An expanded readership for English-language fiction and non-fiction has developed in a symbiotic relationship with the profusion of literary festivals that dot middle-class India's cultural calendar.

At the same time, the sphere of public expression in India is marked by an ever-increasing hostility to freedom of speech. With dismaying regularity, there is some controversy involving free speech, often accompanied by threats of physical violence and/or legal action against an artiste, scholar, or citizen for offending the sentiments of one Indian group or another. Those who make such threats and act on them often do so in the name of being members and representatives of religious communities: Hindus, Muslims, Sikhs, or Christians, as the case may be. Cultural or religious organizations as well as political parties often join in such protests as well. Highlighting a few important events in the long history of opposition to free speech in India will both illuminate this pattern and emphasize important questions relevant to the objective of this chapter. While the history of censorship in the Indian context is extensive (and other events from it will be noted later in this chapter), a brief overview suffices at this point to bring these salient issues into focus. The events indicated here also serve as reference points to which this chapter will return in the context of other arguments.

The honor of authoring the darkest chapter in the history of Indian censorship arguably still belongs to former Indian Prime Minister Indira Gandhi, for her imposition of the "Emergency" of 1975–7, a twenty-one-month-long period that saw elections suspended, an assault on rights, a crackdown on the press, and widespread arrests. Another critical moment was the de facto banning of Salman Rushdie's novel, *The Satanic Verses*, by the Indian state in 1988.[2] The following year, the Iranian religious leader Ruhollah Khomeini issued a *fatwa* ordering Muslims to kill Rushdie for committing blasphemy in his novel. Indian Muslims have continued to criticize Rushdie and oppose his presence in India on literary visits. Other writers have also drawn the wrath of Muslim groups and communities for their portrayal of Islam. The Bangladeshi poet Taslima Nasreen, who has intermittently made her home in India after her forced exile from her country in 1994, continues to be routinely threatened with humiliation, assault, and death by Indian Muslim groups.

Hindus in India and across the globe have responded similarly to speech they consider insulting to their faith and identity. In 1998, the Shiv Sena, a Hindu nationalist political party, shut down theaters in Indian cities that were screening Deepa Mehta's film, *Fire*. Party members were angered by the portrayal of a lesbian relationship in the film, which they deemed to be against Indian culture. The film was seen as especially offensive to Hindus since the characters in the relationship were named Radha and Sita, the former sharing her name with the companion of the Indian deity Krishna and the latter with the wife of the deity Ram. After facing unrelenting threats of violence and death since the 1990s in addition to being deluged with lawsuits for his paintings of Hindu goddesses, M. F. Husain, one of India's greatest artists, had to leave India in 2006.[3] He died five years later in Qatar, unable to return to his homeland. In 2010, Wendy Doniger, a scholar of Hinduism at the University of Chicago, drew the ire of Hindu right-wing organizations for her book, *The Hindus: An Alternative History*, published by Penguin. Dinanath Batra, a Hindu right-wing activist with a long history of waging battles against the representation of Hinduism in educational and academic works, filed a lawsuit against Doniger, Penguin India, and Penguin USA for intentionally seeking to denigrate Hindus and create discord between Hindus and

---

[2] The Indian state technically engineered the ban by prohibiting the book from being imported under the Customs Act (BBC 2012), although reading the book itself in India was not illegal.

[3] While this is the version of events widely reported in Indian and international media, Husain, in the final interview of his life, claimed he had left India of his own volition in 2005. See PTI, "I have not fled India, said MF Husain in his last interview," *The Times of India*, June 9, 2011. Available at: http://timesofindia.indiatimes.com/india/I-have-not-fled-India-said-MF-Husain-in-his-last-interview/articleshow/8791202.cms.

non-Hindus.[4] The lawsuit explicitly invoked section 153A of the Indian Penal Code, which criminalizes those guilty of "[p]romoting enmity between different groups on grounds of religion, race, place of birth, residence, language, etc., and doing acts prejudicial to maintenance of harmony" and section 295A which penalizes "[d]eliberate and malicious acts, intended to outrage religious feelings of any class by insulting its religion or religious beliefs."[5] Penguin finally settled the case in 2014, agreeing to stop publication and to pulp the remaining copies of the book.

As with attacks on other scholars of Hinduism, the Internet was a critical tool for the Hindu Right to mobilize opinion and campaign against Doniger. Online vigilante groups serving the cause of the Hindu Right are also exceptionally adept at using Internet platforms such as Twitter and Facebook to safeguard the reputation of Hinduism and the rights of Hindus. The Bharatiya Janata Party has been especially proactive in recognizing and exploiting the political potential of the Internet. The party ran a superb social media campaign in the recent election, shaming Congress's shabby efforts in this regard.

Several important facts related to the state of free speech in India need to be highlighted from this brief overview. First, state and religious groups often use the same grounds to ban or demand a ban on particular works of expression and speech. The relevant legislative provisions here are sections 153A and 295A of the Indian Penal Code, colonial in provenance but kept alive in post-colonial India. Even if members or spokespersons of religious communities do not intend to pursue legal redress, they often use the language of these provisions, which are now well integrated into normative public discourse in India. In free-speech controversies, the reflexive defense of traditional Hindu, Muslim, or Christian "values" is inextricably interwoven with the somewhat odd and dramatic complaint of hurt "feelings" and "sentiments." Second, the state's response indicates that it is unable or unwilling to take up the cause of individuals, especially when they are pitted against communities (regardless of whether or not the individual is from the offended community). Third, the modes and strategies for protesting against speech that is perceived to be offensive are shared across communities, although protesting Hindus, Muslims, and Christians might hold their own specific grievances against the state and media for insulting particular aspects of their faith. Hindus, for instance, routinely complain of being victims of the double standards of the state and

---

4   The full text of the lawsuit is available on the website of an Indian magazine. See "Your approach is that of a woman hungry of sex," *Outlook*, February 11, 2014. Available at: www.outlookindia.com/article/Your-Approach-Is-That-Of-A-Woman-Hungry-Of-Sex/289468.

5   Secs 153A and 295A are available respectively at: http://indiankanoon.org/doc/345634/ and http://indiankanoon.org/doc/1803184/.

media, both of which they see as making exceptions for Muslims. Muslims, in contrast, often accuse the state and media of acting in majoritarian Hindu interests despite the professed commitment of the state and media to secularism. Finally, the question of free speech is entangled with the desire of Indian religious groups to control the representation of religion in imagined national and global spaces. When speech threatens to destabilize a presumed equilibrium between such groups or between groups and the state, it provokes anxiety and violence.

FREEDOM AS A GENERAL VALUE IN THE HINDU TRADITION

One useful way of approaching free speech as a value in Hinduism is to locate it at the heart of what may be seen as the general paradox of freedom in lived and textual Hinduism. On the one hand, the limits and license of freedom in Hinduism are determined at the juncture of the vast fold of Hinduism, which includes a remarkable diversity of practices and forms of orthodox and heterodox life, including what are called the "great heterodoxies of Jainism and Buddhism" (Raghavan and Dandekar 1988, p. 204). On the other hand, these aspects reflect the severe curtailment of the rights and freedoms of entire categories of people, whether women, so-called lower castes, or those outside the caste system. An important Hindu text such as the *Manusmriti*, for instance, provides the textual basis for circumscribing the behavior of different groups. The *Manusmriti* locates the "essence of dharma or righteousness" in the "proper functioning of the organization of the four classes" (Raghavan and Dandekar 1988, p. 221). These are the categories of priest, warrior, trader, and serf, who are born respectively from the "mouth, arms, thighs and feet" of Purusha or the cosmic being (Raghavan and Dandekar 1988, p. 221). The narrative serves at the very least as a metaphor, but also as an organizing principle and source of legitimacy for the unequal distribution of power, privilege, and voice as they exist among different castes, with the Brahmin or priestly class sprung from the mouth as the embodiment of voice or speech itself.

It is important to recognize a conceptual distinction between Hindu traditional sources as the basis for social authority and as the foundation of a narrower conception of law. The *Encyclopedia Britannica*, for instance, describes the *Manusmriti* as "traditionally, the most authoritative of the books of the Hindu code (Dharma-shastra) in India."[6] However, Menski, a leading authority on Hindu tradition and law, argues that the idea that traditional Hindu sources prescribe rules is deeply problematic (Menski 2003, p. 5). Menski sees

---

[6] See www.britannica.com/EBchecked/topic/363055/Manu-smriti.

the Hindu cultural universe as much more expansive, dynamic, and flexible than a narrow conception of the law might admit. Yet, as Patel argues with regard to women's rights, the *Manusmriti* does possess a near-hegemonic status in providing social codes that circumscribe the freedom of women:

> Although it is undoubtedly correct that the *Manusmriti* cannot be held up as "the" lawbook of the Hindus as it is mistakenly claimed to be, it is nevertheless important to note the importance of this text as a primary instrument for the attempted progressive homogenization of Indian society. Within this, it is also a significant text as embodying various normative codes for the appropriate behavior of women. (Patel 2007, p. 75)

A similar argument can be made about the text with regard to caste hierarchies in Hinduism and Indian society. The paradox of Hindu tradition then is that it offers a richly imagined repertoire of numerous ways of being and an endorsement of values that we could recognize as supporting free speech in a modern, liberal sense while other sources with antithetical values hold a dominant place in that tradition.

Thus, one can find Salman Rushdie invoking the *Natya Shastra*, a Hindu treatise on theater, as offering a ringing endorsement of free speech: "[s]o in one of the most ancient of Indian texts we find as explicit and extreme a defense of freedom of expression as you can find anywhere in the world."[7] However, for B. R. Ambedkar, scholar, leader, and architect of India's constitution, Hinduism as a religion was incompatible with the principle of free speech. Born into an untouchable caste, Ambedkar renounced Hinduism for Buddhism in 1956. "A Hindu must surrender his freedom of speech," argues Ambedkar in a devastating indictment of the faith "so long as you are in the Hindu religion, you cannot expect to have freedom of thought" (Ambedkar 1936). The inherently undemocratic nature of Hinduism, says Ambedkar, warrants Hindus to follow a hierarchy of authoritative texts and imitate others at the expense of reason.

This tension may also be reflected in a certain self-limiting quality of the nature of Hindu universalism, at least according to one reading. In an argument related to the limits of freedom of religion in Hinduism, Sharma shows that the particular way in which the value of universalism is understood in Hindu thought serves to bring it into conflict with faiths like Islam and Christianity. Through a reading of the story of Prahlada, Sharma argues that, since Hinduism itself is understood as a universal way of life, with universal precepts, it can accommodate believers who may follow another god,

---

7 See text of speech, above at note 1.

such as, for instance, Jesus Christ (Sharma 2010, pp. 26–7). What Hinduism and Hindus find difficult to accept, according to Sharma, is the rejection of Hinduism itself as the foundational ground of being, which is what conversion to other religions requires (Sharma 2010, pp. 39–40). For these reasons, Hindus are opposed to religious conversion, even though Hinduism as a larger framework of life is consistent with the commitment to religious freedom.

Sharma's argument can be critiqued as claiming an exception for the universalism of Hinduism, for it can be argued that Islam and Christianity both offer similar normative frames of universality.[8] However, it points to a tension which can be seen playing out today in India. In the wake of the recent assumption of power by the BJP-led government, there have been efforts by Hindu Right groups like the World Hindu Council to "reconvert" Indian Muslims and Christians to Hinduism, under the aegis of so-called "Ghar Wapsi" or "Homecoming" movements (Krishna 2015). The claim here is that the ancestors of these Indians were originally Hindus, and accordingly such Muslims and Christians need to go back to the faith of their forefathers. A key objective of the Ghar Wapsi movement is to force a ban on *all* conversion, thus depriving religious groups of one of their rights and freedoms under the Indian Constitution.

Salman Rushdie's invocation of the tradition of Indian theater as exemplifying the value of free speech is instructive here. In both Ambedkar's act of renouncing Hinduism for Buddhism and the curtailment of religious rights through initiatives such as the Ghar Wapsi movement, the public performance of freedom is linked strongly to the issue of religious identity. Control over one necessarily requires control over the other. The relationship between speech and religious values is subject to the same dynamic of the politics of visibility. That relationship is partly shaped by the particular nature of authority within Hinduism, as outlined above. It is also a product of historical contingency, emerging from a series of colonial operations in the domains of religion, custom, and the law.

THE COLONIAL CONSTRUCTION OF RELIGIOUS IDENTITIES IN INDIA

As a member of an untouchable caste, Ambedkar experienced and challenged the Hindu prejudices laid out in ancient authoritative texts. Yet these abiding prejudices were also reshaped, like Hinduism at large, by the colonial

---

[8]   Raghavan and Dandekar point out that Hinduism too possesses to a degree "the creedal statements of other religions" (1988, p. 205).

encounter. The main transformation effected during British colonial rule that is significant for the relationship of free speech, religion, and traditional values today pertains to the legal reforms introduced by the colonial state. These reforms reinscribed the logic of community in India in chiefly religious terms through the instrument of the law. The result was a homogenized conception of law that prioritized textual sources over customary practice as the basis of law. Separate bodies of Anglo-Hindu and Anglo-Muhammadan law were developed for Hindus and Muslims. Agnes argues that, by conflating custom with religion, the British colonial state created the "legal fiction that the laws of Hindus and Muslims [were] rooted in their respective scriptures and further that Muslims and Hindus [were] homogeneous communities following uniform laws" (Agnes 1999, p. 43). The British colonial administration accordingly parsed Indian communities of Hindus, Muslims, and Christians as distinct peoples, each defined by their own rites, practices, and laws.[9]

The template for the relationship between tradition or custom, religion, and law that continues to inform matters of free speech in India today was set in place here. Importantly, too, the construction of community along these lines vested identity as a characteristic of the group as opposed to the individual. Colonial governance during British rule then became a matter of the management of relations between different Indian groups, as organized by religion but also by place, ethnicity, language, and so on. It is here that we can see the basis for the reasoning that informs section 153A of the Indian Penal Code, which considers it a crime to promote "enmity between different groups on grounds of religion, race, place of birth, residence, language, etc." Section 295A extends this logic, expanding the troubling notion of group rights at the expense of individual rights and the principle of free speech.[10] The origins and scope of sections 153A and 295A, as well as precedents for the manner in which they have been invoked by the state and communities, are rooted in the historical particularities of colonial political economy, characteristics of which have been inherited by the post-colonial Indian state. If community identity is predicated on religious or group belonging,

---

[9] Menski has a contrary view about the scholarly consensus regarding the codification of Indian laws (2003, p. 554).

[10] Sec 295A has its roots in controversy surrounding a text, *Rangila Rasul*, about the life of the Prophet Muhammad, published in the 1920s in India and attributed to Pandit M. A. Champati. On the basis of Muslim protest, the state arrested the publisher, Rajpal, seeking to hold him guilty under sec 153A. Rajpal, however, was acquitted, since the judge held that the offense did not qualify for punishment under the law (Daniyal 2014). Since the ruling appeared to contribute to communal tensions in Lahore at the time, the state enacted sec 295(A) following the judge's recommendation of the need for a law that would criminalize such publications (ibid.).

then the *performance* of the defense of such a principle, through legal or other means, becomes a means of asserting that group identity. This suggests that the invocation of the reasoning that informs sections 153A and 295A has become entrenched as a ritual of religious belief and assertion. The logic of colonial legislation and the culture of taking offense at speech have led to a perverse state of affairs in which conspicuously visible violent protest and indeed threats have become de facto religious and socially sanctioned forms of religious assertion. For the state in independent India, whether out of pragmatism, cynicism, caution, or helplessness, has chosen to keep these colonial laws alive without amendment, even though the Constitution of India guarantees citizens the fundamental right to freedom of expression under Article 19.

SECULARISM, SPEECH, AND RELIGION IN INDEPENDENT INDIA

Article 19(1)(a) of the Constitution of India grants Indian citizens "the right to freedom of speech and expression," while Article 19(2) lists the conditions that limit the exercise of such a right, imposing "reasonable restrictions ... in the interests of the sovereignty and integrity of India, the security of the State, friendly relations with foreign States, public order, decency or morality or in relation to contempt of court, defamation or incitement to an offence."[11] The language articulating the right and the limits imposed upon it conform to a classic liberal template. Yet, in the Indian case, several items in this list of restrictions immediately provide a mechanism for sections 153A and 295A to come into play in determining the scope of the right of freedom of expression in particular cases. "Public order," "decency," "morality," "defamation," and "incitement to an offence" can all be, and have been, mobilized by the state and judiciary as reasons in challenges to free speech, as indeed they can by community spokespersons in the court of public opinion.

The Indian media routinely presents the view that the Indian state should repeal sections 153A and 295A. Ramachandran, for instance, argues that the Indian state is excessively cautious in preserving these laws, which are applied widely, broadly, and unfairly (Ramachandran 2013). However, doing away with them is more complicated than might appear, since the laws owe their continued existence in part to the peculiar secularism of the Indian state.[12]

---

[11] Article 19 is available at: http://indiankanoon.org/doc/1218090/.
[12] The scholarly literature on Indian secularism is vast. Two excellent collections are Bhargava (1999) and Needham and Sunder Rajan (2007).

Unlike in other societies, Indian secularism is not defined in the negative as a separation of religion and state or the exclusion of religion from the public sphere. The ideal of separation, the so-called "wall" between church and state, arguably does not exist in any secular society, whether in France or the United States. Indian secularism, however, seeks to treat all religions equally or not to discriminate between citizens on grounds of religion. In this sense, the ample presence of religion in public, or rather religions in public, does not contradict the reality of Indian secularism. Equal visibility of religions, in fact, is viewed as one barometer of Indian secularism. As described above, the right to claim belonging in India is contingent on demonstrating membership of a religious group, which, in turn, is linked to the right to assert collective religious identity in public.[13] Indian secularism itself provides an ideological basis for this logic of expressing religious identity.

The traumas of the partition of India and the daunting task faced by the leaders of the newly born nation meant that India had to be visualized as a capacious, inclusive community at the time of independence in 1947. A claim had to be made that the political value of Indian secularism was consistent with India's inclusive history. This project would necessarily have to be an interventionist one, requiring the state to ensure space and security for India's minorities. It would also require the state to interfere proactively in the domain of religious life to secure social equity.[14] The Indian state has faced difficult challenges in striving to balance its treatment of different religious groups. Concessions given to one group, against the rights of individuals within that group or other groups, have often been followed by concessions to other groups.[15]

---

[13] Given the Hindu nationalist dispensation of the party that heads the current coalition government, however, it seeks to deny this right to non-Hindus in India. The BJP has been a constant critic of what it terms the "pseudo-secularism" of the Congress and Indian Left parties.

[14] This point is owed to Govind Shahani (in a personal conversation with the author). Smith, in his landmark analysis of Indian secularism, has drawn attention to the constitutional problem of "reconciling the principles of protective discrimination and non-discrimination by the state," an abiding tension that applies to religion and caste in the Indian context (Smith 1999, p. 209).

[15] For example, the 1985 *Shah Bano* case, in which the Supreme Court of India upheld that a divorced Muslim woman was entitled to maintenance, met with protests from the Muslim community as constituting interference in the personal laws of Muslims or their traditional values. Rajiv Gandhi's government passed a new law in 1986, which, critics held, was a weak act of appeasement aimed at the Indian Muslim community. In 1986, the government also unlocked the gates of the Babri Masjid or Babri mosque, following an order from a district judge. The move was seen as giving Hindus their corresponding due since the government was perceived to have overridden the Supreme Court under pressure from Muslims.

It is a fair generalization that judges have been more interventionist when it has come to effecting changes in Hinduism than in Islam through judgments pertaining to personal laws.[16] Smith suggests that reforms to Hindu law, "while painful to the orthodox," were accepted because "the vast majority of legislators were Hindu" (Smith 1999, p. 227). However, the cost of the perception of the Indian state meting out unequal treatment to different groups has been significant. There has been a disproportionate burden on Indian judges to balance the principles of individual free speech (or freedom of religion) and secularism, often in the knowledge that the Indian state expects them to rule in keeping with the community interest. It is worth noting that, in independent India, section 153A was struck down in a 1951 judgment by the East Punjab court, but the addition of the phrase on "public order" in Article 19(2) under an amendment to the act in 1951 restored the validity of 153A (Gaur 2011, p. 262). A related observation here is that sections 153A and 295A also perform the function of hate speech laws in India and have been used to arrest divisive religious and political figures who have threatened violence against a religious community. It is the threat to Indian secularism that is generally viewed, even if cynically, as the implicit ground for action against these figures. For this reason, progressive Indian activists like Jyoti Punwani caution against knee-jerk reactions that scapegoat the laws for free-speech controversies and seek to remove them (Punwani 2015).

A rethinking of sections 153A and 295A with regard to free speech must also then necessarily involve a rethinking of the legal protections for Indian secularism. Mehta, in fact, locates the failure to defend free speech in independent India within a failure of the broader political culture of the modern Indian state itself: in its liberalism, statism, and means-ends rationality of Congress, which, in the aftermath of independence, "was willing to use an oppressive legal order to further progressive social ends" (Mehta 2015). Mehta's argument implies that the political and social context for the exercise of free speech in India will need significant transformation for the liberation of speech from restrictive laws.

Over the last two decades or so, India has experienced enormous changes wrought by cultural and economic globalization. New kinds of compacts between individuals, communities and the state have emerged, and tensions between commitments to free speech and other values have flared up. The

---

[16] An official archival resource of the Government of India defines personal law thus: "The people of India belong to different religions and faiths. They are governed by different sets of personal laws in respect of matters relating to family affairs, i.e., marriage, divorce, succession, etc." Available at: www.archive.india.gov.in/citizen/lawnorder.php?id=16.

relationship between free speech and traditional Hindu values has mutated in new directions, seen most clearly on the Internet, an apt symbol of the globalization of India's voice and aspirations.

FREE SPEECH AND HINDU VALUES IN THE ERA OF GLOBALIZATION AND THE INTERNET

Several important factors have influenced developments over the last quarter of a century regarding the relationship between free speech and traditional religious, particularly Hindu, values. The first is the integration of India's economy into the global economy, beginning with the reforms initiated in 1991, commonly referred to as "liberalization." These changes have culminated in the so-called Indian growth story, which, while criticized for promoting inequality, environmental degradation and disenfranchisement among India's most vulnerable, has also created new kinds of opportunities and aspirations for many Indians. The second factor is the increased legitimacy of the ideology of Hindu nationalism among a large swath of Indians. The electoral success of Narendra Modi, India's current prime minister, reflects the latest ideological phase in the history of the Hindu Right. Modi's campaign promises forged goals of technocratic development with the proposition of Hindu cultural and political primacy in India. The third factor is the impact of the Internet on Indian public discourse. Even though a fraction of India's population of 1.2 billion has access to the Internet, in the context of Indian society these 243 million users include elites, opinion-makers and those with educational, cultural, and political capital (Chari 2014).[17]

These developments have created new audiences for the message of Hindutva in India and abroad, even as they have generated fresh anxieties among Hindus regarding the possibility of controlling the representation of Hinduism. The global Hindu diaspora has long been a vital source of support for Hindu nationalist organizations in India. Counting highly educated and affluent professionals in the United States in its ranks, the Hindu diaspora has played a role in numerous initiatives related to the representation of Hinduism, such as challenging the portrayal of Hinduism in US school textbooks. Working with Hindu organizations in India, a range of diasporic Hindu organizations have been at the forefront of smear campaigns against scholars such as Paul Courtright, Jeffrey Kripal, and Romila Thapar (Bal 2014; Prashad

---

[17]   Internet access is also growing rapidly, especially with the massive number of mobile phone users in India, and promises to reach wider audiences who will enter into all kinds of conversations online.

2014). Global Hindu communities have made very effective use of the Internet in such campaigns, to intimidate so-called "anti-Hindu" voices and generally to promote their perspective (Chopra 2008, pp. 155–71; Lal 2001; Mazumdar 2003; Rajagopal 2000).

Here we see the politics of visibility at work again, as a response to the compulsions of Indian political modernity in the era of globalization and the Internet. The objections to free speech arise precisely when speech, in the form of a book, film, or even tweet, threaten to enter a *secular* public domain or space in Indian society. Within nominally internal religious econ-omies of circulation, *even if public*, defamatory and slanderous statements about other religious communities are commonplace. Peter Manuel, for instance, has described the crucial role played by audio cassettes with anti-Muslim messages in fostering religious tensions in north India (Manuel 1993, pp. 250–5). Publications of fundamentalist or hard-line Hindu and Muslim organizations are filled with diatribe against the Muslim or Hindu enemy. Hindus or Muslims do not necessarily litigate or resort to violence about such negative depictions in the so-called Hindu or Muslim press. It is when these messages enter a perceived national and global space that the protests start. This is a pattern seen with *Rangila Rasul*, which, released with the name of a distinctly Muslim-sounding publisher, was clearly meant to cross audience boundaries and reach Muslims. This is precisely the threat represented by the secular forms of the novel and cinema and by the paintings of artists such as Husain. Such anxieties are compounded in the Internet age, with the technol-ogy's promise of reach across national and global audiences. Whether it is a member of the community in question or an outsider, speech is considered subversive of traditional religious values when it is articulated in secular space or when it leaks into secular space. The crime, then, is not just the content of the utterance but also the very right to speak about the community which is the bearer of traditional values. As shown in the conclusion to this chapter, the general right to speak is itself under duress in India from these older prec-edents as well as from newer pressures.

CONCLUSION: TRADITIONAL VALUES BETWEEN STATE, RELIGIOUS COMMUNITY, AND INDIVIDUAL

Recently there have been several major controversies involving free speech in India, in each of which the speakers stand accused of some form of secu-lar or religious blasphemy, or both. Perumal Murugan, the Tamil writer, was attacked by local Hindu groups for allegedly denigrating the religion in his 2010 book, *Madhorubagan (One Part Woman)*, and has given up writing in protest (Biswas 2015); the comedy troupe, All India Bakchod, was attacked by film industry unions, Christian groups, and politicians for engaging in obscene speech and denigrating Christianity in a video recording roasting Bollywood stars on YouTube ("Please note AIB"), and Shireen Dalvi, the editor of the Urdu newspaper *Avadhnama*, had to go into hiding after being sued by Muslim groups for reprinting a recent cover of *Charlie Hebdo* showing the Prophet Muhammad. All these parties had to face legal action for their alleged offenses.

In these cases, and others, the domains of traditional values, religious morality, and Indian culture are often invoked on flimsy pretenses. The sensitivities meant to be reserved for religion are extended to any number of realms, giving rise to a frivolous and vindictive culture of litigation. Dina Nath Batra's initiative reflects this culture, in that it used lawful means to attempt to shut down Doniger. The culture of invoking tradition for instrumental and cynical uses dovetails with two other recent developments in the Indian media landscape. The first is the accelerated corporatization of the media as well as a more aggressive role in media organizations by owners who had previously allowed editorial autonomy in media organizations. In 2014, Reliance Industries, owned by India's wealthiest man, took over the Network18 Media group, which owns numerous media companies in the cable television, magazine, and Internet space. The takeover has been followed by the removal of journalists perceived to be critical of Narendra Modi from CNN-IBN, one of the channels owned by the group. The same trend has also been seen in other publications like *OPEN* magazine and the venerable *Hindu* newspaper. The obsequiousness shown by media and the alarming idea that the nation's leader should not be criticized are not so much a function of a sudden shift in journalistic culture (the Indian press has too long and deep a tradition of independence for that) as a shift in the political economy of the Indian media. The second development is the unwelcome readiness of the Indian state, in its avatar of past and present government, to clamp down strategically on and censor the Internet. The previous UPA coalition government passed the draconian and sweeping section 66(A) of the Information Technology Act, which can be used to prosecute anything on Twitter or Facebook that could be construed as offensive, defamatory or even annoying. As Datta notes in pointing out the potential for misuse and revenge, section 66(A) is often combined with "the provisions dealing with the offences of blasphemy or spreading communal hatred" (Datta 2014), that is, sections 153A and 295A. Additionally, like other states in a global post-9/11 world, the Indian state uses the threat of terrorism to clamp down on speech online. Around the end of 2014, the Department of Telecommunication blocked thirty-two websites in response to a possible threat by the so-called Islamic State fundamentalist group (ISIL) (Ghoshal and Dutta 2014).

It is problematic to make a case that the intolerance committed by one religious community is worse than that committed by another. However it is worth noting that, since the BJP has formed a government, the Hindu Right has embarked on a number of projects to control the representation of Hinduism, revise existing scholarship that it sees as critical of Hinduism, target religious minorities, and muzzle dissent. The challenge to this state of affairs will need to come from both religious and secular domains in India, and from a wide cross-section of Hindus within the religious domain. The battle for free speech will need to be fought on the terrain of Hinduism, and the attempt to establish a culture of defending speech on grounds of traditional Hindu values will also require a reclaiming of tradition that does not pit it as antithetical to secular modernity. The task will no doubt be daunting but, at the very least, we need to begin imagining the possibility.

REFERENCES

Agnes, F. 1999. *Law and Gender Inequality: The Politics of Women's Rights in India*. New Delhi: Oxford University Press.

Ambedkar, B. R. 1936. "Speech delivered by Dr. Ambedkar to the Bombay Presidency Mahar Conference, 31st May 1936, Bombay," translated by V. W. Moon and edited by F. W. Pritchett. Available at: www.columbia.edu/itc/mealac/pritchett/00ambedkar/txt_ambedkar_salvation.html.

Bal, H. 2014. "Pulped: Why have publishers failed to stand up to Dina Nath Batra?," *The Caravan*, December 1, 2014. Available at: www.caravanmagazine.in/reportage/pulped.

BBC 2012. "Salman Rushdie: India banned *Satanic Verses* hastily," BBC News India, September 12, 2012. Available at: www.bbc.com/news/world-asia-india-19566894.

Bhargava, R. (ed.) 1999. *Secularism and its Critics*. New Delhi: Oxford University Press.

Biswas, S. 2015. "Why Indian author Perumal Murugan quit writing," BBC News India, January 15, 2015. Available at: www.bbc.com/news/world-asia-india-30808747.

Champati, M. A. 1920s. *Rangila Rasul*. Delhi: Mohammad Rafi Publishers. Available at: https://archive.org/stream/RangeelaRasul/RangeelaRasul1#page/n0/mode/2up.

Chari, M. 2014. "As internet use rises, five global websites that Indians have come to dominate", *Scroll.in*, August 19, 2014. Available at: http://scroll.in/article/674798/As-Internet-use-rises,-five-global-websites-that-Indians-have-come-to-dominate/.

Chopra, R. 2008. *Technology and Nationalism in India: Cultural Negotiations from Colonialism to Cyberspace*. New York: Cambria Press.

Daniyal, S. 2014. "A short history of the blasphemy law used against Wendy Doniger and why it must go," *Scroll.in*, February 18, 2014. Available at: http://scroll.in/article/656608/A-short-history-of-the-blasphemy-law-used-against-Wendy-Doniger-and-why-it-must-go.

Datta, S. 2014. "The repugnant section 66A of India's Information Technology Act", *Index on Censorship*, June 16, 2014. Available at: www.indexoncensorship.org/ 2014/06/the-repugnant-section-66a-of-indias-information-technology-act/.

Gaur, K. D. 2011. *Textbook on the Indian Penal Code* (fourth ed.). New Delhi: Universal Law Publishing.

Ghoshal, D. and Dutta, S. 2014. "A threat from ISIL prompted India to block Github and 31 other sites," *Quartz India*, December 31, 2014. Available at: http://qz.com/ 319866/a-threat-from-isis-prompts-india-to-block-github-and-a-handful-of-other-sites/.

Jaffrelot, C. 2007. "Introduction: The invention of an ethnic nationalism," in Jaffrelot, C. (ed.),*Hindu Nationalism: A Reader*. Princeton: Princeton University Press, pp. 3–5.

Khilnani, S. 1999. *The Idea of India*. New Delhi: Penguin Books.

Krishna, T. M. 2015. "As I see it: In the name of ghar wapsi," *The Hindu*, January 17, 2015. Available at: www.thehindu.com/opinion/columns/t_m_krishna/as-i-see-it-in-the-name-of-ghar-wapsi/article6788990.ece.

Lal, V. 2001. "The politics of history on the internet: Cyber-diasporic Hinduism and the North American Hindu diaspora," in Paranjpe, M. (ed.), *In Diaspora: Theories, Histories, Texts*. New Delhi: Indialog Publications, pp. 179–221.

Manuel, P. 1993. *Cassette Culture: Popular Music and Technology in North India*. Chicago: University of Chicago Press.

Mazumdar, S. 2003. "The politics of religion and national origin: Rediscovering Hindu Indian identity in the United States," in Kaiwar, V. and Mazumdar, S. (eds.), *Antinomies of Modernity: Essays on Race, Orient, Nation*. Durham, NC: Duke University Press, pp. 223–60.

Mehta, P. B. 2015. "The crooked lives of free speech," *Open*, January 30, 2015. Available at: www.openthemagazine.com/article/voices/the-crooked-lives-of-free-speech.

Menski, W. 2003. *Hindu Law: Beyond Tradition and Modernity*. New Delhi: Oxford University Press.

Needham, A. D. and Sunder Rajan, R. (eds.) 2007. *The Crisis of Secularism in India*. Durham, NC: Duke University Press.

Neufeldt, R. 2003. "The Hindu Mahasabha and Gandhi," in Coward, H. (ed.), *Indian Critiques of Gandhi*. Albany: State University of New York Press, pp. 131–52.

Patel, R. 2007. *Hindu Women's Property Rights in Rural India: Law, Labour and Culture in Action*. Surrey: Ashgate.

"Personal Law," *Archive*: www.archive.india.gov.in/citizen/lawnorder.php?id=16.

"Please note AIB: Here is a list of nine people/organisations angry with you," *The News Minute*, February 5, 2015.

Prashad, V. 2014. "Wendy Doniger's book is a tribute to Hinduism's complexity, not an insult," *Guardian*, February 12, 2014. Available at: www.theguardian.com/ commentisfree/2014/feb/12/wendy-doniger-book-hinduism-penguin-hindus.

PTI 2011. "I have not fled India, said MF Husain in his last interview," *The Times of India*, June 9, 2011. Available at: http://timesofindia.indiatimes.com/india/I-have-not-fled-India-said-MF-Husain-in-his-last-interview/articleshow/8791202.cms.

Punwani, J. 2015. "In Charlie Hebdo's name, chauvinistic Urdu journalists in Mumbai are going after a female editor," *Quartz India*, February 5, 2015. Available at: http:// qz.com/339334/in-charlie-hebdos-name-chauvinistic-urdu-journalists-in-mumbai-are-going-after-a-female-editor/.

Raghavan, V. and Dandekar, R. N. 1988. "The Hindu way of life," in Embree, A. T. (ed.), *Sources of Indian Tradition: Volume I: From the Beginning to 1800* (second ed.). New York: Penguin, pp. 201–378.

Rajagopal, A. 2000. "Hindu nationalism in the US: Changing configurations of political practice," *Ethnic and Racial Studies* 23(3): 467–96.

Ramachandran, C. R. 2013. "Little reason to restrict freedom of speech," *The Hindu*, September 26, 2013. Available at: www.thehindu.com/todays-paper/tp-opinion/little-reason-to-restrict-the-freedom-of-speech/article5169173.ece.

Savarkar, V. D. 1969. *Hindutva: Who Is a Hindu?* 5th edition. Bombay: Veer Savarkar Prakashan.

Sharma, A. 2010. *Hindu Narratives on Human Rights.* Santa Barbara: Praeger.

Smith, D. E. 1999. "India as a secular state," in Bhargava, R., Bagchi, A., and Sudarshan, R. (eds.), *Multiculturalism, Liberalism and Democracy.* New Delhi: Oxford University Press, pp. 177–233.

Vanaik, A. 1997. *The Furies of Indian Communalism: Religion, Modernity, and Secularization.* London: Verso.

14

Cyber-Leninism: The Political Culture
of the Chinese Internet

Rogier Creemers

Oh steam whistle! Oh Lenin![1]
Computers don't do what you want them to do, but what you tell them to do.[2]

INTRODUCTION

In March 2000, Bill Clinton laid a challenge at the door of China's rulers. Optimistically assessing the catalyst that communications technology could be for liberty in China, he famously likened cracking down on the Internet to nailing Jello to the wall (Clinton 2000). Clinton's sanguinity was exemplary for a zeitgeist characterized by techno-optimism and a firm belief in the ineluctable progress of liberal democracy and market capitalism. Information communication technologies (ICTs) and new media would become a panacea for political strife and contradiction, while the economic potential of the Internet promised a new era of economic welfare and entrepreneurialism. Moreover, Clinton's statement evinced a libertarian belief, deeply held in the technological community, that the Internet's transnational nature effectively rendered it uncontrollable by national governments. In the decade-and-a-half since, there has been ample cause for moderating these ideas. Internet giants, such as Apple, Google, and Amazon, or the glorified taxi service Uber, are now routinely castigated for their creative engagement with tax authorities worldwide, the low salaries they pay bottom-level employees and the extent to which they monitor users' behavior. Not every internet user is a civil democratic citizen; the Internet has become a recruiting, communication, and propaganda tool for despicable organizations such as so-called Islamic State. Perhaps most importantly,

---

[1] Lu Xun's satirical rendition of Communist poetry (Lu, cited in Mitter 2005, p. 233).
[2] Anonymous.

the Snowden revelations have shattered the myth that a democratic government would not use the tools available to it to expand its capabilities, often
through a discourse of securitization.

   The allure of the democratization discourse has also strongly influenced
hopes and expectations for the Internet in China. Social movements, activ-
ism, and the development of civil society became the leading themes in the
field of Chinese Internet study, often with an unspoken assumption that these
would be the fountainheads of an ineluctable stream of political progress.
Much of this work was inspired by Chinese dissidents and liberals, such as
Ai Weiwei and Liu Xiaobo, the latter describing the Internet as "God's present to China" (Liu 2009). Yet this romanticized conception of the Internet
obfuscated many of its less democratic elements. Chinese liberal voices were
merely one part of a broader spectrum of participants that also included patriotic hackers, ethnic nationalists, and dark-red Maoists. The government, in
particular, often remained a black box: a locus of abstract power that sought
to oppose its dictatorial will on a to-be-liberated citizenry. It is (often at the
same time) portrayed as a formidable oppressor and a paper tiger that must
inevitably bend to the tides of history. Possibly in order to avoid the accusation
of abetting authoritarianism, questions of legitimate authority (as opposed to
legitimization) have been kept at arm's length, with most attention directed
to the tactics that governmental actors used to counter social activities. It is,
perhaps, therefore no surprise that few studies have sought to elucidate the
government's point of view, even if merely to identify the logic that animates
local notions of governmentality and its interaction with the effects of internet
use. Yet, as Bruce Gilley suggests, the state remains the dominant actor in the
Chinese sociopolitical order and a state-centered approach is indispensable
in understanding how new media and information technologies will interact
within the Chinese context.

   There is another, methodological point that further explains the paucity of
analyses of Chinese governmental approaches to Internet governance. What
news is there to be learnt by examining China's brand of authoritarianism? Is
it not typical of all nondemocratic governments, or indeed of all governments,
that they seek to censor and manage information? Isn't ideology superseded
by brutal, but simple, calculations of power and interest? At a certain level of
abstraction, these claims may be valid, yet they do not enlighten us about the
particular and subjective elements that give meaning to the political system. It
is not incorrect that the Chinese Communist Party (CCP) seeks to maintain
its hold on power through using the internet as a platform for legitimization,
but the issue of how the notion of legitimacy is understood and interpreted
requires a deeper knowledge of China's political experience and history,

including the way political objectives are defined and operationalized, and the way the bureaucracy works. In the end, to discuss how the internet is perceived and governed in the Chinese context, we must be able to understand the assumptions, motives, fears, and aspirations of the individuals staffing the political system. Still, against the Scylla of a Procrustean approach that leaves little space for cultural specificity stands the Charybdis of cultural exclusivity. Nothing in this chapter should be construed as a claim that the Chinese case is exceptional or unique. Apart from the empirical validity of any such claim, it would exclude the Chinese case from analysis rather than open it up for comparative scrutiny or as a contribution to a more global picture. Instead, this chapter seeks to explore the particularities of China's political culture, discuss how they might shape ideas on the role of the internet in contemporary Chinese society, and present them as one possible path for the development of the Internet, with its own idiosyncrasies as well as points of overlap with the other cases presented in this book.

In particular, this chapter will attempt to discuss how the Internet was introduced in a specific, historically developed, political-cultural context, which shaped the parameters for its development. In other words, while previous observers have often sought to describe how the Internet would change China, it aims to discuss how China has changed the Internet, particularly with respect to questions of political discourse and organization. Of course, China's Internet has become as flourishing a platform for commercial activity and social engagement as that anywhere else in the world. Politically, however, it has been shaped by a tension that has characterized Chinese governance for centuries: the oscillation between centralization, hierarchy, and order on the one hand, and decentralization, rebellion, and disorder on the other. This chapter first discusses how the elements of this dialectic process developed during imperial times, and how the subsequent Leninist state reinterpreted and added to it. Second, it explores how the reform process changed this political culture. Next, it discusses how the advent of the Internet brought both challenges and opportunities for the party leadership, before exploring the implications of China's cyber-Leninism for its future.

BELIEF SYSTEMS IN CHINESE POLITICAL CULTURE

In the same way that notions of free speech and access to information have profound roots in the European political culture of the Renaissance and Enlightenment, some of the central elements of Chinese views on Internet governance originate from the political culture of the late empire. The politically dominant worldview at that time was state Confucianism, a system in which the emperor governed a bureaucratic administration through ritual, demonstrative virtue, discipline, and obedience. The ultimate Confucian objective was harmony, which could only be achieved if all members of the social organism understood and performed their duties correctly, and cultivated their virtue. To that end, officials were appointed through a meritocratic system of civil examinations, which tested their comprehension of the canon of Confucian classics.

Yet, while Confucianism was the dominant culture of a genteel political elite, it was counterbalanced by a set of popular cultural elements, shaped by Daoist and Buddhist mysticism, which stood diametrically opposed to most of its fundamental tenets. Where Confucianism required hierarchy and obedience, popular culture romanticized the fraternity of secret societies and individual heroism. Confucianism mostly eschewed the supernatural, but religious sects, sorcery, and magic were part and parcel of its popular counterpart. Lucian Pye describes these as the two poles of a political-cultural spectrum, whose tensions have historically animated the nature of political contestation (Pye 1988, p. 165) In other words, rather than a pendulum between different policy options, identified as left-wing or right-wing for example, the dynamic of Chinese politics might be better imagined as a piston alternating between centralization, orthodoxy, and order on the one hand, and decentralization, heterodoxy, and rebellion on the other. Yet at various times, these two cultures have overlapped. Not unlike the acceptance, or even expectation, of eccentricity or the adoption of bohemian lifestyles in the British aristocracy, individual members of the Confucian gentry would seek scholarly inspiration in Buddhist or Daoist work or adopt hermitical lifestyles. Successful leaders of uprisings, on the other hand, would be quick to discard their rebellious roots and take on the Confucian garb of imperial rule.

The Confucian quest to forestall the delusion and confusion of the people by witchcraft and heterodox sects goes some way to explain the norms and actions by which the state sought to regulate the public word. State control over printing, which had become a fully fledged industry by the time of the Song dynasty (AD 960–1279), provides an illustrative example. First, both the Imperial Court and local governments were active producers of print materials, ranging from the calendars and almanacs that were essential in an agricultural society to authorized editions of the Confucian classics and approved commentaries needed for preparation for the examinations. A new dynasty would also be expected to compile the orthodox history of the preceding dynasty.[3] Local governments published gazetteers, but also engaged

---

[3]　Interestingly, the CCP has undertaken to finish compiling the history of the Qing.

in commercial printing, publishing literature upholding Confucian values. The Qing government in particular was very active in patronizing the compilation of dictionaries, encyclopedias, and literary compendia (on the largest of these projects, the *Siku Quanshu*, see Guy 1987). Illustrating the close connection between these efforts and orthodoxy, the Tongzhi emperor (1861–75) ordered the establishment of printing houses in provinces affected by the Taiping rebellion, in order to replace works lost during the uprising (Rawski 1979). Also, the government employed criers to travel from village to village, reminding the populace of their moral obligations and narrating instructive tales. Secondly, general and specific censorship rules were imposed. While a Song-era pre-publication review system was rapidly abandoned after it fell into disuse, the legal codes made explicit reference to "devilish books and writings" (*yaoyan yaoshu*), the production of which was made a capital offense (Vittinghoff 2002, p. 325). The government had a monopoly over calendars and almanacs, while "licentious" literature and the publication of sensitive government information were also circumscribed (Mote 2003, p. 927). The early Qing era saw repeated waves of literary censorship, particularly targeted at works subversive to the new, non-Han, dynasty, although it must be added that the efficaciousness of such campaigns in the provinces is dubious.

Two millennia of a remarkably constant political and institutional structure came to an end at the end of the nineteenth century. While previous dynastic changes had little effect on the architecture of the Chinese state, the end of the Qing dynasty was characterized by successive clashes with modernizing European powers and, perhaps most humiliatingly, Japan. This caused an intellectual crisis in a country that had until then considered itself to be the center of the civilized world, spurring a search for a new orthodoxy. This upended the traditional tensions between the center and the periphery that had animated Chinese political culture; elite and popular cultures, despite their differences, agreed on the fundamental elements of the imperial system: the worldly and religious power of the Emperor, and the pursuit of harmony and perfection. As the old order disintegrated, successive waves of reformers, often still raised within the Confucian tradition, sought recipes for national deliverance. Some claimed that a purified version of Confucianism would reinvigorate the Chinese nation, although, in a phenomenal bout of cultural patricide, the majority held Confucianism responsible for China's corruption and backwardness and looked abroad for new ideas. One of these was Marxism, which was attractive to many modernizing intellectuals as it provided both a credible explanation of China's plight at the hands of imperial powers and a promise of restoration and glory.

Yet, as the Republican project failed and political authority fragmented among provincial warlords during the 1910s and 1920s, the search for a new orthodoxy primarily became a quest for organizational efficacy, rather than substantive progress. Both the Guomindang (GMD) and the CCP sought inspiration, and received assistance from, the Soviet Union through the Comintern, and were structured along Leninist lines (Dickson 1997). Some aspects of the imperial Confucian tradition, as well as popular political culture, were quite congenial to the Leninist project that the GMD would attempt and the CCP would perfect. Both Confucianism and Leninism are predicated on the belief that legitimate rule is an intellectual effort that can only be performed by those understanding orthodoxy well enough to lead the faceless masses. The Confucian inheritance, as well as both the GMD and CCP projects, eschew value pluralism, the idea that different legitimate values or interests may be incommensurable, assuming instead that all virtuous preferences can, in the end, be harmonized. Confucian notions of hierarchical obedience and filial piety resonated with Leninist notions of party discipline, and the Utopian Leninist promise of progress to a worker's paradise devoid of class struggle can, with a little good will, be compared to imperial notions of harmony. In both Confucianism and Leninism, the primary political challenge was disciplinary: bridging the divide between the center and the locality, in order to ensure that the center's will is implemented across the land.

Leninism also brought appreciable innovations and, unsurprisingly, tensions. First and foremost, its communitarian ethics notwithstanding, self-cultivation in Confucian terms was largely an individual project of intellectual and moral inquiry, not a disciplinarian inculcation of a rigid ideology or belief system. The Chinese empire has never known an equivalent of the Catholic Church, with an inflexible theology, substantial political influence, separate hierarchy and administration, and its Inquisition. Instead, during various periods, intellectual exploration flourished. In the late Ming period, for instance, an active printing industry produced wildly diverging interpretations of the Confucian canon, often laced with Daoist or Buddhist elements. In contrast, the Leninist doctrine of democratic centralism would come to see self-cultivation not as a personal project, but an organizational necessity as exploration was replaced with indoctrination. Secondly, with regard to legitimate rule, Confucianism externalized and abstracted ideas concerning virtue and the common good into the concept of "Heaven" (*Tian* 天). Legitimacy was conferred on a dynasty by a "Mandate of Heaven" (*Tianming* 天命), which would be withdrawn if an emperor failed to rule virtuously. On the one hand, this legitimized rebellion against tyranny or, at least, was invoked as such *ex post* by the newly enthroned leaders of a successful uprising. On the other hand, it provided a rhetorically objective standard against which rulers' behavior could be evaluated. This fostered an enduring Chinese political tradition of virtuous officials remonstrating negligent or delinquent monarchs. No such super-authority existed in Leninism, where it is the center of the vanguard party that possesses the fundamental truths and insights necessary for governance, which must gain and maintain the levers of power necessary to propel society towards eternal sunrise. Democratic centralism provides little room for loyal opposition once the party line has been determined. Lastly, Confucianism was imbued with a particular kind of conservatism: it did not seek to overthrow China's sociopolitical order, rather to ensure that the individual rulers and officials themselves were morally up to the task. Leninism, on the other hand, introduced the notion of progress, as it sought to mobilize and organize society as a whole in pursuit of wholesale revolution along a historically determined path forward.

Both the GMD and, later, the CCP set up remarkably similar structures to govern public communication. Both created propaganda departments, in charge of all important media outlets and tasked with spreading the Party's message to the rank-and-file, as well as the population. However, although the forms were similar, they developed substantively different ideological programs. The GMD, taking nominal command of the Chinese republic at the end of the 1920s, developed a syncretic system mixing elements of Confucianism, Christianity, nationalism, and authoritarianism, which it called the "New Life Movement." The CCP, on the other hand, forced into an underground existence as a rebel movement in the barren mountains around Yan'an, in northern China, adopted a more rigorously Socialist project of class struggle, land reform, and, most of all, thought control.

It was during this formative period, during World War II, that a pattern for CCP engagement with intellectuals was established. The immediate catalyst was the arrival in Yan'an, the CCP's headquarters, of a number of young urban idealists, such as the writers Wang Shiwei and Ding Ling, enamored with the Communist cause and the romanticism of sacrifice for the revolution. Yet the increasingly rigid Party hierarchy, together with the meticulous sumptuary rules they found, grated against their egalitarian predilections. In good Confucian tradition, they decided to remonstrate, using large-character posters (*dazibao*) in public spaces. Retribution was swift. Mao organized a Party Forum on Literature and Art, where Wang Shiwei in particular was lambasted for acting as a traitor to the Communist cause. Writers should, instead, serve the Party and the masses, maintain a close connection with the center's political line and act as "spiritual engineers" to create a new kind of progressive citizen (Mao 1942). The subsequent purge and rectification became a cauldron for the development of enduring ideological and governance tactics and tools, many of which are still used and referenced today. It also resulted in the ruthless elimination of Mao's political opponents. Wang Shiwei himself was summarily executed on trumped up charges of Trotskyist espionage as Yan'an came under GMD attack in 1947.

This cycle would, with slight variations, play over repeatedly in the People's Republic. Political circumstances would create opportunities for criticism and debate; intellectuals would come forward with energetic participation; the leadership would, after some initial dawdling, silence the debate; intellectual leaders would be sanctioned, and a conservative backlash would follow. Never would intellectual risings result in enduring liberalization. The Hundred Flowers movement and the subsequent Anti-Rightist Campaign of 1956–7, the Democracy Wall movement of 1979, the protests of 1986, the subsequent Anti-Bourgeois Liberalization campaign of 1986 and the tragic events in Tiananmen Square of June 1989 have all been iterations of this pattern. To a certain degree, one could argue that the evolution of internet use and governance, particularly after the Beijing Olympics, again follows this script, albeit in slow motion.

Over that period of time, however, the self-perception and nature of the party-state underwent profound change. The first three decades after the establishment of the People's Republic were characterized by an often violent struggle to define the new regime and its policy orientation. The mercurial romantic Mao sought to bring China to a state of permanent revolution. Throughout his life, Mao kept an anti-establishmentarian streak, even as he became the establishment. By the mid-1960s, he had come to distrust the Party apparatus to such an extent that that Cultural Revolution was unleashed as an attack on an entrenched bureaucracy. Leaders such as Liu Shaoqi and Deng Xiaoping, on the other hand, sought to construct a more institutionalized form of governance, with a meticulously planned economy and hierarchical administration, inspired by the Soviet example. In other words, the CCP contained conflicting elements that harked back to both poles of imperial political culture, overlaid with Leninist notions of progress and internal discipline.

THE DEVELOPMENT OF POLITICAL CULTURE AFTER MAO

After Mao's death, support for violent class struggle and permanent revolution crumbled rapidly and Deng Xiaoping restructured the party-state in a manner reminiscent of the Confucian approach. The Party bureaucracy was strengthened, more constant norms of political life were instituted, and, most importantly, the people were ejected from participation in politics. In return, the state started progressively to withdraw from many aspects of citizens' private lives. A society tired of the constant upheavals of the Mao era and yearning for order and stability complied with surprising speed and obedience. This had a considerable impact on the position and social standing of intellectuals. Where Mao had instinctively distrusted scholarship, preferring the spontaneity of the masses, Deng recognized that expertise was as important as political loyalty. More leeway was now permitted in research, particularly in the natural sciences, and opportunities for policy debate and input widened. Yet ambivalence remained, as this enhanced space remained conditional on support for the Leninist Party system and fealty to the party line, and dependent on the fluctuations of politics.

In discursive terms, many of the symbols and tropes of Maoism remained, albeit in a less intensive form. Near-superhuman heroes, such as Lei Feng, remained part and parcel of propaganda efforts, but were increasingly ignored by a public more interested in pop music and video games. The personality cult of the genius Great Helmsman was recast in intellectual terms: the legitimizing narrative of the CCP relied, and relies, for a large part on its claim to possess the correct, scientific wisdom to drive progress. Consequently, whereas British monarchs' visible legacies are the names of parks, squares, and their initials on pillar-boxes, every leader since Mao has sought to add his own theoretical contribution to the Party's body of accreted ideological statements. However vague or vapid, these have been celebrated as major advances in the human understanding of objective laws of social development. The near-magical element of Maoist sloganeering, which purported that great achievements were possible simply through the triumph of the will, still resonates in today's claims to realize the Chinese Dream and the great rejuvenation of the Chinese nation.

Some elements of the Chinese information order have deeper historical roots. The drive to create a new, enlightened citizenry, which was a central element of GMD and Maoist ideology, is still pursued through a "Socialist core value system" that in both form and content resembles the Kangxi Emperor's Sacred Edict and its predecessors. Intellectuals continue to use allegorical references to well-known figures from the past, often Confucian officials, in criticizing the present. The law scholar He Weifang, for instance, closed his Weibo account by posting a picture of Tao Yuanming, a fifth-century poet who resigned from government service out of disgust with the corruption of the Jin court he served (SCMP 2013). The ruthless crackdown against Falun Gong echoes the way in which dynasties sought to eradicate heterodox sects.

These elements are mobilized at a time when the limitations of both Leninism and imperial political cultures are becoming clear. First, the pursuit of harmony has tyrannized Chinese political culture. The idea of monism, that all legitimate values, preferences, and interests can not only be harmoniously combined but, moreover, be combined in a manner that will resolve contradictions in society, remains a foundational touchstone in Party ideology and discourse. Loyal opposition and recognition of the irreconcilability of different purposes are rejected. The definition of harmony and the question of how to achieve it have evolved between different stages of Party rule. During the Maoist era, it was held that harmony (or Communism) could only be reached after the violent eradication of all remnants of bourgeois suppression. Claiming that thirty years of class struggle had succeeded in removing most pre-revolutionary feudal dregs, the new Dengist regime proposed a broader vision of modernity, aimed at being as inoffensive as possible. This was a sanitized, clinical, and often inane vision of modernity, consisting of gleaming skyscrapers and bullet trains that, while impressive, was mostly bereft of human individualism. The party-state still sponsors works of art, films, and television programs to propagate this vision, most notably around Chinese New Year and the anniversaries of important political events. Yet these are rarely attractive beyond their immediate spectacle value; investment in these projects is high. More problematic in the political context, disagreement is still often viewed through the prism of disobedience. Drafters of policy documents, even at the highest level, still take pains first to demonstrate that a particular policy is designed to conform to the spirit of a leader's speech or a previous decree. Further, even though the space for debate on political matters was greater during the Deng era, its boundaries were unlimited and shifted with the political winds. Particularly those on the periphery of the party system, such as activist lawyers and academics, have found themselves on the other side of the boundary of permissibility without having changed their position.

Second, the perfectionist element of political and intellectual culture tends to see social issues as problems that can, and must, be solved. The technical side of Party ideology, developed by Mao in the late 1930s, is based on the notion that every historical era is characterized by a chief contradiction, which causes all other contradictions. Social progress is therefore generated by resolving all subordinate contradictions and, in the end, the chief contradiction. In turn, this reflected an intellectual current of patriotic worrying with its roots in the modernization movement of the late Qing. Deng Xiaoping's exhortation to "seek truth from facts" (*shishi qiushi* 实事求是)(Schoenhals 1991) was a pragmatic exhortation to look towards numbers to guide policy solutions, rather than ideological exegesis. However, as China grew less poor and less backward, it transpired that development not only solved problems, but generated new ones. Moreover, as economic and social relationships grew more complex, it became concurrently more difficult to find unequivocal win-win answers to policy questions.

Third, the essence of the Party's Leninist system is that it is purposive: its prime function is to achieve a single, defined future goal. This is easiest when the status quo is one of destitution or clear danger, as was the case in the first decades of the People's Republic. The mission was to construct a powerful Socialist state and economy, in defiance of hostile foreign nations. After the death of Stalin, this also included the Soviet Union. However, growing welfare has undermined this dynamism. An interesting parallel is perhaps the development of the pharmaceutical industry. Leninism relates to politics like emergency surgery relates to a healthy lifestyle. It is a form of political organization designed to deal effectively with a crisis and pursue single-minded objectives. It is less able to function in a situation where there is no clear immediate purpose or where various different possibilities and risks need to be balanced. In other words, Leninism might have played an important role in bringing an ailing China from the ruins of war and division, but is less well equipped to preside over a mature political order in which different interests, objectives, and processes must constantly be balanced. Put differently, the irony of a successful Leninist system is that it renders itself superfluous. However, just as the pharmaceutical industry has responded to increasing levels of general health by medicalizing ever-more trivial afflictions and mental conditions, the party-state has sought to imbue new challenges with the same sense of threat and urgency as in the national crises it faced in the past. For instance, the maintenance of sufficient ideological accomplishments among cadres under Xi Jinping has is seen as a matter of "life and death" for the Party.[4] Leninism has created a pathological need for an enemy to fight against and a mission to struggle for. However, the popular unity necessary for this is increasingly challenged by rising living standards, which reduce the attraction of mobilization and social change, and by the realities of commerce and market capitalism, which drive individualized preferences and identity-based commercialism. As a result, the Party's call must compete ever more with the distractions that a modern and prosperous market economy provides.

These tensions, partly pre-existing and partly the result of the profound social and economic changes that China has undergone, explain the contradictory nature of Party discourse. It has extolled the wisdom of the masses while raising barriers to public speech, and has excluded the masses from the political process while calling upon them to join an "historical struggle." It seeks to

---

4 This is, of course, not a tactic limited to the Chinese government. It merits remembering, for instance, that objectionable but minor satraps are often rapidly dubbed "the new Hitler."

claim credit for China's undeniable process, while attempting to create a sense of crisis that requires further, Party-led progress. It portrays its enemies as both a lethal risk and paper tigers that can be vanquished with ease, and depicts its mission as a labor of struggle that nevertheless is entirely feasible on the basis of Party pronouncements. These contradictions, the logical consequences of the first principles of China's political culture, have emerged regardless of the actual quality and performance of the administration. The CCP's failure to resist corruption and abuse within its ranks merely exacerbates the perceived hypocrisy and resulting social cynicism. This is reflected in the continuing influence of the historical traumas of the late 1980s: Tiananmen and the collapse of Communism in Central and Eastern Europe. The former remains an enduring warning of the possible consequences of visible splits within the Party, while the latter demonstrated that regime change could come swiftly and unexpectedly. Both highlighted the pernicious role of intervention by amorphously named "foreign hostile forces." However strong the Party's hold on power may be, a predominant concern of the leadership is it might have overlooked new ways for opposition to coalesce. Its response has been to increase control, which has become a goal in itself (Minzner and Wang 2015).

THE EVOLUTION OF POLITICAL CONTROL OVER THE INTERNET

It is difficult to overestimate the importance that the internet has had in transcending many of the barriers to communication that the party-state has erected. Starting with urban, educated elites and expanding to all strata of society, affordable tools of mass information generation, distribution, and reception are now in the hands of Chinese citizens. Internet technology broke down the regional and sectoral fragmentation of traditional media (which had been a deliberate effort to prevent cross-boundary opposition) and the licensing obligations that kept alternative voices out of public discourse. The speed with which information circulates online vitiated the ability of censorship authorities to develop unified responses to viral news. The online sphere fostered public intellectuals, sometimes with tens of millions of followers, whose influence vastly exceeded that of Party media.

Yet the leadership had, from the earliest advent of personal telecommunications, been wary of their organizational potential. One particular spur to action came when Falun Gong members formed a human chain around the Party's headquarters in Zhongnanhai that was organized by mobile phone and e-mail. In response, the roots were laid for what is now one of the most advanced and intricate surveillance mechanisms worldwide. As the Internet became a publicly accessible information and communication platform, there was no debate about whether it should fall under government supervision, only about how such control would be implemented in practice. Over time, different strategies have been employed. Websites, like other media outlets, are required to register with propaganda authorities; Party-led industrial associations promulgate self-regulatory documents and, as the user base has grown, individual censorship duties have been outsourced to the Internet companies.

These measures notwithstanding, Internet use skyrocketed in the 2000s (Creemers 2016) and netizens increasingly found intricate ways to satirize, organize, and publicize. This was partly due to the fact that propaganda authorities mainly saw the Internet as merely a novel platform for the publication of traditional processes of persuasion and content control. They had not anticipated the enormous expansion of user-generated content, in particular through social media, but also through the "self-media" (*zimeiti* 自媒体), that convenient production and editing software had enabled. Technology authorities, on the other hand, did not see content management as a priority. As a result, the traditional strength of the propaganda bureaucracy in managing the publication and dissemination of information was deeply eroded, as viral tweets and blog posts sped across China before the censors had even pulled on their proverbial boots. A particular illustration of the new power of technology came in the form of built-in cameras in smartphones, which made it possible to produce powerful images and distribute them in real-time. Many cases of local corruption and social problems were exposed in this manner. One symbolic incident was the Wenzhou rail crash of 2011, where individuals uploaded photos on Weibo which allegedly showed attempts to bury the wrecked carriages, even as rescue efforts were still ongoing (Bondes and Schucher 2014). Yet already during this high tide of online communication, which reached a symbolic zenith with the Wenzhou rail crash of 2011, there was brewing a counter-oscillation towards discipline and order. Even as liberal-leaning intellectuals claimed that the government would be unable to control the social forces that had been unleashed online, that government became ever more determined to prove them wrong.

As a reaction to the liberal stance, a growing chorus of pro-control voices called for greater self-confidence and "cultural self-awareness" in influential Party media, such as *Red Flag Manuscripts*, while various Party and state bodies initiated research projects to formulate counter policies to an online sphere that was increasingly seen as out of control.[5] Initial restructuring measures

---

[5] Such projects often resulted in cadre training materials or policy recommendations for stricter ideological guidance (*zouxiang wenhua zijue*).

were taken within the propaganda administration from 2011 onwards, including the establishment of the State Internet Information Office (SIIO), a specialized body tasked with managing online content, and the dedication of a plenary Central Committee session to the important role of culture in fostering national self-consciousness in October 2011 (Central Committee 2011). Yet the SIIO was largely a department of the State Council Information Office, the government spokesperson, without its own staff, and the sixth plenum of the seventeenth Party Congress still referred to the Internet only superficially. The administration of Xi Jinping, which came to power in November 2012, dealt with the Internet much more energetically. Most importantly, the SIIO was given enhanced powers and an independent staff, and its new director and vice-director, Lu Wei and Ren Xianliang, became the most visible faces of the new propaganda-and-control offensive.

To a certain degree, the authorities availed themselves of the traditional media control toolkit that the Party had developed over the years. New ethical rules for online celebrities and ordinary users, the "Seven Baselines," were laid down first (People's Daily 2013). The most influential online voices were approached individually, at first in an effort to co-opt them, later through more coercive means. A media campaign across official channels sought to soften the ground for the inevitable crackdown, by presenting the stricter approach as a remedy for the various risks and dangers the Internet harbored. The authorities also took a more direct approach in managing Internet use: the previous system in which censorship duties were largely outsourced to Internet companies was supplemented with new rules that directly targeted individual behavior online and demonstrated an increasingly sophisticated understanding of the online communication ecology (Creemers 2015). The dynamism of public social media, for instance, was countered by rules that imposed prison sentences for publishing particular kinds of undesired content if it was re-tweeted 500 times or more (Supreme People's Court 2013). Moves towards a more effective real-name registration system were taken to ensure culprits were identifiable.

Yet, gradually, the reconfiguration of Internet governance also revealed a fundamental shift in attitudes towards technology. Where previous propaganda administrators had primarily seen technology as a source of risk, Lu and Ren sought to harness its potential for their own purposes, including its use as a propaganda platform. Whereas previously private Internet companies were kept at arm's length, government departments and officials, as well as official media at all levels, are now encouraged to use the platforms these enterprises provide to connect better to a populace that has left traditional media behind. The corporations operating these platforms have themselves been brought into decision-making structures and are often touted abroad as national champions of China's innovation and development agenda. However, propaganda is now only one part of a much broader agenda to restructure the Party's governing framework through technology. Illustratively, the SIIO, whose English name was changed to Cyberspace Administration of China in 2014, became the host department for the office of a new Central Committee leading group, the Central Leading Group for Cybersecurity and Informatization. This combined the previously separate bureaucracies responsible for propaganda, technological innovation and development, and security. In particular the technology administration had, over the previous years, produced ambitious plans for "informatization" (*xinxihua*): the introduction of ICTs in all aspects of social and economic life, in order to enhance efficiency and the delivery of public services, support urbanization and economic growth, but also to be better able to monitor "social thinking trends."

The potential ramifications of this plan are mind-boggling. As it is now mandatory that user accounts for online services and mobile phone subscriptions are registered on the basis of real-name information, it will be technologically possible to mine the vast amount of data that will be generated through user activities in increasingly sophisticated and granular ways. Yet the plan does not stop there. It is connected to new forms of social management based on camera surveillance and monitoring by on-the-ground teams. China's Internet has been referred to as a Panopticon, Jeremy Bentham's conception of a circular prison in which a central, invisible watchman can observe the inmates, who have no means to perceive whether or not they are being watched at a given point in time and so are driven continuously to conformity (Bentham 1843). Yet technological potential is causing this static mode of governance to evolve into what Branden Hookway calls a "panspectron," which entails a much more dynamic approach not only to information-gathering, but also to processing and analyzing that information in order to intervene in social and economic processes (Hookway 2000).

This signals an important shift in the tactical arsenal that the Party has at its disposal. The problem of coercion damaging the Party's image and causing a domestic and international backlash is overcome by modifying the space for action, and subtly employing less prominent means, including technology and code, either to nudge individuals towards compliance or to make it impossible for them to engage in undesired activities. These powers are primarily seen, and utilized, as a tool to prevent organized opposition and dissent. Control has developed a logic of its own, connected to the Party's essential program that it, and it alone, has the legitimate authority to govern China. However, these powers are also utilized as part of a broader project of socioeconomic reform, raising questions about the purpose of such control within a broader strategy of national development.

WHITHER CHINA'S POLITICAL CULTURE IN THE DIGITAL ERA?

The powerful levers of social management will allow the Party to manage the inevitable tensions between its perfectionist narrative and the messiness of everyday life. The citizenry's autonomy to raise topics or expose painful truths has largely been constrained, and these are channeled into controlled paths that ensure key decisions about publication and response remain within the Party. The authorities are therefore again able to prioritize certain claims over others, marginalize particular interests and groups, and recast critical narratives into forms that are consistent with the Leninist ideal to maintain the dominant voice in the public sphere. For instance, the tension between the manufactured satisfaction of Socialism and the manufactured dissatisfaction of the market economy is, at least rhetorically, resolved by portraying consumer complaints as a call for government protection of consumer rights, without addressing the foundational iniquities of the system.

One interesting illustration of this tension is found in defamation law. So long as all media were controlled by the party-state, defamation law functioned as an alternative form of supervision over individual news outlets as much as it provided legal protection for individuals' rights to reputation. Now, the internet permits individual Chinese citizens to slander or insult each other without any immediate relevant political connection. Yet to define defamation doctrine clearly would entail a public commitment to a jurisprudential delineation of acceptable speech, something the leadership has strenuously avoided. As a solution, judges are left relatively free to employ the necessary tools to solve the problems before them, as binding precedent does not exist in Chinese law. Some judges have, for instance, actually cited the US case of *New York Times* v. *Sullivan*[6] in verdicts. This practice ensures that defamation cases can be dealt with in a manner conducive to generating procedural legitimacy, as well as that the broader system of undefined and vague boundaries can continue to exist.

These trends allow for increasing ways to stabilize the system, and to manipulate rules, norms, and computer code in such a way that citizens are nudged into rationally acting out the leadership's will. Where Confucian officials had to rely on persuasion and acceptance to inspire action, technology makes consent superfluous. Still, one central tension of the Leninist system

---

[6] *New York Times Co. v. Sullivan*, 376 U.S. 254 (1964).

remains: its need for an enemy and a mission. Whether and to what extent Chinese officials and citizens believe in or support Leninist ideology is an open and complex question. However, the rhetorical demands of obedience require declaring dedication to the Party's plan and vociferously struggling against its enemies. However, doing so may politicize issues that would otherwise not have gained prominence, and antagonize individuals who might otherwise have remained peaceful. The fanatical focus on security and controllability is thus, to some extent, self-exacerbating. A further challenge is the guardsman's problem. The internet has also been used as a tool to impose stricter control over officials in departments and localities. They are now required to publish various kinds of information that is not only useful for the local populace, but also for their Beijing overseers. The Party's anticorruption watchdog has gone so far as to develop a mobile phone app to report venality directly to the central authorities, bypassing the often-treacherous path of having to travel physically to Beijing to present a petition in person. The internal Party system will have to adjust to this new mode of control and there is a continuous risk that the few senior officials in control of the system pose a political danger of their own, not unlike the previous head of internal security, Zhou Yongkang.

These developments give cause for reflection, also outside China. In the same manner that Internet and digital technology have mercilessly exposed the hypocrisies and tensions within the liberal-democratic order, they have revealed the dysfunction and contradictions of the Sino-Leninist project. In both cases the response has been the enthusiastic embrace of more technology. In the West, the silicon mantra of techno-optimism, data-driven solutions and disruption remains current, despite damning criticism. In China, where such criticism is quickly circumscribed, ICTs are marshaled to induce the discipline and compliance that has eluded the system for so long. Everywhere, big data analysis is now being proposed as a legitimate means to tackle harms generated by political and commercial interests. It is a painful awakening to find that the libertarian ethos underpinning much of the evolution of technology has fostered systems that enable more total control over individual lives than at any time in the past. Not unlike Leninism, technology designers often consciously or unconsciously impose particular preferred lifestyles onto individuals, equally denying them autonomy and individuality. However, as Isaiah Berlin warned:

> Once I take this view, I am in a position to ignore the actual wishes of men or societies, to bully, oppress, torture them in the name, and on behalf, of their "real" selves, in the secure knowledge that whatever is the true goal of man (happiness, performance of duty, wisdom, a just society, self-fulfillment) must be identical with his freedom – the free choice of his "true", albeit often submerged and inarticulate, self. (Berlin 2004, original 1958, p. 180)

REFERENCES

Bentham, J. 1843. *The Works*, 4. Bowring, J. (ed.). Edinburgh: William Tait.

Berlin, I. 2004. *Liberty*. Oxford: Oxford University Press.

Bondes, M. and Schücher, G. 2014. "Derailed emotions: The transformation of claims and targets during the Wenzhou online incident," *Information, Communication & Society* 17(1): 45–65.

Central Committee 2011. Central Committee of the Chinese Communist Party Decision Concerning Deepening Cultural Structural Reform, October 18, 2011. Translation available at: https://chinacopyrightandmedia.wordpress.com/2011/10/18/central-committee-of-the-chinese-communist-party-decision-concerning-deepening-cultural-structural-reform/.

Clinton, W. 2000. Remarks at the Paul H. Nitze School of Advanced International Studies, Washington, DC.

Creemers, R. 2016. "Cyber China: Upgrading propaganda, public opinion work and social management for the twenty-first century," *Journal of Contemporary China*, Online First.

2015. "The privilege of speech and new media: Conceptualizing China's communications law in the internet era," in DeLisle, J. et al. (eds.), *The Internet, Social Media and a Changing China*. Pennsylvania: University of Pennsylvania Press.

Dickson, B. 1997. *Democratization in China and Taiwan: The Adaptability of Leninist Parties*. Oxford: Oxford University Press.

Guy, K. 1987. *The Emperor's Four Treasuries: Scholars and the State in the Late Ch'ien-lung Era*. Cambridge: Cambridge University Press.

Hookway, B. 2000. *Pandemonium: The Rise of Predatory Locales in the Postwar World*. Princeton, NJ: Princeton Architectural Press.

Liu, X. 2009. "The Internet is God's present to China," *The Times*, April 28, 2009. Available at: www.thetimes.co.uk/tto/law/columnists/article2048790.ece.

Mao, Z. 1942. Talks at the Yenan Forum on Literature and Art. Translation available at: www.marxists.org/reference/archive/mao/selected-works/volume-3/mswv3_08.htm.

Minzner, C. and Wang, Y. 2015. "Rise of the Chinese security state," *China Quarterly* 339: 222–46.

Mitter, R. 2005. *A Bitter Revolution: China's Struggle with the Modern World*. Oxford: Oxford University Press.

Mote, F. 2003. *Imperial China 900–1800*. Cambridge, MA: Harvard University Press.

People's Daily 2013. "Wangluo mingren gongshi gongshou 'qige dixian'" ("Online Celebrities' Common Understanding and Joint Respect of the 'Seven Baselines'"), August 11, 2013. Translation available at: http://chinacopyrightandmedia.wordpress.com/2013/08/13/online-celebrities-common-understanding-and-joint-respect-of-the-seven-baselines/.

Pye, L. 1988. *The Mandarin and the Cadre*. Ann Arbor: University of Michigan Press.

Rawski, E. 1979. *Education and Popular Literacy in Ch'ing China*. Ann Arbor: University of Michigan Press.

Schoenhals, M. 1991. "The 1978 truth criterion controversy," *The China Quarterly* 126: 243–68.

SCMP 2013. "Prominent scholar He Weifang says 'goodbye' to online debate," *China Insider,* December 31, 2013. Available at: www.scmp.com/news/china-insider/article/1394040/prominent-scholar-he-weifang-says-goodbye-online-debate.

Supreme People's Court 2013. "Interpretation Concerning Some Questions of Applicable Law When Handling Uses of Information Networks to Commit Defamation and Other Such Criminal Cases." Translation available at: https://chinacopyrightandmedia.wordpress.com/2013/09/06/interpretation-concerning-some-questions-of-applicable-law-when-handling-uses-of-information-networks-to-commit-defamation-and-other-such-criminal-cases/.

Vittinghoff, N. 2002. *Die Anfänge des Journalismus in China (1860–1911).* Wiesbaden: Harrassowitz.

15

French National Values, Paternalism, and the Evolution of Digital Media

Julien Mailland

INTRODUCTION

France has a long tradition of supporting free speech, critical thinking, and political criticism, dating back to the Enlightenment. Some of France's finest political writers, such as Diderot, Voltaire, and Rousseau, were hugely influential around the Western world, and Thomas Paine, Benjamin Franklin, and Thomas Jefferson all spent time in France, mutually contributing to thinking on freedom. The Declaration of the Rights of Men and the Citizen of 1789 established liberty as a natural right, and set the basis for the French regime of freedom of speech. Later it would be a key source of inspiration for the 1948 United Nations Universal Declaration of Human Rights. One might therefore be surprised to learn that the positive law for freedom of speech in France, the Law of July 29, 1881 on the Freedom of the Press, is actually a criminal law that prohibits the expression of a number of ideas. Further, that there have been multiple attempts by government to censor the Internet, to such a degree that in 2012, Reporters Without Borders placed France on its list of countries under surveillance and denounced "the legislative straitjacket" being deployed with regard to digital networks (Reporters Without Borders 2012). If France is so inclined in promoting free speech, why are things such as libel and hate speech crimes? Why are journalists prohibited from broadcasting in any language other than French and radios required to play a minimum amount of "French content?" Why is it that, as France moved into the digital age, it imposed censorship systems on digital information distribution networks? And why did all four branches of government come to consider the Internet to be a danger, with the executive branch of government busy fighting the free-flow-of-information theory promoted by the United States with its own version of digital contraflow?[1]

---

[1] Contraflow refers to the "proliferation of multilingual and multifaceted growth of media content, emanating from regional hubs of creative industries," made possible by "[t]he availability

This chapter examines the tensions between freedom and regulation of speech in the digital age, by reference to the traditional role of the French language and content in state-society relations, in nation-building and in French foreign policy. Throughout the chapter, this analysis sheds light on French Internet policy, at both the domestic and international levels.

SPEECH AND STATE-SOCIETY RELATIONS

The French constitutional order, and in particular the ways civil liberties, including free speech, are balanced, rests on assumptions that are fundamentally different from those that exist elsewhere, such as in the United States of America. Speech is constitutionally regulated in the USA through a negative command to Congress: "Congress shall make no law … abridging the freedom of speech, or of the press."[2] In contrast, the French Constitution gives a positive role to Parliament in regulating speech for the good of society: "[a]ny citizen may … speak, write and publish freely, except what is tantamount to the abuse of this liberty in the cases determined by Law."[3] This difference reveals a contrasting approach to the role free expression should play in state-society relations. The positive law of the USA reveals a model of distrust for the government: "the forefathers did not trust any government to separate the true from the false for us,"[4] once wrote Justice Jackson. Unrestricted speech is considered a tool through which good ideas can triumph over bad ones in the marketplace of ideas, and through which the people can realize their sovereignty and control their government. As a result, speech such as hate speech that is banned in most countries is protected in the USA. As summed up by influential First-Amendment theorist Alexander Meiklejohn, "in a society pledged to self-government, it is never true that, in the long run, the security of the nation is endangered by the people … Freedom is always wise. That is the faith, the experimental faith, by which we Americans have undertaken to live" (Meiklejohn 1955, pp. 6–7).

France, in contrast, grants a positive role to government in regulating social activity, including speech, for the good of the people. There is no such thing

---

of digital technologies and satellite networks," and a "privatized and deregulated broadcasting and telecommunication environment," which have enabled "an increasing flow of content from the global South to the North," resulting in "non-Western production center[s] making [their] presence felt in a global cultural context." (Thussu 2006, 180).

[2]   US Constitution, Amendment I (1791).

[3]   Declaration on the Rights of Men and the Citizen, Article 11.

[4]   *Thomas v. Collins*, 323 US 516, 545 (1945) (Jackson, J. concurring).

as popular self-government. While France is a democracy, "the people" are not sovereign; rather, the Nation is, and its infallible will is expressed through parliamentary law-making. This trust that social relations are most properly organized from the top-down, as opposed from the bottom-up as in the USA, is one of the reasons why the possibility of constitutional review in France has historically been extremely limited. "The Law has the right to forbid ... those actions that are injurious to society,"[5] proclaims the Declaration of the Rights of Men and the Citizen.

The regulation of speech in France is underpinned by these fundamental assumptions about the role of government in organizing social relations and, in particular, in protecting the people at large against abuses of liberties by a minority. Parliament is a protector. This vision for state-society relations is reflected in specific regulations, chiefly the Law of July 29, 1881 on the Freedom of the Press. This law, it is essential to stress, is a criminal law. Its basic tenet is that speech is free. The law begins with brief statements of the principles, that the press is free (Article 1), and that the printing and distribution of content requires no prior authorization (Article 5). However, these statements are followed by forty-two Articles listing specific exceptions to the principles and providing for a criminal regime, all of which are supported by the underpinning principle that the majority must be protected from the minority, and that Parliament is the wisest body to balance rights and obligations to ensure social peace.

The underlying assumption behind this approach is that "the people" are weak and incapable of determining right from wrong. This paternalistic style is reflected in a number of criminal speech offenses: hate speech, broadcasting ideas in any language other than French (see the next section below), insulting the President of the Republic (an offense that had not been applied since President De Gaulle, until it was revived by the courts under President Sarkozy); and "[presenting] narcotics in a good light," an offense used to prosecute proponents of marijuana legalization (Mailland 2001, p. 1186).

In addition to the protective-state rationale, some authors have provided alternative underlying principles. For example, James Whitman suggested that the French criminalization of hate speech is "only one aspect of a more complex cultural pattern," (Whitman 2000, p. 1282), in this case a French cultural tradition of civility, which Whitman traces back to the eighteenth-century tradition of "revolutionary redistribution of honor" that was previously

---

5   Declaration on the Rights of Men and the Citizen, Article 5.

reserved to the aristocracy (Whitman 2000, pp. 1395–6 and 1398). While this theory is not widespread, it could be used to explain certain speech crimes, such as criminal insult (Article 29), which is frequently used, often successfully, by politicians trying to silence journalists and pundits whose criticism is not sensitive enough to their taste. Such critics are sometimes sentenced to fines in addition to civil damages. However, by and large, the "protection of the people" rationale is the most significant principle when it comes to explaining the regulation of speech in France, in both the analog and digital ages.

France has over thirty-five years of experience regulating digital marketplaces. Starting in 1979, the state launched a high-modernist digital information distribution network, Minitel, as part of its plan to digitize the national telephone network, jumpstart a hardware and content industry, and compete against the American behemoth IBM (the international relations aspects of the plan are discussed below). Following the seminal Nora-Minc report, *The computerization of society* (Nora and Minc 1981), the Post, Telegraph and Telephone Ministry (PTT) distributed free computer terminals to every French person and soon all of France was online, surfing for news, games, things to buy and, of course, pornography (Mailland 2001, p. 1179; Mailland 2016). Digital speech regulation issues that would not appear in most countries until 1995 when the Internet became a public network had to be addressed in France much earlier, including how to control online networks to ensure compliance with speech laws.

In 1981, a century after the press law had been passed, the PTT, and then Parliament a year later, opted for a censorship system. One was not allowed to publish anything over the network unless the site had been authorized in advance by the executive branch of government; authorization was granted (or denied) by the Prefect, a Napoleonic institution of local representatives of the Emperor spread throughout the country to enforce the uniform application of centrally determined rules of behavior. What is most interesting is not so much that the state opted for a censorship system, but why. Originally, PTT leaders wanted to create a fully open network, through which anyone could publish anything without prior authorization. After all, such a system would have been in line with the press law of 1881 that established the principle of freedom to publish, with speech crime exceptions punished by the judicial branch *a posteriori*. However, the print press industry cleverly foresaw its impending demise and considered Minitel an enemy that should be destroyed or, at least, adjusted to fit the existing information-economy order. But this selfish argument would have failed in the court of public opinion, so the press crafted its public rhetoric around an appeal to fear.[6] Through a massive campaign waged in 1981, the print press warned of "the lack of a rulebook ... which has led to a certain state of anarchy at the start, and created the illusion for many service providers that everything was permitted and possible."[7] That argument relied on the aforementioned underpinning principles for speech regulation in France, specifically the necessary role of the centralized state to protect the people against abuses of freedom by a minority. Lest the government intervene to regulate Minitel and constrain it within a monopoly system for the press, or at least a prior-authorization system (the censorship system adopted later), then service providers would risk thinking that "everything [is] permitted and possible,"[8] an outcome that might sound like music to the ears of Alex Meiklejohn, but not to the French people.

There is evidence to suggest that the PTT, and the administration of newly elected President Mitterrand, felt such angst from the people, created by the press's relentless rhetoric of fear when it came to Minitel, that they felt they had no choice but to bring the debate before Parliament, which then subjected Minitel to the prior-authorization censorship regime in 1982. This highlights the subconscious need of the French to have social relations regulated from the top down, as well as the direct impact that the tradition of centralization and content control by the state has had on digital speech regulation in France. To borrow from James Scott, digital communication networks were hardwired in the early 1980s, in the same ways that road and rail communication networks in France had been "hardwired" (Scott 1998, p. 73) to embed the French political tradition of centralization: the latter "systems increasingly favored movement to and from Paris over interregional or local traffic" (Scott 1998, p. 73) and "reflected the centralizing ambitions of local lords and the nation's monarchs" (Scott 1998, p. 74). These communication networks were "devised to maximize access and to facilitate central control" (Scott 1998, p. 75). Pointing to a "centralizing aesthetic," Scott shows how the networks "defied the canons of commercial logic or cost-effectiveness" and instead "severed or weakened lateral cultural and economic ties by favoring hierarchical links" (Scott 1998, p. 76). Borrowing from Eugen Weber, Scott concludes that

---

[6]   As explained by Tom Hollihan and Kevin Baaske, "appeal to fear" refers to an argument that "relies in fear to convince someone to agree ... Such appeals do not provide real choice, and thus they are not really reasons for agreement – even if they are sometimes successful in gaining compliance." (Hollihan and Baaske 2005, p. 166).

[7]   Contribution of the National Syndicate for the Regional Daily Press on the report of the Commission of Telematics Monitoring: Its experience and subsequent monitoring, October 18, 1982.

[8]   Ibid.

the layout was "designed to serve the government" (Scott 1998, p. 75, quoting Weber 1976, p. 195). Scott shone a light on the ways in which communication networks have historically been designed in ways that reflect the political traditions of information control and, more broadly, of state-society relations, in the states where they were built. Arguably, the censorship regime imposed by positive law on Minitel reflects the same tradition. Parliament granted the executive branch the power to decide whether or not one would be allowed to distribute digital speech. This set the centralized state at the heart of the network and precluded those lateral ties that would come to characterize, in contrast to Minitel, the open Internet.

At this point, the great global Internet scare entered the French consciousness. Shortly after the US government privatized the Internet and made it a public network, multiple criminal prosecutions were initiated in France where content otherwise banned under French law was accessible by French residents who simply connected to foreign servers, mostly in the USA. This yielded a fragile regulatory arbitrage in the realm of speech.[9] The landmark case was *Yahoo!*. In 2000, the Paris courts ordered the US company to remove neo-Nazi content from its US servers because the availability of such content to French households contravened the criminalization of hate speech in the French press law of 1881.[10] What is interesting is the underlying rationale of the ruling. The criminal damage on which the court asserted its jurisdiction was, in the mind of Judge Gomez, "the offense to the country's collective memory." (Ibid.) Here again appears an old principle: the state must protect the people at large (in this case, the people's "collective memory") against abuses of liberties by some (in this case, the "offense" committed by the US company that facilitated the speech act). In the same vein, former French Interior Minister Jean-Pierre Chevenement also urged the international community to "restrain the excesses of an unfettered freedom" by harmonizing laws and participating in a world convention on cybercrime (Reuters 2000).

Further attempts by France to regulate Internet speech through positive law can also be explained by reference to the central role of the paternalistic state in organizing social relations from the top down. For example, Parliament, always eager to reassert its role as a protector of the masses, decided in the spring of 1996 to replicate for the Internet the censorship scheme that was set up for Minitel. The "Amendment Fillon," named after the future prime minister who introduced it, amended the 1986 Telecommunications Act and

---

[9] On regulatory arbitrage in the realm of speech, see Froomkin (1997).
[10] TGI Paris, May 22, 2000 (*UEJF et Licra* v. *Yahoo! Inc and Yahoo France*); TGI Paris, November 20, 2000 (*UEJF and Licra* v. *Yahoo! Inc and Yahoo France*).

extended the jurisdiction of the Minitel censor to the Internet.[11] It mandated that the censor (now named "CST") develop a code of conduct with restrictions on speech content that all French Internet service providers would be required to impose contractually on their customers. Content could only be uploaded to the Internet if it met content-quality criteria set by an administrative authority, outside the legislative or judicial process.

The Constitutional Court struck down the law for establishing an unconstitutional censorship regime.[12] That decision, however, was not the end of centralized command and control. A few months after the court's decision, Isabelle Falque-Pierrotin, a state council justice, wrote in a report on behalf of the telecommunications and culture ministers that "the post-sixties libertarianism" spirit of the Internet, and the standards and regulatory choices made to date, "did not correspond to the French and European approach nor to its values" (Falque-Pierrotin 1997, p.11). She described the network as a place of danger, and called for state action to "civilize" the network (Falque-Pierrotin 1997, pp. 8, 11, 68, 85). She noted that the Internet "sometimes escapes French Cartesian logic" (Falque-Pierrotin 1997, p.12) and, rejecting technological determinism, concluded: "[t]he best way to protect ourselves against the Internet … is to be there!" (Falque-Pierrotin 1997, p.12). The justice suggested that the government step up its efforts, started by the Amendment Fillon, even though they were deemed unconstitutional by the High Court. Cynically, she argued that "contracts [entered into between users and service providers] can give legal grounds to content filtering without creating negative reactions such as in the case of censorship" (Falque-Pierrotin 1997, p. 72). Although the Falque-Pierrotin report did not become law (after all, Parliament had just been censored by the High Court), its inspiration lived on. In 1999, the Pierret Report again suggested the creation of a French "safety bubble" through censorship (Abramatic, 1999).

The discourse around Internet regulation, played out in all four branches of government, reflects a political tradition of state-society relations where the state micro-manages relationships between the state and civil society and within civil society itself, as a protector of a people considered weak and unable to organize itself.

Even today, the fear rhetoric, the discourse about the dangers of the Internet that require state micro-management of the network and control of the content being distributed over it, remains omnipresent. A recent controversy surrounding the distribution of the results of election exit polls is indicative. On

[11] Law no. 86–1067 of September 30, 1986, Article 43.
[12] Cons. const., DC No. 96–378 of July 23, 1996, JO, July 27, 1996, p. 11400.

election days in France, it is illegal to disclose exit polls before 8.00 pm. This rule was challenged in the 2007 presidential election, when Swiss and Belgian news websites began disclosing results during the afternoon, to the delight of French Internet users and the dismay of French media outlets that could not compete with their foreign colleagues for fear of prosecution. In the 2012 presidential election, faced with rumors that French media outlets might disclose exit polls before 8.00 pm since the election code was, at that point, a joke (given the ready availability of the information elsewhere), the state made it clear that it would prosecute any offenders. It warned not just the media but also all Internet users that any leaks over social networks such as Facebook or Twitter would lead to prosecution. As a result, the Twittersphere filled with humorous and not-so-cryptic messages, celebrating such things as the increasing smell of roses, a reference to the flower that is the symbol of the socialist party of victor François Hollande. Regarding the infamous French three-strike law for copyright law violators, which adopted a graduated response culminating in the withdrawal of Internet access, Trisha Meyer noted:

> [T]his was … often accompanied by a strong discourse on the dangers of the Internet. The French Ministry of Culture and Communication, the president, and the culture industry have described the Internet as a jungle and as an uncivilized environment where only the fittest survive. They strongly urged regulation of the Internet, something that the following quote illustrates well: 'Art is the highest expression of civilization. It is up to us to make sure that a civilized Internet exists' (Meyer 2012, p. 120) She concluded: "[t]he discourse on the dangers of the Internet in France is strong and not limited to the debate on copyright. President Sarkozy has continued to use the term 'civilization of the Internet' in Internet governance discussions" (Meyer 2012, pp. 120–2).

We will see below how this discourse around France's role in civilizing the Internet plays out in international relations.

THE FRENCH LANGUAGE AS A TOOL FOR NATION-BUILDING

One might be surprised to learn that, in France, it is illegal to speak any language other than French on broadcast media, or to advertise in any media in any language other than French. Further, under a 1994 law (Toubon Law),[13] radio stations are required to play a certain quota of French music per broadcast segment. This law, as well as the inbound aspects of French Internet policy, is rooted in the traditional role of the French language as an instrumental and essential tool in nation-building. For example, the French Marxist

---

[13] Law No. 94-665 of August 4, 1994.

philosopher Etienne Balibar shows how, like "the progressive formation of absolute monarchy brought with it effects of monetary monopoly, administrative and fiscal centralization," the institution of state language is rooted in "the process by which monarchical power became autonomous" (Balibar 1991, p. 132). In France, that is through progressive extreme centralization, from the High Middle Ages to the time of Louis XIV, the Sun King. James Scott remarks that "the imposition of a single, official language" (Scott 1998, p. 72) is a crucial element that supports the imposition of vertical state control, because a distinct language "represents a formidable obstacle to state knowledge, let alone colonization, control, manipulation, instruction, or propaganda" (Scott 1998, p. 72). "At the top of the pyramid," Scott remarks, "sat Paris and its institutions: ministries, schools, academies (including the guardian of the language, l'Académie Française)" (Scott 1998, p. 73). And to conclude, quoting Alexandre Sanguinetti, "[i]t was centralization that permitted the making of France despite the French" (Scott, 1998, p. 73).[14]

Here again, the contrast with the USA is striking and highlights the influence of state-society traditions, including that of information control, on communications policy. Unlike in France, where the state imposes a national language as part of its centralized control apparatus, there is no official language at the federal level in the USA, and state laws mandating the use of English in certain administrative processes such as taking a driving test have been struck down by courts[15] as discriminatory, which indicates a more bottom-up, popular-sovereignty-centered, market-based mode of state-society organization (Garza 2000).

In contrast, the French language and a unified French culture have historically been cores of national cohesion forced onto the people from the top down. Not only did the "French 'revolutionary nation' accord a privileged place to the symbol of language in its own initial process of formation" (Balibar 1991, p. 86), it also served as a crucial tool in creating what Etienne Balibar called a "retrospective illusion," that of the "self-manifestation of the national personality" (Balibar 1991, p. 86). From a pragmatic standpoint, this served to support the establishment of a centralized power, when local particularism and rule had been the reality. The 1539 Ordinance of Villers-Cotterêts, which mandated the use of French to record all court judgments, "was a step in the Crown's long match to establish its authority over a diversity of rivals" (Weber 1976, p. 70). With the Revolution of 1789, language unity as a means to establish centralized power became intertwined with ideology, as "the ideal of the

---

[14] Alexandre Sanguinetti, quoted in *Le Figaro*, November 12, 1968.
[15] *Sandoval v. Hagan*, 197 F.3d 484 (11th Cir. 1999).

Revolution lay in uniformity and the extinction of particularisms" (Weber 1976, p. 72). Language unity was key to grounding the myth of national unity. This coincidence of practical and ideological motives is perhaps best summed up by Eugen Weber: "teaching the people French was an important facet in 'civilizing' them, in their integration into a superior modern world" (Weber 1976, pp. 72–3).[16] Contrary to Ernest Renand's self-congratulatory remarks (Renand 1882), unity of language (and, by extension, unity of the state), was obtained by coercive measures (Weber 1976, pp. 67–94).

Such coercive measures persist today, and are materialized in particular in the Toubon Law on the use of the French language. The Toubon Law is a protectionist tool that operates at a domestic level in international relations, as a levee against foreign cultural penetration that would endanger national culture and, by extension, national unity. Back in 1949, French communists started warning against what *L'Humanité*'s editor-in-chief Pierre Hervé called "coca-colonization" in a famous editorial (Hervé 1949, pp. 1–2). The term exemplifies the "emerging resistance to 'Americanization'" and plays on the fact that "perhaps no commercial product is more thoroughly identified with America than Coca-Cola" (Kuisel 1991, p. 97). In fact, a Coca-Cola official suggested, at the time, "apparently some of our friends overseas have difficulty distinguishing between the United States and Coca Cola" (Kuisel 1991, p. 98). By asking "will we be coca-colonized," French Communists stressed the fact that "Coca-Cola was part of the Marshall Plan's strategy of colonizing France," and "only one feature of a multifaceted American 'invasion' that included Hollywood films, the *Reader's Digest*, and tractors" (Kuisel 1991, pp. 101–102).

> [Even the more moderate] *Le Monde* argued Coca-Cola represented the coming American commercial and cultural invasion … "What the French criticize is less Coca-Cola that its orchestration, less the drink itself, than the civilization – or as they like to say the style of life – of which it is the symbol … What is now at stake is the moral landscape of France … Coca-Cola seems to be the Danzig of European culture." (Kuisel 1991, p. 113)[17]

Turning to the Internet, "cocacolonization" has been captured by "omnigooglization," a term introduced in January 2005 by Jean-Noël Jeanneney, head of the French National Library, to mean "a crushing domination by America on

---

[16] Here, one can observe the premises of what would become, on the international scene, modernization theory. Associated in particular with David Lerner, "modernization theory arose from the notion that international mass communication could be used to spread the message of modernity and transfer the economic and political models of the West to the newly independent countries of the South" (Thussu 2006, pp. 42–3).

[17] Citing *Le Monde*, December 30, 1949 and *Le Monde*, March 29, 1950.

future generations' understanding of the world" (Jeanneney 2005). Jeanneney "argued that Google's plans to digitize books and make their content available on the Internet represented a threat to France because this would, in the long-run, reflect a unipolar world view with a strong bias towards English works and American culture" (Jeanneney 2005). Jeanneney's characterization was picked up by many French intellectuals, and even President Jacques Chirac called for a French "counterattack" by asking the National Library to draw up plans to accelerate the digitization of its collections and to work with other European nations to put their libraries online (Nunberg 2005). This approach to the role of speech in French society echoes the critique of Herbert Schiller. In his seminal essay, "Communication and cultural domination," Schiller warned that:

> [A] largely one-directional flow of information from core to periphery repre-sents the reality of power. So, too, does the promotion of a single language – English … [c]ultural-informational outputs represent much more than conventional units of personal-consumption goods: they are also embodi-ments of the ideological features of the world capitalist economy (Schiller 1976, p. 6)

The theoretical approach to the role of information, and of the French lan-guage, in French society continues to underpin both existing positive law and attempts to reform positive law. Recently for example, the same press industry lobby that had successfully imposed a censorship system on Minitel demanded that Google be taxed for indexing news articles. The rationale was to prevent the evil US behemoth from destroying a fledging French press industry. As it had in 1981, the appeal to fear worked on the government. Demands by the press were embraced by the communications and culture minister. And, when Google threatened to stop indexing French news articles, François Hollande summoned Eric Schmidt, CEO of Google, to the presidential palace. Once again, the appeal to fear that decentralized networks will destroy the fabric of French democracy, lest the centralized state impose rules from the top down, drove the discourse around the role of speech in digital France.

Many of the tensions surrounding the role of language and speech in state-society relations domestically have also had an impact on French foreign policy.

TOWARDS A FOREIGN POLICY FOR COMMUNICATIONS IMPACT

French international Internet policy focuses on France's version of a multi-stakeholder model, a reinforced role for government, and co-operation through traditional institutions such as UNESCO and the ITU. The USA advances its "free-flow" doctrine which focuses on free-market distribution mechanisms (Thussu 2006), whereas cultural diversity (i.e., French culture as an alternative to US culture) is at the center of France's international digital policy. Consider this 2011 policy summary statement by the French Ministry of Foreign and European Affairs (MAEE) regarding France and the global challenges of information and communication technologies:

As shown by the Arab revolutions in 2011, the internet is a powerful tool for demanding fundamental freedoms. It plays a key role in providing access to knowledge and culture.

In his speech for the inauguration of the e-G8 Forum on 24 May 2011, the president of the French Republic recalled that the internet has 'provided all citizens of the world with a freedom of speech that is unprecedented in history. This outstanding leap in individual freedoms cannot be taken at the expense of the rights of others.' In France's view, all fundamental freedoms must be protected and safeguarded to the same extent in the internet area and the real world.

The MAEE conducts actions to promote freedom of expression on the internet, notably through its operator Canal France International (CFI) which organizes training courses for journalists wishing to gain a command of digital tools.

Digital technology is crucial to the future of cultural and creative industries and MAEE cultural policy.

The issues surrounding the new opportunities provided by the internet for the development of cultural and creative industries, and for defending cultural diversity and copyright in this new environment, are priorities for the French Ministry of Foreign and European Affairs. Exceptional appropriations (of about €3.5 million) were therefore allocated in 2009 and 2010 to adapt tools for promoting French cultural and creative industries and our cultural network overseas.

MAEE support for the festival www.myfrenchfilmfestival.com, the first online French film festival staged by Unifrance Films, the operator responsible for promoting French cinema overseas, is a further significant example of this cultural development. Lastly, the French Institute (IF), set up in January 2011 and supported by MAEE, plays a significant role in cultural development online.

The MAEE fully incorporates ICTs in the various co-operation actions it conducts with developing countries (DCs) in a great variety of areas, including ... development of related content and services.

Canal France International (CFI), the MAEE operator specializing in media sector co-operation, provides assistance to the media in DCs to help them switch to digital technology. (Directorate-General of Global Affairs, Development and Partnerships 2011)

This focus on culture as part of French Internet policy is not surprising, as it has been a cornerstone of French foreign policy for well over a century. The process of domestic colonization through the imposition of a unique language was replicated in the colonies, where subjects of colonization were also provided with French cultural goods as part of "France's *mission civilisatrice* (civilizing mission), the notion that a thoroughly particular French culture had universal relevance for all of humanity" (Schloesser 2005, p. 153, citing Conklin 1997). The focus in colonial Africa after World War II was on "the quality of the cultural product" (Schloesser 2005, p. 153, citing Conklin 1997). Such projection through diffusion of language and culture has been performed both directly through colonization and indirectly through international organizations such as La Francophonie, an international organization of fifty-six states and a key tool of French global influence.

Going forward into the digital age, while the USA is not mentioned specifically in the digital policy statement quoted above, it is clear that France has been eager to pose as an alternative to US hegemony in the Internet governance and digital content spheres. The primary enemy to French "intellectual radiance" (Schloesser 2005, p. 153) (read: French imperialism through cultural hegemony) has traditionally been the USA. As noted by Pierre Bourdieu, "a large part of what we are observing in Franco-American relations is the product of a relationship structure that we must think of as the confrontation of two universalist imperialisms" (Bourdieu 1992, p. 149). Stanley Hoffman concurs (though some may quarrel with his statement):

[T]he USA and France are the only nations that present their values as universal, and give themselves as models to the rest of the world. Foreign policy conflicts that have opposed both countries since 1945 often have been economic, strategic or diplomatic struggles, but the rivalry of universalisms often has given these struggles a passionate twist. (Hoffman 2000, p. 65)

Cultural flows originating from the USA are an impediment to France's civilizing mission, since they provide a counter-narrative to French claims of universalism.

The Nora-Minc report of 1978 was a first attempt to devise a French foreign policy as an explicit reaction to the rise of the USA in the digital age. The report's authors outlined the dangers to French sovereignty presented by US hardware and content providers, represented by IBM in the role of the villain. US-influenced information systems were threatening the top-down model so central to French state-society relations. "In a country shaped by centuries of centralization, publicly criticized and secretly craved" (Nora and Minc 1981, p. 4), telematics (telecommunications and informatics) will not only "affect the economic balance" but also "modify power relationships, and increase the stakes of sovereignty" (Nora and Minc 1981, p. 4). Well-aware that the development of cross-border networks, by empowering the people directly without mediation from the state (in a US popular-sovereignty fashion), threatened "the social consensus" (Nora and Minc 1981, p. 1) and that France should "avoid excessive pressure from foreign governments or groups whose objectives may run counter to hers" (Nora and Minc 1981, p. 2), the authors suggested that France:

> ... has to take into account the renewal of the IBM challenge. Once a manufacturer of machines, soon to become a telecommunications administrator, IBM is following a strategy that will enable it to set up a communications network and to control it. When it does, it will encroach upon a traditional sphere of government power, communications. In the absence of a suitable policy, alliances will develop that involve the administrator of the network and the American data banks, to which it will facilitate access. Only action by the authorities, standardizing the networks, launching communication satellites, and creating data banks, can give an original model for society with room to develop ... In some cases, to improve France's position in a contest with competitors not under her sovereignty, the authorities must make unrestrained use of their trump card, which is to decree. (Nora and Minc 1981, pp. 6–7)

The authors understood the role of digital information networks as power, not just domestically, but also in the "international market for loyalties," to borrow Monroe Price's expression (Price 1994, p. 667; Price 1995a, p. 802; Price 1995b, p. 67; Price 1997, p. 445; Price 2001, p. 1885; Price 2002, p. 32). An explicit goal of the report, and of the subsequent Minitel plan, was to make France a powerhouse as an exporter of digital technologies and content, to reinforce France's international influence in the digital age. The comparative-law literature has shown that iconography is not just "finery," it is also a "great purveyor of lessons," including to understand policy (Legrand 1996, p. 289). It is in this spirit that the advertisement for Teletel (Minitel's other name) as an export is reproduced below in Figure 15.1, because it shows quite clearly that French digital content is indeed a tool for "intellectual radiance" (Schloesser 2005, p. 153) on the international scene, France's own version of US hegemonic efforts embodied in Coca-Cola, the *Reader's Digest*, IBM, and Google.

FIGURE 15.1 Teletel et l'International, Intelmatique, circa 1985: French cultural radiance through digital information technologies.

The projection part of the plan, however, did not work. All attempts to export Minitel to foreign countries to provide an alternative to IBM failed (Mailland 2016). Even in neighboring countries, England and Germany, digital information systems (Prestel and BTX, respectively) were based on IBM hardware and protocols. However, the Nora-Minc analysis was pertinent nonetheless, and their rhetoric of providing a counter-narrative to that of the USA, mitigating US hegemony on the world scene, and using French culture and language as a projectionist tool unsurprisingly appeared again in the discourse about digital foreign policy when the Internet was privatized and became a global public network. For example, State Council Justice Falque-Pierrotin argued, "[t]he best way to protect ourselves against the Internet ... is to be there!" (Falque-Pierrotin 1997, p. 12). She suggested that an offensive, rather than defensive, policy be adopted to develop French Internet services (Falque-Pierrotin 1997) and that France should build on the Minitel experience to develop French content. It was important, she wrote, to pursue the development of "francophone spaces, for those are the means to favor the respect of personal rights and freedoms to which we are attached" (Falque-Pierrotin 1997, p. 12). It also was critical to "reinforce the role of the French language as the communication language between Internet users in order to move beyond the current rate of only 2 percent of Internet exchanges being in French" (Falque-Pierrotin 1997, p. 12). This position seems to be a natural extension of the traditional role France has given to its language and culture in the expansion of its sphere of influence, as for example in the colonization of West Africa. Shortly after the Falque-Pierrotin report was published, the Martin-Lalande report recognized that "the Internet is a wonderful tool to contribute to the influence of France at an international level for our culture and our language" (Martin-Lalande 1998, p. 1). It presented the Internet as "a major cultural tool, especially in the context of La Francophonie," and noted "[d]istance learning is a 'global market' where the French content industry must be present and where La Francophonie must be well represented. Therefore, synergies between Radio France International, the [distance learning center], TV5, ... and [other public service broadcasting organizations] must be encouraged" (Martin-Lalande 1998, p. 20).

The IBM/Google threat, therefore, was seen as both a domestic and a foreign policy issue. When the head of the French National Library, Jean-Noel Jeanneney, referred to omnigooglization as a "risk of crushing American domination in the way future generations conceive the world," (Jeanneney 2005) he was referring not only to French generations, but to generations of peoples around the world who, but for the flow of US-produced content, would benefit from what is considered to be the higher level of civilization brought to them by the French, not through swords, but through culture. When it comes to the role of digital information in shaping the world, French foreign policy doctrine is positioned as a contraflow designed to protect "cultural diversity" (Directorate-General of Global Affairs 2011). It is ironic because contraflows are usually thought of as "an increasing flow of content from the global South to the North, for example, the growing international visibility of telenovelas, while the Indian film industry is an example of a non-Western production center making its presence felt in a global cultural context."[18] Daya Thussu suggests that these "contraflows" can be largely explained by discontentment of non-Western countries with the West, "partly as a reaction to perceived Westernization of their cultures and partly as a reaction to the alleged distortion in representations of non-Western cultures in the global media," something referred to in terms such as "Westoxication," or "McWorld."[19] And here comes a country nostalgic of its imperial past, a former colonial power, one of

[18] Thussu (2006, p. 180).
[19] Ibid., p. 183.

few countries with an explicit claim to cultural universalism, which presents itself as the spearhead of resistance against "Westoxication," or "omnigooglization:" the "defence of cultural diversity and copyright in this new environment … [are] priorities for the French Ministry of Foreign and European Affairs."[20] Whether characterized as benevolent contraflow, or hegemonic projection, it is clear that the role of the French language and of French content is a crucial part of French foreign policy in the digital age, as the modern continuation of a time-honored practice.

CONCLUSION

Positive law and other governmental behavior shaping speech in digital France can be explained by traditional conceptions of state-society relations domestically and of France's role in international relations. The existence of a criminal press law reflects the time-honored conception of the top-down role of the state in organizing social relations and protecting a "weak" people from itself. In the digital age, this translated into a censorship regime for Minitel, as well as attempts to control the Internet to protect the masses from domestic and foreign "dangers." A unified French language and French content imposed through coercive measures had been a way to civilize the French "in their integration into a superior modern world" (Weber 1976, p. 73). The historic importance of this nation-building tool explains the domestic reaction to omnigooglization, the digital manifestation of "cocacolonization," something the French government perceives as "a crushing domination by America on future generations' understanding of the world" (Jeanneney 2005). On the foreign policy stage, the French language and French content distributed globally through the Internet with the political and financial support of the executive branch of government are simply digital ways to replicate (framed this time as contraflow and the fight against "Westoxication") the traditional hegemonic practice of spreading French culture around the world to establish power, either through colonization or international organizations. Going forward, analysts of French digital policy should continue to turn to the traditional conception of speech and culture in French policy, both domestic and international, to gain an understanding of the normative behavior of the four branches of government.

---

[20] Directorate-General of Global Affairs, Development and Partnerships (French Ministry of Foreign and European Affairs), *France and the global challenges of information and communication technologies* (2011).

REFERENCES

Abramatic, J.-F. 1999. *Développement technique de l'Internet: rapport remis à M.Christian Pierret, secrétaire d'Etat à l'industrie (Technical Development of the Internet: Report to M. Christian Pierret, Deputy Minister of the Industry)*. Paris: La Documentation Française.

Balibar, E. 1991. "The nation form: History and ideology," in Balibar, E. and Wallerstein, I. (eds.), *Race, Nation, Class: Ambiguous Identities*. London: Verso, pp. 86–106, republished in Eley, G. and Suny, R. G. (eds.) 1996, *Becoming National: A Reader*. New York: Oxford University Press, pp. 132–49.

Bourdieu, P. 1992. "Deux impérialismes de l'universel" ("Two universalist imperialisms"), in Fauré, C. and Bishop, T. (eds.), *L'Amérique des Français*. Paris: Editions François Bourin, pp. 149–55.

Conklin, A. 1997. *A Mission to Civilize: The Republican Idea of Empire in France and West Africa, 1895–1930*. Stanford: Stanford University Press.

Directorate-General of Global Affairs, Development and Partnerships 2011. *France and the Global Challenges of Information and Communication Technologies*. Paris: French Ministry of Foreign and European Affairs.

Falque-Pierrotin, I. 1997. *Internet: Enjeux juridiques. Rapport au Ministre Délégué à la Poste, aux Télécommunications et à l'Espace et au Ministre de la Culture (Internet: Legal Stakes. Report to the Deputy Minister of the Post, Telecommunications, and Space, and to the Minister of Culture)*. Paris: La Documentation Française.

Froomkin, A. M. 1997. "The Internet as a source of regulatory arbitrage," in Kahin, B. and Nesson, C. (eds.), *Borders in Cyberspace*. Cambridge, MA: MIT Press, pp. 129–63.

Garza, C. A. 2000. "Measuring language rights along a spectrum," *Yale Law Journal* 110: 379–86.

Hervé, P. 1949. "Serons nous Cocacolonisés?" ("Will we be coca-colonized") *L'Humanité*, November 8, 1949.

Hoffman, S. 2000. "Deux universalismes en conflit" ("Two conflicting universalisms"), *La Revue Tocqueville* 21(1): 65–71.

Hollihan, T. and Baaske, K. 2005. *Arguments and Arguing: The Products and Process of Human Decision Making*. Long Grove: Waveland.

Jeanneney, J.-N. 2005. "Quand Google défie l'Europe" ("When Google challenges Europe"), *Le Monde*, January 22, 2005.

Kuisel, R. F. 1991. "Coca-Cola and the Cold War: The French face Americanization 1948–1953," *French Historical Studies* 17(1): 96–116.

Legrand, P. 1996. "Comparer" ("To Compare"), *Revue Internationale De Droit Comparé* 48: 279–318.

Mailland, J. 2001. "Freedom of speech, the Internet, and the costs of control: The French example," *New York University Journal of International Law & Politics* 33(4): 1179–234.

2016. "101 online: American Minitel network and lessons from its failure," *IEEE Annals of the History of Computing* 38(1): 2–18.

Martin-Lalande, P. 1998. *L'internet: Un vrai défi pour la France: Rapport au premier ministre (The Internet: A Real Challenge for France: Report to the Prime Minister)*. Paris: La Documentation Française.

Meiklejohn, A. 1955. "Testimony on the meaning of the First Amendment, address before the US Senate Subcommittee on Constitutional Rights," *Senate, Committee on the Judiciary, Subcommittee on Constitutional Rights, hearings, eighty-fourth Congress, first session.*

Meyer, T. 2012. "Graduated response in France: The clash of copyright and the Internet," *Journal of Information Policy* 2: 107–27.

Nora, S. and Minc, A. 1981. *The Computerization of Society.* Cambridge and London: MIT Press.

Nunberg, G. 2005. "Letting the net speak for itself: Fears of an 'Anglo-Saxon' take-over of the online world are unfounded," *Mercury News*, April 17, 2005. Available at: http://people.ischool.berkeley.edu/~nunberg/weblg.html.

Price, M. 1994. "The market for loyalties: Electronic media and the global competition for allegiances," *Yale Law Journal* 104: 667–705.

1995a. "Law, force and the Russian media," *Cardozo Arts & Entertainment Law Journal* 13: 795–846.

1995b. *Television: The Public Sphere and National Identity.* Oxford: Clarendon Press.

1997. "The market for loyalties and the uses of 'comparative media law'," *Cardozo Journal of International and Comparative Law* 5: 445–65.

2001. "The newness of new technologies," *Cardozo Law Review* 22: 1885–913.

2002. *Media and Sovereignty: The Global Information Revolution and its Challenge to State Power.* Cambridge, MA: MIT Press.

Renand, E. 1882. "What is a nation?" (M. Thom, trans.), in Eley, G. and Suny, R. G. (eds.), *Becoming National: A Reader.* New York: Oxford University Press, pp. 50–5.

Reporters Without Borders 2012. "2012 Surveillance – France," March 12, 2012. Available at: http://en.rsf.org/france-france-12-03-2012,42071.html.

Reuters 2000. "G8 complains of digital havens: French hate 'unfettered freedom'," May 13, 2000.

Schiller, H. 1976. *Communication and Cultural Domination.* New York: International Arts and Sciences Press.

Schloesser, S. 2005. *Jazz Age Catholicism: Mystic Modernism in Postwar Paris, 1919–1933.* Toronto: University of Toronto Press.

Scott, J. 1998. *Seeing Like a State: How Certain Schemes to Improve the Human Condition have Failed.* New Haven: Yale University Press.

Thussu, D. K. 2006. *International Communication: Continuity and Change.* 2nd ed. London: Hodder Arnold Publication.

Weber, E. 1976. *Peasants into Frenchmen: The Modernization of Rural France, 1870–1914.* Stanford, CA: Stanford University Press.

Whitman, J. Q. 2000. "Enforcing civility and respect: Three societies," *Yale Law Journal* 109: 1279–398.

16

Strategies and Tactics: Re-shaping the Internet in Ethiopia

Iginio Gagliardone

Many countries in Africa have become battlefields where rival conceptions of the role of speech in society are competing for attention and hegemony. Afrobarometer's latest opinion polls in 2016 indicate citizens' strong support for the role of media as watchdogs (Nkomo and Wafula 2016). Heading in the opposite direction, governments are becoming more confident and assertive about the need for the media to "play along" with the ruling agenda, to support development and avoid fueling "destabilizing forces." China's increasing influence in Africa, including in the media and telecommunication sectors, has been suggested as one of the causes of this latter tendency (Farah and Mosher 2010; Kurlantzick 2007). To date, however, African heads-of-state have been just as likely to refer to the US-backed "war on terror" to justify restrictions to freedom of expression, than to the appeal of a supposed "Chinese model" of the information society (Fisher and Anderson 2015; Gagliardone 2014, 2016).

Focusing on the recent history of Ethiopia since the fall of Colonel Mengistu Haile Mariam in 1991, this chapter examines how these competing forces interact in one of Africa's fastest-growing economies and most tightly controlled countries. It reflects on the emergence and contradictions of an Ethiopian developmental model under the guidance of the Ethiopian People's Revolutionary Democratic Front (EPRDF) that has sought to innovatively refashion the role of the media in society. In place of the prevailing focus amongst the international community that relates the media to debates on policies, politics and development strategies, the EPRDF have instead emphasized *delivery* of information, services, and knowledge.

The greater assertiveness and appeal that derives from a developmental model that privileges stability and economic growth over political freedoms and disruptive innovation, however, does not mean this model has become conclusive or hegemonic. If we compare national and international reactions to the death of Singapore's first prime minister and the nation's founding father, Lee Kuan Yew, in 2015 as reported in Cherian George's chapter in this collection, with the responses to the death of Meles Zenawi in 2012, who played an arguably similar role in contemporary Ethiopia, the fragility and contradictions of the Ethiopian variant become particularly apparent.

The development of Singapore and Ethiopia's media systems share numerous features. These include private media's longstanding hostility toward the state and the nation-building projects elaborated by the government, efforts to prevent free media from getting in the way of the job of elected officials, and the emphasis by the government on the need to promote social cohesion over debates of difference (as argued in Cherian George's chapter). However, while Lee's vision received much posthumous praise at home and abroad, signaling some acceptance of the model he championed, "including in the liberal democratic West, whose finger pointing he had so scornfully rebuffed during his career" (ibid.), most posthumous international commentaries on Meles' vision struck a difficult and more ambiguous balance. Commentaries tended to emphasize the skills of a premier who brought sustained economic growth to one of the poorest countries on the continent, but also the ruthlessness he used to crush political opponents, including ordering firing on protesters in the aftermath of the contested 2005 elections. The reactions to Meles' death hosted by social networking platforms offered an even more confused and divided picture. On Facebook, the words "dictator," "savior," "murderer," and "visionary" blended together in an ambiguous whole. This ambiguity continues to characterize Ethiopia, a country whose government is openly challenging orthodoxy in development aid while remaining its largest recipient in Africa, and achieving sustained economic growth but also marginalizing many national actors that could play an active role in promoting innovation and change.

A CONTRADICTORY PROJECT

On November 8, 2006, the Ethiopian Telecommunication Corporation and the Chinese telecom giant ZTE signed the largest agreement in the history of telecommunications in Africa. Backed by the China Development Bank, ZTE offered a loan of $1.5 billion to overhaul and expand Ethiopia's telecommunication system. Six years later, another $1.6 billion was entrusted to ZTE and Huawei (one of China's most successful multinational corporations), bringing Chinese government support for Ethiopia's Information and Communication Technology (ICT) sector to over $3 billion.

Despite these unprecedented investments, however, Ethiopia has continued to score at the bottom of regional and global rankings in terms of access to ICTs. In 2006, when the contract with ZTE was signed, mobile connectivity in Ethiopia was 1.1 percent. Though this rose to 31 percent in 2014, comparisons elsewhere failed to flatter Ethiopia. In neighboring Kenya, 74 percent of people had a mobile phone in 2014, a population that also had 43 percent of people regularly connecting to the Internet. In Ethiopia, in contrast, only 3 percent of the population were using the Internet in 2014 (International Telecommunications Union 2015). In addition, the quality of the service provided to customers in Ethiopia is appalling, so bad in fact that even tightly controlled official government media have been allowed to criticize technical glitches and incompetence.

And yet, the Ethiopian government has developed some of the most ambitious projects in Africa, employing ICTs to support development and improve service delivery, penetrating even the most remote parts of the country. Two flagship e-government projects developed by the Ethiopian government, Woredanet and Schoolnet, have employed satellite connectivity and the same protocol the Internet is based upon to expand the reach and capacity of the state over Ethiopia's vast territory. Woredanet ("woreda" refers to the administrative units of Ethiopia) has been used to improve and straighten governmental communication between the center and the peripheries, enabling ministers and cadres in Addis Ababa to videoconference with distant woreda offices and instruct them on what they should be doing and how. Schoolnet has used a similar technological architecture to ensure that every secondary school student in the country has access to education of the same quality (and content), even if this has to come in the form of pre-recorded classes broadcast through plasma television screens.

Furthermore, in a country well known to the world for its food insecurity, the state has innovated how food demand and supply are matched, creating the first Commodity Exchange in Africa. The Ethiopian Commodity Exchange (ECX) has used ICTs to link the trading floor in Addis Ababa with grading centers assessing the quality of the products, warehouses and display sites all around the country. It has also allowed inventories to be updated in real time, payments to be made the day after purchase, and information to be provided to different audiences through the web, the radio, and mobile phones.

This commitment to investing in new technologies for development, however, has been matched by an equally strong resistance toward uses of ICTs that are perceived to challenge central power and threaten to destabilize the country. Ethiopia is the nation in Africa that most pervasively filters the Internet and surveils communications. Most government opposition websites are not accessible within Ethiopia and the use of proxies and anonymizers to circumvent these restrictions have been made increasingly difficult (OpenNet Initiative 2007). Companies headquartered in China, Italy, and Britain have offered equipment and expertise to the Ethiopian government to monitor communication and even spy on opposition leaders living abroad (Human Rights Watch 2014). In April 2014, six bloggers were arrested for "planning to destabilize the country using social media."[1] In October 2016, following widespread protests in the regions of Oromia and Amhara, the government declared a six-month state of emergency, leading to a shutdown of mobile Internet across the country, and criminalizing uses of social media that could be considered supportive of the protesters (BBC 2016; Dahir 2016).

When examined together, these projects, policies, and events appear to offer a paradoxical image of how innovations in communication have been both resisted and embraced to fit into a specific nation-building project. However, the recent history of ICTs in Ethiopia can be better explained when greater attention is paid to the ideologies and discourses that have been used by the EPRDF to inform and justify the evolution of Ethiopia's information society and to how domestic and international power balances have shifted, allowing greater room for the EPRDF to assert their own conceptions of the role speech should play in society.

The next sections trace this evolution in the last twenty-five years of Ethiopian history, explaining how a specific ideology, grounded on the concepts of ethnic federalism, revolutionary democracy, and the developmental state, has shaped the relationship between speech, innovation, and development in Ethiopia today. Inflected with the assumptions of high modernity that "bureaucratic enclaves of excellence and huge infrastructure projects can qualitatively reconfigure domestic political-economic systems" (Jones et al. 2013, p. 6) this trajectory has been echoed elsewhere in Africa. In the case of ICTs this has meant, at the national level, placing the state in the conditions to act as the prime mover in most large-scale technical projects and ensuring its prominence over other actors. On the international stage, these governments have devised innovative practices leading to embrace key elements of donors' agenda – improvements in service delivery above all – and use tangible results in these areas to counterbalance deficits in others, such as the lack of respect for freedom of expression and for oppositional views.

---

[1] For a full account of the charges against the bloggers, see https://trialtrackerblog.org/home/.

TACTICS AND STRATEGIES IN THE EVOLUTION
OF INFORMATION SOCIETIES IN AFRICA

A distinction between tactics and strategies, as suggested by the French historian and philosopher Michel de Certeau in *The Practice of Everyday Life* (1984), can help appreciate some important qualitative aspects that have characterized the shift from the dependency African nations experienced from donor countries in developing ICT policies and projects, to a relationship characterized by greater assurance and independence, but also by greater tension and mistrust.

De Certeau's exposition of tactics and strategies was developed to better understand the possibilities of individuals and groups to subvert an order that overwhelms them. Referring to the relationship between Spanish colonizers and the colonized, for example, de Certeau illustrated how the latter were able to use:

> laws, practices, and representations that were imposed on them by force or by fascination to ends other than those of their conquerors; they made something else out of them; they subverted them from within – not by rejecting them or by transforming them (though that occurred as well), but by many different ways of using them in the service of rules, customs or convictions foreign to the colonization which they could not escape. (de Certeau 1984, p. 32)

This analysis can be extended to other relations that involve an imbalance of power. Weak actors, whether they be states or individuals, resort to tactics to achieve their aims while strong actors possess the opportunity to develop a strategy. Strategies demand locations of power, they define what is proper and legitimate, and aim to remain conclusive. Successful strategies are able to circumscribe a place that can be used as a basis to generate relations with an exterior that is distinct from it (e.g., a competitor or a client), and to measure, include and control foreign forces and objects. Tactics, however, are courses of actions that lack power and are employed to achieve short-term aims. They play with resources owned by an adversary and, as they occur within its "field of vision" (de Certeau 1984, p. 37), they can be observed and sanctioned by it.

Reframed using the perspectives and language informing this edited collection, we can think of strategies as belonging to the realm of the normative, and tactics as modes of operation seeking to challenge the norm, or to subvert it. The use of the Internet to challenge a regime and denounce its wrongdoings is a tactic when the regime remains in control, even if it is forced to make concessions. But it can become a strategy if, for example, it forces that regime to institutionalize the practice of publishing all public acts online and create a proper space where citizens can legitimately obtain and demand information. Similarly, the censorship of a blog by a government is a tactic when it is a temporary measure in the face of an imminent threat and can be sanctioned by a higher order as illegal. It can also become a strategy when it is grounded in a norm that circumscribes a space as legitimate and recognized by that higher order (e.g., when the censoring is justified by the need to prevent ethnic violence and endures over time). Being able to distinguish a practice as a tactic or a strategy is important in understanding where power lies and where it may shift. In the particular case of the evolution of new communication technologies, it is essential to understand whether or not an assemblage of technologies, discourses, and actors have the potential to endure and acquire momentum, or to lose impetus and eventually fade.

The evolution of government practices toward the Internet and other communication technologies in Ethiopia illustrated in the following sections is an example of how governments in developing countries can shift from a tactical to a strategic approach toward charting national information societies. As is maintained in this chapter, while in an initial phase the Ethiopian government adopted short-term measures to contain critical voices and resist external pressures to open up the national information space, in a latter phase following the millennium it progressively managed to incorporate new technologies into its own agenda. In the 1990s the EPRDF-led regime had to relate to norms and resources that were "owned" by others but as the new century dawned it embarked in a complex process to create a space it could own and control and where it could experiment with innovation without necessarily relating to externally imposed norms and templates. What seems paradoxical and confounding at first glance, then, is rather a peculiar product of history, a unique model stewarded by ambitious government officials informed by a revolutionary struggle and determined to consolidate rule.

TACTICAL RISK: OPENING A SPACE FOR DEBATE WITHOUT ENGAGING WITH THE DEBATES.

The EPRDF took power in 1991 after almost two decades of guerrilla war against the military dictatorship led by Mengitsu Haile Mariam. Almost immediately, a very tense relationship emerged between the EPRDF and the national media. Caught in two minds seeking to balance public pressure for freedom of expression with the desire to use the media to support its own political agenda, the EPRDF responded by committing what can be considered its original sin in the contemporary history of the media in Ethiopia: when the new leaders came to power they opened the space for debate but refused to engage with the very debates they had allowed to bloom.

In the early 1990s, the EPRDF had to show it was different from its oppressive predecessors. In the ostensibly unipolar world that emerged after the fall of the Soviet Union, the pressure to respect certain rights and freedoms was significant and, as a tactic, promoting free media represented an opportunity to boost the new government's international legitimacy. At the domestic level, the liberalization of the press also helped signal to a population traumatized by decades of war that a new breed of rulers was now in power.

The Transitional Federal Government, which was established to write a new constitution and build the foundations for a new Ethiopian state, soon created the conditions for the first private papers to start publishing and later spelled out their rights in the relatively progressive Press Law passed in 1992. However, these ostensibly strict legal safeguards were to be undermined by the EPRDF's lack of commitment to the freedoms it had allowed and its failure to understand what it really meant to allow a plurality of voices to compete in a postconflict scenario.

As some of the individuals who oversaw the transition from one regime to the other later admitted, they expected the discussions in the newspapers to be around policies and not to challenge the government's very mandate to rule (Stremlau 2011). Reflecting on this period, Amhed Hassen, the former Deputy Chairman of the Information and Culture Affairs Commission, stated:

> We saw this initial phase as a transition period. We hoped that a democratic process would have come through the civil society and we hoped also through the media. But the media did not participate. They were just adversarial. And so our approach was to just ignore them. At the time of the transitional government they were attacking Meles personally but he decided just to ignore them.[2]

As the criticisms in this newly created civic space took on an increasingly adversarial tone, the EPRDF leadership initially stuck to its "head-in-the-sand" policy, ignoring dissenting voices or brusquely dismissing them as "anti-peace" and "anti-constitution" (Ethiopian Herald 1991, p. 7). This approach found justification in the belief that those writing for the private press were not part of the EPRDF's constituency in any case, so there was little need to expend political capital either repressing or engaging them.[3] Over time, however, the

---

[2] Interview: Amhed Hassen.
[3] For a broader analysis of the press under the EPRDF see Nicole Stremlau 2011. "The press and the political restructuring of Ethiopia," *Journal of Eastern African Studies* 5(4): 716–32.

trading of accusations and the inability of opposing factions to command each other's attention progressively poisoned the debate in ways that would have repercussions beyond the press.

When the Internet started to be employed as a space to discuss Ethiopian politics, the debates were just as polarized as those witnessed in the pages of the newspapers. Launched by Ethiopians in the diaspora, platforms such as the Ethiopian Review, Nazret, and Ethiomedia hosted articles that could have equally appeared in the newspapers printed in Addis Ababa. Indeed, real connections between the spaces did exist. From the very beginning it became common to find references and connections between online and printed articles. New media, rather than being seized by a new generation of leaders and advocates as an opportunity to test innovative ideas, was largely bound to the limits of old political mindsets. Instead of debating new issues as occurred in Kenya, where new media were seized at an early stage by activists and civil society groups to launch initiatives to check on those in power,[4] authors returned to old grievances that had their roots in the 1960s and 1970s when the movements challenging the Emperor and later the Derg started to appear. While some new ground did emerge both online and offline, the discussions they promoted tended to remain in the background and were unable to galvanize or mobilize passions in the same way as the more extreme pieces that polarized old debates.[5]

Thus, when international organizations and NGOs began to hail the potential of the Internet for development in the second half of the 1990s, the Ethiopian government remained largely indifferent to such ideas, even if it did not challenge them openly. In the absence of a clear understanding of how the new technology could be used to serve the state's interests and remaining fearful it could be turned against it, the government simply prevented other actors from entering the market. Telecommunications continued to be a state monopoly, no private Internet Service Provider (ISP) was licensed and the cost for connectivity was kept out of the reach of the vast majority of Ethiopians.

In this first phase of EPRDF rule, roughly 1991–2000, preoccupied with the difficult task of turning a military victory achieved by the labors of a small

---

[4] A famous example of this tendency is Mzalendo, a platform launched by Kenyan activists Ory Okollo to check on the activities and performance of Kenyan MPs.

[5] *The Reporter*, a newspaper started by Amare Aregawi, a former TPLF member and editor-in-chief of TPLF's clandestine radio during the guerrilla, was started to provide a form of constructive criticism to the EPRDF. The presence of papers such as *Meznania* were representative of a younger generation trying to move the debate to the center. Similarly moderate online spaces were those created by bloggers such as Dagmawi or Enset.

but committed army into a legitimate mandate to rule over a diverse country, the Ethiopian government balanced uneasily between defenses of sovereignty and appeals to legitimacy. On the one hand, the EPRDF needed the support and resources of the international community to rebuild a country fractured by decades of civil war. In the media sector this meant accepting the calls to "democratize" that dominated the post–Cold War scenario. But the government was also fearful that opening too much, especially in areas seen as potentially revolutionary such as the Internet, could lead to losing control of its state and nation-building project completely. Either accepting or resisting external influences meant having to relate to norms and resources that were "owned" by others, a conception of freedom of expression that had little to do with the ideas that had been forged in the field of battle. It meant deploying technologies that appeared monolithic, difficult to unpack and little understood given the lack of an adequate knowledge-base in the country. Both acceptance and resistance, however, were doomed to fail or produce unexpected and unwanted consequences. Caught between these poles, the EPRDF instead reached for the forbidden fruit, opening a space without engaging with content. This tactic, however, meant poisoning the public debate for years to come. As would become clear during the elections in 2005 and the protests in 2016, even the government monopoly over telecommunications, the strict censorship of oppositional blogs and websites and the surveillance over online communications was not enough to prevent uses of the Internet that could support dissent and mobilization against the government.

TOWARD A STRATEGY: ADAPTING THE INTERNET FOR STATE- AND NATION-BUILDING

In 2001, Meles emerged from a series of profound ruptures and disagreements within the EPRDF that followed the two-year long war with Eritrea, scathed but still in control. Meles responded to this insecurity by launching an ambitious project to reinforce the state. The institutional connections between the center and the peripheries were to be strengthened and the state was reformed to function as a more active player in social and economic renewal. In this climate, the Internet, while still cautiously viewed for its potential to allow external and critical voices to gain prominence in national debates, began to be perceived differently as a potential tool for the EPRDF in promoting transformation and capacity-building.

Underpinning this shift in perceptions was an unprecedented exposure to new technologies. Between 1999 and 2001, the international community organized innumerable events in Addis Ababa to demonstrate how new technologies could be used for development. While many of the ideas put forward in these international fora were challenged by the Ethiopian government, they nevertheless offered Ethiopia's leaders the chance to reflect on which aspects of the new technologies were more compatible with their political and development plans and thus to develop a more nuanced approach than either liberalization or repression.

In this period of state consolidation, rather than hastily adopting a policy it could not master or refusing to adopt a technology for fear of its destabilizing potential, the government acted to ensure it had better control over innovation in communication technologies and was able to create the conditions to firmly root them in the principles at the core of its political project. The opportunity to start developing a more strategic approach toward the Internet was offered through the launch of Woredanet and Schoolnet that incorporated discourses at core of the EPRDF state- and nation-building project: revolutionary democracy, ethnic federalism and, at the later stage, the developmental state.

The concepts of ethnic federalism and revolutionary democracy emerged within the EPRDF during the guerrilla war waged against the military dictatorship of the Derg, which was initially fought in the name of the rights for self-determination for the people of Tigray, but later expanded in scope and ambition to become national liberation. Once the guerrilla fighters came to power, the ideology of ethnic federalism was used to reframe Ethiopia from a unitary nation into a federation of ethnicities, which at least on paper were all entitled to the same rights to self-determination. By connecting the Tigrayan minority to other oppressed groups and offering them the opportunity to participate in the re-founding of the nation, the EPRDF presented its de facto capture of the state as a victory for all marginalized groups. Ethnicity emerged as both a means and an end. It served as an operational principle for the redistribution of resources to those recognized as separate ethnic groups, but the provision of material benefits along ethnic lines was also aimed at convincing people on the ground that it was in their interests to be recognized as ethnically diverse. By building the state and creating new institutions and new rules for citizens to relate to central and local authority and claim their rights, the EPRDF aimed to build the nation through ethnicity, offering new categories and ideational referents for Ethiopians to think of themselves as citizens.

The concept of revolutionary democracy also emerged during the military struggle, but its definition continued to evolve after the EPRDF came to power. Revolutionary democracy rejects the focus on the individual that characterizes liberal democracy, preferring to stress group rights and consensus. It favors a populist discourse claiming a direct connection between the leadership and the masses, bypassing the need to negotiate with other elites who advance competing ideas of the nation-state and the role different groups have within it.[6] Through the contribution of Meles Zenawi himself, new concepts were progressively added to the core tenets of ethnic federalism and revolutionary democracy, borrowed largely, but selectively, from the models of the developmental state and stressing in particular the importance of state stability and the role of a determined developmental elite in supporting economic performance and avoiding rent-seeking.

At the turn of the millennium, Woredanet and Schoolnet became the technological substantiation of these principles. They represented a pioneering endeavor for an African government to sustain a process of state- and nation-building through the support of new communication technologies. Woredanet employs the same protocol that the Internet is based upon, but rather than allowing individuals to independently seek information and express their opinion, it enables ministers and cadres in Addis Ababa to videoconference with the regional and woreda offices and instruct them on what they should be doing and how. Schoolnet uses a similar architecture to broadcast pre-recorded classes in a variety of subjects, from mathematics to civics, to all secondary schools in the country, while also offering political education to schoolteachers and other government officials.

In its first rollout, Woredanet was intended to link the central government with the eleven regional and 550 district administrations so that through a forty-two-inch plasma television screen installed in the regional and woreda offices, local officials could receive training and instructions from teacher trainers in the capital, high-level civil servants, government ministers and even the Prime Minister himself. In the case of Schoolnet, 16,686 plasma television screens were initially deployed to allow 775 secondary schools in the country to receive broadcasted lessons, from mathematics to civic education. In the most remote areas of Ethiopia, which were without electricity and were not served by the main roads, petrol generators were installed and the military was employed to airlift some of the equipment. After Schoolnet was installed, schools could be used out of term time as training centers to offer political education programs of the kind that was imparted during the struggle.

Revolutionary democracy offered the core framework for the design and implementation of Woredanet and Schoolnet. The two systems were aimed at improving service delivery and the quality of life in rural communities, but the fervor with which they were pursued can only be understood with reference

---

[6] For a recent overview of the debate on revolutionary democracy, see the special issue of the *Journal of Eastern African Studies* (2011) on "Ethiopia's Revolutionary Democracy, 1991–2011," 5(4): 579–817.

to the goal of increasing the presence of the state on the ground by opening new communication channels between the vanguard and the grassroots. At a practical level, Woredanet was intended to build the capacity of the peripheral nodes of the state by training and instructing individuals, some of whom had little formal education, to enable them to provide better services. This was to benefit the whole community, but at the same time it symbolized the commitment of the government to the rural population. Conveying a unified message was intended to bond the entire country around similar principles, despite its diversity. Through Woredanet, the EPRDF leaders at the center hoped to reach the grassroots in a mediated way, turning the members of the state apparatus in the peripheries into messengers of ideas and policies formulated in the capital.

As a complement to Woredanet, Schoolnet was also designed to reach targets in the peripheries more directly. Its main objective was enabling students living in the countryside to have access to the same quality of education as those in the major towns and cities. The goal was for students in remote areas to no longer have to rely on poorly trained teachers for their education, as had often been the case. Schoolnet was a powerful symbol of the EPRDF's commitment to guarantee every citizen equal opportunities and address the urban-rural education divide. An advantage for the government of having students exposed to the same programming was that they could be trained in the founding principles of the state as defined by the EPRDF. Notably, civic and ethical education was among the first subjects to be included in the Schoolnet programming.

The principle of ethnic federalism, however, was not only present in the content transmitted though Woredanet and Schoolnet, but also in the very ways in which the systems were deployed, in their scale and in their convoluted design. Realizing ethnic federalism on the ground required the allocation of the same rights and resources to every ethnic group. In resonance with Benedict Anderson's analysis of nations as "imagined communities" (Anderson 1983), the symbolic value of equally distributing resources among different regions was seen to be as important as their material value. It was essential that each node of the federal state had equal access to use the system, even if this might constrain its effective functioning.

Through the implementation of Woredanet and Schoolnet, the government started charting a distinctive and confident *strategy*, bringing new technologies within a space it owned and could control, rather than adhering to a policy advocated and imposed by others. This strategy had both strengths and weaknesses, though. Numerous technical problems encountered in the first phases of implementation caused frustration and required constant patching. Also, the government's hope that Woredanet and Schoolnet could offer an efficient channel to communicate with the rural constituencies, allowing it to continue ignoring the critical voices in the papers and online, were partially frustrated by the ability shown by political opponents to combine new and old media during the 2005 elections. The two programs, however, offered a concrete example of how locally rooted discourses could influence technological adoption and adaptation, creating the pre-conditions for similar courses of actions to be employed in subsequent projects.

NEW STRATEGIES MEET TACTICS: ETHIOPIA'S INFORMATION SOCIETY AFTER 2005

Despite their complexity, Woredanet and Schoolnet took shape at a remarkable speed, responding in part to the EPRDF's ambition to use them before the elections in 2005 to gain a competitive advantage over political opponents. Prior to 2005, elections under the EPRDF had been mostly held for the party to reaffirm its control over the territory and for external consumption rather than to provide a real opportunity for political competition. Opposition parties historically had been harassed and, in most cases, boycotted elections in protest (Aalen 2002). However, in an effort to consolidate its domestic and international legitimacy, the EPRDF accepted the challenge of having the first openly contested polls in the history of Ethiopia. As was later confirmed by international observers, the EPRDF allowed the voting process to be comparatively free and fair (Carter Center 2005). Opposition parties were given unprecedented access to the state media and numerous oppositional newspapers were able to circulate in Addis Ababa and other major cities (Stremlau 2011). The relative openness, however, required the government to develop new tools to make sure that it retained control and occupied the political spaces necessary to win the election through consensus and not coercion alone. As an international civil servant who had been involved in developing Woredanet and Schoolnet argued:

> Before the elections in 2005 it was key for them [the EPRDF] to reach the population in the rural areas. To speak with the peripheries. And they saw technology as an opportunity to do that ... But because of this the political dimension created problems. Technical decisions were made by political figures creating a convoluted combination ... In fact at the end it did not really serve the purpose they had in mind. And the technology did not make such a big difference in the elections of 2005. But at the same time by investing and

implementing so much they realized that this tool was powerful for politics and for other reasons too.[7]

Contrary to the EPRDF's expectations, in 2005 it was not Woredanet and Schoolnet, but rather the way in which oppositional forces and their supporters used the Internet and new technologies, that changed old forms of communicating and political mobilization. The government's policy toward maintaining monopoly of the Internet and mobile phones had kept their penetration at 0.22 and 0.55 percent of the population, respectively (International Telecommunications Union 2015). However, new media had a potential that went well beyond what these numbers alone might suggest. This is especially true when analyzed as part of a wider communication network that emerged after 2005.

By 2005, the Ethiopian blogosphere was blossoming. In the years preceding the election many bloggers had not only joined already popular platforms such as Nazret, Ethiomedia, and the Ethiopian Review, but had started creating their own spaces. Bloggers such as Enset were influential commentators from the diaspora, while others like Ethio-Zagol were contributing to the online debate from Addis Ababa.[8] The key, though, for the fruition of these disruptive trends was the association of the press. In a move that dramatically multiplied the possibilities of these voices to be heard in Ethiopia despite the limited Internet connectivity, many newspapers reproduced opinion pieces and news originally published online. Eskinder Nega, who has been sentenced to jail multiple times for his critical reporting of the government, and who used to be the editor and columnist of the newspapers *Menelik*, *Asqual*, and *Satenaw*, explained how his papers served as platforms to promote awareness within Ethiopia about debates occurring outside of the country:

> We were publishing articles by prominent people in the diaspora. Fundamental debates were going on in websites such as Ethiomedia and the Ethiopian Review and we were translating them because we wanted to make sure they were known to the public in Ethiopia.[9]

The quest for information also led people to download and print commentaries, and political manifestos, turning them into leaflets to be distributed to

---

7 Interview: international civil servant.
8 For an overview of the role of the diaspora in Ethiopian politics see Terrence Lyons 2007. "Conflict-Generated Diasporas and Transnational Politics in Ethiopia," *Conflict, Security & Development* 7(4): 529–49; and of the Ethiopian blogosphere up to 2005 see Nancy J. Hafkin 2006. "'Whatsupoch' on the Net: The role of information and communication technology in the shaping of transnational Ethiopian identity," *Diaspora* 15(2/3): 221–45.
9 Interview: Eskinder Nega.

those who could not access the Internet. Mobile phones, and especially SMS, were used to mobilize people in real time and to disseminate calls for action which had first emerged on other platforms. Word-of-mouth continued to play a paramount role in further disseminating information, especially in urban settings.

After polling closed, the EPRDF realized it had suffered greater losses than it was ready to accept despite winning the election. This was particularly the case in urban areas where people started protesting over the delay in issuing the results, leading the government to shut down some of the channels used to mobilize protestors. In the aftermath of the first wave of demonstrations initiated by university and secondary school students on 6 June, SMS service was discontinued, to be restored only some two years later.[10] However, it took some time for the government to realize how a variety of media were being used by opposition groups in the creation of another imagined community as part of a more complex network where information could be relayed across multiple channels. As a cadre working in the communication sector explained:

> The post-election period showed how technology can also affect society negatively … Short messages were used to defame people and you could not really know the source. If I send an SMS to you, then you can act as a multiplier. Also the websites were publishing a lot of factious articles. All this was making people confused. There was an uncontrolled circulation of unfiltered and unbalanced information. I think that it was a strategy of certain groups who know how to use the media. The strategy was to turn down this government and many different media were used to reach this single goal.[11]

After shutting down the SMS messaging service, the Ethiopian government continued to close down other communication channels so as to reduce their capacity to be employed, singularly or in combination, to serve the protest and disseminate alternative information and narratives. In early November 2005, some of the most vocal Ethiopian journalists who challenged the results of the election and called for more democracy were arrested and their papers were forced to close. In May 2006, one year after the contested election, access to online spaces such as Nazret and Ethiomedia, and to a number of individual blogs, started to be blocked (Poetrano 2012). These actions received harsh criticism from the international community, and while Meles sought to justify the

---

[10] The service was restored only on the occasion of the celebration of the Ethiopian millennium. The first message Ethiopian citizens received on their mobiles after a long silence was a greeting by Ethiopian Telecommunication Corporation's CEO, Amare Anslau, wishing them a happy new Ethiopian millennium.
[11] Interview: Desta Testfaw.

violence that was used to suppress street protests, no justification was initially provided for the shutting down of SMS and the censoring of blogs. Instead, these moves were presented simply as technical glitches, rather than deliberate measures undertaken to defend national security.

As the EPRDF closed avenues for popular protest and forcefully consolidated power, however, it began an ambitious project to legitimize these measures and weave them into a more coherent strategy. Initiatives such as the Anti-Terrorism Proclamation and the Telecom Fraud Offences Proclamation, drafted by the Information Network Security Agency (INSA), Ethiopia's equivalent the US National Security Agency (NSA), emerged as central components of this process. A new discourse hailing security and stability as fundamental ingredients for Ethiopia's path toward development started to be articulated more widely and visibly. Since coming into force, the Anti-Terrorism Proclamation has been used to override existing norms regulating the media in Ethiopia and to silence, attack or threaten critical journalists inside and outside of the country.[12]

The government also sought, and found, new partners that could support it in this new endeavor. China emerged as the most significant ally. At an ideational level, China's ability to balance control of information and dramatic growth of Internet users became a model and source of legitimation for the restrictive practices the Ethiopian government employed in the aftermath of the elections. In a cable reporting a meeting between Sebhat Nega, one of the Ethiopian government's ideologues, and the then US ambassador Donald Yamamoto, Sebhat was reported to have openly declared his admiration for China and stressed that Ethiopia "needs the China model to inform the Ethiopian people" (US Embassy in Addis Ababa, 2009). As stressed by Meles, China's presence opened up space for new forms of experimentation. The Chinese government not only aided Ethiopia indirectly, by offering legitimation for alternative models of media engagement, but also directly, through the provision of essential technical and financial support.

---

[12] Existing laws regulating the media in Ethiopia are the already mentioned Press Proclamation No. 34/1992, the Broadcasting Proclamation No. 178/1999 as amended by Proclamation No. 533/2007 and the Freedom of the Mass Media and Access to of Information Proclamation 590/2008. These laws do incorporate most international standards of freedom of expression and access to information and in theory offer a conducive environment for media pluralism in Ethiopia, both in the field of old and new media. These laws, however, seem to have been developed mostly for donors' consumption and are seldom implemented. By contrast, the Anti-Terrorism Proclamation No. 652/2009 has more often been embraced against the media. See Caelainn Barr 2011. "Ethiopia uses anti-terror laws to silence critical journalists," *Guardian*, September 29, 2011. Available at: www.guardian.co.uk/media/greenslade/2011/sep/29/press-freedom-ethiopia?.

Privatized telecommunication markets were now booming in most of Africa, providing increasingly cheaper and more reliable access to mobile phones and the Internet. Against this backdrop, the Ethiopian government faced the challenge of how to balance its decision to retain a monopoly over telecommunication against the need to expand access – which, it was proving, was far easier to do if markets were opened up to competition from multiple providers. As the Minister of Communication and Information Technology, Debretsion Gebre Michael, argued in 2008:

> Monopoly is a crucial factor in this. It is exactly because ICTs [Information and Communication Technologies] are so important and they have the capacity to penetrate every aspect of our lives that we have to make sure that it is the state that is in charge of using and implementing them. In this phase we cannot leave it to the market. ICTs are too key for our development. They are a priority. Behind the decision of leaving the monopoly in the ICTs and telecommunication market there is big philosophical thinking. It is not just because we want to make money from the use of telecoms.[13]

Without an external partner to fund a massive expansion of services, it would have been impossible for the EPRDF to square this circle. China's offer of a $1.5 billion loan, the largest in the history of telecommunication in Africa, was thus critical to the government's ability to expand mobile service and Internet connectivity while keeping the Ethiopian Telecommunication Corporation as the only player in the market (Zhao 2013). Some of these resources also went to upgrading the infrastructure of Woredanet and Schoolnet. Connectivity through fiber optic was provided to different nodes of the network, replacing the satellite communication and allowing a system that many had considered unsustainable to become even more central to the government's communication strategy toward the periphery.

These proactive and reactive measures, taken together, delineate the traits of an increasingly cohesive media system, emerging in opposition to one advocated by Western donors, but also increasingly dependent on new forms of external support, most notably from China. While the first deployment of censorship measures was disguised as a technical glitch, only a few years later Meles Zenawi declared his right to defend Ethiopia's sovereign information space as part of a developmental media strategy, jamming international broadcasters. With the Telecom Fraud Offences Proclamation adopted in 2012 and the Computer Crime Proclamation passed in 2016, the government

---

[13] Interview: Debretsion Gebre Michael.

continued in the same vein, expanding the legal foundations of its claim to be able to legitimately block and censor information.

CONCLUSION: A FRAGILE MODEL OF THE
DEVELOPMENTAL INTERNET

The evolution of EPRDF policy toward the Internet in Ethiopia offers a significant illustration of a wider trend where governments in Africa have become increasingly assertive in developing their national information societies in ways that often challenge mainstream conceptions of the Internet as a medium able to blur national boundaries, increase public participation, and allow a plurality of actors to contribute to a country's development. The progressive re-nationalization and centralization of the information space in Ethiopia has been achieved through a mix of reactive and proactive measures, and legitimated through attempts to theorize policies and projects as components of a relatively coherent strategy for development.

Reactive and repressive measures, including the censoring of blogs and the disruption of SMS messaging, have been put in place to minimize criticism, prevent mobilization, and marginalize alternative ideas of the Ethiopian nation. While the Ethiopian government initially made weak attempts to explain or defend these measures, over time it has begun to seek opportunities and partners that could help to justify them and increase their legitimacy. At the same time sophisticated attempts have been made to capture new communication technologies for development goals, undergirded by strong ideological and developmental agendas that are often overlooked or misunderstood by outsiders. Woredanet and Schoolnet are just an example, and have been followed by other large-scale projects employing new media for development – most notably Ethiopia's Community Exchange (ECX), Africa's first digitally supported market for trading coffee and seeds.

As argued throughout the chapter, this evolution is also indicative of a progressive shift from a tactical to a strategic approach to the development of the Internet; from the forced acceptance of standards and technologies imposed from above to the development of applications, projects, and norms that are more contextually grounded and may actually compete with more widely accepted ones. This shift might be heralded as an indication of a lessening of a relationship of dependence between North and South, and of an increased sense of self-reliance, if it were not for two major pitfalls.

First, in countries such as Ethiopia and Rwanda, this evolution has corresponded to a progressive reduction in the number of actors actively contributing to the development of national information societies, or at least to the significant subordination of some actors to others. Academia and the civil society, which have played a paramount role in the shaping of early innovations in the field of ICTs, have progressively been marginalized, while it has been left to governments to take the lead in theorizing alternative conceptions of the role of information – and speech – in society. As explained elsewhere (Gagliardone and Golooba-Mutebi 2016), some governments have offered greater room to maneuver to local private companies or NGOs, as long as they operated within the boundaries defined by a vision emanating from the center of power. This relative freedom, however, is distant from those early hopes that the Internet could lead to reconfiguring and rebalancing relationships of power. Greater agency acquired by the state vis-à-vis donor countries in charting independent conceptions of the information society hardly means that a more equitable distribution of authority within national boundaries has been achieved. As the arrest of bloggers and political opponents seeking to assert different visions of how new media could be used in Ethiopia indicate, governments have sought to monopolize the right to shape national information spaces, often masking this attempt as a struggle to break a relationship of dependence on the Global North.

This leads to a second major problem affecting emerging conceptions of developmental information societies: the new strategies have emerged more as the result of the exploitation of the fragilities of dominant actors than from the implementation of a vision that can rally a plurality of actors and become hegemonic. These fragilities of dominant actors include the scandals related to extensive global surveillance by the US government and the inability of donors to reconcile their emphasis on security with the aspiration of promoting human rights globally. African institutions were among the first seeking to exploit the information revolution to promote human development (as illustrated by the African Information Society Initiative, that already in 1997 sought to chart a path to shape the African Internet). Yet models of the information society of the kind emerging in Ethiopia have little of the pan-African spirit that inspired the first wave of decolonization. They are framed in the context of a re-nationalization of the information space that responds to and is justified by the interests of distinctive elites. While the developmental model proposed by leaders of the caliber of Kwame Nkrumah and Julius Nyerere had major shortcomings – and they similarly favored the state over other actors in charting national media systems – they were also strategically visionary, seeking to connect Ghanaians and Tanzanians to other African citizens in a shared path toward progress. Little of this spirit has been evoked by the Ethiopian government to develop its information strategy. The risk is that the increased assuredness and agency of African governments today will be increasingly used to develop an insular project, rather than an alternative one that can stand on its own feet, one where the rebalancing of global inequalities is achieved at the cost of greater inequalities suffered within a re-nationalized information space.

REFERENCES

Aalen, L. 2002. "Ethnic federalism in a dominant party state: The Ethiopian experience 1991–2000," *Chr. Michelson Institute*. Available at: www.cmi.no/publications/769-ethnic-federalism-in-a-dominant-party-state.

Anderson, B. 1983. *Imagined Communities: Reflections on the Origin and Spread of Nationalism*. London: Verso.

Barr, C. 2011. "Ethiopia uses anti-terror laws to silence critical journalists," *Guardian*, September 29, 2011. Available at: www.theguardian.com/media/greenslade/2011/sep/29/press-freedom-ethiopia.

BBC 2016. "Seven things banned under Ethiopia's state of emergency," BBC News, October 17, 2016. Available at: www.bbc.co.uk/news/world-africa-37679165.

Carter Center, (The) 2005. "Final statement on the Carter Center Observation of Ethiopia's 2005 National Elections," September 2005. Atlanta, GA: Carter Center.

Dahir, A. L. 2016. "Internet shutdown could cost Ethiopia's booming economy millions of dollars," *Quartz Africa*, October 19, 2016. Available at: http://qz.com/812689/oromo-protests-ethiopias-internet-shutdown-could-drain-millions-of-dollars-from-the-economy/.

de Certeau, M. 1984. *The Practice of Everyday Life*. Translated from French by S. Rendall. Berkeley, CA: University of California Press.

Ethiopian Herald, The. 1991. "Editorial," *The Ethiopian Herald*, June 6, 1991, p. 7.

Farah, D. and Mosher, A. 2010. "Winds from the East: How the People's Republic of China seeks to influence the media in Africa, Latin America, and Southeast Asia," *Center for International Media Assistance*, September 8, 2010. Available at: www.cima.ned.org/wp-content/uploads/2015/02/CIMA-China-Report_1.pdf.

Fisher, J. and Anderson, D. M. 2015. "Authoritarianism and the securitization of development in Africa," *International Affairs* 91(1): 131–51.

Gagliardone, I. 2014. "New media and the developmental state in Ethiopia," *African Affairs* 113(451): 279–99.

2016. *The Politics of Technology in Africa*. Cambridge: Cambridge University Press.

Gagliardone, I. and Golooba-Mutebi, F. 2016. "The evolution of the Internet in Ethiopia and Rwanda: Towards a 'developmental' model?," *Stability: International Journal of Security and Development* 5(1): 1–24.

Hafkin, N. J. 2006. "'Whatsupoch' on the net: The role of information and communication technology in the shaping of transnational Ethiopian identity," *Diaspora* 15(2/3): 221–45.

Human Rights Watch 2014. "'They know everything we do': Telecom and Internet surveillance in Ethiopia," *Human Rights Watch*, March 15, 2014. Available at: www.hrw.org/report/2014/03/25/they-know-everything-we-do/telecom-and-internet-surveillance-ethiopia.

International Telecommunications Union 2015. "Information society statistical profiles: Africa."

Jones, W., de Oliveira, R. S., and Verhoeven, H. 2013. "Africa's illiberal state-builders," *Refugee Studies Centre, University of Oxford, Working Paper Series No. 89*, January 2013. Available at: www.rsc.ox.ac.uk/files/publications/working-paper-series/wp89-africas-illiberal-state-builders-2013.pdf.

Kurlantzick, J. 2007. *Charm Offensive: How China's Soft Power Is Transforming the World*. New Haven, CT: Yale University Press.

Lyons, T. 2007. "Conflict-generated diasporas and transnational politics in Ethiopia," *Conflict, Security & Development* 7(4): 529–49.

Nkomo, S. and Wafula, A. 2016. "Strong public support for 'watchdog' role backs African news media under attack," *Afrobarometer*, May 3, 2016. Available at: http://afrobarometer.org/sites/default/files/publications/Dispatches/ab_r6_dispatchno85_media_in_africa_world_press_freedom_day.pdf.

OpenNet Initiative 2007. "Internet filtering in Ethiopia in 2006–2007," OpenNet Initiative. Available at: https://opennet.net/studies/Ethiopia2007.

Poetrano, I. 2012. "Update on information controls in Ethiopia," OpenNet Initiative. Available at: https://opennet.net/blog/2012/11/update-information-controls-ethiopia.

Stremlau, N. 2011. "The press and the political restructuring of Ethiopia," *Journal of Eastern African Studies* 5(4): 716–32.

US Embassy in Addis Ababa. 2009. Cable #09ADDISABABA149.

Zhao, L. 2013. "Contributing to the development of Ethiopia with wisdom and strength," ZTE, June 12, 2009. Available at: wwwen.zte.com.cn/endata/magazine/ztetechnologies/2009year/no6/articles/200906/t20090612_172517.html.

Part V

Conclusion

17

Conclusion: Philosophies and Principles in Turbulent Times

Monroe Price and Nicole Stremlau

This is a time – echoing a similar moment after World War II – where theories of speech and society are under intense examination with contestation as to what international norms will or should emerge. In the 1940s, it was war and devastation that gave birth to a Universal Declaration of Human Rights (UDHR). In the current environment, there are a variety of provocations and realizations. New technologies, as detailed in the Introduction and in many of the chapters, are causing a reexamination of existing arrangements. States seem weaker and intermediaries such as television networks and new media are growing ever stronger. Rising populism and geopolitical changes are altering the political environment that undergirded the 1940s settlement on defining human rights. The globalization of terrorism creates a new psychological and material framework for thinking through the regulation of speech and press in society. In this much-changed context, traditional practices lead to novel results and novel approaches are necessary to reach traditional consequences.

First the satellite and then the Internet, new technologies have transformed the capacity of states and individuals to reach across borders, resulting in movements of information that have placed historic models of national sovereignty at risk. The formula of information and data flowing "regardless of frontiers," as set out in Article 19 of the UDHR, has taken on new meaning as the way in which individuals receive and transmit data alters, almost daily. Long intense concerns about language, national identity, and modes of assuring loyalty reappear with significant new challenges, from fake news to information warfare. And in this new geopolitical world, rising powers join those who have been more constantly sat at the bargaining table and seek, often, different formulae for approaching controversial issues.

With the world in transformation, the stakes are high. Whole economies, ways of life, understandings of the world – all seem to be at issue. In many places, this even includes debates on what constitutes the basic elements of a democratic society, questions asked of the media's role in ensuring that a society is truly democratic and what is needed to support or undergird a "free and independent media." In these debates it is important both to assert and defend what are increasingly deemed old "universal" principles and understand the new forces combining to alter those seemingly unalterable principles. To make a difficult task harder, there are counter-principles lurching towards power and also seeking legitimacy; massive economies, more statist, more illiberal, and more authoritarian are on the march, and with Brexit Britain and Donald Trump's America, to some degree on the ascendancy or at least moving from the periphery and margins to the center of debates. Many of the chapters in this volume remind us about the difficulties, but also possibilities, in finding shared ground on what should be called universal.

Max Weber (1970, p. 78) famously defined a state as a "human community that (successfully) claims the monopoly of the legitimate use of physical force within a given territory." Increasingly, this search for a monopoly directs attention to speech, perceived so often as the incubator of violence and a crucial factor for consolidating power, advancing interests or world views. This can be witnessed in the efforts by some governments to combat and block Islamic State propaganda online, for example, or growing evidence and concerns about fake news emanating from state actors, or even young people half-a-world away with limited knowledge of the politics they are intervening in but doing so for the advertising money, influencing democratic elections. Indeed, one of the signals that come through the chapters in this book is that the often long-standing yearning for protection and stability reduces differentiation among states. The chapters are sometime reminders of efforts by states and other actors to address violence and instability through apprehensions concerning speech. Societies coming from different traditions are examining transforming aspects in ways marked by those traditions. While all states are confronted with technological change, threats to national security, the crisis of secularism, and the powers and limits of the nation state, each brings a particular history to the issues. It is precisely for this reason that identifying and understanding competing speech-related philosophies are so important. What is intriguing is the interplay among varying philosophies and bodies of ideas and their endurance in the face of major centripetal forces. Philosophies of speech and society become envelopes of authority. Raising a philosophy to a level of universality gives it a special heft. Those who seek to introduce competing worldviews, even for local application, seek an ideology, a set of beliefs, a framework, which makes their political program more attractive.

A major question from this recognition of diversity is how proponents of varying philosophies adjust themselves to globalization. States that advocate classic "freedom of expression" in the form most famously embodied in the First Amendment to the United States Constitution, for example, must ensure that in a cross-border world the ability to maneuver without controls follows carefully the production of knowledge and data in different localities, and does not shift with each state crossing. States that thrive or depend on control to maintain authority must seek cooperation to maintain their coercive regimen, or expend large amounts of national treasure. This need to look globally for solutions regarding speech in society (however it is valued) takes place at a time when the capacity of states to exercise authority to regulate entry into such a market is lessened in the face of the large-scale strategic communication of others (including other states). Powerful strategic communicators often appropriate the language of reigning speech philosophies to justify the power that they exercise and to build a circle of immunity around themselves from those who seek to reduce their effectiveness.

In the process of appropriating the traditional language surrounding free speech to cloak their true intent, a chasm between the ideological imaginings and reality often emerges. Increasingly, the contrast between ideology and direct experience occurs where there are campaigns of communication that constitute a substantial and effective effort that is initiated from outside a target society and is designed to alter an existing consensus vital to the future shape of a particular society. Faced with such intense campaigns, target societies react in many ways. Some change organically. Others are powerless to assert themselves. Some are inherently repressive and necessarily act inconsistently with international norms. But all must cope with the circulation of information and ideas that may be at odds with their idealized domestic notions of speech and society.

Although operating in a shadowy world where the full extent of these practices are hard to witness, examples of such subversive and interventionist practices proliferate. These include Salafist plans to impose a fierce religious order within and across borders, as, for example, in efforts to install a caliphate in Iraq and the Levant, collective efforts to increase the influence of moderate Islam vis-à-vis the influence of those classed as "fundamentalists;" efforts by evangelical groups in the United States to spread the Word (of God) in Africa and efforts to promote democracy in the former Soviet Union. Readers will have their own judgment on the efficacy, wisdom, or morality of such approaches. But such efforts can encourage conflict and instability by spreading ideas of hate or ethnic tension, or they may be designed to reduce conflict through "peace broadcasting" or supporting particular groups to maintain a precarious status quo. Just as the canvas for imagining interventions shaping the relationship between speech and society is a large one, so too is the number of methods used to pursue these objectives. State-supported stratagems can include efforts to amplify or lessen the importance of particular voices (increasing or decreasing, for example, public service broadcasting) as well as the now familiar approach to seek control of the media and deny media power to the enemy in conflict contexts. And while many communications may be initiated outside the target society, this is an ever-more artificial distinction, not least of all because the question of intent is significant; a set of broadcasts or channels may not have the goal of altering mores or changing consensus in a target society but have the effect of doing so nonetheless.

The point here is not to distinguish "good" or warranted speech-related interventions from those that are in the service of more "evil" purposes, although, of course, these distinctions between the benign and the destructive exist and are ultimately significant in the making of policy. It is rather about understanding actions pursued in the pursuit, tested or not, of a desired impact and evaluating the extent of that impact.

SPEECH IN A FREE-EXPRESSION CONTEXT

We can examine this relationship between ideal and practice in a free-expression context. The work of the late C. Edwin Baker offers a starting point to think through these transnational interactions. Baker devoted his academic life to understanding and strengthening arguments for free expression by rigorously questioning relatively standard arguments about the principles said to undergird them, testing how these concepts were being applied in practice and checking to ensure that the goals behind free expression were not being misrepresented and re-engineered in the modern world. It was Baker's mission to strengthen commitments to free expression by ensuring greater understanding of the foundation, role, and implications of free-expression concepts and thereby strengthening our confidence in them. False invocations, twisted applications, and deceptive claims about freedom of speech could destroy the integrity of the principle.

Take, for example, the ubiquitously invoked phrase, "the marketplace of ideas" that has come to be the standard and most-heard argument used by those advocating a free-speech regime unencumbered by regulation. The answer to problematic speech, in this view, is almost always more speech. Of course, Baker welcomed deeper and further reaching conversations in the face of intractable problems, but he saw fundamental problems with this standard formulation. Given the contemporary information environment he was writing within, Baker saw the necessity of challenging most modern inflections of John Milton's foundational idea, namely that in the marketplace of ideas, ultimately, "Let her [Truth] and Falsehood Grapple. Who ever knew truth put to the worse in a free and open encounter?" Showing his strongly iconoclastic side, Baker asked in *Human Liberty and Freedom of Speech*, "Why bet that truth will be the consistent or even the usual winner?" (1989, p. 6).

For Baker, the wisdom of the bet depended upon a more detailed understanding of the market in which the bet took place. In the Miltonian market, falsities may be traded but they would ultimately always be shown as meretricious and dismissed when compared to the persistent and enduring radiance of "Truth." Milton could believe that truth would prevail because he held a deeply Christian view of truth and its relationship to divine revelation. Yet the patience of modern society is not so long and its beliefs are not so deep (Baker, 1989: pp. 4, 12–17; Haworth, 1998). In the contemporary marketplace of ideas, falsity may have a very long tail. And in a "post-truth" era, persuasion, not truth, is often the most prized quality. Set against this rather more complex backdrop, to write about the contemporary marketplace of ideas requires more specific and developed understandings of how ideas emerge, how they are sustained, and what elements can assure "fairer exchange" than a now-anachronistic Miltonian formulation can provide.

Further complicating matters, for Baker (and also for a line of questioning followed by the philosopher Bernard Williams), for the "marketplace of ideas" to make sense, "truth must be 'objective' or 'discoverable'." (Baker, 1989, p. 6; Williams, 2010). "Truth", as Baker writes, "is able to outshine falsity in debate or discussion only if truth is there to be seen." (1989, p. 6). If what is "true," however, is only what is seen or felt to be true, then, "an adequate theory must explain why and how the usually unequal advocacy of various viewpoints leads to the 'best choice'." (Baker, 1989, p. 6). Much of what leads to conflict and division might be resolvable by recourse to "truth," if only it were the kind of truth that could be established by a blue-ribbon commission dedicated to rooting out the facts. However, a great deal of what the modern world debates has to do with belief systems and emotive appeals founded on religion, affiliation, class, history, and alternate perceptions of the world. In this competitive milieu, "truth" can become a path to legitimating power rather than a power in and of itself. For that reason alone, those in power, or seeking power, try to capture definitions of "truth" and keep them within their preserve.

This "post-truth" perspective explains the unease that develops as different actors, sometimes wealthy, powerful, and significant, in other cases marginal or virtually working alone, attempt to shape an information space with outsized influence and gain the ability to deprive subordinate groups of opportunities to compete. Increasing access to social media was once seen as an antidote, flattening or democratizing influence, to such challenges whereby social media becomes a tool of subordinate groups to gain greater equality in the "marketplace of ideas." In recent years, and particularly after the 2016 US elections, such idealism has largely faded away.

In these tumultuous times where challenges to longstanding consensuses on social and political issues and alternative social realities abound (Rogers, 2012), the relationship between media and democracy has arguably never been more important and provides a major justification for free-expression campaigns. But, too often in these campaigns, the link between "democracy" and media is rendered in terms that simplify and atrophy both alternative structures of the media and alternative conceptualizations of democracy.

The point here is that, often, free-expression arguments do not sufficiently take into account such substantial variegation in models of governance, including democratic governance, both real and radically imagined. The superimposition of patterns of communication from outside may change the balance among proponents of different styles. The correspondence of media systems and political systems underscores another complexity of the general free-expression advocacy sphere: the design of press and media strategies for societies that feature few of these dominant variants of democratic practice, such as societies that are semi-authoritarian, conflict-ridden, or without government authority. An analytic framework like Baker's that seeks to match media to political system works best in a background that is aspirationally democratic but fits uneasily with societies that may have different political and economic agendas. In the absence of a preferred theory of democratic practice that can be reinforced by a media system, the fallback is an idealized template.

Richard Danbury, in his chapter in this book, distinguishes between consequentialist or deontological arguments for freedom of expression. Many of the authors emphasize what is often called an "instrumentalist" theory of freedom of expression. These are theories tied to output or impact, in this case impact on democratic political development. Certain kinds of efforts to shape information environments – what is called "democracy promotion" – feeds from these theories of freedom of expression by Thomas Emerson, Ronald Dworkin, Robert Nozick, Thomas Scanlon, and others, which are chiefly deontological: freedom of expression is adopted, celebrated, and followed not because of its impact on democratic development or other attractive consequences that ensue, but because of principle or moral determinant or sense of what it means to be human. In an instrumentalist world, other information interventions might trump freedom-of-expression principles if the ultimate objective can be achieved; in a frame of principle (often captured by international norm), it is the mandated ideal that is decisive (Schauer, 1990).

Indeed, the furtherance of international norms of free expression, such as Article 19, is particularly significant in societies where the capacity for self-determination is extremely limited in terms of formal (and actual) democratic practices.

In this spirit, the chapters in this book have explored the tension between the instrumental and the deontological. And they asked whether, in this particular moment, it is the instrumental arguments that are the most convincing. These arguments suggest an emphasis on governance, capability of coping with the world's new threats and dangers, and the capacity for stability, creativity, and economic growth. How philosophies of speech will be molded to help reach these goals will be the project of the next decades.

REFERENCES

Baker, C. E. 1989. *Human Liberty and Freedom of Speech*. New York: Oxford University Press.

Haworth, A. 1998. *Free Speech*. London; New York: Routledge.

Rogers, D. T. 2012. *Age of Fracture*. Cambridge, MA: Belknap Press of Harvard University Press.

Schauer, F. 1990. "Who Decides?," in Lichtenberg, J. (ed.), *Democracy and the Mass Media: A Collection of Essays*. Cambridge: Cambridge University Press.

Weber, M. 1970. "Politics as a Vocation," in Gerth, H. H. and Mills, C. W. (eds.), *From Max Weber*. London: Routledge and Kegan.

Williams, B. 2002. *Truth & Truthfulness: An Essay in Genealogy*. Princeton, NJ: Princeton University Press.

   2010. *Truth and Truthfulness: An Essay in Genealogy*. Princeton, NJ: Princeton University Press.

Index